European Approaches to International Management

Editors:
Klaus Macharzina and Wolfgang H. Staehle

Walter de Gruyter · Berlin · New York 1986

This book is dedicated to
Louis Perridon
for his academic contribution towards
European management thinking

Library of Congress Cataloging in Publication Data

European approaches to international management.
Bibliography: p.
1. Corporations, European—Management—Addresses, essays, lectures.
2. International business enterprises—Management—Addresses, essays, lectures. 3. International economic relations—Addresses, essays, lectures.
I. Macharzina, Klaus, 1939 –.
II. Staehle, Wolfgang H., 1938 –.
HD2844.E9 1985 338.8'8 85-20599
ISBN 0-89925-018-1

CIP-Kurztitelaufnahme der Deutschen Bibliothek

European approaches to international management / ed.: Klaus Macharzina and Wolfgang H. Staehle. – Berlin ; New York : de Gruyter, 1986.
ISBN 3-11-009827-X (Berlin)
ISBN 0-89925-018-1 (New York)
NE: Macharzina, Klaus [Hrsg.]

 – Typesetting and Printing: Wagner GmbH, Nördlingen. – Binding: Dieter Mikolai, Berlin. – Cover Design: K. Lothar Hildebrand, Berlin. – Printed in Germany.

Preface

Europe has been one of the most attractive places in the world economy to invest and to do business with. Now tables are turning and European companies spread internationally not only by way of still intensifying and expanding their traditionally high exports but also by sole direct investment, joint ventures, and transfer of technological and managerial know-how. The cross direct-investment position between the US and Europe has come close to par.

This book aims at introducing the features and strategies of European business and management when turning to the international market place. Emphasis is placed on the role which they play in international competition, particularly vis à-vis the United States and Japan. Another focus is on the state and potential of Europe's important industries. The discussion of some European concepts of managing the business function is to round up the picture. An international group of twenty-three experts in their respective fields have contributed to this volume which addresses the international business and academic community who are interested in exploring the actual strengths, problems, and the future potential of European business.

European business plays a focal part in today's rapidly changing international economy, particularly with respect to the solution of the dismal problems facing it. Some years ago the new international economic order was expected to change dramatically the existing beneficial to all-climate of international investment flows into a situation where the developing countries push at restraints and alterations in the balance of benefits. Today there are signals that world economic recovery may lead to a new North-South problem through a combination of higher interest rates and rising protectionist barriers in the industrial countries. Europe as a traditionally globalist partner in the international economy may well provide for market oriented adjustment in order to overcome these problems eventually. These measures may include open door economic policies, avoidance of exchange controls, reduction of public sector borrowing and the gradual conversion of debt into equity to reduce debt service at floating interest rates and the cost of debt rescheduling.

For the time being, however, European nations seem to be forced to cure their own international market problems which are mainly caused by competitive pressure exerted through the US and Japan. As a result of the analyses presented in this book one might conclude that the domesticist economic attitude followed by these major competitors in recent years can only be overcome by an even stronger European belief in open door economic strategy, based on an active industrial policy, and a sound industrial culture. While expanding further into world economy, Europe should attempt to restructure the relative weight of European policies to influence world economic relations. It should recall the notion of European authority and should seek to revive consensus and capacity at European level in order to be a strong and efficient partner in international economic cooperation.

Analysis of this book reveals clearly that technological, process and market innovation will be the engine of revival of European influence in world economy. In a time of telescoping life cycles of innovation the latter is critical to productivity. We can expect a new European entrepreneurial revolution which may be technology, process or market initiated, and which may take place both at corporate and industry level.

While in parts one and two of the book the focus is on such features of European corporations and industries, part three looks at European management and business concepts. This part was designed in the spirit of a **Festschrift for Louis Perridon** who has been pioneering for excellence of European thought throughout his academic service as a scholar at several European universities. It is for this very reason that the group of authors who contributed to this part, including the editors, solely consist of former students and researchers who worked with Professor Perridon at Munich and Augsburg universities. The Festschrift is dedicated to him on the occasion of his retirement from Augsburg University, and his removal to Caën – another European approach.

May the book serve its purpose which is to allow for better judgement as to what can and cannot be expected from European business in the world's big economic village in the foreseeable future.

Stuttgart and Berlin,
December 1985

Klaus Macharzina and Wolfgang Staehle

Contents

Part 1
Features of European Multinationals

introduced by Klaus Macharzina

The growth and decline of nations is largely dependent on their economic development. Economies grow, industrialize and trade internationally; in a more advanced stage of development their enterprises invest directly across domestic borders and become multinational in nature. Finally, they are referred to as multinational, international or transnational corporations. This is the case when these enterprises conduct business in more than one country under a system of decision-making which includes coherent policies and a common strategy, and when their subunits are linked by ownership or contract in a way that a central seat of management exerts significant influence over their activities and with respect to their sharing of resources and knowledge. Transnationally operating businesses bare an undisputed importance for international economic developments. This is particularly true of Europe where due to the specific natural conditions and resources international trade has traditionally been a fundamental necessity. In fact the early Italian and German merchant houses and agents of the middle ages, and later the Dutch and British international trading companies of the 19th and early 20th century can be looked at as predecessors of today's multinationals which developed since the fifties of this century. During the seventies the foreign operations of multinational corporations gained in importance compared to their domestic operations. Empirical evidence suggests that multinationals have continued to expand their foreign operations faster than their domestic ones. The recent UN Third Survey on Transnational Corporations' Influence on World Development[1] shows that for the largest 380 TNCs the ratio of sales by foreign subsidiaries to total sales rose from about 30% in 1971 to 40% in 1980; among them are 88 European, mainly British, German and French based, besides 179 US and 47 Japanese multinationals. This suggests that there is a growing trend of transnationalization across industries which is underlined by growing cross-currents of investment among industrialized countries and an increasing globalization of production – inspite of conditions of global economic recession and intensifying protectionism. Investment outflows continued to increase faster than domestic investment expenditures in home countries but more slowly than domestic investment

1 Cf. United Nations, Document E/C. (10, 1983, p. 2).

expenditures in developing countries. Available data also show a diversification in the origins and destinations of foreign direct investment flows. While the increase of relative shares of the total outflow by Canadian, West German and Japanese outflows compensated for more than a 50% drop in the US share the latter's share in inflows has increased to about one third of the total, making the US the largest recipient and source of foreign direct investment.

In the sixties European business was fighting back to the wall against the American challenge and dominance in industry and finance which was mainly exerted by financially and technologically strong US multinationals. The latter created or seized control of European markets in a way that one feared that Europe as the world's third greatest industrial power after the US and the USSR would be replaced by American business in Europe. The major reasons for this being the dollar gap, the technological gap and the managerial gap from which European business suffered and which gave rise to a hegemonial type of industrial and economic power to the US and a permanent structural disequilibrium in the world's balance of payments. As Europe's business had recovered from these structural shortcomings new problems arose in the seventies.

Firstly, European multinationals were constrained in their operations not only by the oil-crisis and economic recession. Secondly, being a mature type of economy both with respect to individual nations and Europe as a whole the loss of international competitiveness in important industries, and thirdly protectionist trends, have affected and will even more affect European multinational business activity in the future. The latter comprises the United Kingdom, the Federal Republic of Germany, France, The Netherlands, Belgium, and Sweden as the most important nations when ranked in the order of foreign direct investment flows. When measured by the volume of exports Germany and Britain followed by France and Switzerland lead the European nations because of their emphasis on exports in manufactured goods. Measured by the share of foreign in total sales in the period between 1971 and 1980 France took a leading position with 54% over Germany with 51% and the UK with 41% in 1980 compared to 44%, 46% and 29% respectively in 1971. Other Western European countries' share rose from 53% to 62%, the one of the US from 23% to 31% between 1971 and 1980. According to these statistics[2] Britain and France were relatively successful as regards their international business growth but fall still far behind Japan which managed to increase its international activities of its major companies by 23% from 20% in 1971 to 43% in 1980[3] – a well-known and remarkable success which made Japan the best performing nation in the international market place of the seventies.

2 Cf. loc. cit. Note that this only refers to the UN sample of 380 largest TNCs. Foreign sales of say medium and small business which is very strong in Europe are not included.

3 Cf. loc. cit.

There is no doubt that Europe's leading nations and their multinationals have undergone relative changes in their world market shares. General reasons for this are certainly maturing industries such as West Germany's manufacturing industries, new multinationals such as France's focus on high technology, information oriented and other new industries, but on an overall scale the Japanese pressure on international markets. Certainly, there is a growing influence of Third World multinationals which specialize in mature standardized technologies and certain labor-intensive industries where they are able to compete successfully against industrialized nations' multinationals or co-operate through joint venture-type activities with them. The latter can be expected to still increase and may be particularly important for European multinationals; this is because of the technological and marketing deficits of Third World companies, and the fact that advanced technology seeks the local production know-how of newly industrializing and developing countries.

Whereas most European countries – apart from France – directed their operations mainly to industrialized nations in the past there may be a redirection following particularly the Japanese example which to date is the only country whose multinationals have more subsidiaries in developing than in industrialized countries.

According to the UN corporate profile data base[4] as of 1980 there were about 57% of foreign subsidiaries located in Western Europe while 9% were located in North America and about 25% in developing countries. Australia, France and the US have over 30% of their foreign subsidiaries located in developing countries whereas Scandinavian countries have less than 15% of their total in the latter region. Among Europe's multinationals British foreign subsidiaries are predominant in both developed and developing regions where they account for about 60% together with the US. While UK, Dutch and Scandinavian based subsidiaries are evenly spread among developing regions, France has a strong concentration in Africa.

It is interesting to note that the numerical representation does not always compare to the foreign performance of a country – a fact which is evident for the UK as a numerically predominant but not so important country when looked at in terms of her foreign operations share; the same is true of the US. On an overall scale the contribution of foreign operations of European multinationals to their profitability has grown faster than that of their domestic activities.

Taking into account this background the following chapters focus on the important features of European multinationals, particularly their present and future competitive constraints and potential, and their international perfor-

4 Cf. The CTC Reporter (No. 15, Spring 1983, p. 8).

mance. Special consideration is given to the future development vis-à-vis the US and Japanese challenge, the development of new multinationals in Europe and the industrial relations pattern. The major focus is, however, on an indepth analysis of the *country-specific* features of multinational business activities which due to diverse socio-economic environments even within Europe bring about different constraints and possibilities which have to be taken into account when assessing future developments. The most important countries are dealt with in separate chapters apart from France and The Netherlands which are partly covered in the contributions on New Multinationals in Europe and on Belgian multinationals, respectively.[5]

5 The reason for this is that the authors who were selected for the chapters on France and The Netherlands did not see themselves in a position to submit their respective papers within the permitted time.

International Competitiveness of European Industry

John M. Stopford

Summary

The paper addresses the problem from an integrated standpoint by combining macro and micro level issues with the hard- and software dimensions of equipment and people. This framework of analysis allows for key proposals to solve Europe's problems of competition in its international environment. Required adjustments to reassure international competitiveness relate to the area of managerial behaviour, strategy, and public policy, and in that order of priority from the business manager's standpoint.

1. Introductory Remarks

Europe, like other industrialised parts of the world has faced monumentous changes in the last decade. We have not adapted to a world of slow growth and to the new competitive conditions as well as our competitors in Japan, and more recently in the United States. I was much struck by the analogy drawn some time ago by Mr. André Danzin, the Adviser to the Economic Commission for the ESPRIT Programme. He compared Europe to a violin with dampeners placed inside the frame to prevent resonance. It was no use complaining the violinist was awful. Nor was it any use sending him to Japan for training for he would produce the same dreadful sounds on his return. One had to find ways of removing the dampeners before one could expect resonance.

I shall argue that it is managers that must find the ways and that there is some urgency in the task. Industry cannot wait in the hopes that our governments will change their policy direction, for there are few signs that they have learned much from their past mistakes.

Before developing my theme, let me confess that I am uncertain how to generalise about competitiveness across European industry. My academic antennae are sympathetic to the reverberations of a recent management conference of the European Management Forum that concluded there were 240 variables to be considered, most of which could not be qualified. My more practical antennae tell me that I should distinguish between successful and unsuccessful firms, and between prosperous countries and less prosperous ones. My dilemma is no doubt a familiar one.

As Charles Kindleberger once said of a particularly nasty problem of international economics, getting to grips with the concept of competitiveness is rather like wrestling with a bear under a rug. When you launch yourself at the mound under the rug, you find that by the time you land the bear has moved somewhere else. If you measure competitiveness in terms of costs or prices, you get one set of results. If you measure it in terms of export shares, you get another result. And so on. Competitiveness is at best a composite of different variables for any one firm at a particular time. It is difficult enough to be sure that one is looking at the appropriate composite – or if you will, the mound under the rug – for any one firm. It is far more difficult to define the composite for European industry in general.

Nevertheless, there are various factors that have affected all European countries and most of their firms to varying degrees in the past decade. These common factors, discernible in the immediate past, provide some of the clues about where the difficulties of adjustment have proved most acute and where the future challenges lie.

2. Framework for Analysis

To deal with the complexities and to hear signals amongst all the noise, one needs a simple framework of analysis. I have found it helpful to use the structure developed by Abernathy and others in the USA (Abernathy, Clark and Kantrow 1981). In their review of US competitiveness they first distinguished between analysis and prescription of "macro" issues and "micro" ones. Macro issues have to do with general national problems such as monetary and fiscal policy, whereas micro issues apply to particular firms. They then went on to examine a second basic distinction between "hardware" (equipment, etc.) and "software" (people, organisational systems, corporate stategies and so on). They thus produced a simple matrix. Macro issues were divided between the hardware of economic policy and the software of social policy. Micro issues were equivalently divided between the hardware of supply capabilities and the software of corporate management.

The quadrants in this matrix are rough and ready categorisations of sets of issues. Yet they can be used to focus attention on priorities. I shall review each quadrant in turn to establish my argument that Europe's problems are not evenly distributed around the matrix. They are concentrated in the zone of corporate management and its internal adjustment to the new competitive rules.

3. Economic Policy

3.1 Fiscal and Monetary Policy

At the level of macroeconomic policy the diagnosis by Jim Ball and Michel Albert for the European Parlament deserves considerable attention (Albert and Ball 1983). What they say at the macro level is all too often reflected at the micro level. They point to two grave mistakes: Europe has sacrificed the future to the present; and Europe has been run at the national level, every man for himself, rather than at the Continental level. One might add to those mistakes a third one, the growing belief in a "Fortress Europe" as a protectionist response to continuing external threat.

The symptoms of sacrificing the future to the present are widespread and disturbing. Over the last decade, all European countries have increased wages at the expense of corporate profits and increased consumption at the expense of investment. Europe's institutions, especially its social security systems, were built up during the years of rapid expansion and were dependent upon continuing growth. Faced with the abrupt transition to a world of low growth after 1973, Europe chose to maintain increases in purchasing power regardless of cost. This was really a social choice, and one based on very short-term calculations. It is now apparent that, lacking competitive investments, European firms had lost their ability to create jobs. Between 1973 and 1983 Europe lost 3 million jobs, whereas the USA, faced with equivalent external threat, increased its jobs by 15 million.

Industry has borne the brunt of this choice. Whereas most European governments have publicly espoused the priority of supporting industrial investment, they have in practice given priority to public finances. One can argue that European countries have lost control of their public finances. Social welfare spending, to take but one aspect, has continued to rise twice as fast as overall wealth. Our social institutions, for health care, for unemployment compensation, for pensions for an increasingly elderly population, have not been adjusted by any considerations of an ability to pay at an affordable social cost. Given the rigidity of these institutions, for perfectly understandable political reasons, there is little hope for the trend towards every greater public expenditure to be reversed.

The second mistake of "every man for himself" is in direct contradiction of Article 2 of the Treaty of Rome which states that "the Community shall have as its task . . . to promote . . . a harmonious development of economic activities . . . and closer relations between the States belonging to it." The achievements in the first 15 years were considerable, but faced with slow growth, national attitudes have hardened and, as Albert and Ball put it "member states . . . were disposed to regard the Community, not as a collective investment asset based on the principle of a 'fair return', but as one where each was convinced of its entitlement to a larger share than the others."

In the last ten years, the European Communities (EC) have been paralysed by budgetary disputes and interminable legal wrangles over issues that have little to do with creating wealth. Narrow nationalism is a far more serious problem than some of our politicians would have us believe. Sir Geoffrey Howe, the British Foreign Secretary, characterised the Community as a perfectly respectable car that happens at the moment to have a flat tyre. Sir Geoffrey needs to take a closer look at the car itself, not the state of its tyres. He could learn from the General Motors executive who remarked: "We took a look at the Honda Accord and we knew the game had changed." GM has reacted with a sense of urgency to the new game and has gone far to reassert its competitiveness and profitability; European politicians have done little to recognise the common external threat to the Community and to change accordingly.

The symptoms of inertia are all around us. Despite two oil shocks, we neglect our energy investments, spending proportionate to GDP, at about only one-third of the US or Japanese rate. Our national monetary policies continue to diverge. The European Monetary System has been one substantial achievement, but currencies like Sterling need to join it before it can become a powerful instrument of convergence.

Agriculture is protected at the national level, as are all of the Service sectors. The Community is decades away from establishing the common financial infrastructure that has such an important part to play in the efficient allocation of scarce investment resources. To compound these difficulties, national bodies such as the German Cartel Office hate not appreciated the magnitude of the competitive threat from outside the Community and continue to block moves to rationalise competition across internal borders.

It is bad enough for policy makers to take a protectionist line at home; it is much more serious when they extend that sentiment to the Community at large. With the notable exception of the recent trade agreement with the remaining EFTA countries, the, so far faltering, steps taken to create an EC level trade policy seem to be based on the belief that "Fortress Europe" will somehow buy time to allow adjustment to a more competitive tomorrow. This belief takes no account of the fact that national protectionism has failed to induce a transformation of national firms. All the evidence is that it has allowed firms to continue to behave as they did before. Why then should continental-scales initiatives such as the voluntary restraint agreements with the Japanese have a different result?

3.2 Regulatory and Social Policy

The forces of inertia are equally apparent in my second quadrant of regulatory and social policies. Internal divisions continue to impede the creation of an integrated internal European market.

Despite the valiant efforts of such bodies as the Kangaroo Group – a body of Euro-MPs and others dedicated to the task of removing internal barriers to trade – European industry continues to pay substantial cost penalties because of the lack of common Community-wide practices. Border customs and delays, even when the French lorry drivers are working, add 5–10% to transport costs. Add to such costs, the costs in product design and production of different technical standards and the cost penalty compared to the USA can run as high as 30% in some industries.

Other types of regulatory policy and nationalistic behaviour add further penalties. Governments tend to prefer national suppliers for items of public procurement. Telematics and defence procurement are notorious examples of the trade consequences of the failure to establish a common continental-scale "home" market. IBM is fond of pointing out that the taxes it has paid in France approximate the entire Government investment in its 'Plan Calcul', so far with little return. Where there have been EC-inspired initiatives to reduce capacity in Europe's most troubled industries – steel and fibres for example – there is ample evidence that the agreements fail to preserve or reward the most efficient producers and that the agreements are frequently broken when it suits a government to do so.

All of us would like to be more hopeful of future progress than I am suggesting. There are, to be sure, a few gleams of sunshine in this gloomy scene, such as the ESPRIT initiative in information technology. But such initiatives are small scale and tend to alleviate the symptoms rather than attack the root cause of the disease. We desperately need better ways of harnessing our innovative efforts at a continental scale rather than dissipating them among competing projects. We do not get the same return on R & D investments as do our foreign competitors.

Solutions to the problem are elusive, and the search frustrating. The sense of frustration that led Peer Gyllenhammer to establish his much-publicised group of senior industrialists – the so-called G16 – is probably shared by many. If governments will not act, then industry itself must point the way. But will the vision of industrialists be sufficient to exchange the macro conditions within which European competitiveness is determined to be sufficient? I fear not. The political balance of forces is such that rational arguments will command lip service but litte more. Rather the answers lie in the behaviour of firms. Here the examples of success and the possibilites for progress are much more promising.

4. Business Policy

4.1 Production Capability

Let me turn therefore to the micro side of my framework of analysis. First, there are the questions of the hardware affecting the capacity of firms to supply competitive output. With respect to this problem, I wish to make only two points.

First, there is the question of the use existing hardware. Under-invested though many firms may be, there is still much potential for getting better results without extensive further investment in plant and machinery. A recent study of the European textile industry concluded that, even after the massive redundancies of the last decade and the rationalisation of much capacity, productivity could be still increased by a further 30–40% *on average**. In the author's view, the keys to improvement lay in better work practices, machine layouts, control and product design. In other words in management, not in the hardware. Startling increases in productivity have recently been achieved by some UK firms in other sectors, and I am sure equally by other European firms, as management has begun to tackle head-on the difficult problems of curing years, if not decades, of benign neglect of their internal procedures. Though better use of existing hardware will not provide all the answers, it would go a long way to restoring more acceptable levels of profitability and buy time to permit longer-term reconstruction.

My second point is to do with the adoption of new technology. Europe, and particularly the UK, has been very slow to perceive and use the new technologies that are now available. In robotics, for example, Japan is a clear leader and, as yet, only Swedish firms have come close to emulating the leader.

Robotics, electronics and other "hightech" developments are only part of the story. There are more humdrum types of technology affecting such parts of the process as materials handling that lower overall costs. Even in the so-called mature industries, careful applications of "low-level" technology can in some cases yield cost reductions to the point where imports for the NICs can successfully be resisted. A new shoe factory opened in the UK recently is one such example. The wonder is that it took management so long to perceive the possibilities.

The choice of technology has been argued in terms of a race between the tortoise and the hare. The hare represents the great leap forward into new technology, while the tortoise represents the slow, detailed and incremental use of existing technology, wherever in the world it may have been developed.

* A private survey by an US textile consultant.

There is much European preoccupation with hares. They are of enormous importance in such strategically important industries as information technology. But one shoud not be so preoccupied with them that the tortoises are forgotten. Indeed, contrary to the pervasive image, much of Japan's international competitive success has been based on tortoises, not hares.

Taken together, *all* the now available technologies have the effect in many industries of lowering the minimum economies of scale. This development opens new possibilities for producers to take advantage of the diversity of the European markets and can go a long way towards offsetting the cost penalties of continuing fragmentation. Many mature industries, like automobiles, are beginning to feel stirrings of new blood. The curious jargon is "a process of dematurity". How extensive are the possibilities and how fast they may be exploited depends upon management – in the fourth and last quadrant of my matrix.

4.2 Corporate Strategy Adjustments

Faced with adverse macroeconomic conditions it is understandable that so many European firms should have pulled in their horns and worked to ensure short-term survival. Some have sacrificed the future to the present, though they would argue, perhaps with reason, that they had no option. The cost in terms of reduced R & D spending, limited new product development and rigidity in organisational structures and processes has, however, been immense. That is past history. We now need to look forward. In most sectors there is a resumption of growth in demand, albeit at a slow rate in real terms. There is thus a breathing space when we can attempt to catch up with the international leaders. But to do so will require significant shifts in attitudes about how business should be conducted and what resources need to be created to meet the new competitive demands.

One of the most profound changes to be faced is in the structure of competition itself. Just as the oil and pharmaceutical industries experienced years ago, competitiveness is shifting from national to international, if not global, scale. It is quite clear that, without government protection, few segments remain defensible at the national level in consumer electronics, telecommunications, industrial machinery, wholesale banking and a growing list of others.

Though global competition is a somewhat vague term, the symptoms are discernible. At least one competitor has found a way of gaining benefits of extra-national scale. The benefits may lie at any stage of the value-added chain of the business from design to sales. In some business, they may be in terms of designing products for many markets and thus lowering production costs below that of purely national players. Worldwide designs may cover 80% of the needs, with 20% for local adaptations. All too often European firms design products for the home market and then search for exports. System X, the new British telecommunication system, is a dramatic example of the inadequacies of this approach. In other businesses, the benefits may lie in exploiting an international distribution system with families of related products. One might note on this score how many very successful Japanese exporters are spending more money on international distribution than on plant modernisation or product development at home. Too many Europeans pay scant attention to overseas distributive investments as a means of exploiting production or technological advantages. The successful global competitor can use these and other benefits of extra national scale to deliver a superior price/value ratio to customers in many markets simultaneously.

One must be extremely cautious about making any general statements on the trend towards global competition. Some industries now seem to be retreating from full-blown globalisation, partly for the technological reasons cited earlier. A few years ago, the chase for the "world car" preoccupied the automobile industry. Today it seems clear that the world car, as a design concept, has failed and local variations of basic designs proliferate. World-scale competitors like Ford may still reap benefits from common parts, brand identity and so on, but their current assessment of the trends is quite different from that of 1980. Troubled national producers like British Leyland are no doubt encouraged by these signs of change for they can now see future protectable niches, provided they can transform their factories to keep costs competitive.

These are cross-currents in the drift towards internationalisation of production. To identify with some precision how the battle among competing forces is being played out puts great stress on management's strategic vision of the future. Given the complexities involved it should be well understood that any such vision cannot be the exclusive property of those at the centre. Coordination at many different levels is essential, so that effort can be focussed on common tasks and change managed quickly and effectively.

We are often told by international managers how difficult it is to weld previously autonomous national subsidiaries into a coordinated body, where the whole is greater than the parts. There is the familiar problem of product specifications. In a case where three subsidiaries scattered across Europe had resisted head office's attempts to create common standards local management had become enormously creative in finding reasons why head office was wrong to suggest change. They might have been right, yet the major competitor had adopted a common specification and was rapidly gaining market share. Clearly there was a gap in communications, and serious problems in motivation and in the performance measurement and reward systems. In short, there was a failure to define and articulate strategy in terms that could be implemented at the unit level.

I do not mean to imply by this example that growing global competition means growing centralisation of management. It may do so in some circumstances, but far more often it means that local management must be kept far better informed about group affairs in ways that permit them to make better judgements about local strategies and locally defined action plans. Successful international competitors are characterised by large investments in senior management meetings and other, largely informal means of communication and of pooling experience. Unsuccessful ones still rely heavily upon formal manuals of procedure.

This message will not come as news to many American companies with well developed European networks. They are in many respects the most European companies in that they seem to work more naturally at continental scale and have found ways of minimising the problems of cultural difference that still plague indigenous firms. Take the case of IBM again. I understand that all fifteen of IBM's European plants are, exchange-adjusted, competitive at world scale with their facilities elsewhere. IBM has not allowed itself to become mesmerised by the difficulties of working within the fragmented, macro framework of European economies. The echoes of Servan-Schreiber from the 1960s are still important.

If some companies can find ways of continental-scale benefits across Europe, others must surely be able to follow suit. Does this mean that one should advocate a wholesale movement of cross-border mergers to shorten the time it would take to build new powerful groups capable of matching world leaders on equal grounds? Would a single European telecoms firm be the answer? Would combinations such as Bosch and Lucas in automobile components provide a new level of European competitiveness? I fear not. Shotgun marriages are seldom successful. The European record from previous attempts – Dunlop-Pirelli, Estel-Hoogovens and others – is a sorry one. Quite apart from the appalling complexities of harmonising different systems of management, such mergers lacked a crucial ingredient for success. They were too similar in important strategic respects. As Mr. De Benedetti of Olivetti has been saying recently, such collaborations or mergers must be able to trade technology for markets. Collaboration with American and Japanese partners is likely to be of much greater benefit, provided – and this is an important proviso – that the rewards are shared equally among the partners.

Though cross-border mergers of major firms are unlikely to work organisationally, they may however work for smaller firms where the organisational challenge is lesser. Future competitiveness rests just as much on the small firm as on the large.

5. Future Challenges

In the main I see the priority needs for raising levels of competitiveness to lie in the management of internal change. Change must come organically and, to be effective, incrementally. Human organisations have only a limited capacity to adapt. To create change, I suggest that there are major challenges ahead in three broad areas: strategic, behavioural, and in the realm of public policy. As agenda items, let me merely list them:

Strategic Challenges

- to understand world-scale competition and competitors more fully.
- to become technologically more involved, either as creators or users, and to break the barrier that still separates research from production.
- to give quality a far greater emphasis.
- to link national units more effectively so as to achieve extra-national scale benefits in those parts of the value-chain most affected by new competition.

Behavioural Challenges

- to invest more in improving the processes of management, especially communications.
- to upgrade managerial skills.
- to upgrade skills at all levels in the organisation.
- to improve union bargaining relationships.

Public Policy Challenges

- to increase pressure on governments to behave as Europeans and to encourage all initiatives that create better continental infrastructure.
- to demand better quality from our educational systems to support the necessary skill developments at work.

Of all these, I consider the behavioural issues to be the most important, for improvement on the other fronts will be impossible until European firms can create their own internal conditions for change. Above all lies the challenge with senior management to set the pace and the tone of the change.

Alfred Sloan of General Motors once said years ago of Henry Ford, "The old master failed to master change". Europe, as we all know, is rich in old masters. Let not the same be said of them.

Bibliography

Abernathy, W. J./Clark, K. B./Kantrow, A. M.: The New Industrial Competition. *Harvard Business Review,* September/October 1981.

Albert, M./Ball, J.: *Towards European Economic Recovery in the 1980s, a report to the European Parliament.* July 1983.

European Management Forum, *Report on Industrial Competitiveness.* 1981.

European Multinationals: An International Comparison of Size and Performance

Alan M. Rugman

Summary

The 50 largest European multinational enterprises are identified and their financial performance over the last ten years is contrasted to that of a group of North American multinationals. It is found that the European multinationals are less profitable due to the extent of state ownership or participation in a large number of these firms.

1. Introduction

In this paper the largest European multinational enterprises (MNEs) are identified and their financial performance is contrasted with that of the largest North American MNEs. Data on the size and degree of multinationality of these firms are also reported. As an indication of financial performance the mean return on equity over 10 years (1973–1982) is calculated and as a proxy for risk the standard deviation of this rate of return is used.

The difference in financial performance of the European MNEs relative to the U.S. MNEs (and also a group of Canadian MNEs) is analyzed in terms of the size and degree of multinationality between the two groups. The presence of state-owned enterprises (SOEs) in Europe is also examined as a possible factor to explain the difference in the financial performance between the European and North American MNEs.

2. Size and Performance of European Multinationals

The 50 largest European and U.S. MNEs were selected from the Fortune International 500 and the Fortune 500 Industrials respectively (Fortune 1974a–1983a and 1974b–1983b). MNEs with less than 20 percent foreign sales to total sales (F/T), as reported in Stopford (1983), were deleted from the lists. Sales by foreign affiliates to total sales would have been a preferable criteria as (F/T) includes export sales. However, this information is not segregated for a sufficient number of MNEs to enable its use as a measure of multinationality.

The performance measure employed is the rate of return on equity (ROE), defined as net income over the year-end stockholders' equity (net worth). The data on stockholders equity for European MNEs were difficult to interpret due to the non-uniformity of accounting conventions used in various European nations. It is assumed that the different treatment of accounting practices balances out across nations and thereby does not introduce any systematic bias in the ROE calculation.

The mean ROE over the 1973–82 period is used as a proxy for the expected rate of return. The standard deviation (S.D.) of the observed ROEs about their mean is used as a proxy for total risk. A substantial portion of the MNEs experienced losses in one or more years, and both for simplicity and to avoid a downward bias these losses were taken as a zero ROE.

From Tables 1 and 2 it is clear that the European MNEs are less efficient in economic terms relative to U.S. MNEs. The European MNEs have an ROE of 8.5 percent and an S.D. of 5.16 versus an ROE and S.D. of 14.3 and 3.58 respectively, for U.S. MNEs. Thus European MNEs earn less return and at a higher risk than do their U.S. counterparts. The disparity is even more pronounced than during the 1970–79 period when the European MNEs' ROE and S.D. were 8.36 and 4.47 respectively as compared to the U.S. MNEs' 12.95 and 4.38 (Rugman 1983). Although it is not the intent of this paper to analyse the specific causes of the European MNEs less efficient performance vis-à-vis U.S. MNEs, a few reasons initially come to mind.

First, it might be argued that European MNEs are not as multinational as U.S. MNEs. The European MNEs conduct a large proportion of their foreign operations in neighboring countries or within the EC whereas U.S. MNEs' foreign operations are at much greater distance from the home country (with the exception of Canada). The argument then, would centre on the U.S. MNEs achieving greater benefits of international diversification where markets more remote from the home country offer a higher degree of risk reduction through offsetting market covariances. However, offsetting market covariances have been found to occur just as much within Europe as occur on a worldwide basis (Rugman 1979).

Added to this is the fact that most international trade and investment is conducted East-West rather than North-South, so European and U.S. MNEs operate in each others home markets. In fact as the F/T ratios in Tables 1 and 2 demonstrate, European MNEs derive a significantly higher percentage of their total sales from foreign markets than do U.S. MNEs (58 versus 37 percent).

Thus it is unlikely that the risk return disparity between European and U.S. MNEs is attributable to the locations or extent of foreign operations.

Table 1: Performance of the 50 Largest European MNEs (1973-82)

Firm	1982 Sales (US Millions)	1981 F/T (percent)	ROE Mean	ROE S.D.
Royal Dutch Shell	83,759	60[2]	18.0	4.63
British Petroleum	51,322	74	14.4	7.97
ENI[10]	27,506	28[1]	2.7	5.38
Unilever	23,120	40[2]	13.3	4.83
Francaise des Petroles	20,029	59	11.6	13.40
Elf-Aquitaine[10]	17,785	26[2]	15.3	7.86
Siemens	16,963	56	8.6	1.52
NV Philips	16,093	93	4.9	2.92
Daimler-Benz	16,023	59	18.6	12.80
Renault[10]	15,837	84	3.3	4.43
BAT	15,648	78	12.1	2.61
Volkswagenwerk	15,417	72	7.0	7.51
Fiat	15,331	na	3.0[3]	3.73
Hoechst	14,409	72	7.3	3.22
Bayer	14,346	76	8.4	3.02
Nestle	13,611	97	10.5	9.34
BASF	12,960	60	8.4	2.92
Thyssen	12,947	45[2]	5.8	4.70
Imperial Chemical	12,873	60	11.1	5.70
Volvo	12,027	77	9.8	6.93
Peugeot-Citroen	11,522	45	9.6	9.04
Generale Electricite[10]	10,004	40	6.7	1.85
Petrofina	9,209	na	15.5	4.24
General Electric plc	8,007	55	18.1	3.29
Saint-Gobain	7,805	61	6.8	3.15
Ruhrkohle	7,246	na	3.3[4]	2.85
Thomson Brandt[10]	7,152	46	10.1	12.61
Friedr. Krupp	6,886	38	4.2[5]	3.82
NV DSM[10]	6,802	64	6.9	9.83
Ciba Geigy	6,794	60[2]	3.6	1.24
Mannesmann	6,783	60	12.8	7.63
Montedison	6,664	37	3.2	7.10
British Steel[10]	6,579	26	1.0	3.68
Rio Tinto Zinc	6,439	77	11.8	3.32
Gutehoffnungshütte	6,386	50	7.1	2.12
Schneider	5,973	50	4.3[7]	7.67
Robert Bosch	5,689	56	10.0	4.46
Rhone-Poulenc[10]	5,656	61	3.2	4.27
Michelin	5,567	56	7.3	5.05
AEG Telefunken	5,460	45	3.0	7.91
British Leyland[10]	5,374	48	2.9	4.55
Akzo Group	5,298	90	4.8	4.97
Imperial Group	5,146	20	11.9	5.21
Electrolux	5,035	72	14.7[8]	5.70
Brown Boveri	4,773	85	5.3[6]	0.85
Dalgety	4,685	49	14.1[9]	3.96
Thorn-EMI	4,655	33	17.0	3.94
Pechiny-Ugine Kuhlmann	4,415	57	5.2	3.99
Metallgesellschaft	4,120	57	4.5	1.59
Salzgitter[10]	3,972	38[2]	1.6	2.85
Average		58	8.5	5.16

Notes: 1. 1980 2. minimum F/T 3. 1981–82 not available 4. 1973 not available 5. 1982 not available 6. 1981–2 and 1976 not available 7. 1975 not available 8. 1974 not available 9. 1978, 76, 75 and 74 not available 10. State-owned.
Source: Fortune (1974b–1983b) and Stopford (1982)

Table 2: Performance of the 50 Largest U.S. MNEs (1973–82)

Firm	1982 Sales (millions)	F/T (percent)	ROE Mean	ROE S.D.
Exxon	97,173	74	16.8	3.28
GM	60,026	25	12.0	8.11
Mobil	59,946	65	15.0	4.52
Texaco	46,986	67	13.5	4.53
Ford	37,067	49	8.6	7.40
IBM	34,364	54	19.9	2.06
Standard Oil (Ca.)	34,362	53	15.1	3.63
E. I. du Pont	33,331	29	12.7	3.70
Gulf	28,427	38	12.5	2.57
General Electric	26,500	36	17.2	2.51
Occidental Pet.	18,212	37	18.1	12.40
I. T. and T.	15,958	47	11.1	1.97
Phillips Pet.	15,698	24	16.5	3.59
Sun	15,519	26	14.6	4.09
Tenneco	15,241	22	15.0	1.74
United Technologies	13,577	46	13.1	1.37
Proctor and Gamble	11,994	32	17.1	1.06
R. J. Reynolds	10,906	26	18.0	1.04
Eastman Kodak	10,815	39	17.7	1.79
Dow	10,618	49	18.5	5.62
Chrysler	10,045	20	3.1	5.29
Dart and Kraft	9,974	28	13.5	1.24
Westinghouse	9,745	27	9.5	5.37
Philip Morris	9,102	32	19.3	1.40
Union Carbide	9,062	31	13.6	4.17
Beatrice Foods	9,024	25	14.1	3.18
Goodyear	8,689	41	9.5	1.67
Xerox	8,456	43	16.4	2.59
General Foods	8,351	31	13.6	4.61
PepsiCo	7,499	23	17.8	2.43
3M	6.601	46	17.8	3.70
Caterpillar	6,469	56	16.3	6.19
Monsanto	6,325	37	11.9	5.11
Coca Cola	6,250	45	20.7	1.32
Allied	6,167	32	11.3	4.94
W. R. Grace	6,128	21	13.9	2.24
Consolidated Foods	6,039	25	13.0	4.08
Nabisco	5,871	34	16.0	2.58
Johnson and Johnson	5,760	44	17.0	0.87
Sperry	5,571	43	12.1	1.43
Raytheon	5,513	27	18.1	3.28
Honeywell	5,490	32	12.0	2.81
Gulf & Western	5,486	20	13.3	3.34
TRW	5,132	30	15.4	1.49
Continental	4,979	25	13.1	2.08
Litton	4,941	24	10.5	9.74
Signal	4,936	32	12.1	5.36
Colgate Palmolive	4,888	59	15.3	0.92
Ralston Purina	4,878	23	14.0	2.97
Int'l Harvester	4,725	36	7.4	5.85
Mean		36.6	14.3	3.58

Source: Fortune (1974a–1983a) and Stopford (1982)

Table 3: Comparative Sales of European and North-American MNEs (in U.S. dollars, billions, 1982)

	European MNEs		U.S. MNEs		Canadian MNEs	
Stratum	Mean	S.D.	Mean	S.D.	Mean	S.D.
1–10	28.8	22.09	45.7	21.64	3.0	1.40
11–20	14.0	1.26	14.0	2.58	1.5	1.72
21–30	8.1	1.60	8.9	0.99	0.9	0.26
31–40	6.1	0.50	6.1	0.31	0.4	0.12
41–50	4.8	0.50	5.1	0.30	na	na
all 50[1]	12.4	13.00	16.0	17.97	1.6	1.22

Note: 1. All 36 in the case of Canadian MNEs.

The second possible explanation of the risk return disparity might be the bias introduced by the size differential between European and U.S. MNEs. Table 3 summarizes the sales of the MNEs in five stratums or quintiles. Although the segration of MNEs is somewhat arbitrary the results are consistent with the notion that size is not a factor in the performance disparity.

The mean sales level for U.S. MNEs is greater at $16 billion compared to $12.4 billion for European MNEs. However, only in the top quintile is there a significant difference between sales levels. The variability of sales levels are also consistent with the exception of the second quintile where U.S. MNEs experience a far greater range. The top quintile reveals a mean sales levels of $ 44.7 billion for U.S. MNEs as opposed to $ 28.8 billion for Europeans. The difference is largely due to petroleum firms which make up five of the top 10 U.S. MNEs. European petroleum firms, while accounting for four of the top 10 European MNEs, have only two, Shell and BP, in the same league as the U.S. petroleum MNEs. Yet the mean ROE and S.D. for the top 10 U.S. MNEs is 14.3 and 4.23 respectively. This mean return is equal to the top 50 U.S. mean ROE and the risk is actually *greater* than the U.S. top 50. Thus it is not the size differential of the top 10 U.S. MNEs that creates upward bias of the overall risk return disparity.

To underscore the irrelevance of the size differential as a factor in performance, data on the top 36 Canadian MNEs are presented in Table 3. The Canadian MNEs are the highest ranked (by sales) on the Financial Post 500 with an F/T of 20 percent or more. The Canadian MNEs are one-tenth and one-thirteenth the size of U.S. and European MNEs respectively. However, their mean ROE at 12.9 percent, exceeds the European ROE although at a greater risk of 5.74 percent (Table 4).

The top 50 U.S. MNEs are all privately owned. Within the top 50 European MNEs there are at least eleven firms with a state-interest of more than 50

Table 4: Comparative Performance: State-owned versus Private MNEs

	Mean 1973–82	
	ROE	S.D.
U.S. MNEs		
All 50 (all private)	14.3	3.58
Canadian MNEs		
All 36 (all private)	12.9	5.74
European		
All 50	8.5	5.16
Private: excluding MNEs more than 50 percent state-ownership	9.4	5.04
Private: excluding MNEs with more than 10 percent state-ownership	9.7	4.55
State-controlled MNEs (greater than 50 percent)	5.4	5.57
State-participating MNEs (between 10–50 percent)	8.2	6.68

1. Eleven MNEs have greater than 50% state-ownership: ENI, Elf-Aquitaine, Renault, Generale Electricite, Thomson Brandt, DSM, British Steel, Rhone-Poulenc, British Leyland, Pechiney-Ugine, and Salzgitter.
2. Nine MNEs have between 10–50% state-ownership: British Petroleum (39%), Francaise des Petroles (35), Volkswagenwerk (40), Daimler-Benz (14-Kuwait Government), Saint-Gobain (being nationalized), Ruhrkohle (through Veba and Salzgitter-38), Fried. Krupp (25-Iranian government), Montedison (13-through ENI), and Metallgesellschaft (20-Kuwait government).

percent. A conflict exists between economic efficiency and social benefit in SOEs. The expectation is that SOEs will not maximize their return as they have other objectives, such as social responsibility to satisfy. In SOEs it is probable that a certain amount of economic performance will be offset in the name of social benefits.

The three types of European MNEs; private, state-controlled (more than 50 percent), and state-participating (10–50 percent) are segrated in Table 4. As expected, the mean ROE of state-controlled MNEs is considerably less than that of the private MNEs at 5.4 and 9.4 respectively. Their risk is also greater at 5.57 versus 5.04. When the state-participating MNEs are also excluded from the top 50 the result is the same, although the performance of private versus state-participating firms is only marginally different. The mean return of European MNEs increases with each exclusion of the two types of state-interest firms. The mean risk also decreases with each exclusion.

The relatively higher performance of privately-owned MNEs is not limited to the U.S. MNEs. The Canadian MNEs, also all privately-owned, have a mean ROE just slightly less than the U.S. MNEs albeit at considerably more risk.

It can be concluded that the state's participation in European MNEs has impaired their performance. In fact the impairment is actually greater than indicated in Table 4 due to the method of ROE calculation. To reiterate, loss years were treated as zero ROE. If these loss years were included as negative returns rather than zero the mean ROE would be considerable less and the mean risk considerably more.

This result is illustrated by the data in Table 5, which calculates the total number of loss years as a percentage of total years for which observations were available. The U.S. MNEs exhibit a three percent loss year rate and the Canadian MNEs an eight percent loss year rate while private European firms experience only a 9 percent loss rate. State-participating MNEs are marginally worse off with a 13 percent loss year rate. The state-controlled MNEs have a dismal 35 percent loss year rate.

Table 5: Comparative Loss Years: State-owned versus Private MNEs

	1973–82 Percent
U.S. MNEs	
All 50 (all private)	3%
Canadian MNEs	
All 36 (all private)	8%
European MNEs	9%
Private MNEs (less than 10 percent state-owned)	
MNEs 10–50 percent state-owned	13%
MNEs more than 50 percent state-owned	35%

3. Conclusions

European MNEs are less efficient than U.S. MNEs in terms of their risk-return performance, as measured by mean ROE and its variability. The degree of multinationality of U.S. and European MNEs is not considered a factor in the risk-return disparity as essentially the MNEs operate in the same markets and industries. Europe's market covariances are comparable to world market covariances and European MNEs are just as multinational in terms of foreign to total sales.

The greater mean sales level of U.S. MNEs is also not considered a factor as only the top 10 are significantly larger and the mean ROE and the risk of these 10 is not found to bias upward the U.S. MNEs' performance.

Finally, the presence of state-interest MNEs is found to decrease the overall return and increase the risk of these returns. This is particularly true of state-controlled MNEs and only marginally true of state-participating MNEs. However, state-interest MNEs do not account for the entire risk-return disparity. Here it is observed that state-interest firms account for 21 percent of the mean ROE disparity and 39 percent of the mean risk disparity. It is also shown that these amounts are likely minimum accountabilities as the method of ROE calculation counted loss years as a zero rather than a negative return.

An interesting point is that only a marginal disparity is exhibited by state-participating MNEs when compared to private European MNEs. This implies that perhaps the social objectives of European nations can be met with only a small sacrifice in performance if the state were to take a minority rather than a majority interest in European MNEs.

Bibliography

Fortune: The Fortune 500 Largest U.S. Industrial Corporations. *Fortune,* May Issues, 1974a–1983a.

Fortune: The Fortune International 500. *Fortune,* August Issues, 1974b–1983b.

Rugman, A. M.: *International Diversification and the Multinational Enterprise.* D. C. Heath. Lexington 1979.

Rugman, A. M.: *Inside the Multinationals.* Columbia University Press, New York 1981.

Rugman A. M.: The Comparative Performance of U.S. and European Multinational Enterprises, 1970–79. *Management International Review,* Vol. 23, No. 2, 1983, pp. 4–14.

Stopford, J. M.: *The World Directory of Multinational Enterprises 1982–83.* Macmillan Publishers, London 1983.

Japanese and European Multinationals in America: A Case of Flexible Corporate Systems

Yoshi Tsurumi

Summary

Japanese and European multinational firms reveal that they are expanding their manufacturing activities in the U.S. while their American competitors are cutting back their manufacturing operations inside the U.S. This "Japanese and European Paradox" is to be explained by the product life cycle of foreign trade and the corporate culture as a firm-specific determinant.

1. Japanese and European Paradox

Of late, the Pacific Age of the U.S. has produced important changes in the international environment of the American economy (Tsurumi 1984). Ever since 1978, more American trade and investment have crossed the Pacific Ocean than the Atlantic, ending the 350 years of the Atlantic Age for the U.S. scarcely a decade ago, Western European countries and Canada dominated the U.S. trade and investment, with Latin America and Asia competing for the distant third position. In 1983, in two-way trade flows alone, of $461 billion of the U.S. trade, the Pacific trade ran up $183 billion, leaving further behind the Atlantic trade of $113 billion and the Canadian trade of $87 billion.

In direct investment areas, from 1979 to 1983, American investments in Japan and other Pacific countries were increasing at an annually compounding rate of 20%, about three times as rapid as American investments in Europe. In turn, increased American investments in Japan and other Asian countries have increased the tempo of Japanese firms' investments in the U.S. From 1979 to 1983, Japanese direct investments in the U.S. have increased by about 340% from $3.4 billion to $15 billion. In 1982, Japan's investments in the U.S. surpassed investment positions held by Germany and France. By the mid-1984, Japan's investment positions in the U.S. were estimated to have surpassed comparable positions held by the U.K. and the Netherlands, former leaders of foreign direct investments in the U.S.

Meanwhile, partly to offset slower growth of the Atlantic trade, European direct investment positions in the U.S. have doubled from about $40 billion in

1979 to about $78 billion in 1983. Together with increasing Japanese investments in the U.S., steady increases in European investments in the U.S. have contributed much to closing the asymmetrical gap between American investments abroad and foreign investments in the U.S. As late as in 1979, foreign investment positions in the U.S. were merely about one-fourth of American investments abroad. By the end of 1983, however, foreigners had closed this gap to about two-thirds of American investments abroad. By the year 1990 the familiar asymmetry in the cross investment features between America and the rest of the world, most notably, Japan and Europe, will be easily reversed and foreign investment positions in the U.S. will exceed American investment positions abroad. Between Japan and the U.S. alone, this reversal already occurred in 1982.

More importantly, even a cursory analysis of Japanese and European multinational firms active in the U.S. reveals that they are expanding their involvements in manufacturing activities in the U.S. This is happening at a time when their American competitors are even cutting back their own manufacturing operations inside the U.S. This is what I call the "Japanese and European Paradox" in the U.S. When many American manufacturing firms are fleeing the U.S. to countries where wages are lower, their Japanese and European competitors are coming ashore to the U.S. to manufacture their quality products with high cost American labor. Some Japanese firms have taken over even unionized plants which their American competitors have abandonned as uneconomical and have turned them around successfully (Y. and R. Tsurumi 1984).

What does then enable Japanese and European multinationals to succeed where their American multinationals have failed in their own home territory? In particular, the three-way competition inside the U.S. among American, European and Japanese firms is moving into even high-tech fields in addition to steel, auto, machine, tools, tires, und pharmaceuticals. This situation challenges us to freshly review two theoretical paradigms of foreign trade and investment: namely (1) product life cycle theory of foreign trade (PLC) and (2) corporate culture as a significant firm-specific determinant of foreign direct investment.

2. A Revised Theory of Product Life Cycle (PLC)

In February 1983 Atari Corporation in the so-called silicon valley of California suddenly laid off 2,000 American workers, engineers, and managers and shifted its production operations of home computers and games to Taiwan. Over the past two decades or so, this sort of reaction to the first sign of intensifying price competition even in the growing U.S. market has gripped one American manufacturer after another. In order to meet their budgeted profits, American managers have ditched their employees and salvaged their equipment by moving familiar production processes to lower wage countries.

Many American economists and business executives, using a prototype PLC theory of international trade and investment (Vernon 1966), still defend the behavior of the "Atari Syndrome". According to them, the profit maximization goals of any firm would logically dictate an international migration of manufacturing operations of mature and standard products from the U.S. to low wage countries in a search for lower production costs. The mythology of the free enterprise system reinforces the effects of the Atari Syndrome to the extent that economists, business executives, politicians, and even labor leaders seem to equate the Atari Syndrome behavior with the sacred rights of management.

U.S.-trained economists and business scholars in particular still cling to the assumption that the rate of firm- and industry-specific technological innovation will decline as products enter the mature phase of the product life cycle. Accordingly, the behavior of the Atari Syndrome fits the prognosis offered by this prototype paradigm of the PLC theory. If firms do not achieve innovation in their production processes and upgrade the skills of their workers, they have little choice but to seek lower wage rates to cut average production costs. The Japanese and European Paradox in the U.S. confronts us with the task of revising the PLC theory. For example, in the U.S. automobile industry, in addition to earlier manufacturing investments by Volvo of Sweden and Volkswagen of Germany, Renault's partial acquisition of American Motors have brought the three European auto manufacturers to face off with three Japanese auto makers, Honda, Nissan, and Toyota, in the U.S. productions of subcompact cars. In the product development and subsequent production of subcompacts, all American auto manufacturers have all but conceded to their Japanese and European competitors. Although Volkswagen has somewhat stumbled, Honda, Nissan and Toyota have already shown that quality subcompacts can be profitably manufactured in the U.S. How did this happen?

Using the example of the Japanese automobile industry, I would like to demonstrate conclusively that even after the product reached its maturing stage in Japan the rate of technological innovation in the industry continued to grow. To ascertain this empirical proposition econometrically, I used the Bayesian estimation method of the production function (Y. and H. Tsurumi 1980). The results are summarized in Table 1. The methodology of the relevant econometrics is summarized in the Appendix to this paper. (Cf. 35 et seq.)

The Japanese automobile market reached the maturing stage around the second quarter of 1970. But even after 1970, the industry continued to register

Table 1: Coefficients of Technological Progress of the Japanese Automobile Industry*

Growth Stage	
1st Quarter of 1962 to 2nd Quarter of 1966	0.022
Maturing Stage	
2nd Quarter of 1970 to 2nd Quarter of 1980	0.035

* Estimated on the basis of quarterly production data, with the use of CES production function.

technological progress, as shown by the significantly larger coefficient of technological progress for the latter of the two periods indicated in Table 1. As market competition in Japan intensified throughout the 1970s among seven major firms, the Japanese invented and perfected flexible manufacturing systems (FMS). In addition, these technological innovations in both production processes and corporate management knowhow soon spread to other batch-system production operations, such as consumer appliances, IC chips, machine tools and electronics and precision equipment. These advances enabled many Japanese firms to attain two goals simultaneously – higher productivity and zero-defect production – which would enable the firms to cope swiftly with whimsical shifts in market demand at home and abroad without loosing production efficiency. These FMS-related management skills are now helping Japanese manufacturers to succeed in doing in the U.S. what their American competitors often failed to do: namely, to produce mature products in a high-wage country like the U.S.

Although Japanese auto makers have produced a number of product innovations such as the transversed front wheel drive engines of Honda Accord, their distinct technological innovations have been related to their manufacturing processes and institutional skill. Contrary to a popular belief in the U.S., the productivity and quality of Japanese firms do not stem from a static economy of scale like a longer production run of the same model than their American competitors (Garvin 1984). As shown in Table 2, when one compares the production systems of subcompact cars of General Motors and Toyota, for example one must notice that Toyota's system is radically different from that of General Motors.

In short, the manufacturing processes of Japanese firms like Toyota are not only far more productive but more importantly far more flexible than a typical manufacturing process of American firms like General Motors. As shown by the smaller number of quality inspectors inside their plants, Japanese manufacturers have integrated their quality control into their production processes. Whereas, their American competitors still try to "inspect quality" mainly after products are finished. Rather than using inventories of finished goods, parts,

Table 2: Comparisons of Manufacturing Systems of General Motors and Toyota, 1981 (Subcompacts)

	GM	Toyota
Average production run	10 days	2 days
No. of parts stamped per hour	325	550
Worker per press line	7–13	1
Average time needed to change dies	4–6 hours	5 minutes
Daily absenteeism	11.8%	3.5%*
No. of quality inspectors	1 per 7 workers	1 per 30 workers
Time needed per finished car	59.9 hours	30.8 hours
No. of outside suppliers	3,000	300
Inventory/sales ratio	17%	1.5%
No. of worker job categories inside plant	26	4

* This number includes people away from work on business and training assignment that make up most of Toyota's absenteeism rate.

and work-in-process products to cushion uncertainties of market demand, suppliers, and production operations, Japanese firms use frequent changes in the number of production shifts and the flexibility of production runs to cushion cyclical demand fluctuations. Rather than playing one supplier off against another, Toyota and other Japanese firms have long built up their organic and cohesive relationship with those fewer suppliers that operate equally flexible production systems to meet rigorous delivery schedules and quality standards (Y. Tsurumi 1982).

We can easily recognize the economic superiority of the flexible manufacturing system like the one developed by Toyota over the typical rigid manufacturing system of many American firms. More importantly, we need to acknowledge that the economic superiority of the flexible manufacturing system does not stem so much from such "hard ware" as robots – important as they may be – as from such "soft ware" technologies as the firm's abilities to obtain workers' willing cooperation for incessant retraining and rotational assignments. In 1981, a similar comparison of Ford and Mazda manufacturing systems revealed that Mazda's overall production cost was about $1,300 lower per car than Ford's comparable subcompacts (Y. Tsurumi 1983). The difference in the degree of automation and product engineering was found to contribute only 17% of the overall cost differences. The wage rate differential was found responsible only for 4% of the total cost difference. The rest originated from the difference in the production process yields and human resource management factors between Mazda and Ford. After all, the fact that over three-quarters of advanced industrial robots installed today in the world are found inside Japanese factories in Japan reflects their management-employee relations conducive to workers' total cooperation with introduction of new machines into their factories. In fact, one prevailing fallacy of American management today is to equate the flexible manufacturing systems mechanically with the robotization. Many American managers disregard the corporate culture underlying the successful robotization of manufacturing processes.

More dramatic comparisons of Japanese and American firms can be made with the example of 64 K RAM integrated circuits (IC chips). This comparison includes European-owned factories of Fairchild Camera in California which Schlumberger, a French firm, acquired in 1980. Japanese semiconductor makers in Japan pay roughly the same price as their American and European competitors in the U.S. for raw silicon materials. However, Japanese firms have to pay about four times as much as their American competitors for energy and chemicals and twice as much for direct labor. As a result, Japanese production costs per wafer are today about $159 as opposed to American competitors' costs of $94. However, Japanese firms dominate the American and European market of 64 K RAM IC chips. How is this possible?

In 1984, Japanese semiconductor firms were voluntarily restraining their supply quantity to the U.S. and European markets in order to maintain the price of $4 per IC chip. This price level provides a protective umbrella to higher-cost producers in the U.S. and Europe. Naturally, Japanese firms are found to be making 50% to 90% more profit contribution per IC chip over the cost of its wafer than their American competitors. The difference is due to the higher chip yields per wafer of Japanese firms. When American and European firms are making only 176 good chips per the same sized wafer, their Japanese firms are found making anywhere from 264 to 380 good IC chips per wafer.

Accordingly, once transplanted to the U.S. by Japanese firms, their flexible production processes make Japanese semiconductor firms far more competitive when they can work with cheaper labor, cheaper chemicals and energy in the U.S. Unlike the semiconductor operations, however, Japanese auto firms have to pay about 50% more for American labor than for their Japanese labor. Yet, the higher monetary wage rates in the U.S. are more than offset by the higher productivity of Japanese auto assembly systems. Today, General Motors is counting on its joint venture with Toyota in California for learning Toyota's superior manufacturing systems (Reich 1984). In Europe where the wage rates are already generally lower than Japanese rates, the flexible manufacturing systems of Japanese multinational firms have helped them more readily to overcome start-up problems.

All told, manufacturing firms can continue to pursue the technological innovations as they ride their product life cycle well beyond the growth stage. The innovation of production processes and management skills – institutional technology – often turn out to become the ultimate competitive strength of firms operating in the worldwide markets.

3. Corporate Culture as a Firm-specific Technology

The Japanese and European Paradox needs one additional explanation. Otherwise, we are still left with one mystery that Japanese plants of high-tech related products in Japan, Korea, Taiwan, Malaysia, Singapore, and Europe have been able to cope with dynamic shifts in U.S. market demands for IC chips, consumer electronics, and other high-tech related goods better than American plants located in the same areas.

The Atari Syndrome would not have placed American operators of off-shore supply bases at a disadvantage vis-à-vis their Japanese competitors if the mature demand in the U.S. market had remained rather static. In reality, however, maturing markets for many consumer durables and industrial products continued to reflect dynamic changes in the tastes and requirements of the users of those items. As seen in the case of color t.v. sets in the U.S., the maturing market demand often showed sudden surges of rejuvenated growth when new product innovations were added to what until that point had been considered standardized products.

Cut-off geographically from the American market, many of the manufacturing systems that American firms had moved overseas frequently proved too inflexible to cope with dynamic shifts in demand in the American market. For example, when U.S. demand for IC chips shifted from 16 K RAM to 64 K RAM during the period from 1980 to 1983, American suppliers failed to respond quickly. This void in the U.S. and European markets were filled by their Japanese competitors. Moreover, American IC chip manufacturers with off-shore plants in low wage countries frequently found themselves faced with new problems of defective product quality. Loosing out in the market to their Japanese competitors, American chip manufacturers ran to the U.S. government for protection from Japanese competition.

In order to remain competitive in dynamic markets firms must be able to supply newer products quickly in ample quantity to their markets. This move requires closer and simultaneous coordination among R & D, product development, marketing and manufacturing operations (Fraker 1984). This kind of corporate flexibility is only sustained by free and instantaneous flows of necessary information back-and-forth among diverse operational units of the same firm. Many American manufacturers could not cope with dynamic market changes because of not only vast geographical distance but more importantly, fatal communication gaps between their R & D and marketing centers in the U.S. and their manufacturing centers abroad. Unlike their Japanese competitors, manufacturing operations of many American firms abroad were informationally isolated from American markets.

In contrast, Japanese executives when encountering similar market competition invariably move to save their human resources. They tend to seek technical rather financial or legal solutions. If they must cut personnel costs immediately, they cut their own salaries first. They strive to lower production costs and improve product quality by building more flexibility into their production processes, through automation and worker retraining. The offshore plants of Japanese firms are closely linked with their parent plants and suppliers in Japan, all of which are alert for market changes worldwide.

Theoretically the Japanese solution is available to American firms. But it requires closer coordination of such diverse functions as research and development, manufacturing, and marketing. Such coordination demands that the corporate culture nurture an atmosphere of comraderie among different individuals so that they can develop a shared commitment to the same corporate goal. Unfortunately, to many American executives, management leadership means the manipulative power to pit one profit or cost center against another, or one individual against another. They are quick to take credit for their firms' financial success, yet equally quick to find someone else – often foreigners – to blame for their failures. Accordingly, production managers are told to cut the costs of production within their own limited means. As a result, one company after another falls prey to the deadly "Atari Syndrome". Their offshore plants are informationally and managerially isolated from the U.S.

Successful transfer of Japanese manufacturing systems and Volvo experiments of factory management to the U.S. have shown that even the production of mature products can be made economically feasible in a high wage country like the U.S. A strong case can also be made to show that sustained successes in the high-tech related markets of industrialized areas like the U.S., Japan, and Europe require multinational firms to develop flexible corporate and manufacturing systems to cope with dynamic shifts of such markets. Elsewhere, I have shown that successful Japanese and American firms in such markets have developed rather similar corporate structures and cultures and that corporate cultures of firms can be generally divided into two dominant types, namely Model J and Model A (Y. Tsurumi 1976 and 1979).

Model J type firms are found predominantly among Japanese, European and American firms whose business environment is characterized by technological innovations, global competition, and rapid growth. Unlike Model A type firms which include many American firms involved in mature technologies and markets in the U.S., Model J firms share such internal characteristics as (1) management commitment to the job security of employees; (2) a shared corporate goal as the effective management control device; (3) lateral and informal communication across different departments and individuals of the firm; (4) strong identification of both management and employees with their firm; and (5) management emphasis on continued training of corporate members.

Implicitly, the job security of Model J corporation members becomes the foundation of the long-term orientation of the firm's employees. The job security also serves to support cooperative rather than adversarial relations among various subunits of the firm or between management and rank and file members. The job security of Model J firms often negates the need for cumbersome measures of arbitrating job grievances or policing individual members' behavior. Because of the job security, few resist the introduction of new machines and changes in work rules that are necessary to remain competitive in dynamic markets. Inasmuch as a manager's misjudgement concerning the market or the competition that produces a decline in sales and profits is not offset by expedient layoffs of rank and file employees, managers must always concern themselves with their organization's flexibility to cope with rapid shifts in the business environment.

The Japanese and European Paradox in the U.S. has demonstrated that Model J corporate structures are far more flexible than Model A corporate structures in their ability to make high-speed adjustments to dynamic changes in technological and market environments. Similarly, even after having acquired unionized factories in the U.K., the successes of Hitachi and Toshiba, two leading electronics firms of Japan, have shown that even militant British trade unions moderate their adversarial behavior and accept no-strick clauses in their contracts under Model J types of management of Hitachi and Toshiba. Michelin's success in transplanting its plant management know-how to South Carolina in the U.S. also underscores the fact that the firm's emphasis of training American labor and honoring the job security of its rank and file employees has enabled Michelin to develop superior production systems to those rigid manufacturing systems of its American competitors in Ohio and other mid-western areas of the U.S. In fact, Model J corporate culture has shaped its corporation to be "a learning entity" which encourages much experimental adaptation to their new technological and competitive environment.

Structural and cultural differences between Model A and Model J types of corporation can best be observed by the following four components of the corporate structures. All these four components are interrelated with one another.

3.1 Management Leadership Style and Ideology

Ideologically, management treats human labor as most important and renewable assests of the firm. Management leadership style is expressed in management's keen attention to actual details of manufacturing and sales operations of the firm. Management is not prone to shift the blames for management mistakes to the lay-off of rank and file employees. The costs of adjustments are absorbed, often first by the top management echelon, through temporary reduction of salaries and wages rather than through reduction of employment level. In shaping Model J types of firms after World War II, the Japanese brand of Confucian ideas of moral courage, self-sacrifice, and benevolence was consciously applied to enriching the management leadership style and substance (R. Tsurumi 1983). In fact, Japanese management's conscious efforts from 1949 onward were devoted to combining the Japanese Confucian notion of managerial leadership and entrepreneurship with the best of American industrial ideologies of efficiency, quality, and growth (Kodansha 1983).

3.2 Human Resource Development

In order to develop the corporate culture to turn the firm into a learning entity, continual training of management and rank and file employees is emphasized. Many individuals are often rotated among different jobs so that they could develop their own views of how different functions of their firm are intertwined with one another. Each corporate member is encouraged and even required to share his or her job skill, knowledge, and even work assignments with fellow employees.

3.3 Personnel Rewards and Job Performance Evaluation

In order to ease job rotations and frequent changes in job assignments, wages and salaries are tied more to such personal factors as the seniority and training backgrounds than to specific job categories. When one links job categories to wages and benefits, one should maintain as few job categories as possible to facilitate job rotations. As shown in Table 1, Toyota's four job categories were far less than General Motors' 26 job categories inside a comparable auto assembly factory. Rather than relying on strict job descriptions for guiding individuals' job performance, their shared acceptance of their firm's goals and their assigned tasks is emphasized to guide individuals' job performance. In order to reward the cooperative work among employees as well as to help develop every member's commitment to the corporate goals, various forms of profit sharing plans are actively maintained (Marsh and McAllister 1981).

3.4 Management-Labor Relations

Both formal and informal information sharing about the firm's goals and operations between management and labor (employee) is extensively practiced. This shared information serves to reduce conflicts and tensions between management and labor. In addition to management's sharing the responsibility of honoring the job security of rank and file employees, the extensive and frequent sharing of information between management and labor was carried out by both Hitachi and Toshiba when they needed to avoid destructive labor relations developed under former British owners. In 1971 when Hitachi Metals acquired a special alloy plant in Edmore, Michigan in the U.S. from its former owner, General Electric Corporation, Hitachi Metals faced the militant labor union (the United Auto Workers) that had grown distrustful of the management under conflict-ridden relationships with GE management. By sharing the responsibility for the job security of rank and file members with the UAW, and by sharing the management information and operational information with the UAW and rank und file employees, Hitachi Metals rebuilt the management-employee relationship toward more cooperative mode. During the economic recession of 1974–76, Hitachi Metals opened its books to the UAW and asked the employee (union members) to choose between a temporary but across the board wage cut with no lay-off and the lay-off of about 25% workers with no wage cut for the remaining group. By an overwhelming margin, the union members decided to accept the wage cut across the board.

4. Conclusions

Flexible manufacturing systems of many Japanese firms and some American and European firms are integral parts of their flexible corporate systems. The Japanese and European Paradox in the U.S. is made possible by the flexible corporate systems of Japanese and European multinationals. Flexible corporate systems are already found more suitable for uncertain global competition in the 1980s and the 1990s. Accordingly, the final outcome of the global competition among multinationals of different nationality will depend on their ability to develop their flexible corporate systems with their own employees of different nationalities worldwide. The firms will have to learn to integrate even those foreign managers, specialists, and employees, not born and trained in the home country of the firms, into their informal and formal communication networks across different functions and locations of the same firm (Y. Tsurumi 1978; Japanese Business 1978).

In this regard, increasing successes of Japanese and European direct investments in the U.S. are confronting many American multinational firms in auto and other mature industries to reconsider their global strategies and corporate structures. Besides, as exemplified by IBM, there are already some American multinational firms in computers and other high-tech fields which have developed their own flexible corporate systems beyond those prototypes offered by their Japanese and European counterparts. The three-way competition among American, Japanese, and European multinational worldwide will take on far greater complexities as they grope for cooperation and competition among them through innovative business tie-ups and defensive manoeuvers in one another's territories.

More immediately, the Japanese and European Paradox in the U.S. helps us answer one tantalizing empirical question of multinational firms' investment behavior: why are many American multinationals prone to move their manufacturing operations to lower wage countries even before their products reach their maturity stage in the U.S.? Why do their Japanese and European competitors often wait until the end of the maturing stage of their products at home before they transfer the production of standard products to lower wage countries? Hypothetically, if American firms learn to behave like their Japanese competitors, they would collectively offer at least 4 to 5 years of additional employment time to their employees. Since this is no small matter for the U.S. struggling to ease employment adjustment problems, a host of public policy issues will be further illuminated by further analysis of the Japanese and European Paradox in the U.S.

Just as Japanese managers have successfully combined the Confucian entrepreneurship values of human resources with the modern capitalism based on the Judeo-Christian mores, European multinational managers have much to contribute to the ideological enrichment of flexible corporate structures. Many of them have already been bred in the tradition of humanistic and social democracy and have been exposed to pragmatic management-labor codetermination. Their successes in the U.S. will add a new dimension to the modern management of multinational firms.

Bibliography

Fraker, S.: High-Speed Management for High-Tech Age. *Fortune*, March 5, 1984.

Garvin, D.: Comparisons of American and Japanese Manufacturing Systems. *Columbia Journal of World Business*, Winter 1984.

Japanese Business: Annotated Bibliography and Research Guide. Praeger, New York 1978.

Kodansha Encyclopedia of Japan, Vol. 1. Harper & Row, New York 1983.

Marsh/McAllister: ESOPs Tables. A Survey of Companies with Employee Stock Ownership Plans. *Journal of Corporation Law*, Spring 1981.

Reich, R. B.: GM's Pact with Toyota Is a Cover for Surrender. *The New Republic*, February 27, 1984.
Tsurumi, H./Tsurumi, Y.: A Bayesian Test of the Product Life Cycle Hypothesis as Applied to the U.S. Demand for Color TV Sets. *International Economic Review*, October 1980.
Tsurumi, R. R.: American Origins of Japanese Productivity. *Operation Management Review*, February 1983.
Tsurumi, Y.: *The Japanese Are Coming*. Ballinger, Cambridge 1976.
Tsurumi, Y.: The Best of Times and the Worst of Times. *Columbia Journal of World Business*, Summer 1978.
Tsurumi, Y.: Two Models of Corporation of International Transfer of Technology. *Columbia Journal of World Business*, Summer 1979.
Tsurumi, Y.: Managing, Consumer and Industrial Marketing Systems in Japan. *Sloan Management Review*, October 1982.
Tsurumi, Y.: The U.S. in the Pacific Age: New Challenges to Corporate and Government Policies. *World Policy Journal*, Summer 1984.
Tsurumi, Y./Tsurumi, R.: *A New Mechanism of Employment Adjustment for the U.S.* Work in America Institute, Scarsdale, New York 1984.
Vernon, R.: International Investment and International Trade in the Product Cycle. *Quarterly Journal of Economies*, May 1966.

Appendix: Estimation of Technological Progress of the Japanese Automobile Industry

Production Function: We need to estimate econometrically longitudinal changes in important parameters of production function. In other words, we need to capture quantitatively changes over time in such variable as technological coefficient along the PLC curve. This requires us to utilize the transitional functions.

We estimated the production function of Japanese passenger cars by introducing a gradually shifting technological coefficient to the CES production function in which the two primary inputs, capital (K), and labor (L) are the only arguments. We ignored any other inputs in our study. The elimination of nonprimary inputs such as enegry and raw materials from the production function is allowed if and only if the primary inputs and technical change are separable from nonprimary inputs. Otherwise the estimation of the production function will be subject to specification errors. We assumed here the separability of the primary inputs from nonprimary inputs since there was the evidence that capital and labor are separable from energy and raw material inputs. Accordingly, we specified the production function as:

(1) $Q = f(K, L, A)$

where Q is output; K, capital: L, labor and A, technological index.

Taking the logarithm of equation (1) and introducing the transition function, trn(·), we specify the production function to be

(2) $\ln Q_t = \lambda t + \lambda' \mathrm{trn}(s_t/\eta)t + \ln f(K,L) + u_t$

where u_t, is the error term, and $\mathrm{trn}(s_t/\eta)$ is a transition function. We assume neutral technical change. The transition function satisfies

(3) (i) $\lim_{s_t \to \infty} \mathrm{trn}\,(s_t/\eta = 1$

(ii) $\mathrm{trn}(0)=0$

(iii) $\lim_{\eta \to 0} \mathrm{trn}\,(s_t/\eta) = 1$

and s_t, is given by

(4) $s_t = \begin{cases} 0\ , \text{ for } t \leqq t^* \\ t-t^*, \text{ for } t > t^* \end{cases}$

where t* is a join point and η is a reaction coefficient which indicates how gradual the parameter shift is from one regime of the product life cycle to another. f(K,L) is in CES form

(5) $f(K,L) = \gamma[\delta K^{-\varrho}+(1-\delta)L^{-\varrho}]^{-v/\varrho},\ v, \gamma > 0,\ \varrho \geqq -1, 0 \leqq \delta \leqq 1.$

Substituting (5) into (2) we obtain

(6) $y_t = \alpha_1 + \alpha_2 t + \alpha_3 \mathrm{trn}(s_t/\eta)\, t + \alpha_4 \chi_t + u_t$

where $y_t = \ln Q_t$, $\alpha_4 = v$, and $\chi_t = -\frac{1}{\varrho} \ln\,[\delta K^{-\varrho}+(1-\delta)L^{-\varrho}]$. Assuming the noninformative prior probability density function for the parameters and $u_t \sim$ NID $(0, \sigma^2)$, we obtain the joint marginal posterior pdf for t*, η, δ, and ϱ:

(7) $p(t^*, \eta, \delta, \varrho \mid \text{data}) \propto \mid X'X \mid^{-1/2} [S(\hat{\alpha} \mid t^*, \eta, \delta, \varrho)]^{-(n-4)/2}$

where $S(\hat{\alpha})=(y-X\hat{\alpha})'(y-X\hat{\alpha})$, $\hat{\alpha}=(X'X)^{-1}X'y$; X is the matrix whose t-th row consists of $\{1, t, \mathrm{trn}(s_t/\eta)t, \chi_t\}$, and $y' = (y_1, \ldots, y_n)$. Since the marginal pdf of any of the four parameters in (7) is not exactly expressible in analytical form we resort to a numerical integration procedure to obtain marginal posterior pdf's.

Using semi-annual data from 1955 to 1977, we derived the posterior means and posterior standard deviations of all the parameters, and the results are given in Table 3. The transition function is given by the hyperbolic tangent function. Important inferences are summarized in the following paragraph.

From Table 3 we see that the estimate of α_3 is positive indicating that technological progress increased in the second regime. Also we see that the join point, t*, i.e. the point at which the parameter shift occurs, is the 2nd half of 1966, and the reaction coefficient, η, of 4.1 indicates that the adjustment to the new regime took about three and a half years, since $\mathrm{trn}[(t-24)/4.1] \geqq .95$ for all t greater than the year 1970. This indicates that by early 1970 the industry reached the mass production stage.

Table 3: Posterior Means and Standard Deviations of the Parameters in Equation (6)

Coefficients	Posterior Mean	Posterior Standard Deviation
α_1	3.1742	.0889
α_2	.0221	.0069
α_3	.0131	.0029
α_4	.679	.0458
t^*	1966.II	1.9
η	4.4	1.6
δ	.3	.014
π	3.3	4.8
R^2	.96	
DW	1.71	

R^2 and DW are respectively the coefficient of determination, and the Durbin-Watson test statistics. They are computed using the posterior means of the parameters. We present R^2 and DW as descriptive diagnostic checks of the goodness of fit and auto-correlation.

Table 4: Investment on Plant and Equipment by the Japanese Automobile Industry, 1965–74

Year	Plant and Equipment Investment (millions of 1975 yen) I_t	I_t/I_{t-1}
1965	217,818	.973
1966	211,077	.969
1967	368,352	1.745
1968	440,491	1.196
1969	434,128	.986
1970	522,286	1.203
1971	419,057	.800
1972	466,241	1.110
1973	554,345	1.323
1974	496,186	.896

Source: *Planning on Plant and Equipment Investment*, Payment Basis, the Ministry of International Trade and Industry, Tokyo, Japan, various issues.

Can we support our findings with some other information on the Japanese automobile industry? Table 4 presents the real investment expenditures on plant and equipment by the Japanese automobile industry. From this table we see that during the period from 1967 to 1970 when the production function was experiencing the transition to a new regime, plant and equipment investment grew at the annual average rate of 28.3%, and after the new regime was reached, the rate of growth of the capital investment went down to 3.2% per annum for the period from 1971–74.

New Multinationals in Europe

Michel Ghertman

Summary

In the paper two topics are selected for discussion out of the wide research area concerning the multinational enterprises: the respective roles of U.S. multinationals in Europe and the European multinationals in the U.S.A. in the history of international oligopolistic competition between 1945 and 1980 and on the other hand the internationalization of European public enterprises. The paper is completed by a look at the change of the image of multinationals in Europe.

1. Some Present Research Results about New Multinationals in Europe

The theme of "the new multinationals in Europe" covers many ideas. The following list, eventhough non-exhaustive, should cover most of them.

Multinationals develop in new industries like robotics and biotechnology along different patterns in Japan, the U.S.A. and Europe (Shiino 1983 and Horwitch 1983).

The service industries become increasingly multinational with some leading figures in European banking, insurance, transportation, tourism, hotels and restaurants. This trend cannot encompass all services for many are either public or limited to a single country such as education, health, city transit, army, police and government services (Ghertman and Allen 1984, p. 34).

Small and medium-size business also become multinationals (Newbould 1978).

Japanese firms increase their degree of multinationality at an extremely rapid rate and their European and American competitors react in many different ways (Franko 1983).

American investment in Europe is of an entirely different nature than other types of foreign investments originating in other industrialized countries. The former are in their mature stage, when foreign subsidiaries grow on their own financial resources as 80% of new investments are based on reinvested foreign earnings, in the period 1978–80 while the latter are in their infant or growing stages: 1% und 17% respectively for French and German multinationals during the same period. The only mature European based multinationals are British: reinvested earnings account for 53% of foreign investment (Centre des Nations Unies 1983, p. 20).

Multinationals originating in lesser developed countries (LDCs) are also present in Europe, eventhough to a much smaller extent than their American and Japanese competitors. And Europe represents a very small share of the foreign investments of LDC multinationals. For example Europe represents 0,6% of total direct Indian investment abroad, 1,6% if one includes Greece within Europe and 3,6% with Cyprus and Yugoslavia. These figures are compared to 49,1% for South-East Asia and 28,8% for Africa (Lall 1983, pp. 26–28).

Multinationals from Eastern Europe and the U.S.S.R. are also present in Western Europe, especially in banking since 1919 in order to finance East-West trade, but also in distribution to promote Eastern goods, in transportation and in industry, eventhough to a smaller extent. But the investments of socialist countries in Europe are quite small compared to their Western competitors and they are less important than socialist assets in LDCs, mainly in raw materials extraction (7) (Zaleski 1983).

Public enterprises are becoming an increasing part of multinational activity. From 14 amongst the 483 largest industrial companies in 1962, they turned 37 in the same group in 1978 with their share of total sales of that group raising from 2,4 to 7,8 percent during the same period (Centre des Nations Unies 1983, p. 57). Public multinationals are essentially European companies. Out of the list of the main 41 state firms 38 originate in Europe, two in Canada and one in South Africa (Centre des Nations Unies 1983, p. 58). Public companies are also numerous in LDCs, some are multinationals but to a smaller extent than European ones.

In such a short paper it is not possible to cover all the above topics. Therefore, we have selected two:

First, the respective roles of U.S. multinationals in Europe and European multinationals in the U.S.A. in the history of international oligopolistic competition between 1945 and 1980.

Second, the internationalisation of European public enterprises.

They will be the matter of parts one and two of this paper. We have chosen to write the third part about the old and new image of multinationals in Europe. *At the request of the editors of this volume we shall put special emphasis on French multinationals.*

2. U.S. and European Multinationals in International Oligopolistic Competition

The dynamics of competition between U.S. based and European based multinationals were first considered with a static approach by the literature until the beginning of the seventies; it is only recently that a dynamic framework was considered (Graham 1978). Let us review the major conclusions of these two models.

2.1 The Static Model

Hymer and Rowthorn have compared the growth rate of U.S. (G_p), European multinationals (G_E) and the European subsidiaries of U.S. multinationals (G_s) between 1957 and 1967 (Hymer and Rowthorn 1970).

Their results read:

$G_s \geq G_E \geq G_p$ (Hymer and Rowthorn 1970, p. 72)

Eventhough these authors did not explain why the leader of the U.S. oligopoly first invested in Europe, they insisted on how the other U.S. competitors followed their leader's European move. They were forced to invest abroad because the leader's action could endanger the stability of market positions in the home territory by imports at a lower cost from foreign subsidiaries, or a faster move down the learning curve for standard volume goods. Knickerbocker (1973) tested this explanation empirically. Half of U.S. subsidiaries in Europe were created within three years of the leader's move and 75% after seven years.

Hymer and Rowthorn predicted that European firms would retaliate by investing in the U.S.A. creating a cross-investment pattern between the U.S.A. and Europe. This reaction would end up in the creation of a new stable oligopoly with an international scope for territories and players.

International competition gave different results than the above forecast. The dynamic model helps to explain this new reality better than the static one.

2.2 The Dynamic Model

The U.S. leader invested in Europe because of the rigidity of the home oligopoly. As marginal gains of market share were costly, it was more promising to invest first on new and fast growing markets. This explanation of the leader's behavior is formulated in Lanteri (Lanteri 1982). But his major contribution to the literature lies in his analysis of the reaction of European firms.

If U.S. firms were successfull in their European countries it is because they could exploit a proprietary advantage over local competition. Their is little reason for European companies to set foot in the home territory of their U.S. competitors if they are already at a disadvantage on their own base. European firms reacted in two directions (Lanteri 1982). First an important movement of restructuring occurred amongst European firms by mergers and acquisitions during the sixties and the seventies. This increase in industrial concentration took place on a national rather than pan-European basis. The large European firms, some already multinationals other to become so, are not European as such but rather from British, German, Dutch, Swiss, French or Italian origin. The second move lies in foreign investments by these firms in the neighbouring European countries. U.S. foreign investment was therefore as much an explanation to European economic growth and concentration as the Treaty of Rome.

It is only after this double reaction of concentration and foreign investments in Europe that firms from European countries built their own specific advantage which they could in turn develop in the U.S.A. This double reaction took a period of approximately ten years, which explains why European foreign investments in the U.S.A. increased mostly after 1974. Table 1 is a good illustration of the above.

Table 1: Relative shares of foreign investments to the six E.C. countries and relative shares of foreign investment from the six E.C. countries (1970–78)

Period	1970–73	1974–78
Investments from other countries of which		
E.C.	41,2	40,8
U.S.A.	26,9	19,8
Investments to other countries of which		
E.C.	47	38,9
U.S.A.	7,9	18,8

Source: Lanteri (1982, pp. 169–173)

European firms invest more in neighbouring European countries than in the U.S.A. eventhough the attraction of the latter more than doubles in 1974–78 compared to 1970–73.

American multinationals in Europe in the eighties are quite a new breed compared to the same multinationals twenty or thirty years before. Instead of penetrating different territories, their foreign subsidiaries develop on their own financial strengths (up to 80% of their needs) and they repatriate half of their profits to the U.S.A. in the form of dividends. U.S. multinationals are mature and stable in Europe, there is no decline in their market position.

European multinationals moving into the U.S.A. in the late seventies and the eighties have many similarities to the thrust of U.S. firms in Europe twenty years before. Their subsidiaries in the U.S.A. reinvest two-thirds of their profits and their parents provide most of the equity required for the penetration stage. Between 1966 and 1980 the ratio of European investments in the U.S.A. to U.S. investments in Europe is less titled towards U.S. dominance: from 37 to 49% (Pelkmans 1982). Europe, however, is still much more invested by U.S. firms than the reverse eventhough the gap is narrowing. There is no evidence to conclude the continuation of this trend or the stabilization of the oligopoly.

As European firms reacted to U.S. investments, U.S. firms are reacting to the current move of European and Japanese investments by a movement of concentration of a magnitude never seen in the past. The merger of Dupont with Conoco in 1982 and the joint-venture between General Motors and Toyota in 1983 are recent examples. The reaction of U.S. firms to European investments is probably as important an element of explanation of U.S. economic growth in the beginning eighties as the economic policy of the Reagan administration. The continuation of U.S. economic concentration may have consequences for the behavior of U.S. multinationals abroad. A stabilization of international oligopolistic competition is therefore highly unlikely. Furthermore new entrants in the game may change the results in a manner requiring new theoretical developments in the future.

3. European Public Multinationals

Public enterprises mainly exist as a result of public policy to secure raw material resources (petroleum, mining) or high technology goods necessary for national independence (aerospace, armament). When the local private enterprise is able to fulfill the needs of such public policies, like in the United States of America, there is no need for a public enterprise. In Europe, however, lack of sufficient indegenous raw materials and the small size of internal proprietary military or high technology markets paved the way for a sustained need of public enterprise.

A second reason – complementary to the first one – for public enterprise is ideological. Social-democrats in France, Great-Britain and Austria after world war II, but also national-socialists in Germany before, because of anti capitalist feelings, prefer direct control of certain very large firms or banks rather than indirect control by regulation or continuous subsidies. The result may not be drastically different for the strategies of the units concerned, but respect is paid to political symbolism.

Ideology and its impact on direct economic control by governments is not the sole prerogative of many European socialists (but for the Germans). The French post world-war II government used patriotic feelings to take over Renault because the family which owned and directed it collaborated with the occupants during the war. The desire of direct control of monetary matters following the tradition of French kings and of the revolution of 1789 explain the takeover of the major French banks in 1945. The remainder, nationalized in 1982, are quite small in comparison. The economic component of liberal ideology is also present in the movement initiated by the Thatcher government to denationalize companies. Ideology is clearly responsible for the recent expansion of the public sector in France and its shrinking in the U.K. in the beginning eighties and in Germany in the fifties and sixties.

In case of a loss of the government and the presidency by the French socialists in 1986 and 1988, it will be interesting to see if their liberal followers will or will not cut the size of the French public sector. Theory cannot predict which will be the strongest: their liberal economic ideology or their tradition of economic centralization.

A third reason for European public enterprise lies in the importance for public policy in some countries to help ailing sectors of the economy for a mix of social and sometimes strategic considerations: steel, chemicals and computers in France for example.

Table 2: Employment size of public multinationals and uninationals in three countries

Employment statistics	United Kingdom (1976)		France (1980)		United States (1976)	
Categories of economic agents	Number 000s	% of total employment	Number 000s	% of total employment	Number 000s	% of total employment
Government services	5 300	21.37	2 546.5	12.21	18 060	20.64
State controlled firms (including multinationals)	2 000 360	8.06	1 602.6 330	7.68	1 013	1.16
Local subsidiaries of multinationals	926	3.73	818	3.92	1 128.80	1.3
Private indigenous multinationals	2 527	10.19	3 433	16	11 830	13.52
Other	14 047	56.64	12 455	60.20	55 453	63.38
Total employment	24 800	100	20 856	100	87 485	100

Source: Ghertman, (1984, p. 92)

When all the three reasons (national security, ideology and helping ailing firms) are present, they reinforce each other and state controlled firms are an important part of the home economy, like in France or the U.K. before the Thatcher government. When these reasons are absent, the reverse is true as in the U.S.A. The above table gives an idea of the size of public enterprise measured by the employment level for the U.K., France and the U.S.A. It also indicates the size of public multinationals in these countries.

In the U.K. (1976) and France (1980) the public sector accounts for about the same figure: around 8% of total home employment. It is quite large when compared to the employment due to the local subsidiaries of foreign multinationals: close to 4% in each case. But it is not as important as the employment of private indigenous multinationals: 10% in the U.K. and 16% in France or of government services: 21% and 12% respectively. Public multinationals account for 18% of the public sector employment in the U.K. (1976) and 21% in France (1980). If one accounts for the 490 000 employees (all in multinationals) added to the French public sector in 1982 (Ghertman 1982) the percentage of employment due to public enterprise rises to a little over 10% and French public multinationals account for 37% of the employment of the public sector, quite an extension, indeed. Public firms are amongst the largest enterprises in their countries. The concentration of public enterprises is much higher than that of the private sector. In comparison, the figures in the U.S.A. illustrate the lack of importance of public enterprises in general and public multinationals (non-existent on the record) in particular.

We have already mentioned that out of the 41 main state enterprises listed by the C.T.C. in 1981, 38 are European. Out of these 8 are French, 7 Spanish, 6 British, 4 Italian, 3 German, 3 Swedish, 2 Austrian, 2 Finnish, 2 Norwegian, 1 Dutch, 1 Belgian and 1 Portuguese. If one adds the six French firms who became public in 1981 and 1982, the French count rises to 13 in 1982. Out of these thirteen, eight are multinationals.

The French military industry is worth looking into because it is a case of international success (Anastassopoulos and Dussauge 1981). Armament requires a high technology which needs heavy R & D investments. Some are paid by the French budget through preferential purchases from French firms because of the policy of national military independence. However, as France is a middle size industrial country her budget would not suffice; therefore, the need to export is vital for the survival of its armament industry. Two factors explain the success of firms like Areospatiale (public), Matra (51% state-owned) of Aeronautique Marcel Dassault. The first is the high caliber of French technology developed by a corps of engineers nurtured by the Napoleon-build system of engineering schools. The second is the image of political independence of France amongst its foreign clients. French military equipment is sold in competition with those of the two largest exporters: the U.S.S.R. and the U.S.A., far larger than France in military exports. French diplomacy is not under Russian influence and has shown less dependence from U.S. influence than its British competitor who ranks fourth in the world armament export business. Eventhough Aerospatiale is a multinational, it exports much more than it manufactures overseas. Little possibility exists of changing this result because of national security requirements in this industry.

Good engineering and good diplomacy explains the French military export (and to a lesser extent multinationalization) success. Do other French public enterprises apply the same international strategy? The answer looks positive. A national telephone network, nuclear reactors, helicopters, radars, subways, satellites are sold by a combination of diplomats, industrialists and bankers (Anastassopoulos and Dussauge 1983). They all have high technological content. However, the independent image of French diplomacy does not help to sell subways or telephone systems like it does military equipment. Indeed, these systems are not as highly sensitive for defense purposes. Also competition comes from European countries and Japan, not only the U.S.A. Furthermore competition from the U.S.S.R. is frequently absent in the examples mentioned above. The factors of success for French military exports and transfer of technology, with its multinational component, do not apply as well to other French public multinationals. Competition arises from companies stressing marketing and production skills, i.e., cost effectiveness, while the French prefer technological innovation. This highly risky path, deeply rooted in French tradition, is certainly a major element to explain the difficulties of French public multinationals in international competition.

4. New Multinationals, Old and New Image

The transformations of multinationals, i.e. their new characteristics in the eighties are fairly well captured by the existing literature. However, very little research is available on the old and the new image of multinationals in Europe. A study exists on the old image in the major European countries mainly for the year 1974 (Peninou et al. 1978). The new image is only captured for French multinationals by research done for the years 1976, 1979 and 1982 (Cotteret, Ayache and Dux 1984). Let us analyse the image in 1974 and 1982.

4.1 The Image in 1974

In 1974, public opinion considered multinationals from an ethical point of view. It was a controversial topic which produced a majority of negative value judgements about the validity of the existence of such firms.

"First of all, there is an element of *active imagination*, i.e. an interpretation of the phenomenon nourished by arbitrary and evocative images and dominated by the idea of power and covert activity – two variants of the same basic fear. This interpretation brings forth many associations of ideas such as the cold and hybrid monster and hidden and evil machinations ... The favourite image is that of a shapeless 'thing' forever expanding in its rapaciousness (a monster with 'twitching feelers', a 'tentacled' octopus, a hydra 'with a thousand arms') ... Then the idea of *size* takes over, provoking that malaise which always goes with *immensity*. Immensity is the very essence of the multinationals, whose power and worldwide field of actions is evoked" (Peninou et al. 1978, p. 30).

Immensity is quite well captured by the attribute of "gigantic" the shapeless monster by the attribute of "supranational", i.e. which cannot be tagged with a label of national origin. Table 3 illustrates this perception in four countries.

Table 3: Spontaneous Attributes Applied to Multinationals in 1974

	France	West-Germany	Netherlands	United-Kingdom
Gigantic	12	19	20	16
Supranational	20	31	9	11
No reply	37	39	42	30
Others	31	11	29	57

Source: Peninou et al. (1978, p. 5)

It is quite striking that in France and Germany the fear of supranationality was much larger than that of gigantism while the reverse was true for the Netherlands and the United Kingdom. A possible explanation arises if one differentiates foreign from indigenous multinationals in the following table.

In Germany and in France the most quoted names of multinationals were foreign rather than indigenous: respectively six and one in Germany (where the supranational image is at its peak) and four and two in France. The reverse is true in the Netherlands and the U.K. In the Netherlands the three indigenous firms in the list are quoted with a much higher frequency than the four foreign firms: Philips is quoted over ten more times than I.B.M. In the four foreign firms we have included Shell, eventhough it is Anglo-Dutch, because it is largely perceived by Dutch opinion as an American firm (Peninou et al. 1978). In the U.K. four indigenous firms are quoted against three foreign. The two following hypotheses seem well grounded in the above tables and observations:

– The more foreign multinational names arise spontaneously in public opinion, the more multinationals have the image of supranational monsters and the less of giants.

Table 4: How well are Multinationals known?
Q. Which multinational companies do you know at least by name?

France	%	West Germany	%	Netherlands	%	Great Britain	%
Automobile companies	25.3	Shell	24.0	Philips	42.2	Ford	23.1
Non-American petrol companies	15.3	American petrol companies	22.3	Shell	33.3	I. C. I.	19.7
Péchiney	9.9	Ford	11.6	Unilever	21.0	Shell	17.9
I. B. M.	9.7	Coca Cola	10.6	Akzo	17.3	General Motors	11.4
American petrol companies	9.3	I. B. M.	9.8	American petrol companies	8.1	B. P.	8.5
Philips	9.0	General Motors	9.6	I. T. T.	5.3	American petrol companies	8.0
		Volkswagen	8.6	I. B. M.	3.9	Unilever	5.9

Source: Peninou et al. (1978, p. 54)

– The more indigenous names of multinationals arise in public opinion of the home of the parent, the less multinationals have the image of supranational and the more of giants.

Therefore nationalist feelings appear to determine which negative attribute comes first: supranational or gigantic.

4.2 The Image in French Public Opinion in 1982

The controversial and negative image of 1974 was confirmed for French newspapers and weeklies in 1976 (Cotteret, Ayache and Dux 1984). However, a major turnaround occurred in 1979: instead of having become factual. They deal with their economic role in specific industrial sectors. While in 1976 the gigantism of multinationals was condemned, their power considered abusive and their competence noxious, in 1979 their giantism was perceived as ordinary, their power tolerated and their competence evident. 1979 is clearly a year of the fall of the negative myth of multinationals in the French press. In 1982 the image becomes more ambivalent: less positive than in 1979 but less negative than in 1976 (Cotteret, Ayache and Dux 1984).

French public opinion in 1982 has an image of multinationals similar to that of the French press. From 1974 to 1982 the improvement of the image of multinationals in French public opinion paralleled a decrease of the number of names of foreign firms quoted spontaneously and an increase in the same for indigenous multinationals: 4 to 3 for the former are and 2 to 3 for the latter. This reinforces slightly the two hypotheses formulated above.

Overall two conclusions coincide for the period under observation:

– a drastic change of image: economic replace ethical considerations and the national identity perceived becomes more national.

– a stability of the image of giantism, power and competence eventhough its content turned from very negative in 1976 to ambivalent in 1982.

The two major explanations to the above changes are the following. First, economic difficulties turned the multinationals from a potential threat to national sovereignty into economic partners during hard times. Second, the nationalization of public firms in 1982, all of which are multinationals, gave rise to comments in the media about multinationals with a "French flag". The daily "Liberation" played the role of an opinion leader in that respect.

5. Conclusion

American multinationals in Europe differ markedly from what they were thirty years ago, while multinationals from several European countries, mainly Germany, the Netherlands and Switzerland are strongly investing in the U.S.A. Public multinationals have changed the picture of the European multinational scene. The image of multinationals is a new one in France in 1982 compared to 1974.

The three above conclusions give an idea of the transformations of multinationals in Europe in the past thirty years. The next years are likely to see even faster changes. The new European multinationals of the year 2015 will certainly be very different from the ones we have described.

Bibliography

Anastassopoulos, J. P./Dussauge, P.: L'armement, une spécialité industrielle à la française. *Revue Française de Gestion,* Mai–Juin 1981.

Anastassopoulos, J. P./Dussauge, P.: Transformer les avancées technologiques nationales en avancées stratégiques mondiales, *Revue Française de Gestion,* Sept.–Oct. 1983, pp. 6–12.

Centre des Nations Unies sur les sociétés transnationales: *Les sociétés transnationales dans le développement mondial,* troisième étude. Nations Unies, F. 83. II. A. 14 ST/CTC/46, New York 1983.

Cotteret, J. M./Ayache, G./Dux, J.: *L'image des multinationales en France.* P.U.F., 1984.
Franko, L.: *The Threat of Japanese Multinationals; How the West Can Respond.* Wiley, Chichester 1983.
Ghertman, M.: *Les multinationales, Que sais-je?* PUF, Paris 1984.
Ghertman, M./Allen, M.: *An Introduction to the Multinationals.* Macmillan, London 1984.
Graham, E. M.: Transatlantic Investment by Multinational Firms: A Rivalistic Phenomenon? *Journal of Post Keynesian Economics,* Vol. 1, 1978.
Horwitch, M.: La nouvelle complexité dans l'innovation technologique et la concurrence multinationale: le cas de la naissance d'une industrie bio-technologique multinationale. In: Cotta, A./Ghertman, M.: *Les Multinationales en mutation.* PUF, Paris 1983, pp. 89–105 and 107–131.
Hymer, S./Rowthorn, R.: Multinational Corporation and International Oligopoly: The Non-American Challenge. In: Kindleberger, Ch. ed.: *The International Corporation: A Symposium.* MIT Press, Cambridge 1970, pp. 57–97.
Knickerbocker, F. T.: *Oligopolistic Reaction and Multinational Enterprise.* Harvard University Press, Boston, Mass., 1973.
Lall, S.: *The New Multinationals, the Spread of Third World Enterprises.* Wiley, Chichester 1983.
Lanteri, M.: *Analyses des investissements directs entre les Etats-Unis et les pays européens,* thèse des doctorat de 3ème cycle, Université de Nice, 1982.
Newbould, G. et al.: *Going international, the experience of smaller companies overseas.* Associated Business Press, London 1978.
Pelkmans, J.: *Intereconomics,* HWWA, Vol. 17, No. 2, Mars–Avril 1982.
Peninou, G./Holthus, M./Kebschull, D./Attali, J.: *Who's Afraid of the Multinationals?* Saxon House, Teakfield 1978.
Shiino, K.: Les multinationales de la robotique. In: Cotta, A./Ghertman, M.: *Les Multinationales en mutation.* PUF, Paris 1983, pp. 89–105.
Zaleski, E.: Les multinationales des pays de l'Est. In: Cotta, A./Ghertman, M.: *Les Multinationales en mutation.* PUF, Paris 1983, pp. 195–213.

Role and Structure of German Multinationals: A Comparative Profile

Anant R. Negandhi

Summary

This paper examines the organizational structures, control processes and decision-making in German multinational companies and compares those aspects with their counterparts American and Japanese multinational companies. It is based on an empirical study undertaken with 244 subsidiaries of three types of multinational companies and 31 headquarters of those companies.

The purpose of this paper is to examine the changing role and structure of German multinational companies. The competitive pressures in the world's market place have increased the need for reducing cost and achieving economies of scale for all international companies. Particularly such competitive pressures are more intensive in industrialized countries. Usually American multinational companies have responded to competitive challenges by rationalizing production and marketing processes. This strategy of global rationalization is now being adopted by both the German and the Japanese multinational companies. Adoption of such strategy has led to corresponding changes in the structuring, decision-making, and control processes.

In the following pages, we will examine the changing structures, decision-making and control aspects in German multinational companies. In so-doing, we will compare and contrast German MNCs with their American and Japanese counterparts. Such comparative profiles will enable us to see the relative, instead of the absolute, positions of the German companies.

In order to place our analysis in some perspective, attempts will be made to briefly outline the relative position of German foreign direct investments.

1. Factual and Methodological Framework

1.1 German Foreign Direct Investments

As shown in Table 1, German foreign direct investments have increased tenfold, that is, from US $3 billion to $31.8 billion during the period of 1967 to 1978. Their total share in the world's foreign direct investment increased from 2.6 percent to 8.6 percent during the same period.

Table 1: Stock of Direct Investment Abroad of Developed Market Economies, by Major Country of Origin, 1967–1978

Country of Origin	Billions of Dollars End of: 1967	1971	1975	1978	Percentage Distribution 1967	1971	1975	1978
United States	56.6	82.8	124.1	49.6	49.6	49.3	47.2	45.5
United Kingdom	17.5	23.7	30.4	41.1	15.3	14.1	11.6	11.1
Germany, Federal Republic of	3.0	7.3	16.0	31.8	2.6	4.3	6.1	8.6
Japan[1]	1.5	4.4	15.9	26.8	1.3	2.6	6.0	7.3
Switzerland	5.0	9.5	17.6	24.6	4.4	5.7	6.7	6.7
Netherlands	11.0	13.8	19.0	23.7	9.6	8.2	7.2	6.4
France	6.0	7.3	11.1	14.9	5.3	4.3	4.2	4.0
Canada	3.7	6.5	10.4	13.6	3.2	3.9	4.0	3.7
Sweden	1.7	2.4	4.4	6.0	1.5	1.4	1.7	1.6
Belgium-Luxembourg	2.0	2.4	3.6	5.4	1.8	1.4	1.4	1.5
Italy	2.1	3.0	3.3	3.3	1.8	1.8	1.3	0.9
Total Above	110.1	163.1	255.8	359.3	96.5	97.0	97.3	97.3
All Other (estimate)[2]	4.0	5.0	7.2	10.0	3.5	3.0	2.7	2.7
Grand Total	114.1	168.1	263.0	369.3	100.0	100.0	100.0	100.0

Notes: 1. Fiscal year beginning 1 April of the year indicated on the basis of cumulative flows of direct investment as reported to the International Monetary Fund.
2. Includes Austria, Denmark, Norway, Finland, Portugal, Spain, Australia, New Zealand and South Africa. For 1978: data not available for Denmark and South Africa.

Source: United Nations (E/C.10/38). Reproduced from: Grosse, (1981, p. 5)

Similar to the United States, German investments have been concentrated in the industrialized countries. As shown in Table 2, over 70 percent of their investments are located in developed countries.

Industry-wise, German firms investing abroad are in machine manufacturing and chemicals. As Stopford has indicated, "The industrial composition of these investments reflects traditional German strengths in science and technology" (Stopford 1981). This is vividly portrayed in Figure 1, which shows increasing shares of West Germany in such "high-tech" industries as organic compounds, petrochemicals (plastic), integrated circuits, and aircrafts.

Traditionally, German firms served the world markets through export. However, during the last decade or so, this strategy is being replaced by foreign direct investments in manufacturing operations abroad. This replacement of exported strategies by investment strategies, is shown in Table 3. As one can see from the table, sales of foreign affiliates of major German firms have increased during 1971 to 1976.

Figure 1: Position of Major Industries of the United States in World Markets. Changes in the Shares of Major Industrial Nations in World Markets.

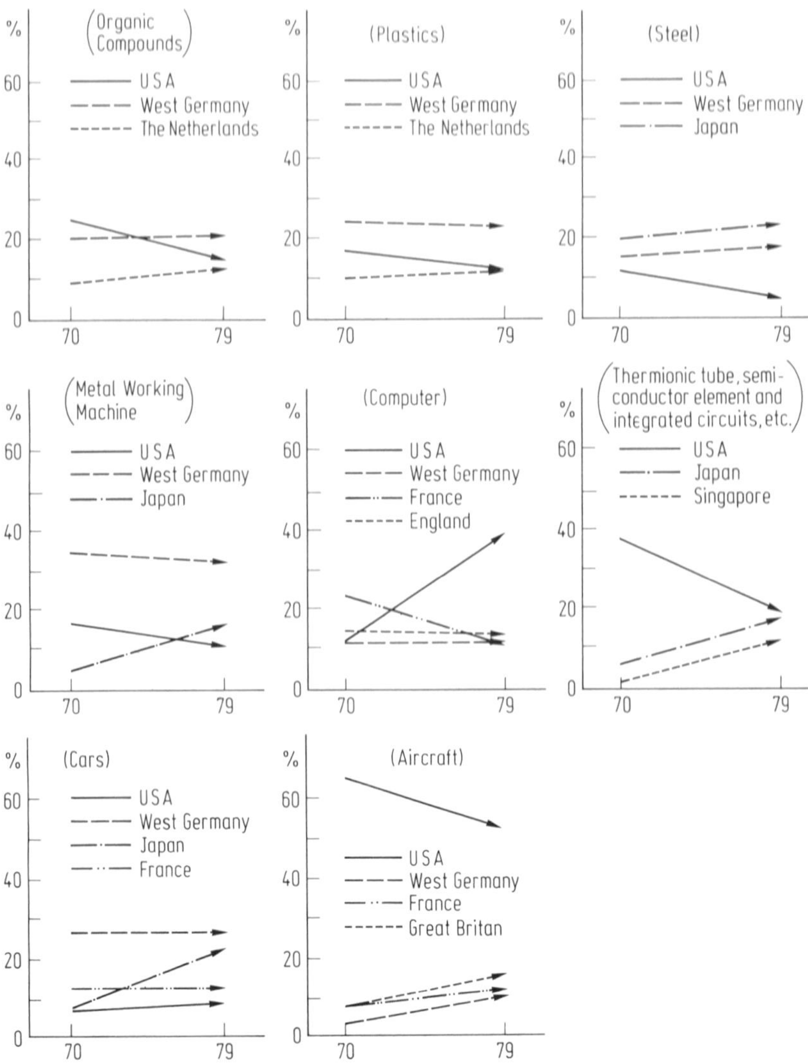

Notes: SITC (Rev. 1) codes of different items are as follows: organic compounds 512, plastics 581, steel 67, metal working machine tools 715, computers 7143, television sets 7241, radio 7242, thermionic tubes, semiconductor elements and integrated circuits, etc. 7293, cars 7321 air craft 734.

Source: UN-YITS. – Reproduced from *White Paper on International Trade Japan 1981,* (Tokyo: Japan External Trade Organization 1981, p. 16.) Permission of the publisher is greatly acknowledged.

Table 2: Location of German Foreign Direct Investments (Percentage)

Country	1971	1976	1984
United States	8.8	11.4	35.17
Belgium-Luxembourg	11.3	10.0	5.12
France	10.5	9.9	5.33
Switzerland	11.0	9.7	2.28
Brazil	6.9	7.3	1.41
Canada	8.2	6.8	2.25
Netherlands	5.5	6.6	6.25
Spain	4.7	6.2	5.75
United Kingdom	3.0	4.2	11.78
Other	30.1	27.9	24.66
Total	100.0	100.0	100.00

Source: Stopford (1980/81, p. 8); 1984 data from Dresdner Bank, Außenwirtschaftsnachrichten, 39. Jg., No. 5, Mai 1985.

Table 3: Changing International Balance of Nine Major German Manufacturers

Firm	Total 1976 Sales (DM billion)	Exports (as % Total Sales)		Sales of Foreign Affiliates* (as % Total Sales)		Export/Foreign Output Ratio	
		1971	1976	1971	1976	1971	1976
Hoechst	23.5	33	28	23	32	1.5	0.6
Daimler-Benz	23.5	30	39	13	21	2.3	1.9
BASF	23.2	26	25	14	20	1.9	1.3
VW	21.4	47	36	25	26	1.9	1.4
Bayer	20.9	30	27	46	48	0.7	0.6
Siemens	20.7	20	26	20	25	1.0	1.0
AEG	13.5	20	28	10	16	2.0	1.8
Mannesmann	11.8	35	47	11	16	3.1	2.9
Bosch	8.3	29	37	13	14	2.2	2.6

* Excluding exports from Germany.
Source: Annual Reports supplemented by author's estimates. Quoted from Stopford (1980/81, p. 13)

1.2 Corresponding Changes in Structures and Decision-making

As mentioned earlier, their changes in strategies from exporting to direct investment abroad coupled with the competitive pressures in the world marketplace, have necessitated corresponding changes in organizational structures and decision-making.

Although the global-rationalization concept and its accompanying global level organizational structure form have been well articulated and selectively implemented (Stopford and Wells 1972; Franko 1976), the real attributes or components of this concept, as well as implications of the process of rationalization, have not been systematically explored or even questioned by many researchers. Especially, answers to the following questions have not been well explored:

- To what extent does the rationalization process lead to a higher level of centralization in decision-making at the headquarters?
- What specific decisions are most likely to be centralized?
- What are the implications of such centralization in decision-making on headquarter-subsidiary relationships and on morale and motivation of the subsidiaries' managers?
- What are the implications of the rationalization process on the MNC-nation state's relationships?

The paper will examine briefly the above questions.

1.3 Research Methodology

The paper is based on two large-scale studies on multinational nation-state relationships conducted by the author during the period 1974–1982. The first study was undertaken with 124 multinational companies (54 American, 43 European and 27 Japanese) operating in six developing countries – Brazil, India, Malaysia, Peru, Singapore, and Thailand. The second study was conducted with 120 MNCs (34 American, 45 German, and 41 Japanese) operating in seven industrialized countries – Australia, Japan, Belgium, France, West Germany, the United Kingdom, and the United States (Negandhi and Baliga 1981; Negandhi and Welge 1984).

The data were collected through in-depth interviews with chief executives and other managerial personnel. A structural, 40-page interview guide was utilized. Each interview lasted about four to eight hours. (For details on the research design and methodology, see Negandhi and Baliga (1981) and Negandhi and Welge (1984).

2. Analysis of Results

We will first examine the level of formalization of policies and practices, degree of centralization-decentralization, and the relative influence of the headquarters and the subsidiaries in decision-making. Secondly, we will explore the impact of these factors on the headquarter-subsidiary relationships. As noted earlier, our aim of examining these elements was to assess the extent of the global rationalization strategies utilized by the three types of multinational corporations, namely the American, the German, and the Japanese. Finally, we will examine the implications of these practices on the relationships between the MNCs and the nation-states.

2.1 Level of Formalization

To assess the level of formalization in the American, German, and Japanese multinational companies, three aspects are examined:

- The subsidiaries' dependence on manuals, policies, and procedures supplied by the headquarters;
- utilization of these policies and procedures for decision-making; and
- the nature and the frequency of the reports required by the headquarters.

An overwhelmingly large number of the American subsidiaries (88 per cent) relied on the headquarters' policies. Approximately 30 per cent of the German subsidiaries did the same, while merely 12 per cent of the Japanese subsidiaries utilized the policies supplied by their headquarters. Conversely, only 16 per cent of the American, 48 per cent of the German, and 66 per cent of the Japanese subsidiaries indicated a very negligible influence on strategic and policy decisions affecting their operations.

A similar picture emerges when one examines the influence of the written policies and procedures (whether those supplied by the headquarters and/or modified by the subsidiaries) on actual strategic and policy-level decisions.

One can also evaluate the headquarters' relative influences on the subsidiaries' operations by examining the nature and frequency of the reports that were required from the subsidiaries' managers.

Almost all the American subsidiaries, and approximately two-thirds of the German and Japanese subsidiaries studied, were required, by their respective headquarters, to provide up-to-date information on balance sheet, profit and loss figures, production output, market share, cash and credit positions, inventory levels, and sales per product. The frequency of reporting was greater for the American (mostly monthly) than for the German and Japanese subsidiaries. The only items with which the subsidiaries were less bothered were the performance reviews of the personnel and the local socio-economic and political conditions. In other words, the stress is placed more on those aspects affecting the short-run financial situation of the company rather than on the factors affecting the firm's long-term survival and growth.

The analyses of the above three aspects of the formalization clearly indicate the increasing levels for formalization that are being introduced by the American

MNCs, while the German MNCs seem to be catching up with the Americans. The Japanese companies, however, are still relying on their informal network.

2.2 The Relative Influence on Decision-making

Centralization versus subsidiary-autonomy is a perennial question. Increasing competition in the world market requires some measure of rationalization of production and marketing processes at a global level, thus requiring a higher degree of centralization. On the other hand, to satisfy the increasing demands form the host as well as the home countries of the multinationals more autonomy on strategy decision-making by the subsidiary is necessary.

To assess the relative influence of the headquarters and subsidiaries in decision-making, we examined the following factors:

borrowing from local banks
use of cash flow by the subsidiary
extension of credit to major customers
choosing public accountants
introduction of new product for local market
servicing of products sold
use of local advertising agency
expansion of production capacity
pricing decisions
determining aggregate production schedules
maintenance of production facilities
appointment of chief executive
use of expatriate personnel
layoff of operating personnel
training programmes for local employees.

Overall, our results indicate that the subsidiaries seem to have at least equal influence on decision-making. American subsidiaries possess the least autonomy and Japanese subsidiaries the greatest. The German subsidiaries are in between those two extremes. However, the picture of the greater autonomy of the subsidiaries changes once we compare strategic versus routine decisions.

To probe further, we computed an overall delegation index by assigning different weights to strategic versus routine decisions. The strategic decisions were weighted three times higher than the routine decisions. The weighing factor was chosen to reflect the approximate ratio of the time-span of feedback of the strategic decisions compared to the routine decisions. Table 4 presents the findings for the overall delegation index and the extent of delegation provided to the subsidiary's management along with a set of decisions. As can

Table 4: Comparison of Delegation in the Various Areas for US, German and Japanese MNCs

	US (N=34)		German (N=45)		US (N=34)		Japan (N=41)		German (N=45)		Japan (N=41)	
	Mean	SD	Mean	SD	Mean	SD	Mean	SD	Mean	SD	Mean	SD
Overall delegation index	−1.68	4.33	0.14	3.72	−1.68	4.33	2.89*	3.38	0.14	3.72	2.89*	3.38
Local personnel decisions	2.40	1.46	2.85	1.24	2.40	1.46	3.51*	0.93	2.85	1.24	3.51+	0.93
Expatriate personnel decisions	−2.10	1.67	−2.49	1.60	−2.10	1.57	−0.65+	2.00	−2.49	1.60	−0.65*	2.00
Routine production decisions	−0.04	2.63	2.59*	1.43	−0.04	2.63	2.24*	1.84	2.59	1.43	2.24	1.84
Strategic production decisions	−1.78	2.21	−1.54	2.21	−1.78	2.21	0.07+	2.26	−1.54	2.21	0.07+	2.26
Routine marketing decisions	1.27	1.62	2.42*	1.19	1.27	1.62	2.85*	1.11	2.42	1.19	2.85	1.11
Strategic marketing decisions	−1.58	2.14	−0.83	2.42	−1.58	2.14	1.14*	2.35	−0.83	2.42	1.14*	2.42
Financial decisions	0.30	2.00	1.61*	1.50	0.30	2.00	1.90*	1.00	1.61	1.50	1.90+	1.00

Key:	−4	0	4
	max. HQ influence	equal influence	max. subs. influence

*#p 0.001
+#p 0.05

Source: Authors' interviews, Negandhi and Welge (1984).

be seen from this table, the overall delegation index is fairly low in absolute terms. The subsidiary's influence on strategic decision-making is minimal. Relatively speaking, the Japanese subsidiaries seem to enjoy the greatest autonomy and the US subsidiaries the least. German subsidiaries are again in between these two extremes.

Organizational structure, formalization of policies, reporting requirements, and the centralized decision-making, with respect to strategic business decisions, are some of the important means through which the multinational companies implement their unification drive. In addition, to implement the global strategies, multinational companies undertake corresponding changes in their policies, controls, and co-ordination devices concerning:

ownership of overseas subsidiaries
technological transfer policies
intra-company sales and purchases
strategic and long-range planning
manpower and staffing policies.

2.2.1 Ownership Policies

As the firm expands its international business activities and accumulates certain expertise in conducting international business, its desire to integrate and unify its overseas units into a global system increases. To accomplish these objectives, besides restructuring the organization, the firm will move to increase its ownership share in the overseas subsidiaries. As Stopford and Wells have found in their study of 187 American MNCs, 'In most cases in which firms showed strong preference for wholly-owned subsidiaries, the issue of control appeared to be paramount' (Stopford and Wells 1972, p. 107). They go on to state that 'certain strategies demanded tight central controls, others did not . . . Strategies that are generally extracted through a tightly controlled organization are also usually associated with a strong preference for wholly-owned subsidiaries' (p. 107). Overall, they found that the firms emphasizing marketing and advertising techniques, rationalization of production processes, and control sources of raw materials tend to prefer wholly-owned subsidiaries.

This trend seems quite visible with respect to the American MNCs. For example, the study undertaken by Booz, Allen and Hamilton (1971), a consulting firm, observed that approximately 60 per cent of the new overseas subsidiaries established by the American MNCs were wholly-owned, another 8–9 per cent were majority-owned, and in only 7–8 per cent, the US parent companies had minor equity interests (Booz, Allen and Hamilton 1971). In spite of increasing demands by the host countries, especially the developing nations, this trend of increased equity holding in overseas subsidiaries continues. As will be seen below, even the German and Japanese MNCs, which were more inclined to enter into joint ventures, now seem to prefer either wholly-owned or majority-owned subsidiaries.

Although our study attempted to secure equal numbers of the wholly-owned and jointly-owned subsidiaries of American, German, and Japanese MNCs, we were not able to find the required number of joint-venture subsidiaries in the various countries. Thus, of the 120 subsidiaries studied in the seven countries (Mexico, West Germany, the UK, France, Spain, Portugal, and the USA), about 107 of them (89 per cent) were wholly-owned, while only 3 per cent were miniority-owned. There were some minor differences among the three types of the MNCs studied; namely, the Japanese companies still preferred joint ownership of their subsidiaries as compared to the American and German multinationals, but this preference, as discussed above, was on a decline.

Our own results, as well as those reported by other researchers, clearly indicate the multinationals' preference for maintaining control through ownership. The drive for global rationalization is pushing the German and Japanese MNCs to acquire even larger equity in their overseas subsidiaries. However, the headquarters have, by and large remained ambivalent about their policies with respect to ownership.

2.2.2 Controlling Through Technology

For sometime now, technology transfer is being emotionally debated both in industrialized and developing countries as a focal issue.

Multinational firms especially the large, and technologically advanced, having control over important commercial technologies, are likely to use this leverage to secure favourable terms from the host countries as well as from their partners in those countries. The MNCs, therefore, create dependency relationships with the host countries as well as their own subsidiaries. Technological know-how provides them the power to control.

To assess the importance of technology as a control device, we collected the following four types of information at the subsidiary-level.

- The level of sophisticated technology used by the subsidiary.
- The relative technology of the subsidiaries compared to what was utilized by other firms in respective countries,
- The extent of technological transfers from the headquarters to the subsidiaries, and from the subsidiaries to the headquarters,
- Research and development activities undertaken by the subsidiaries.

Collectively, the results on these four aspects of technology clearly indicate a heavy reliance on the part of the overseas subsidiaries on their respective headquarters. The subsidiaries not only initially borrow technology from their headquarters, but they also depend on them for new technological know-how from their research and development laboratories. In other words, minimal R and D activities are carried out by the subsidiaries. Some 60, 80 and 78 per cent of the American, German and Japanese subsidiaries, respectively, did not spend significant amounts of money on this account. Among the three types of MNCs, a greater number of American MNCs have begun to decentralize their R and D activities (some 40 per cent of the US subsidiaries claimed to have spend between 1 and 10 million US dollars as compared to 11 and 23 per cent by the German and Japanese subsidiaries). When one considers the fact that the majority of the subsidiaries studied were located in the highly industrialized countries, such as the United States, West Germany, United Kingdom, France and Japan, this amount of expenditure on R and D does not look very impressive. Very few subsidiaries have matured enough to transfer technological know-how to their headquarters.

2.2.3 *Intra-Company Purchases and Sales*

Besides creating a technological dependency, the global rationalization drive by the MNCs may induce the firms to internalize their transactions both to minimize the competitive pressure and to achieve effective co-ordination of the global units of operations. As Buckley and Casson's (1976) study indicates, the multinational firms attempt to grow by eliminating external markets of intermediate goods through internalizing them within the firm. They also found that the incentives to internalize the markets are strongest among the firms with high technology, research and developmental intensity. It has also been shown that the American multinational firms seem to have a greater tendency to internalize their markets.

The United Nations' statistics show that some 23 per cent of sales of the American affiliates were intra-company transactions (UN, Economic and Social Council 1978). Such intra-company dealings are higher in mining and petroleum industries than in the manufacturing sector, and area-wise, they are more significant for the affiliates located in developing than in the developed countries. On the other hand, German and Japanese multinational firms are known to utilize local inputs in greater proportions, both to satisfy the host governmental demands as well as to grant higher degrees of autonomy to their overseas subsidiaries. This is especially true for the developing countries where such demands are most intensive.

Our results show a great deal of convergence in sourcing policies and practices of the three types of MNCs. Approximately two-thirds of the American, German and Japanese subsidiaries purchased one-quarter or more of their requirements of raw materials, semi-finished and finished goods from their respective parent organization.

2.2.4 *Environmental Scanning and Strategic Long-Range Planning*

Environmental scanning and strategic long-range planning are perhaps the most important integrating devices available to the multinational firms to achieve their global strategies. These two functions are conceived as the top-level executives' responsibilities and are concerned with the development of fundamental goals and major policies, assessment of the corporate strengths and weaknesses. Our inquiry on this aspect was mainly directed towards examining the use of strategic planning and environmental scanning as a control device. To explore this aspect, we collected the following data from the MNCs' headquarters and their subsidiaries:

(1) Nature of environmental scanning undertaken by the headquarters and subsidiaries;
(2) use made of the environmental scanning data;

(3) role of the subsidiaries in generating information;
(4) information feedback system;
(5) nature of long-range planning undertaken by the headquarters and subsidiaries;
(6) involvement of the subsidiaries in long-range planning processes.

Our results show that the American MNCs are the most active among the three types of MNCs in utilizing the planning processes as integrating and controlling devices. The majority of the US companies not only undertake long-range strategic planning, but are also involved in scanning the environments in a systematic manner, although the factors examined in the environmental scanning are mainly related to the general economic environments and market conditions. Many of these companies also claim a systematic use of environmental forecasting in their planning processes.

However, both the planning and the environmental scanning functions are to a large extent headquarter-oriented. More specifically, approximately one-third of the subsidiaries of American, German, and Japanese MNCs undertake some sort of environmental scanning, while some 45, 33, and 18 per cent, respectively, are involved in long-range planning. The centralization of these two functions is more clearly seen with respect to the communication patterns concerning the planning and environmental scanning processes between the subsidiaries and their respective headquarters. Among the American MNCs, the nature of communication concerning these two aspects is highly formalized, while the German and Japanese companies seem to be moving rapidly in this direction. Moreover, these communications are transacted through instructions and imperatives rather than constructive exchanges of ideas and information. Only one-third of the subsidiaries surveyed felt that their viewpoints were utilized by the headquarters in formulating long-range goals and objectives.

2.2.5 Manpower and Staffing Policies

There has been a considerable move on the part of the MNCs to localize their foreign subsidiaries' operations and place local nationals in top positions. In an earlier study undertaken by the author (Negandhi 1975) there were less than a dozen or so American nationals in 56 subsidiaries surveyed in the six developing countries. Also, we observed continuation of this trend among the American MNCs in an 1974–76 study of 124 US, European and Japanese multinational companies in developing countries (Negandhi and Baliga 1979). The majority of the top-level executive positions in the US subsidiaries were filled with local nationals. In contrast, the majority of the Japanese MNCs (79 per cent) did not employ even a single host country national in the top-level management ranks. The German MNCs have localized their overseas operations more than the Japanese and less than the Americans.

The drive for global rationalization by the MNCs in industrialized countries seems to be changing the above pattern of localization. Our inquiry concerning the manpower policies and practices for staffing the subsidiaries' top positions, the number of foreign nationals represented in the Corporate Board, and the holding of top-level executive positions in the headquarters, points towards an increasing trend of establishing controls through key personnel from the home offices. An overwhelming proportion of the three MNCs studied filled the key positions of their overseas subsidiaries through expatriates, although policy-wise, they were largely ambivalent in pursuing such policies. In the same vein, there were few foreign personnel represented in the Corporate Board and/or top management echelons at the headquarters.

3. Impact of Global Rationalization

3.1 Headquarter-Subsidiary Relationship

Our earlier studies (Negandhi and Baliga 1979), conducted in the six developing countries, indicate a high intensity of conflict between the headquarters and subsidiaries of the American MNCs. Particularly, the subsidiaries' managers complained a great deal about their inabilities to meet the environmental demands of the host countries due to the centralized decision-making at the headquarters' level. A large majority of the executives interviewed in American subsidiaries (N = 54) felt that they were little more than 'peons' in terms of their head office hierarchy, and that communication between them and the headquarters' personnel was strictly orders and imperatives from the home office.

In contrast to such apparent tensions and misgivings between the US subsidiaries' managers and their head offices, the German and the Japanese managers felt rather comfortable in their relationship with their head offices.

Although there was relatively much less formal reporting to be found in the German and Japanese MNCs, the overseas managers felt that they were involved in, and informed about, the major strategic decisions undertaken back home. Their own voices and viewpoints were seriously considered during the formulation of major policies affecting their operations. They also felt that they had considerable latitude in running their operations. In this respect, most of the American expatriate managers we interviewed, felt that their roles and duties were narrowly defined; they were simply just another cog in the corporate machine.

In the industrialized countries, the scene of greater satisfaction on the part of the German and Japanese subsidiaries' managers has changed considerably.

The global unification plans, pursued by all the three types of MNCs – American, German, and Japanese – have brought about similar problems in their relationship with the respective headquarters.

The capital investment and market and product-related issues dominated the scene in all three types of MNCs. More than one-third of the critical problems between the headquarters and the subsidiaries were related to these two aspects. Overall, the Japanese subsidiaries were less concerned about their decision-making authorities, while for both the American and the German subsidiaries, this was a critical problem by itself. Who has the right and the power to make decisions concerning subsidiary operations, was a highly debated and unsettled issue in the latter subsidiaries. On the other hand, issues related to personnel problems were more prevalent in the Japanese subsidiaries.

Our results indicate the seriousness of these critical problems existing between the headquarters and the subsidiaries. The climate of interaction was most tense in American and least tense in Japanese MNCs. German MNCs were in between these two extremes. In all the three types of MNCs, the top-level executives were directly involved in these issues, and the large majority of the cases were not resolved in less than 6 months. These issues were generally brought up by the subsidiaries' personnel, and they were resolved in formal meetings called by the headquarters.

Besides the differences in the interpersonal-interaction climate, the American, German, and Japanese MNCs differed in the relative influence of headquarters versus subsidiaries in resolving the issues. The German and Japanese MNC's subsidiaries had greater influence in resolving the issues than their American counterparts. Notwithstanding such differences in American, German and Japanese approaches, the critical issues arising due to the implementation of the global unification plans did drain off the executives' energies in all three types of MNCs. Moreover, such issues adversely affected the morale and motivation of the subsidiaries' managers.

3.2 MNC-Nation State Relationships

In developing countries, our results show that a wide gap existed between the expectations of the MNCs and the host governments. Such breakdowns in the understanding of each other have, indeed, created continous tensions and conflicts in their relationships. Many of the developing countries, in order to maximize their returns from foreign private investments, have enacted legislation which requires a majority local equity in foreign enterprises, higher proportion of local nationals in top positions, increase of exports and foreign exchange earnings, and reduction of imports of raw material and spare parts.

Such demands by the host countries have, to some extent, constrained the MNCs to rationalize their worldwide productive capacity. In order to achieve their goals, MNCs on their part have required that host countries provide them with efficient infrastructural facilities, reduce bureaucratic controls and interference in corporate affairs, and provide favourable labour legislation and more flexible expansion policies. (For a detailed analysis of these results, see Negandhi-Baliga 1981).

In industrialized countries, the results show that the host governments were the second most important source of problems the multinationals faced. The specific problems they encountered concerned the controls on foreign exchange, pricing, profits, and expansions. Approximately 50 per cent of the multinational companies studied indicated that the government agencies in the host countries created obstacles by enacting restrictive legislations and erecting unnecessary bureaucratic red tape. This is in line with our previous argument that higher levels of centralization in decision-making at the MNCs' headquarters will create greater tensions in MNC-government relationships. With respect to the consequences of the MNCs' conflicts, approximately one-quarter of the companies interviewed indicated that such conflicts have seriously affected their operational efficiency and demoralized their subsidiaries' managers.

4. Implication

This paper analysed the structure and role of West German MNCs compared to those originating from the US and Japan. In our earlier study in developing countries, it was observed that the German and Japanese companies maintained more organic organizational structures. This situation has changed in recent years, particularly with respect to their subsidiaries in the industrialized countries. Thus, the question should be asked whether or not the German and Japanese multinationals are flexible enough to turn the tide and maintain their organic structures, when the circumstances demanded them to do so in the industrialized countries.

Even the American multinationals, champions of evolving organizational structures for managing expanding international business (from export department to international division, regional structure, worldwide product set-up, and the matrix system) have been warned about the swiftly changing environmental conditions in both the developed and developing countries.

Given the changing economic and political conditions, the MNCs will have to create a responsive organizational structure that will be able to combine the centralization of strategies and policies with increased decentralization of their subsidiaries' operations. Whether the German and the Japanese companies, in their quest to adopt the American model of global rationalization, will be able to achieve a marriage between centralization of strategies and policies (as required by the global rationalization concept) and the needed decentralization or higher autonomy of the subsidiary operation still remains an open question.

Bibliography

Booz/Allen/Hamilton (ed.): Booz, Allen and Hamilton Study. *Business Abroad,* June 1971.

Buckley, P./Casson, M.: *The Future of Multinational Enterprise.* Macmillan, London 1976.

Grosse, R.: *The Theory of Foreign Direct Investment.* University of South Carolina, Columbia 1981.

Japan External Trade Organization: *White Paper on International Trade Japan 1981,* Tokyo 1981.

Negandhi, A. R.: *Organization Theory in an Open System.* Keenikat Press Corp., Port Washington, N.Y. 1975.

Negandhi, A. R./Baliga, B. B.: *The Tables are Turning: German and Japanese Multinational Companies in the United States.* O. G. and H., Cambridge 1981.

Negandhi, A. R./Welge, M.: *Beyond Theory Z: Global Rationalization Strategies of American, German and Japanese Multinational Companies.* JAI Press, New York 1984.

Stopford, J. M.: The German Multinationals and Foreign Direct Investment in the United States. *Management International Review,* 20, 1980/81.

Stopford, J. M./Wells, L.: *Managing the Multinational Enterprise.* Longmans, London 1972.

UN, Economic and Social Council: *Transnational Corporations in World Development: A Re-Examination.* March 1978.

Role and Structure of Swiss Multinationals

Emil A. Brauchlin

Summary

The paper shows how environmental factors together with individual initiatives characterize the Swiss multinationals. The concentration in Swiss multinational business is high. Each firm has pronounced "individuality" – on the base of a common cultural background. It is suggested that the Swiss companies will become even more multinational in future.

1. Introduction

Switzerland offers an impressive example of two facts which in the existing literature are still too often separated because of competing theoretical strands: on the one hand the very existence of Swiss multinational companies is strongly influenced by their national environment. The particularities both of Switzerland and of world politics/world economics have had a strong impact on the rise and development of the Swiss economy and the behaviour of its firms. On the other hand, it is striking to see the extent to which origin, success and failure are the result of special entrepreneurial courage and forsight – or the lack of these crucial elements. At the same time it is illuminating to find how much the companies' present position is determined by their history, i. e. by decisions taken decades ago, which still determine the competitive position as well as the managerial culture of a given firm.

To mention just two introductory cases: That Switzerland has become an important center of finance and at the same time the home country of comparatively large multinational banks can easily be explained by the economic and political legislation (Hirszowicz 1983). That Switzerland is a center of R & D activities relating to ship diesel engines is rather a curiosity. Therefore, we shall combine, in the following pages, pure statistical descriptions with nomothetical "explanations" as well as with ideocratic elements.

2. The National Environment

The following characteristics of Switzerland exert an important influence on all Swiss firms:

Geographical factors:
- Central position in the heart of Europe
- small size (45 000 km^2)
- small population (about 6,4 M.)
- hardly any natural resources.

Socio-cultural factors:
- multidimensional segmentation of population (4 languages and ethnic groups; 3 Christian denominations; social and financial stratification across the whole country)
- socio-liberal basic consensus (mental openness; consideration for minorities; importance of good educational system; balance between state control and private enterprise system.)
- national independence
- absence of war (since 1815 only 1847 small civil war)
- continous development of country
- internal social and political stability.

Economic factors
- early industrialization (beginning of 19th century)
- low inflation
- high wages
- much capital
- limited labour force.

Obviously, Swiss enterprises benefit highly from their social-political and economic environment. On the other hand, the small national markets are a real handicap for many firms, forcing them to become international or multinational.

3. Some Statistics on Swiss Multinationals

Because of the small national markets, exports, direct foreign investments (and to a smaller extent other forms of activities in foreign countries) traditionally play an important part in the Swiss economy. During the last two decades, however, the already strong involvement with foreign economies has considerably increased. Table 1 contains the most important figures since 1913, i.e. since the last year before World War I.

Table 1: Direct investments and exports 1913–1980

Year	Direct Investments			Exports
	Nominal in 1000 M.Fr.	Real (Prices: Base 1980)	In % of national income	Real (Prices: Base 1980) in 1000 M.Fr.
1913	1,2	6,8	20–25	6,9
1919	1,5	4,1		16,4
1960	10,0	22,5	31	14,2
1970	33,8	54,5	44	24,4
1980	58,5	58,5	41	49,6

Sources: SBG (1983 a); SKA (1981)

Table 2: Total work force of Swiss multinationals

		Switzerland		Host Countries		Total	
		work force	%	work force	%	work force	%
Largest	6	80'150	29,4	383'530	69,9	463'680	56,4
	15	160'640	58,9	483'340	88,1	643'980	78,4
	50	233'120	85,5	535'270	97,5	768'390	93,5
	87	272'500	100,0	548'890	100,0	821'390	100,0

Source: Wehrle (1983, p. 63)

Impressive as the global figures are, one should not overlook the fact that the multinational activities of Swiss firms show a very high degree of concentration, and this both in industry as well as in banking and insurance.

Swiss industry is composed of some 55 000 firms, with a total labour force of some 950 000 people. 8800 of these firms employ 6 or more people, which gives a total of some 500 000 men and women working in Switzerland. The figures for the labour force working for Swiss multinationals are set out in Table 2.

Of the 15 largest Swiss companies, only two employ more people in Switzerland than in foreign countries. It is estimated, furthermore, that the 87 largest industrial companies account for virtually all of the personnel employed by Swiss firms in host countries. For the 15 largest companies, the corresponding figure is still about 60%. Concentrated as the multinationals are, they are spread over several sectors of business as shown by Table 3.

The concentration of the personnel employed in foreign countries is paralleled by the amount of sales out of foreign production. Again, we give the figures for the 87 largest companies:

Table 3: Personnel (in 1000's) of the 15 largest multinationals by sectors of business

	Switzerland	Host Countries	Total
Engineering industry	81	154	235
Chemicals	42	118	160
Food processing	7	146	153
Metals	9	36	45
Quarrying	2	17	19
Watches	13	3	16
Electrical Good	6	10	16
Total	160	484	644

Source: Wehrle (1980, p. 67)

Table 4: Sales by 87 Swiss multinationals out of domestic and foreign production (1980)

		Sales out of domestic production		Sales out of foreign production		Total Sales	
		1000 M. Fr.	%	1000 M. Fr.	%	1000 M. Fr.	%
Largest	6	10,9	29,0	53,2	75,9	64,1	59,5
	15	21,1	56,1	61,6	87,9	82,7	76,8
	50	32,0	85,1	68,6	97,8	100,6	93,4
	87	37,6	100,0	70,1	100,0	107,7	100,0

Source: Wehrle (1983, p. 64)

The high degree of concentration of Swiss direct investments in foreign countries contrasts sharply with the much more balanced distribution of the exports between firms of different sizes.

For several years now, the tertiary sector has been employing more people in Switzerland than the secondary. Approximately 150 000 firms account for a total of 16 M. employees. Also in this tertiary sector there are multinational companies, operating in banking and insurance. However, tourism, although nationally highly important, is practically unrepresented in the multinational arena (except the privately owned "national" airline "Swissair").

As far as the banks are concerned, international and multinational banking activities have to be distinguished. Unfortunately, the figures available concern mainly the international dimension. Multinational activities, to our knowledge, have never been thoroughly investigated. Therefore, let us give, first, some information on the Swiss banking system. It comprises (1981) some 550 banks and financial institutions. They have total assets and liabilities of some 560 000

M. Francs. Out of this sum, some 200 000 M. were placed in foreign countries, whereas some 170 000 M. constitute liabilities in foreign currencies.

Concentration in the banking sector is even more accentuated than in industry. The Big 5 account for more than 50% of the total assets and liabilities of all banks (SKA 1981).

As far as multinational activities are concerned, it is known that the three biggest banks dispose of subsidiaries and branches practically all over the world. In addition, they possess affiliated companies in a number of countries, they hold minority interests in other banks and they participate in joint-ventures (Brosset 1983). However, as already mentioned, information on these activities is hard to come by. We know, e.g., that one of the big three employs 4% of its labour force in foreign countries, another big bank states that the sum of the assets and liabilities of its affiliated banks constitutes some 10% of its own. Incomplete as these figures are, they point to one fact. The bulk of the banking operations is rooted in Switzerland. Besides the big banks, some smaller ones specialize in multinational business. However, compared to the total banking system their importance is limited. Our information on the insurance industry is more ample. Here, we dispose of clear figures demonstrating the significance of the multinational companies (Table 5).

Again, in domestic business and much more so in foreign business, the concentration is considerable. Domestic direct business is dominated by five insurance groups (one of which specializes in life-insurance). They earn more than 66% of the life-insurance premiums and more than 50% of the non-life insurance premiums. Professional reinsurance is strongly dominated by one single group. The 6 largest Swiss insurance companies account for approximately 90% of the foreign business.

If one looks at the geograhical distribution of Swiss direct investments abroad, one discovers – naturally enough – a certain predilection for industrialized

Table 5: Insurance premium (Billion Fr.)

	Business		Foreign Business		Total	
	1972	1982	1972	1982	1972	1982
Reinsurance	0,4	0,6	4,4	7,8	4,8	8,4
Life Insurance	2,5	6,3	0,9	2,1	3,4	8,4
Accident, Property & Liability Insurance	2,8	6,1	3,0	4,4	5,8	10,5
Total	5,7	13,1	8,3	14,3	14,0	27,3

Source: Bundesamt für Privatversicherungswesen (1982, 1972)

Table 6: Activities of 15 largest Swiss multinationals (1980, in percent)

	Switzerland	Industrialized Countries	Developing Countries	Total foreign	Total
Personnel	24,9	59,5	15,6	75,1	100,0
Direct Investments	32,4	58,5	9,1	67,6	100,0
Production	25,6	59,6	14,8	74,4	100,0
Cost of R&D	62,0	ca. 35,0	ca. 3,0	38,0	100,0

Source: Wehrle (1983, p.99)

countries, where, by definition, the bulk of the world economy is concentrated. The 15 largest industrial firms mentioned above show the following spread of their acitivities:

Among the industrialized countries Western Europe is by far preferred to the United States, while direct investments in Japan are still very small. The same predilections prevail, incidentally, also for small industrial firms and insurance companies. As far as the developing countries are concerned, Swiss multinationals are particularly active in Latin America, followed by some European, Asian and, finally, African countries.

4. Swiss Multinationals: Result of Environmental Influences and Entrepreneurial Initiatives in Past and Present

The statistics given in section 3 give rise to the following comments:

All important Swiss multinationals have possessed this status for decades. The first firms to go multinational were industrial companies like Nestlé, BBC (both, incidentally established by immigrants to Switzerland), the chemical firms, etc. Soon they were followed by insurance companies. The results of World War I enhanced particularly the position of Swiss insurance companies due to the financial difficulties of their German competitors. The banks, on the other hand, took advantage of the stability of the country and its currency mainly after World War II (the percentage of assets/liabilities in foreign currencies were around 7% before the war).

The end of World War II, and again the 70s brought a new wave of multinational business activity. The reasons for this development were and are manifold:

- Swiss companies, enjoyed a good starting position due to their financial soundness.

- Many of them discovered they could serve market needs better (and earn more) by establishing new production facilities close to the customer.
- At the end of the 60s legal barriers were erected in Switzerland against a further increase of the foreign labor force (at the time some 20% of the labor force was constituted by foreigners).
- Particularly in the 70s high production costs in Switzerland induced some companies to escape to the developing world.
- In the same decade the strong position of the Swiss Franc (the exchange rate for one $ dropped from Fr. 4.30 to less than Fr. 1.60 at the lowest point) exerted considerable pressure on exporters. But it also made it possible to buy or set up new companies at comparatively low cost in other countries.
- Also in the 70s the recession made some firms look for new opportunities abroad.
- Growing protectionism obliged some firms "to become more multinational than they wanted to be", to quote one company's president.
- More and more, a certain number of companies seek to gain advantage from advanced scientific knowledge in other countries like Great Britain, the US or Japan.

Obviously, the primary reason for investing abroad depends very much on the particular core strengths and weaknesses of the individual firms.

It is interesting to state that in some fields a small number of firms managed to grow and to become multinationals, while in other fields such achievements were not realized. To give some negative examples: the Swiss motor car industry never became multinational, with the consequence that the firms in this sector disappeared or discontinued the production of cars. Between the two World Wars this was the case for passenger cars, and, in the last years, it became true for commercial vehicles after national import restrictions were abolished. Swiss hotels, on the other hand, had an extremely strong tradition of being local. Therefore, Swiss cooks and hotel-managers emigrated – but large hotel-chains have not come into existence.

It is also noteworthy that multinational manufacturers of office equipment, of modern communications equipment, etc. do not exist. In both cases, companies operating on a purely national level were not able to compete successfully against their multinational competitors on the world market. Finally, Switzerland is the domicile of a multinational producer of condensed milk and instant coffee, but it has no multinational brewery or mineral water bottling firm – again the result of their earlier strategic decision to serve the national market only.

Growing protectionism and the need for new technologies may well induce Swiss companies (among them also smaller firms) to become more multinational than they are today.

5. Organization and Management

As a rule of thumb, Swiss firms rely on exports or they seek to establish 100% owned affiliated companies – at least in Europe, North America and Australia. But there are indications that majority (or minority) interests are becoming more popular in the course of time. This applies, of course to developing countries, where legal requirements as well as purely economic reasons favor such trends. In Mexico e.g., Swiss firms are organized in the following manner:

Table 7: Management of Swiss companies in Mexico

		51–100% Swiss owned	≤ 50% Swiss minority Tight Swiss Control	Cooperatives
Large Firms	more than 1000 employees and more than 2000 billion Pesos sales	2	2	0
Medium Firms	≥ 200–1000 employees or ≥ 500 billion Pesos sales	7	1	2
Small Firms	> 200 employees and ≥ 500 billion Pesos sales	5	2	5
Total		14	5	7

Source: Wuffli (1984)

It seems, however, that joint ventures with firms in Japan and Newly Industrializing Countries in Asia, but also with Western firms, are becoming somewhat more frequent. There is also a long tradition of licensing agreements with foreign companies. But the commercial significance of this is rather limited (Hunzinger 1983).

From a strictly managerial point of view, Swiss multinationals have some traits in common – and they show some marked differences as well. One common feature is the fact that, as a rule, the members of the board and the top management are Swiss. In addition our impression is that most top managers "think Swiss", i.e. they consider the company as Swiss and take care that financial control over the company remains in Swiss hands. But there are differences as well. As an example, abridging the Perlmutter (Perlmutter 1965; Heenan/Perlmutter 1979) typology, the following pattern of behavior of Swiss firms can be observed in Mexico.

Table 8: Patterns of behaviour of Swiss firms in Mexico

Swiss ethnocentric	*Adaption to Mexico*
Maintain as long as possible 100% ownership of equity capital	Establish a joint venture
Keep the top management swiss	Try to find locals for top management positions
Be »as Swiss as you can«	Try to accommodate to Mexico in as many fields as possible
Try to be a model in the sense of benevolent paternalism	There is no *general* need to be a model
Try to centralize main activities	Try to decentralize activities

Source: Wuffli (1984)

Of course, the two types are grossly oversimplified, but they show the general trands. In this context it might be interesting to list the nationalities of the top managers of the 26 firms in question.

Table 9: Nationality of top managers of Swiss companies in Mexico

	Swiss	British Dutch German	Spanisch, Latin American (without Mexican)	Mexican	Total
Large Firms	2	1	-	1	4
Medium Firms	2	4	2	2	10
Small Firms	6	1	-	5	12
Total	10	6	2	8	26

Source: Wuffli (1984)

6. Financial Results

Traditionally, Swiss firms have a comparatively high equity ratio. This also applies to the Swiss multinationals. Again, however, averages conceal sharp differences between individual companies. Look e.g., at the three largest industrial companies:

Table 10: Equity ratio of Nestlé, Ciba-Geigy and BBC

Company	Equity in % of total assets and liabilities
Nestlé	86,5
Ciba-Geigy	69,4
BBC	32,4

Source: Brown Boveri & Cie. AG (1982); Ciba-Geigy AG (1982); Nestlé AG (1982)

The published financial results are as varied as the amounts of equity. They are strongly influenced by lines of business. Multinationals in the field of machinery and equipment partly suffered losses since 1975. In sharp contrast to this Nestlé, multinational banks, insurance companies as well as chemical firms were hardly hit and they show, for 1983, unprecedentedly good results. Their enourmous efforts to remain profitable and competitive in conjunction with prudent investment policies and recovering markets have led to these excellent figures.

7. Concluding Remarks

Wherever one looks Swiss firms are trying to adapt themselves to the most recent developments in the international economy and in technology. There can hardly be any doubt that the sparkling new technologies and the still increasing neo-mercantilism will oblige Swiss industry to become even more international in various respects:

- Not only production facilities, but also R & D activities will become more regionally diversified.
- In addition to exports and direct investments, other forms of activities like joint ventures and cooperation agreements will gain momentum.
- Smaller industrial firms will have to learn to become (more) multinational.
- As a counterpart, an increased influx of foreign (Japanese and other) knowhow is desirable.

But all these endeavours will not be sufficient. Switzerland as a nation has got to find allies who support her quest for a reasonable international return to liberal trading principles without sacrificing the humanistic ideal which, despite all negativism and pessimism, has been realized at least in part within her own frontiers.

Bibliography

Berweger, G.: *Investition und Legitimation.* Diessenhofen 1977.

Bickel, W.: *Die Volkswirtschaft der Schweiz.* Aarau and Frankfurt a. M. 1973.

Borner, S.: *Produktionsverlagerung und industrieller Strukturwandel.* Bern and Stuttgart 1980.

Borner, S. et al: *Structural Analysis of Swiss Industry 1968–1978: Redeployment of Industry and the International Division of Labour.* Basel 1978.

Brosset, M.: *Multinationale Bankenverflechtungen – Joint Ventures and Partnerschaften.* Bern and Stuttgart 1983.

Brown, Boveri & Cie. AG (Ed.): *Geschäftsbericht 1982.* Baden 1982.

Buckley, P. J./Casson, M.: *The Future of the Multnational Enterprise.* London 1976.

Bundesamt für Privatversicherungswesen: *Die privaten Versicherungseinrichtungen in der Schweiz 1972.* Bern 1974.

Bundesamt für Privatversicherungswesen: *Die privaten Versicherungseinrichtungen in der Schweiz 1982*. Bern 1984.

Bundesamt für Statistik: Eidgenössische Betriebszählung 1975. In: *Statistische Quellenwerke der Schweiz*, Paper No. 631/632. Bern 1978.

Bundesamt für Statistik: *Statistisches Jahrbuch der Schweiz 1983*. Bern 1983.

Burgener, B.: *Strukturwandel und Unternehmungsstrategien: Fallstudien kleiner und mittlerer Unternehmungen*. Basel 1983.

Casson, M.: *Alternatives to the Multinational Enterprise*. London 1979.

Ciba-Geiby AG (Ed.): *Geschäftsbericht 1982*. Basel 1983.

Franko, L. G.: *The European Multinationals*. London 1976.

Haller, M.: *Sicherheit durch Versicherung?* Bern and Frankfurt a. M. 1975.

Heenan, D./Perlmutter, H.: *Multinational Organization Development*. Reading, Mass. et al 1979.

Hirszowicz, C.: *Schweizerische Bankpolitik*. Bern und Stuttgart 1983.

Hunzinger, E.: *Auslandsmarkt-Strategien*. Zürich 1983.

Joggi, W./Rutishauser-Frey, B.: *Auswirkungen der Personalpolitik schweizerischer multinationaler Unternehmungen auf ihre Führungskräfte in den schweizerischen Hauptsitzen und in europäischen Niederlassungen*. Winterthur 1980.

Kneschaurek, F.: Die internationale Wettbewerbsfähigkeit der Schweiz. In: *Mitteilungsblatt d. Delegierten für Konjunkturfragen*, No. 2, 1976, pp. 21–28.

Nestlé AG (Ed.): *Geschäftsbericht 1982*. Vevey 1983.

Perlmutter, H.: L'entreprise international – Trois conceptions. In: *Revue Economique et Sociale*, 1965, pp. 151–165.

Rugman, A.: The Comparative Performance of U.S. and European Multinational Enterprises 1970–1979. In: *Management International Review*, Vol. 23, No. 2, 1983, pp. 4–14.

Schweizerische Bankgesellschaft (SBG) (Ed.): *Geschäftsbericht 1982*. Zürich 1983.

Schweizerische Bankgesellschaft (SBG) (Ed.): *Die Schweiz in Zahlen*, Edition 1983, Zürich 1983 a.

Schweizerische Handelszeitung (Ed.): *SHZ-Liste 1983. Die größten Unternehmen der Schweiz*. Zürich 1983.

Schweizerische Kreditanstalt (SKA) (Ed.): *Swiss Statistical Abstract*. Zürich 1981.

Schweizerische Kreditanstalt (SKA) (Ed.): *Geschäftsbericht 1982*. Zürich 1983.

Schweizerische Kreditanstalt (SKA) (Ed.): *Schweizer Wirtschaftszahlen 1983*. Zürich 1983 a.

Schweizerischer Bankverein (SBV) (Ed.): *Geschäftsbericht 1982*. Basel 1983.

Schweizerischer Handels- und Industrie-Verein (Ed.): *Vorwort Jahresbericht 1981/82*. Zürich 1982.

Vernon, R.: *Storm over the Multinationals*. Cambridge, Mass. 1977.

Wagner, K.: *Die internationale Tätigkeit der Banken als aufsichtsrechtliches Problem*. Baden-Baden 1982.

Wehrle, F.: *Veränderung der weltwirtschaftlichen Rahmenbedingungen und die Internationalisierung der Schweizer Industrie*. Basel 1983.

Wuffli, P.: La presencia suiza en la industria mexicana. In: *Comercio Exterior*, Vol. 34, No. 1, Mexico 1984, pp. 39–49.

Role and Structure of British Multinationals

Neil Hood

Summary

Multinational business remains a vital part of the British economy. This is the case in spite of marked shifts in sectoral pattern and geographical emphasis in recent years. The lower technological base which has characterised British multinationals remains a general feature. While the variety of UK multinational types constitute an opportunity in an era of the emergence of many different modes of international involvement, it has also the potential to be a threat.

1. Historical Context

Overseas investment of various types has long played a critical role in the UK economy. For example, in 1914, the UK was by far the most important creditor nation in the world, accounting for over half of the total outstanding international capital. For some fifty years before that date, the UK invested abroad an annual average of four percent of its national income (Edelstein 1982). Although the majority of the British capital stake at that time took the form of fixed interest portfolio investments (largely in railways and government or municipal securities), many British multinationals emerged. Estimates suggest that some 45 percent of foreign direct investment stock in 1914 was of British origin (Houston/Dunning 1976). Of particular importance in this period were raw material and agricultural investments reflected in the development and expansion of British multinationals such as Dunlop (rubber), Cadbury (cocoa) and Tate & Lyle (sugar). Clearly related were some of the earliest manufacturing operations of Coats in cotton thread and Lever in soap.

In spite of substantial changes in the international economic climate affecting the value of international investments in the inter war years, the UK still accounted for some 40 percent of foreign direct investment stock by 1938, although, the US stock was growing much more rapidly. The British interests, reflecting the country's extensive colonial involvement, continued to be geographically diverse and weighted towards primary products. During this period, British foreign direct investment was not generally associated with the higher technologies of the day and it was focussed on many markets where a degree of protection was enjoyed through Commonwealth preference. Both of these factors, together with the changes induced by World War II, were to be of cricital importance in deciding the role played by British multinationals in the post-war period. Their influence was evident between 1945 and 1960. For example, international direct investment switched in focus from the developing to the developed countries during these years. Some 55 percent of the capital stake was in the former in 1938, as against 40 percent in 1960. This reflected an underlying change of emphasis from supply-oriented investments in which Britain was strong, to those which were market oriented and designed to overcome trade barriers. Thus, for example, by 1960 some 35 percent of US and UK accumulated investment was in manufacturing, as against 25 percent in 1938 and 15 percent in 1914. However, these figures mark the importance of another key component of change, namely the strong surge of high technology investment from the US to Europe and Canada during this period. Set against the background of UK economic weakness, diminuation of technological competitiveness and low levels of internationalisation by higher technology UK companies, the 1938–1960 period recorded dramatic changes in the UK's FDI position. From owning 40 percent of stock in 1938, only 16 percent was of UK origin in 1960; conversely, the US position rose from 28 to 49 percent. The extent of the dramatic change in the role played by British multinationals over this century is evidenced by the fact that the UK outward/inward capital stake fell from 32.5 in 1914 to 1.7 in 1980.

It is against this background that the role and structure of British multinationals over the last two decades will be examined. Subsequent sections will consider the patterns of British outward direct investment; the role which it plays from the perspective of the economy, industrial sector and corporation; and finally, some of the dominant trends in strategic direction will be examined in more detail.

2. Overseas Investment Patterns

Over the past two decades, direct investment has generally accounted for some two thirds of the total of UK private investment overseas. It grew at an average rate of some 8 percent per annum between 1962–71, and thereafter averaged around 16 percent per annum, in large measure due to inflatio and the relative value of sterling. By 1978 there were 1,891 UK enterprises (as defined in Table 1) engaged in overseas direct investment in the form of 14,193 overseas affiliates. British outward investment is heavily concentrated, with 1,290 of the 1978 enterprises accounting for less than 2 percent of book value. Conversely, of the total net assets of £19.2 billion, 39 percent was accounted for by 13 enterprises (with net assets of over £200m each) and 60 percent was represented by 43 UK enterprises.

Table 1: British Outward Direct Investment Stock* (% of total net assets, year end)

	1929	1962	1965	1968	1971	1974	1978
Western Europe	7.4	13.4	15.4	17.6	21.9	27.5	31.0
North America	7.3	23.1	21.8	23.0	22.0	21.8	26.1
Other Developed Countries	10.9	27.1	29.9	30.8	29.8	30.1	23.1
Total (Developed Countries)	25.6	63.5	67.1	71.5	73.7	79.3	80.2
Rest of World	74.4	36.5	32.9	28.5	26.3	20.7	19.8
Total (World)	100.0	100.0	100.0	100.0	100.0	100.0	100.0
Book Value of Total Assets (£ million)	1551.0	3405.0	4210.0	5583.0	6666.9	10435.8	19214.8

* Excluding oil companies, banks & insurance companies.

Sources: Houston and Dunning (1976, p. 113); Business Monitor (MA4, 1978 Supplement, Table 2)

Before examining the changes in pattern the current mix of UK outward direct investment and the outward/inward balance in recent years have to be borne in mind. As Table 2 shows, the latter has continued to be positive, although decreasing. On a sectoral basis the outward rate of bank expansion has far exceeded the inward, with the oil companies being in broad balance. Although manufacturing investment dominates the 'all industries' group it is important to remember the traditional strength of British multinationals in the service industries, especially these relating to finance. For example, the magnitude of the UK stockmarket is evident by the fact that it accounted for 8.5 percent of world equity market capitalisation in 1980. Equally vital are the high levels of earnings from insurance and reinsurance, brokerage and commodity trade which account for some 50 percent of London's foreign earnings. In effect therefore the long history of overseas trade provides the UK with a distinctive framework within which direct investment can operate.

The data in Table 1 provide some broad indication of the geographical distribution of the stock of UK direct investment abroad. As the data suggest, there was a substantial redistribution of UK capital between 1930 and 1962.

Table 2: Stock of UK Outward and Inward Investment at Book Value (1979–82)

	£ Milion (End Years)			
	1979	1980	1981	1982
Outward				
All Industries*	20000	21600	28000	32500
Banks	1910	2310	3060	3295
Oil Companies	6500	7550	9100	10700
Insurance Companies**	800	890	1235	1480
Property	900	940	1120	1350
Total	30110	33290	42515	49325
Inward				
UK Companies*	12800	15100	15600	16500
Banks	1055	1215	1415	1665
Oil Companies	6750	8150	9650	11800
Insurance	330	480	710	825
Total	20935	24948	27375	30790

* Excluding oil, banking & insurance.
** Investment in the US only.

Source: Bank of England Quarterly Bulletin (Vol.23, No.2, June 1983)

This was mainly a shift from the developing to the developed Commonwealth countries, within a context where some 80 percent of all UK direct investment between 1946 and 1960 was in Commonwealth countries. The other major trend suggested in Table 1 is the increasing emphasis given to Europe by British multinationals due in part to the expected UK entry to the European Community and in part to the erosion of economic relationships with the Commonwealth. Further insight into these grographical patterns is provided by the flow data in Table 3, showing the tendency for the flows to Western Europe to decrease compared to the very high proportions flowing to North America (mainly US), since the late 1970s. Even by 1975, for the first time since 1960, there was more UK manufacturing investment in North America than North American investment in the UK (Dunning 1979).

The predominant changes in sectoral distribution were noted in the previous section. By 1962 some 51 percent of book value of the UK's direct investment abroad was in manufacturing, the primary industries' share (excluding oil) having fallen to some 20 percent. During the period covered by Table 1, the manufacturing proportion rose to 65 percent, again largely at the expense of the 'resource-based' investment projects. The sharpest growth in the proportions

Table 3: British Outward Direct Investment Flows*

	Western Europe	North America	Other Developed Countries	Rest of World	Total %	Total (£ million)
1971	44.5	23.1	22.3	10.1	100	675.5
1973	38.5	31.5	17.5	12.5	100	1620.8
1976	32.1	27.6	19.5	20.8	100	2144.8
1978	31.5	40.7	11.6	16.2	100	2709.7
1981	19.5	50.8	13.7	16.0	100	5103.6

* Excluding oil companies

Source: *Business Monitor* (MA4, 1981, Table 1.3)

going into manufacturing were in the developing countries as British multinationals faced host country pressure for local manufacture. On an industry basis, there have been equally marked changes over this period. In the mid 1950s, almost 50 percent of UK manufacturing investment overseas was in food, drink and tobacco, some 12 percent in chemicals and 8 percent in textiles, clothing and footwear. By the late 1970s food, drink and tobacco plus chemicals accounted for almost 50 percent of the investment, but in almost equal proportions. More research and development-intensive sectors such as mechanical, instrument and electrical engineering had grown to some 10 percent of the total, while metal manufacture, textiles and vehicles (including shipbuilding) had continued to decline. However, even with these changes, there remains a sharp contrast between the basic industry orientation of UK outward investment and the focus upon relatively advanced technologies within inward investment in the UK.

A number of explanations can be offered for these changing patterns over the last two decades. The geographical switches reflect a market re-orientation and a shifting of long term political relationships, both in terms of host country industrial development strategies and the emergence of regional trading blocs. The sectoral changes reflect the adjustments in UK competitive advantage to some extent, although the declining role played by food and allied companies relates to both a reduced primary product emphasis and import substitution policies in host countries. Viewed conceptually, the location-specific advantages of British multinationals in Commonwealth countries were seriously eroded. In such markets, many of these companies had probably relatively few durable ownership-specific advantages by the early post-war period. The challenge for British multinationals was thus to adopt corporate strategies to re-establish competitive advantage on both these fronts, almost simultaneously. Up to this stage, only the aggregate effects of these changes have been considered, but later comments will provide corporate-specific illustrations.

It has been suggested (Stopford 1976) that there were two types of investor prevalent among British multinationals, namely a small group with global interests, and the majority, who concentrated overseas production in Commonwealth markets and exported to others from a UK base. The former displayed many of the characteristics of international oligopoly, exploiting technological innovations and economies of scale. To pursue competitive advantage, an investment profile which included high income countries was essential. For the latter, dominant group, the homogenous Commonwealth market was more like a protected extension of the home market where risk was minimised. Predictably, such direct investment flows were closely related to trade flows and, given the long period over which Commonwealth preferential tariffs existed, a clear pattern emerged. One major implication for this second group was their relative lack of international competitiveness as multinationals by the 1960s, this position emerging from high market shares in protected markets. It was thus only the anticipation of substantial environmental change which forced the emergence of the new patterns noted above.

The data in Table 4, however, serve to illustrate the differences between the direction of current investment flows and the returns arising from existing stock. Thus, for example, the Commonwealth still accounts for the highest proportion of net earnings in spite of its decreased importance in relative terms; conversely, the US earnings figures do not yet reflect the magnitudes of the flows during the last decade. Further it should be remembered that some 57.5 percent of UK direct investment overseas in the last decade has been financed out of the unremitted profits accruing from earlier investment.

Table 4: Net Outward Direct Investment Overseas and Net Earnings*

	1976**		1977		1978		1979		1980	
	NODI %	NE %	NODI %	NE %	NODI %	NE %	NODI %	NE %	NODI %	NE %
European Communities	23.1	18.3	20.2	16.4	21.1	19.1	1.0	18.1	13.8	13.4
US	17.6	13.4	24.1	15.7	35.4	18.7	57.3	19.8	51.1	19.4
Commonwealth	33.8	40.8	25.9	39.8	23.1	35.7	29.6	34.8	19.6	37.0
Developing Countries	22.7	31.4	23.1	33.1	18.9	27.2	22.4	27.3	17.6	30.7

* Net earnings (NE) equal profit of overseas branches plus UK companies' receipts of interest and their share of profits of overseas subsidiaries and associates. Earnings are after deducting provisions for depreciation and overseas tax on dividends. Net outward direct investment (NODI) includes unremitted profit; Excluding oil companies.
** Percentages of total UK NODI and NE on a world basis.

Source: Derived from data in *British Business,* (May 14, 1982, Tables 4 & 5)

In addition to the observed overall changes in pattern, British multinationals have adjusted their mode of operation in a number of ways during the study period. There was some evidence (Stopford and Haberich 1976) to suggest that more British multinationals were choosing joint venture routes up until the late 1960s. In part, at least, this was accounted for by their efforts to catch up with their competitors in international investment by gaining direct market knowledge in non-Commonwealth locations. Thereafter, however, there have been two important trends. The first has involved an overall decrease in the use of the joint venture route from 54.0 percent of book value of overseas direct investment in 1963 to 43.6 percent in 1978. This is largely explained by the growing emphasis on developed countries in UK strategy in that period. The second trend, conversely, marks the considerable rise in the importance of such forms in developing countries, where by 1978 some 77.2 percent of UK book values were in subsidiaries where the UK company had less than 100 percent ownership. Both these trends can perhaps be explained by the change in negotiating advantage towards capital importing countries and the improvement in technological capacity in host countries which enabled them to press for more participation in the lower technology end of British multinational activity.

3. The Role of British Outward Direct Investment

In this section, the role of British multinationals is considered in two dimensions: firstly, that of the UK economy, and secondly, that of its sectoral and corporate contribution to competitiveness.

3.1 UK Economy

The predominant macro effects would be expected to fall on capital account and reserves, although the much larger and more significant effects are indirect, through exchange rates and the long term performance of imports and exports via the balance of payments on current account. In the UK and elsewhere, there is a lack of data to enable a full assessment to be made of the benefits and costs of British multinational activity. Covering the mid 1950s to mid 1960s, one study (Reddaway 1968) concluded that on average an addition of £100 to UK foreign direct investment would benefit the balance of payments on current account by £8.1 per annum. This report also documented some of the spillover effects which mainly took the form of the feedback of technical knowledge and the additional employment generated by the exports of finished goods and capital equipment. Much more recently, the overall annual identified effect on reserves has been substantially positive over the past decade or so, with figures ranging between £700–£2,000 million. The potentially negative effects of outward investment on the weak UK balance of payments were factors underlying the exchange control legislation from the early 1960s until 1979, although in the latter years at minimum levels of effective control. These restraints had apparently little effect on UK direct investment which expanded by foreign borrowing and unremitted profits.

There has been some tentative evidence (Panic and Joyce 1980) suggesting that the deterioration in the UK's trade performance in manufactured goods in the 1970s might be partially explained by growing international integration within certain sectors as a result of multinational activity. Most sectors of UK industry are highly concentrated by international standards, while perhaps as much as 40–50 percent of manufactured imports come from 'related' enterprises. Further, as was noted previously, most UK outward investment is in the hands of few firms. Together, these factors might operate as a partial explanation for manufactured good's export performance.

A much more contentious effect in recent years has surrounded the alleged UK export of job opportunities through direct investment. The adjustment processes discussed earlier have undoubtedly led to many British multinationals modifying the distribution of their assets in a quite fundamental way, usually resulting in less emphasis of the UK market. Thus, there are many sectors, especially electronics, engineering and chemicals, where there are substantial disparities between the rate of change in UK and overseas employment over the past five years. The focus of negative views (Hughes 1976; Wilms-Wright 1977) over the recent past in the UK have been in three other areas, namely the subsequent restriction on investment in the UK, the diversion of scarce management from UK activities and export replacement. From a quite different perspective (CBI 1980) some corporate data were generated on 159 UK outward investment projects between 1967–76 in order to examine these negative propositions. Some 80 percent of these were apparently undertaken either because the location was dictated by the activity or because of general expansion of an existing overseas business. Some 85 percent of these appeared to have no material effect on exports and no significant evidence was found on the other counts. The project did, however, generate a number of interesting cases highlighting the complexity and diversity of direct investment decisions.

3.2 Sectoral and Corporate Competitiveness

It is not at all easy to assess these types of effects arising from outward investment. UK firms would appear to invest abroad in those sectors in which they are least internationally competitive. Recent evidence (Dunning and Walker 1982) has shown that UK outward investment is significantly correlated with domestic competitiveness, in that it tends to be concentrated in those sectors which record above average productivity and profitability. At the same time it is not possible to show with authority that outward investment is growing most rapidly in the sectors of the UK which are declining or showing slowest growth. The evidence varies substantially by sector, as does the propensity to engage in foreign production. Part of these problems arise from the quality of data available for aggregate analysis, hence the focus on corporate material in this section.

As elsewhere, UK firms have internationalised in pursuit of a mix of defensive and aggressive strategies which are designed for the long term improvement of their profitability. Outward investment thus plays quite different roles, varying both by sector and by company. Some recent British evidence demonstrates this

Table 5: Largest UK Direct Investments in USA, 1978–80*

	UK Company	US Company	Type of Transaction	Cost ($ Mill.)
1980	Imperial Group	Howard Johnson Co.	Acquisition	630
	Midland Bank	Crocker Natl. Corp.	Acquisition	820
	Lloyds & Scottish	James Talcott Factors	Acquisition	118
	Hawker Siddeley	Fasco	Acquisition	100
	Racal	Decca	Acquisition	147
1979	John Swire & Sons	Bricknell Key	Construction/ Residential	300
	NCS Pension Fund	Continental Ill. Properties	Acquisition	145
	ICI	Corpus Christi Petrochemicals	New Plant/Joint Venture	375
	National Westminster	Natl. Bank of America	Acquisition	429
	Standard Chartered Bank	Union Bancorp	Acquisition/Merger	372
	Davy International	McKee Corporation	Acquisition	106
	Barclays Bank	American Credit Corp	Acquisition	191
1978	BOC	Airco	Equity Increase	298
	BICC	Automation Indust.	Acquisition/Merger	202
	Sir James Goldsmith	Colonial Stores	Acquisition	114
	General Electric	A. B. Dick	Acquisition	103
	BAT Industries	NCR Corporation's Appleton Papers Division	Acquisition	280

* These are the largest transactions where the cost was declared. Only transactions of $100 M. or over have been included. There were no transactions of this size involving UK corporations disclosed during 1976 and 1977.

Sources: Listings of Investment Transactions for 1976–77 data; Mergers and Acquisition, *Journal of Corporate Venture* (Vols. 14 & 15) for 1980 data.

variety. For example, it is possible to discern quite different strategies within the surge of UK investment in the USA since the mid 1970s (Young and Hood 1980). Attracted by the market size and its growth potential, together with the relative values of sterling and the US dollar, many British companies saw the US as offering major opportunities. For many of them, however, the US decision constituted a fundamental re-orientation. Few had oligopolistic advantages in technology, several wished to leap the technology gap between them and their competitors, while also re-orienting their asset distribution. All of these factors have combined to make acquisition the dominant mode of entry adopted by UK firms as some of the illustrative material in Table 5 indicates.

Differentiating between the strategic directions among the UK firms which have not been active in the US is interesting. One group have purchased in order to acquire access to US technology. General Electric (GEC) constitutes an illustration in this case with under 0.5 percent of its global turnover in the US. Traditionally weak in that market and wishing to diversify out of the slow growth, heavy industrial equipment segments, its US purchases have generally been of small high-tech businesses. Similarly, Racal has purchased in the US to repeat its success in the radio communications market by expanding into data communications, using as its distinctive ownership-specific advantages its technological and international marketing expertise. Falling into another distinct strategic category are some of the large UK conglomerates, notably Hanson Trust and Thomas Tilling. Hanson is a classic case of asset re-orientation, in that until 1972 it had no direct investments in the US, while by 1978 some two thirds of its profits were from that market. Its UK operations were primarily in building materials, construction equipment and food products. Aiming to boost earnings per share and net worth, its US purchases have been widespread, including food services and property. A third UK group includes companies with a long outward investment history in the primary products field and who are diversifying from a narrow base. B.A.T. Industries and Rio Tinto Zinc are appropriate examples, the former moving from tobacco and related products, and the latter from a mining and energy related base. A final, and probably the largest, group are multinationals who are broadening their base of operations. Most had strong Commonwealth links and regard vertical and horizontal growth in the US (and Europe) as essential for their long-run strategy. They have tended to stay close to their traditional business area and have made fewer, but often larger, US investments as they selected particular market segments. The Cavenham supermarket and food processing interests, Metal Box in packaging and containers and BOC International in industrial gases, are all examples in this category. So, too, are the major British banking acquisitions in the US, several of which only occurred after difficulties over contested bids and so on (Hood & Young 1981).

Turning from the US case, one of the recent interesting UK phenomena has been the apparent growth of outward investment by smaller firms. Data is, however, generally weak in this area. Some recent studies (Newbould, Buckley and Thurwell 1978) have drawn attention to the lessons to be learned by smaller UK firms from the experience of others in establishing production subsidiaries overseas. These include the higher probability of success associated with a more paced and considered route going in exporting, foreign agents and overseas sales subsidiary, rather than attempting to short-circuit the system. Equally, success was associated with higher proportions of UK equity ownership, selling products aimed at the same market segment in the UK and so on. While there is no general evidence to suggest that British outward direct investment is becoming less concentrated, it is interesting to note the increased involvement of smaller firms in US and Europe. Although motivated by the same factors as the majors, such firms often have relatively few ownership-specific advantages of the traditional type. A third and final illustration within this section surrounds the role of overseas technological royalty transactions in British business.

Table 6: UK Overseas Technological Royalty Transactions (£m)

	Receipts						Expenditure					
	1976	1977	1978	1979	1980	1981	1976	1977	1978	1979	1980	1981
Overseas technological royalty transactions												
(a) Western Europe	61.18	63.65	64.58	70.58	73.86	75.00	50.04	48.15	49.33	45.54	56.21	68.18
(b) European Community	43.77	45.31	44.37	49.19	53.35	47.09	28.45	26.90	33.24	27.33	29.34	40.74
(c) Japan	28.08	34.60	43.31	n.a.	43.78	52.32	n.a.	0.81	0.86	n.a.	1.06	n.a.
(d) USA	51.83	60.27	63.33	98.11	104.50	125.56	150.54	178.69	197.98	n.a.	223.41	250.67
World technological mineral rights	227.69	251.14	273.99	297.67	319.33	368.29	206.32	234.16	258.33	258.29	297.23	337.60

Source: *Economic Trends* (No. 334, August 1981 and No. 359, September 1983)

While not all expenditure transactions in Table 6 are undertaken by multinationals, they benefit from many of the receipts. The interest moreover is in the degree to which surplus and deficit in such data reflect technology gaps. The data suggest that the net deficit position with the US remains large in spite of some quite rapid growth in receipts in recent years. Modest net surplus positions remain with Western Europe, and are greater with Japan. The volume of these figures does not in general suggest that UK companies are making extensive use of inward licensing to offset the dramatic deterioration in manufacturing competitiveness. As has been noted, however, the UK displays an unusual combination of highly aggressive international businesses emerging from sectors which are in sharp domestic decline. In such cases the engine of growth is the company rather than the sector and in this model direct investment has often played a major role.

4. Conclusion

British multinationals continue to play an important role in world terms, with some 9 percent of outward direct investment flows from major developed countries and some 30 percent of the EC stock of direct foreign investment overseas. As regards their contribution to the UK economy this remains substantial by a number of criteria. Not least, for example, is the fact that remitted profits plus other receipts from overseas investment regularly account for around one half of invisible trade surpluses. At the corporate level, the readjusted patterns of investment have provided a vehicle to encompass new economic realities and develop some competitive advantage, often from a weakening base. Perhaps the critical determinant of the future of many British multinationals lies in their lack of technologically-based competitive advantage. While able to shift assets and make the appropriate strategic responses, this gap may ultimately reduce their potential for growth.

Bibliography

Confederation of British Industry: *Investment Abroad and Jobs at Home.* CBI Publications, London 1980.

Dunning, J. H.: The UK's International Direct Investment Position in the mid 1970s. *Lloyds Bank Review,* No. 132, April 1979.

Dunning, H. H./Walker, P. M.: *The competitiveness and allocative efficiency of UK manufacturing industry and foreign direct investment.* Paper presented to the 9th Annual Conference of the European Association for Research in Industrial Economics, September 8–10th, 1982, Leuven, Belgium.

Edelsten, M.: *Overseas Direct Investment in the Age of High Imperialism – the United Kingdom. 1850–1914.* Methuen, London 1982.

Hood, N./Young, S.: *Recent Strategic Expansions by British Corporations in the United States.* University of Strathclyde Business School, Working Paper 8109, 1981.

Houston, T./Dunning, J. H.: *UK Industry Abroad.* Financial Times, London 1976.

Hughes, J.: *Funds for Investment.* Fabian Society Research Series 325, London 1976.

Newbould G. D./Buckley, P. J. Thurwell F.: *Going international: the experience of smaller companies abroad.* Associated Business Press, London 1978.

Panic M./Joyce P. L.: UK manufacturing industry: international integration and trade performance. *Bank of England Quarterly Bulletin,* Vol. 70, No. 1, March 1980.

Stopford J. M./Haberich K. O.: Ownership & Control of Foreign Operations. *Journal of General Management,* Vol. 3, No. 4, 1976.

Wilms-Wright, C.: *Transnational corporations: a strategy for control.* Fabian Society Research Series 334, London 1977.

Young, S./Hood, N.: Recent Patterns of Foreign Direct Investment by British Multinationals in the United States. *National Westminster Bank Review,* May 1980.

Role and Structure of Swedish Multinationals

Erik Hörnell

Summary

Sweden is presumably the country which has the most overseas direct investments in proportion to the size of its economy. Notwithstanding that the Swedish multinational corporations have the majority of their operations abroad their Swedish units are of great importance for Sweden's own industrial employment, exports, and research and development.

1. Introduction

It is taken for granted that Sweden, which is a small, highly industrialized country with rather one-sided natural assets, has a large proportion of foreign trade. But that Swedish companies also have large overseas direct investments is perhaps less self-evident. According to estimates made at U.N. concerning the amount of overseas direct investments Sweden lies ninth, before countries such as Belgium and Italy. If the investment amount per capita is calculated Sweden shares the top place with U.S.A. Moreover, Sweden has 20 companies on Fortune's list of the 500 largest corporations in the world, while the Netherlands has only nine and Belgium six.

In contrast to the outward direct investments the inward are few. The latest information shows that about 6% of those employed in industry work for foreign-owned companies. This is a small proportion in international terms. The disproportion between large outward and small inward direct investments has been a controversial issue which has had the beneficial result that the government defrayed the costs of a detailed investigation of effects on industrial policy of the overseas direct investments. The report thereon, which was published in 1983 (Sov 1983) contained unique material on all Swedish multinational corporations and some of the findings will be presented in this chapter. The data from the investigation chiefly concern the period 1965 to 1978 but certain information has been brought up to date with the help of the corporations annual reports and other public material.

2. Structure

Multinational corporation in this paper denotes such companies which have at least one manufacturing subsidiary abroad. According to this definition, there were in 1978 approx. 120 Swedish multinational corporations with 570 subsidiaries overseas. The group of Swedish multinationals is dominated by the 20 largest, which account for some 80% of the total employees in the overseas subsidiaries (see Table 1).

2.1 Where and When?

Table 2 shows when and where the overseas subsidiaries were established. If we first consider when the establishments occurred, we can confirm that there was a steep increase throughout the period after the Second World War. It is interesting to note too, however, that many subsidiaries came into existence at a very early stage. Already at the end of the 1920s there were 50 or so manufacturing subsidiaries overseas. In 1933 SKF, which is the most internationalized of the Swedish companies, had sales in 56 countries apart from Sweden, sales subsidiaries in 26 and manufacturing subsidiaries in five. Even then about 60% of the group's employees were located in the foreign units (Heckscher 1936, p. 67).

The list of the largest Swedish multinationals (Table 1) shows that several of them have been established long ago. Some of the largest were started already in the 19th century and soon had extensive overseas sales. The origin of each of these companies was an invention, their own or acquired from abroad, which was transformed into a commercially saleable product. The Swedish market was soon saturated and overseas sales became essential for further expansion. The move overseas was no great step when the inventors/company managers had received their education abroad or had other contacts with foreign countries.

The export sales were at first managed by representatives abroad and later to an increased extent by sales subsidiaries.

In some cases it was advantageous, and in others even essential to establish some manufacture abroad. It was then first a question of straightforward assembly or adaptation of the products to the requirements of the local market. This early deliberate contact with the overseas markets and their customers gradually became an increasingly important competitive advantage when other companies began to catch up on the original technological start.

Thus when the great boom occurred after the Second World War the majority of today's large Swedish companies were already multinationals. Of the large number of subsidiaries which have since been formed almost half have been

Table 1: The 20 Largest Swedish Multinationals 1983

	No. of employees abroad	Percent of total no. of employees	Overseas sales/ turnover	Exports/ turnover	Rank according to magnitude of Swedish exports 1981	1965 x=below rank 30	Year of start of company	Establ. of overseas production
Electrolux (E)	58 372	66	76	19	4	25	1910	1921
Ericsson (E)	37 746	54	79	39	6	8	1876	1911
SKF (Me)	34 472	81	92	16	9	6	1907	1910
Volvo[1] (T)	15 541	22	85	25	1	1	1926	1960
Sandvik (Me)	14 807	58	91	82	5	9	1862	1922
Atlas Copco (Ma)	11 996	71	91	25[3]	23[3]	16	1873	1943
Swedish Match (Co)	11 760	64	75	19	28	24	1917[6]	(1917)
Asea[2] (E)	11 582	27	66	31	2	5	1883	1916
Alfa-Lavel (Ma)	10 352	65	90	30	10	20	1878	1892
Esselte (Pa)	8 734	57	65	5[4]	91	x	1912	1965
Skanska (B)	8 502	30	23	0[4]	-	x	1886	1956
Fläkt (Ma)	7 841	58	78	15[4]	36	x	1920	1934
AGA (Ch)	7 662	68	70	5[4]	88	x	1904	1913
Saab-Scania (T)	6 936	18	59	40	3	13	1937/1891	1958
SCA (P)	5 452	36	78	39	7	3	1929	1960
Esab (E)	4 123	71	91	23	53	x	1904	1912
Sonesson (Co)	3 518	53	73	28[4]	61	x	1892	1972
Euroc (Co)	3 436	42	56	23[4]	40	x	1871	1960
Incentive (Co)	3 277	31	56[3]	23[4]	34	x	1963[6]	(1963)
Astra (Ph)	3 206	51	80	33[4]	44	x	1913	1942
LKAB (Mi)				79[4]	20	2	1903	-

B= Building, Ch= Chemicals, Co= Conglomerative, E= Electrical machinery, Ma= Machinery, Me= Primary and fabricated metals, Mi= Mining, P= Pulp and paper, Pa= Paper products, printing and publishing, Ph= Pharmaceuticals, T=Transportation equipment.

Notes: 1. Excl. Sonesson, 2. Excl. Fläkt 3. 1980, 4. 1981, 5. 1982, 6. Merger
Source: Veckans affärer (16, 1984); SOU (1984: 6); Company annual reports.

Table 2: Establishment of Manufacturing Subsidiaries During Different Periods and In Different Regions in 1978

Period of establishment	EC	EFTA	Rest of Europe	North America	other industrial countries	Latin America	other developing countries	All regions	(All regions in 1970)[1]
1875–1919	8	6		3				17	(20)
1920–1929	15	4	3	1	1	6	1	31	(37)
1930–1939	9	5			2	2	1	19	(31)
1940–1949	2	4		2	4	10	1	23	(30)
1950–1959	20	4	1	7	1	12	1	46	(57)
1960–1965	38	10		6	3	9	5	71	(106)
1966–1970	45	17	6	8	3	10	2	91	(146)
1971–1974	59	26	4	14	5	7	3	118	
1975–1978	77	20	5	17	6	22	4	151	
Total	273	96	19	58	25	78	18	567	(427)

1 The difference between the data from 1970 and 1978 is due to closure or sales of subsidiaries in the interval
Source: Swedenborg (1982, p. 69)

established within EC. In 1978 about two thirds of the subsidiaries were in Western Europe and only 10% in North America. Since then, however, some 25% of the permits for overseas investments have concerned U.S.A. so the proportion of subsidiaries located there should have increased considerably.

The vast majority of the subsidiaries are thereby to be found in the industrial countries and lower wage costs abroad were not crucial for the overseas investments. Lower wage costs were in general associated with lower productivity so that the manufacturing costs were no less abroad. The principal reasons for overseas establishments were instead the existence of trade barriers such as the tariffs formerly levied by the EC, requirements for local manufacture, as in Latin America, and in some cases high transport costs. There are only a few cases of so-called resource-oriented investments. It is primarily in the garment industry that lower wage costs were the main reason of overseas manufacture.

2.2 Strategy

An overriding characteristic of the Swedish multinationals may be said to be their preference for specialization and domination via a small range of products where quality, service and market contact are important means of competition rather than the price. Ericsson is one of the world's five largest companies within equipment for telecommunications, SKF is the world's largest manufacturer of ball bearings and has 20% of the world market, Electrolux leads the world for both kitchen appliances and vacuum cleaners, Volvo is one of the five largest producers of exclusive private cars and second as regards lorries, Sandvik holds the lead with respect to rock drills etc. Companies with a small home market could not have reached these positions without a high degree of internationalization. Large foreign sales were essential for product development. This in turn presumed, or was favoured by overseas production.

2.3 Concentration

The combination of high costs for product development and a capacity expansion faster than the increase in the demand has led to continuing concentration in many industries. At the beginning of the 20th century Alfa Laval had 20 domestic competitors which manufactured separators, and in Germany alone there were another 50. Today Alfa Laval has 40% of the world's market for separators, followed by the German Westfalia (30%) and Mitsubishi (10%) (Affärsvärlden, Vol. 24/25, 1982, p. 19). The fact that a concentration of companies has taken place in the last few decades can also be deduced from the evidence that an increasing proportion of the overseas direct investments has taken the form of purchases of existing companies. Table 3 indicates that more

Table 3: Swedish Direct Investments in 1960–1978. Destributed According to Mode of Establishment

Mode of establishment	No. of production subsidiaries established	
	1960–1970	1971–1978
Green-field investments	105	54
Former sales subsidiaries	50	50
Acquisitions	99	163
Total	254	267

Source: Swedenborg (1982, p. 71)

than half of the overseas establishments in the 1970s consisted of acquisitions of foreign companies.

Forsgren & Larsson (1984) studied 280 companies acquired by the 50 largest Swedish multinationals in 1970–82. They found that 32% of the acquisitions comprised purchases of competitors, Sandvik, e.g. which already had a subsidiary in France, bought the French company Le Burin. Sandvik's purpose was to increase its market share, but perhaps primarily to prevent any other competitor from so doing. In 34% of the cases the company acquired had a similar activity on a different market from the Swedish firm. The purpose of the purchase then was to extend the buyer's market. One example is Electrolux, which bought National Union Electric in order thereby to enter the American market for vacuum cleaners. Electrolux previously had no sales of vacuum cleaners in U.S.A. since the trademark "Electrolux" was there owned by another company.

It was less common (10% of cases) for the acquired company to be engaged in similar but not directly competing operations. The acquisitions were then a means of rapidly extending the purchasing company's range and increasing its knowledge. Thus Atlas Copco, which manufactures rock drilling equipment, bought the American company Jarva Ins. which, unlike Atlas Copco, could drill in soft rocks. A more or less equal number of companies (9%) were acquired to effect vertical integration. One example is when ASSI, which manufactures sack paper, bought the British paper sack manufacturer Flexer Paper Sacks. The reamining 15% of company purchases were designated conglomerative acquisitions, which signified that there was no close link with either the technology or the customers of the Swedish corporation. The majority of the acquisitions were small. One of the larger was the American firm Dymo which makes marking equipment, which was bought by ESSELTE which was primarily engaged in printing and publishing.

2.4 Internationalization of Ownership

During the last two years several Swedish multinationals have taken a new step in their internationalization in that they have begun to issue shares abroad. The companies have sold new shares primarily to institutions in the U.S.A. The proportion of foreign owners has increased considerably in a short time. For instance, foreigners – mostly in the U.S.A. – now own 38% of Ericsson's shares (Kontakten, Vol. 5, 1983, p. 7). Nevertheless these shares at present have a lower voting value than other shares.

There are several reasons for the increased share issue abroad. Firstly, the Swedish exchange control at present stipulates as a condition for overseas direct investments that the majority of these should be financed abroad. The capital from new issues can therefore be used for the continued expansion overseas. Secondly, the issues abroad may create good publicity for the companies which may benefit from their sales. If the shares of a Swedish company are quoted on foreign stock-exchanges it will also be easier to buy foreign companies and offer payment in the form of shares in the Swedish company.

3. Role

The Swedish multinationals constitute a vital part of the Swedish industry. Fortyeight per cent of the employees in industry were to be found in their Swedish units in 1978 and they provided 58% of the total Swedish exports. Volvo alone stood for 11.9% of Sweden's exports in 1983. The importance of the Swedish multinationals for industrial policy is also emphasized by the fact that they were responsible for 70% of all industrial costs for R & D. The most controversial political issue in Sweden, as in other countries, is whether the overseas production increases at the expense of operations at home. The data on the 18 largest Swedish multinationals show that their investments abroad in 1980–82 were larger than their investments inside Sweden. These corporations' foreign investments in 1982 amounted to 40% of the total investments in industry in Sweden.

A situation which may provoke disquiet consists in the fact that an increased proportion of foreign sales are based on manufacture abroad. Figure 1 shows that the manufacture in Sweden for export rose at approximately the same rate as the overseas production between 1965 and 1974. In the following four years, however, the overseas production increased much faster and thereby took a larger share of foreign sales. During this period the total Swedish exports developed but little, and lost shares on the world market. Despite repeated devaluations it proved difficult to regain more than a fraction of these market

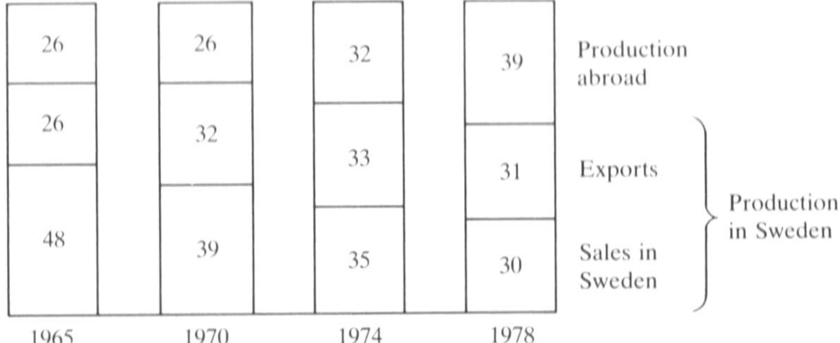

Figure 1: The Swedish Multinationals: Percentage of Sales and Production at Home and Abroad 1965, 1970, 1974 and 1978.

Source: Swedenborg (1982, p. 45)

shares. At the same time it seems that the Swedish multinationals could well defend their shares of the world market.

3.1 Exports

As stated above, the overseas production has increased more rapidly than the exports from the Swedish multinationals' home-based units. The data also show a distinct negative connection between the growth of the overseas production and the increase of the Swedish exports to different geographical regions. Notwithstanding it is not possible to draw the conclusion that the foreign production has had negative effects on the exports. Firstly, relatively speaking, the exports to the countries which have high trade barriers exhibit the worst development. It is therefore unlikely that there would have been a major increase of the exports of finished products to these countries even if there had been no Swedish production companies there. Secondly, overseas manufacture gives rise to export of input goods which would not otherwise have occured. The latter effect is comparatively small, however. This is illustrated by Fig. 2 where only half the exports to the overseas subsidiaries (nine billion Swedish Crowns) consist of input goods, while the remainder are finished products. The latter are sold without further processing by the manufacturing subsidiaries.

The circumstance that trade barriers were the principal reason for the overseas establishments meant that the subsidiaries were concerned merely to supply the local market. The only industry which has any appreciable export back to Sweden is the garment industry. Moreover third country exports were previously of rare occurrence. Figure 2 shows, however, that one fourth of the production in the overseas subsidiaries is exported to a third country. This

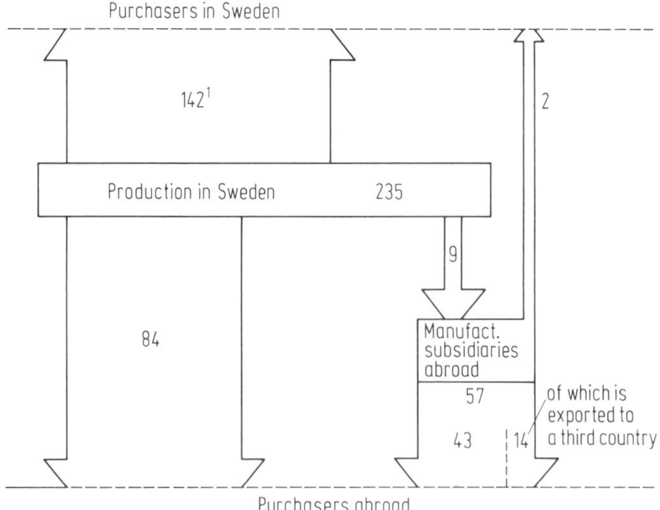

Figure 2: The Sales Production Value and Overseas Sales of Swedish Industry in 1978. (Thousand million Crowns)

Note: 1. This sum, which is a remainder, also includes the exports to the East European States.

Source: SOU (1983: 17, p. 114)

proportion has doubled since 1965. This increase is probably partly due to the fact that certain multinationals have begun to specialize their production among their foreign subsidiaries so that e.g. the subsidiary in France makes one part of the range while its counterpart in Germany is responsible for another. This principle is followed by e.g. SKF and Fläkt.

3.2 Employment

During the period 1965 to 1974 the number of employees increased only half as fast in the multinationals' Swedish units as in their overseas subsidiaries. In 1974 to 1978 the employment in Sweden even declined while it continued to increase abroad. Most of this rise was, however, due to acquisition of companies (see Fig. 3).

In the last five year period the number of employees in the largest multinationals has increased very little in both their Swedish and their overseas units. During the last two years a steep decline has occurred which was greatest overseas (see Fig. 4). This could be interpreted as signifiying that rationalizations and restructuring of operations make their strongest impact on the foreign

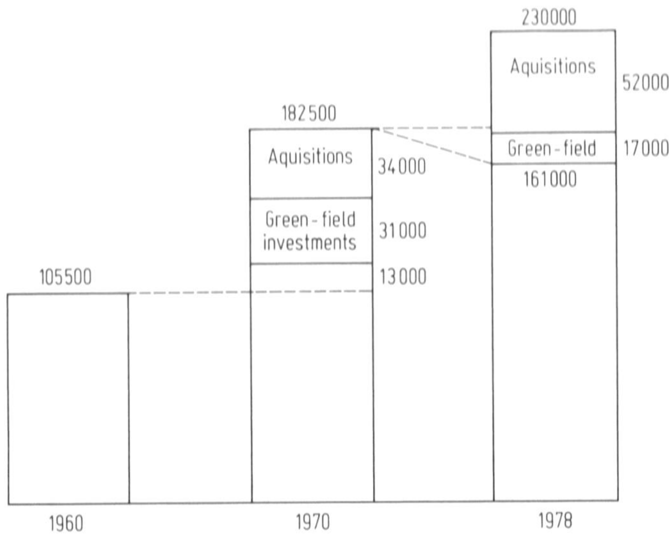

Figure 3: Number of Employees in Swedish Manufacturing Subsidiaries Overseas in 1960–1970 and 1970–1978.

Source: SOU (1983: 17, p. 133)

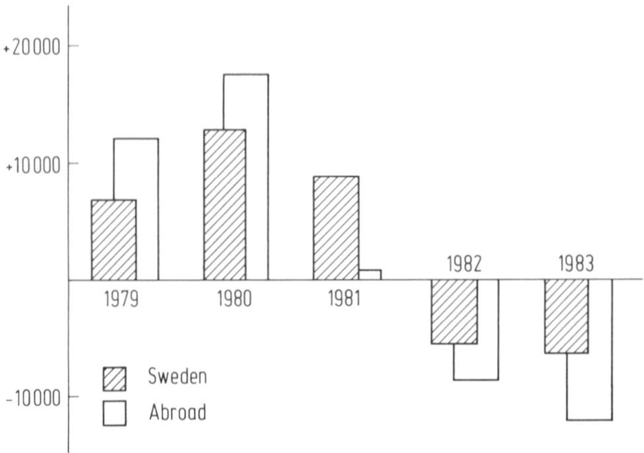

Figure 4: Change in Number of Employment in the Ten Largest Swedish Multinationals 1979–1983[1]

Note: 1. The figures include sales and acquisitions of subsidiaries.

Source: Company annual reports. Veckans affärer (Vol. 16, 1984a)

units. SKF has reduced its overseas employees by about 6,000, and Ericsson by 500 in Mexico alone, since the company went over from manufacture of electromechanical to electronic telephone exchanges (Veckans affärer 1984, p. 54).

3.3 Research and Development

In 1965 14 Swedish multinationals pursued R & D abroad. The proportion of research in their Swedish units was nevertheless as high as 91% for the entire group of multinationals. This proportion fell to 86% in 1970, primarily because SKF transferred its research centre to the Netherlands. Notwithstanding that the number of companies pursuing research overseas increased to 43 by 1978 the proportion of R & D in Sweden remained unchanged, viz. 86%. This means that the intensity of R & D increased in the Swedish units and that a central function of the company was retained in the home country despite the more rapid expansion of operations in general overseas. It is hard to say whether this state of affairs will persist. It may be worth remembering that the percentage of R & D abroad for the 10 largest corporations was as high as 30%.

4. Conclusions

The Swedish multinationals' overseas investments were mainly market-oriented, i.e. they were made in order to overcome trade barriers. Therefore the large foreign sales which the corporations now affect could not have been achieved without overseas production. That the internationalization has been of benefit for the Swedish multinationals is clear from their success in holding their own positions within the growing global oligopoly. Information concerning the localization of R & D and the more qualified stages of the manufacturing process then show that the Swedish multinationals have essentially retained the most competitive parts of their operations in Sweden. The conclusion is therefore that the overseas investments have hitherto improved Sweden's terms of trade and have had overwhelming positive effects.

Bibliography

Det handlar om akier, *Kontakten 5,* Ericsson AB, Stockholm 1983, pp. 6–7.

De utlandsetablerade företagen och den svenska ekonomin. *Bilagedel 2. Särskilda studier, SOU* 1984: 6, Liber, Stockholm 1984.

"Färre jobb utomlands i svenska multisar". *Veckans affärer 16, Stockholm 1984,* pp. 50–55.

Forsgren, M./Larsson, A.: Foreign acquisition and the balance of power in transnational enterprises. The Swedish Case. *Working Paper 1984/2*. Centre for International Business Studies. Uppsala University.

Heckscher, E. F.: Industrins historiska förutsättningar och allmänna karaktär. *Sveriges industri*. Industrins utredningsinstitut, Stockholm 1936.

Näringspolitiska effekter av internationella investeringar. *Betänkande från direktinvesteringskomittén. SOU* 1983: 17, Liber, Stockholm 1983.

"Storföretagen nära 1974 års vinstnivå" *Veckans affärer 17, Stockholm 1984,* p. 52.

"Strategibyte ger nytt avstamp för Alfa-Laval" *Affärsvärlden 24/25, Stockholm 1982,* pp. 14–19.

Sundqvist, S.-I.: *Sveriges största börsföretag 1984*. Förlags AB Marieberg, Stockholm 1983.

Swedenborg, B.: *Svensk industri i utlandet*. Industrins utredningsinstitut, Stockholm 1982. Also published as *SOU* 1982: 27, Liber, Stockholm 1982.

Role and Structure of Belgian Multinationals

Daniel Van Den Bulcke

Summary

This chapter sketches the relative importance of Belgian multinational enterprises and presents their main characteristics and some historical background. On the basis of a small but representative sample the location motives and the preliminary direct investment routes of Belgian foreign subsidiaries are described. The same data base is used to present the organizational structure of Belgian multinationals and the ownership pattern and the autonomy of decision-making of their subsidiaries. To conclude there is a short discussion of the balance of payments and employment effects for the Belgian economy.

1. Introduction

Foreign direct investment (FDI) and the activities of multinational enterprises (MNE) have, especially since the 1960s, attracted a lot of attention. While academics tried to figure out the costs and benefits that went together with multinational business operations, and policy makers were worried about the possibilities of maximising the positive effects and limiting the less favourable consequences, even the general public became gradually aware of the typical characteristics of MNE, i.e. the flexibility of their operations, their global decision-making and their monopolistic advantages. Belgium which favoured inward FDI as part of its restructuring efforts and regional policy objectives since the 1950s, originally devoted little attention to outward FDI. Belgian investment abroad was looked upon as part of its colonial era and identified with the foreign activities of a limited number of larger Belgians firms such as Solvay, Petrofina, Société Générale and Bekaert.

When the Belgian government, at the beginning of the 1970s took certain measures to stimulate and facilitate Belgian companies to establish subsidiaries in foreign countries, the interest as to the role and effects of Belgian MNE on the national economy clearly increased. In 1971 the Belgian International Investment Company was established. This semi-official institution made it possible for the Belgian government to participate in the equity capital in and/or grant loans to Belgian subsidiaries abroad. Also in 1971 the government allowed for "Ducroire", the official institution for the insurance of export risks, to extend its activities to foreign direct investment. It was not until the end of the 1970s that trade unions became more explicit about their objections to Belgian companies investing abroad, as they became increasingly worried about the employment effects of a "runaway industry".

Most of the study results which will be presented furtheron are based upon a research project sponsored by the Belgian Fund for Scientific Research during 1975–1976. (Haex and Van Den Bulcke 1982) Apart from a more limited enquiry about the foreign operations of small and medium sized companies (Andersen and Van Den Bulcke 1981) and the bi-annual survey by the employer's association Fabrimetal, no other studies about Belgian FDI have as yet been undertaken. The research project consisted of a two stage approach. First, a 1975 initial assessment took the form of a standard survey which was sent to all Belgian manufacturing enterprises with more than 100 employees. Although mining, energy, construction and engineering were originally excluded, these sectors were maintained in the first stage of the research in order to present a more complete picture of Belgian industrial activities abroad. In the second stage of the research project, with 1976 as year of reference, these same firms were contacted again and interviewed in more detail about a number of specific aspects of their corporate activities abroad. Only about a third of the eligible firms, chose to participate in this more thorough survey, however.

Two typical characteristics of the Belgian industrial system pose methodological problems for the study of Belgian outward investment. On the one hand the dominating influence of the holding companies somewhat blurs the aspect of direct investment. On the other hand the relative importance of foreign owned subsidiaries in Belgium makes it more difficult to identify indigenous foreign investment ventures.

The first problem results from the fact that holding companies quite often have levels of participation in the equity capital of their subsidiaries that are lower than 10 per cent. This percentage is often taken as a cut-off point to distinguish foreign *direct* investment from indirect or portfolio investment. Direct investment implies an active intervention by the parent company in the decision-making of the subsidiary, while portfolio investment hardly interferes with the decision-making authority of local management. Holding companies do not fit easily in the categories of direct and indirect investment as their determining influence is most often limited to the financial field even if more than 10 per cent is owned. On the other hand even with a degree of ownership of less than 10 per cent the holding company may intervene in the financial management of its affiliates, especially in case of an interlocking ownership structure. The affiliates of so-called 'industrial' holding companies will therefore be included in our estimation of Belgian foreign corporate investment abroad.

A second problem is presented by the outward direct investment activities of foreign subsidiaries located in Belgium. As the 1000 foreign owned companies in Belgium employ about one out of every three employees in manufacturing industry, and more than half of the largest industrial enterprises (more than 1000 employees) are controlled from abroad, it should not be surprising that a number of these firms have themselves subsidiaries abroad which they actively control. This is especially the case with former Belgian enterprises that were taken over by foreign MNE. For practical reasons it was decided that whenever the foreign partner owns less than 50 per cent of the equity capital of a company which has affiliates abroad, it will be included with the Belgian firms. This approach can be justified by the fact that a minority participation by a foreign parent company often leaves the actual control of foreign affiliates with the Belgian owned company.

2. Historical Perspective

Some Belgian ventures abroad go back till the beginning of the 18th century. However, it was mainly during the second half of the 19th century that Belgium ranked high among the dominant investing countries. As Belgium played a predominant role in the industrial revolution during the second half of the 19th century, its enterprises soon acquired monopolistic advantages in railway construction and related businesses which were quickly applied to foreign markets. Especially the Société Générale has been a leading force in Belgium's expansion abroad. Belgian initiatives in foreign countries were based on the technological know-how and the management expertise with respect to the construction and exploitation of railways and steel works. Belgian ventures abroad originally were not so much direct investment projects but rather engineering activities to be compared to turn key plants. At that time Belgian investment abroad often consisted of participations in foreign firms, as Belgian investors felt obliged to accept shares and debentures as payment for the construction of the plants they constructed.

It was only after 1850 that Belgian companies started to engage more systematically in direct investment projects abroad. These direct investments were greatly stimulated by the law of 1873 which established a special legal status for Belgian limited companies which had their principal activity abroad. During 1873–1910 more than 1100 such companies were established, a certain number of which soon disappeared, however. Between 1883 and 1914 more than 200 of these special companies were launched in Russia. In South America about 150 Belgian limited companies with their main activity abroad were set up.

Belgians investors abroad have twice been confronted with important losses because of their too one-sided orientation on a particular country. The first major casualty of Belgian investment abroad took place in Russia. In 1914 as many as 161 Belgian enterprises were still operational in Russia. Sixty four were mining companies and metal works. Belgian groups built four steel plants which expanded into the largest Russian steel firms. Around 1914 Belgian–Russian joint ventures produced one third of Russia's heavy metallurgic products, one fifth of its coal and half of its glass. The Belgian multinational Solvay built its first foreign plant in Russia in 1863. All Belgian possessions were lost during the Russian revolution of 1917. Apart from this important setback Belgian firms in Germany, Austria and France also registered important losses because of World War I.

Although important funds were necessary to restructure the Belgian economy after the first World War, a lot of interest was shown for the promising new initiatives in the Belgian Congo. An important step had been the establishment in 1886 of the C.C.C.I. (Compagnie du Congo pour le Commerce et l'Industrie), the first Belgian colonial enterprise. The C.C.C.I.'s original purpose was to engage in industrial, commercial and agricultural activities as well as the necessary public works, to help with the development of the Belgian Congo. The Société Générale only acquired control of the C.C.C.I. in 1928. At the beginning Belgian financial groups had been rather reluctant to invest in Congo. Until the beginning of the 20th century all important initiatives had been taken by the C.C.C.I.

In 1906 three important enterprises were created which would play an important role in the development of the Belgian Congo and would become the center of new industrial groups. The companies were Union Minière du Haut Katanga (UMHK), the Société Internationale Forestière et Minière du Congo (Formière) and the Compagnie du Chemin de Fer du Bas-Congo du Katanga (BCK). It was only in 1910 that the first manufacturing ventures were established in the Belgian Congo, however.

During the period 1885–1914 the average foreign investment per year in the Belgian Congo amounted to 348 million Belgian Francs. During 1918–1945 969 million Belgian Francs per year poured into the Congo. This latter figure hides that during 1925–1929 there was a very intensive investment activity (2466 million Belgian Francs per year) in the Belgian Congo, and that during and after the crisis of the 1930s this capital inflow diminished tremendously and almost completely dried up during the second World War. After World War II a new burst of investment in the Belgian Congo took place. From 1946 to 1955 2354 new companies were established and 34 billion Belgian Francs of new capital was brought in. This capital inflow represented about two fifth of all new capital investments in the Belgian Congo since 1885 of which one third came from Belgium.

Before the independence of the Belgian Congo in 1960, most Belgian companies had their administrative and social headquarters in Belgium. The law of June 17, 1960 obliged Belgian companies with a colonial status to choose between two alternatives, i.e. either transferring their social headquarter to Zaire or become Belgian companies and transmit their assets to the Zairian subsidiaries. About sixty percent of the Belgian companies preferred the second option. Special problems existed with the mining concessions, however.

After 1965 a gradual "Zairisation" was carried out, which culminated at the beginning of the 1970s. During this period practically no foreign investment projects were started. In 1976 the deteriorating economic situation in Zaire obliged its president to denationalize a number of companies and return them partly to their previous owners. It was stressed that Zaire should at least keep 40 per cent of the equity capital, although earlier on 60 per cent had been put forward. While Belgian direct investment has again become important for the development of the economy of Zaire, Belgian investors have started to diversify their foreign operations much more than before. At the end of the 1970s only one out of four of the Belgian subsidiaries located in developing countries were located in Zaire.

3. Importance and Main Features of Belgian Foreign Direct Investment and Multinational Enterprises

Estimates by the UN Center on Transnational Corporations (CTC) allow to compare Belgian FDI with all or with the 18 major industrial countries which are engaged in foreign direct investment abroad. In order to put the characteristics of Belgian outward investment in a better perspective a comparison will be made with the data available for the Netherlands, a neighbouring country which has many similarities with Belgium (UN, CTC, 1983a).

The Belgian stock of FDI abroad more than tripled from 1.3 billion U.S. dollar in 1967 to 4.7 billion dollar in 1978. This important rate of growth was comparable to the expansion of the FDI of all Western European countries and all developed market economies, however. While Dutch foreign investment only doubled from 11 billion to 23.7 during the same period, it will be remarked that the Netherlands have five times as much outstanding FDI as Belgium. Although the Dutch relative share of the world stock of FDI abroad came down from about 10 per cent in 1967 to 6.4 per cent in 1978, it should be noted that Belgium's relative position barely moved upwards (from 1.1 to 1.3 per cent).

While the flow of Belgian direct investment abroad, as a percentage of gross capital formation, was systematically lower than in Western Europe as a whole, the relative outward flow at the beginning and the end of the 1970s was comparable to the Western European countries. Except for 1979, Belgium's outward investment as a percentage of gross capital formation was systematically lower than in the Netherlands. These latter figures show that although Belgium increasingly invests abroad it has little chance of catching up with entrenched outward investors such as the Netherlands.

Similar conclusions can be drawn from the UNCTC's recent analysis of their Corporate Profile System (1980) of the number of foreign subsidiaries of the large MNE (UNCTC 1983b). Belgium's foreign subsidiaries represent 1.8 per cent of all the subsidiaries of the large MNE, as compared with 4.5 per cent for the Netherlands, 4.2 per cent for Switzerland and 3.4 per cent for Sweden. The global distribution of foreign subsidiaries between developed and developing countries is completely the same for Belgium and the Netherlands, i.e. 82 per cent in developed and 18 per cent in developing countries.

Within the group of developing countries there is a stronger orientation, especially for Belgium towards Africa, the region of their former colony. While 10 per cent of all Belgian foreign subsidiaries are located within African countries only 1.5 per cent have been established in South East Asia. The total of the 18 major industrial countries have 8.4 per cent of their subsidiaries in the fast growing South East Asian region as compared with 5 per cent for Dutch MNE. The concentration of Belgian MNE on the African continent comes out even more clearly if one only looks at the subsidiaries in developing countries. Multinationals from the major industrial countries have only 17 per cent of their subsidiaries in developing countries in Africa, while more than half of the Belgian subsidiaries in developing countries are located on the African continent.

Our own 1975-survey (Haex and Van Den Bulcke 1979) – from which subsidiaries in Zaire were excluded because of the uncertainty as to their actual status due to the nationalisation measures of the government of Zaire – identified 96 Belgian industrial NME with 609 manufacturing subsidiaries abroad. If one includes 81 foreign owned enterprises which control 138 ventures abroad and 8 construction and engineering firms with 44 direct investment projects in foreign countries, and also takes into account that Belgian holding companies control 235 industrial establishments abroad, Belgium owned a total of 1026 foreign subsidiaries. (Table 1).

The 96 Belgian industrial MNE employed about 182 500 people outside of Belgium. This represents about 16.5 per cent of Belgian industrial employment in 1975 and is only slightly higher than their employment within Belgium

Table 1: Geographic distribution of Belgian industrial subsidiaries abroad (1975)

Country of Location	Indigenous industrial enterprises	Holding Companies	Enterprises with > 50% Foreign Interest	Construction and engineering	Total
Netherlands	69	9	30	1	109
France	165	83[1]	30	12	290
West Germany	67	26[2]	18	3	144
Great Britain	41	2	15	3	61
Italy	31	3	9	2	45
Luxembourg	9	24	-	-	33
Ireland	2	2	1	-	5
Denmark	5	-	2	1	8
Total EC	389	149	105	22	665
Norway	5	-	-	1	6
Sweden	7	2	1	4	14
Switzerland	11	2	-	1	14
Spain	48	3	6	2	59
Portugal	13	2	3	1	19
Greece	1	7	2	-	10
Turkey	-	-	2	-	2
Yugoslavia	2	-	1	-	3
Austria	4	5	-	-	9
Total Europe	480	170	123	28	808
North America	38	32[3]	2	3	75
North Africa	7	-	1	2	10
Rest of Africa	20	14[4]	7	-	41
Latin America	35	16[5]	5	8	64
Japan	6	-	-	-	6
Rest of Asia	4	1	-	-	5
Middle East	5	2	-	3	10
Australia	4	-	-	-	4
Others	10	-	-	-	10
Total	609	235[6]	138[6]	44[6]	1026

Notes: 1. Fifteen of these establishments were realized through the Creusot-Loire holding, in which Electrorail holds a participation of 40%.
2. Arbed is responsible for 12 of these settlements. The Société Générale shares control of Arbed with Empain-Schneider (each 14.5%).
3. Twenty of these belong to the Genstar Group (14 in construction sector; 3 in cement – 25 factories; 1 in chemicals – 20 factories; 1 in steel – 4 factories and 1 in packaging). An additional four Genstar firms are engaged in maritime transport activities. The Société Générale is the main shareholder of Genstar (16%). According to the "Canadian Foreign Investment Review Agency" Genstar obtained at a date, which is later than the research assessment, the Canadian nationality.
4. Only included are those firms which explicitly indicated that they were, at the time, still engaged in activities in Zaire.
5. Of which 9 in Brazil.
6. These figures were obtained through the utilization of secondary sources and do not have the same degree of accuracy as applying to the data on indigenous Belgian MNE.

Source: Haex and Van Den Bulcke (1978, p. 27–28)

(163 000 or 15 per cent of Belgian industrial employment). If one calculates the ratio between the employment provided by Belgian and Dutch MNE both outside and in the home country, one finds 1.11 and 2.79 respectively. Dutch MNE provide employment to almost three times as many people outside of the Netherlands than within their country of origin. The actual figures of 1 011 000 jobs abroad and 362 000 inside the Netherlands show again the overall importance of Dutch MNE. The differences in the multinational orientation between Belgium and the Netherlands are largely explained by the dominating influence of a small number of MNE. The employment by the six largest Belgian MNE (both in and outside Belgium) of 166 thousand is dwarfed by the 1 104 000 jobs provided by their six Dutch counterparts. The six largest Belgian MNE were responsible for 114 thousand jobs abroad (see table 2), which amounts to only 13 per cent of the employment provided by their Dutch counterparts.

Other characteristics of Belgian MNE are:

a) the strong concentration of the neighbouring and EC-countries. About half of the foreign subsidiaries are located in the immediate neighbouring countries. France takes the lead with 165 ventures, as compared with 69 for the Netherlands and 67 for the Federal Republic of Germany. Prior to the entry of Greece two thirds of all Belgian subsidiaries abroad were within the European Community. Only 13 per cent of the Belgian manufacturing subsidiaries are established in developing countries.

b) the recent nature of Belgian outward investment. If one excludes Zaire, the great majority of Belgian subsidiaries abroad originated since World War II. Half of the affiliates which were registered in 1975 were started after 1970.

c) the dominance of the traditional industrial sectors of chemicals and metals which are responsible for respectively one half and one fourth of all foreign subsidiaries. Four out of five of the jobs created by Belgian MNE outside of Belgium came about by firms engaged in the chemical or metallurgic industry.

Table 2: Employment by Belgian Multinationals (1975)

Number of firms	Total Employment	In Belgium		In EC (without Belgium)		Other Countries	
		N	%	N	%	N	%
90 Firms	179 512	111 221	62	47 463	26.5	20 828	11.5
"Six Largest"	165 867	51 779	31	80 306	48.5	33 782	20.5
96 Firms (total)	345 379	163 000	47	127 769	37	54 610	16
"Six Largest" as % of total	48%	32%		69%		62%	

Source: Haex and Van Den Bulcke (1978, p. 23)

d) the relative preference for new establishments instead of acquisitions yet within Europe three out of five foreign subsidiaries were acquired by take-over as compared with two out of five for all foreign ventures.

e) the limited multinational network of many Belgian MNE. Fifty of the 96 Belgian outward investors actually are bi-national companies, i.e. they own subsidiaries in only one single foreign country. In the further analysis this group of companies will sometimes be distinguished from the more globally oriented enterprises.

Table 3: Geographic distribution of Belgian metalworking subsidiaries abroad (1982)

Country of Location	Number of industrial subsidiaries			Employment			Sales	
	N		%	N		%	million BF	%
France	30		31.4	4 487		16.5	10 096	18.8
Netherlands	4			225		0.8	765	1.4
West Germany	6			1 299		4.8	2 023	3.8
Italy	4			1 400		5.1	3 410	6.3
Great Britain	2			3 813		14.0	7 533	14.0
Luxemburg	2			112		0.4	137	0.3
Total EC	49		51.6	11 509		42.3	24 275	45.1
Spain	7			2 006		7.4	3 577	6.6
Sweden	2			146		0.5	789	1.5
Portugal	3			4 503		16.5	3 854	7.2
Switzerland	1			-		-	-	-
Norway	3			-		-	-	-
Total Europe	65		67.0	18 557		68.1	33 445	62.1
United States	6		6.2	1 846		6.8	8 694	16.2
Total Industrial Countries	71		73.2	20 403		74.9	42 139	78.3
Africa	5			2 680		9.8	748	1.4
Zaire		3			2 060	7.6	459	0.8
Latin America	15		15.5	3 316		12.2	7 093	13.1
Brazil		4			1 090	4.0	1 294	2.4
Ecuador		3			437	1.6	886	1.6
Chile		1			553	2.0	1 953	3.6
Asia	6			883		3.1	3 753	7.0
Singapore		1			-	-	-	-
Total Developing Countries	26		26.8	6 829		25.1	11 594	21.5
Total	97		100.0	27 232		100.0	53 831	100.0

Source: Fabrimetal (1982)

A detailed comparison of a matched sample of 22 Belgian MNE and 22 uninational companies with at least 500 employees, also showed that:

a) employment of academics was relatively higher in MNE. This was probably related to the higher research intensity of MNE.

b) the net return of uni-national firms surpassed the result for MNE, at least if one excludes the chemical sector.

c) although more MNE are engaged in research activities than uni-national firms, those uni-national firms with R & D expenditures spend – except in the chemical industry – as much as the multinationals. R & D in Belgian MNE is highly concentrated in the home country. Only one out of six Belgian MNE had established a special research budget for their foreign operations. It represented less than 5 per cent of the research expenditures of the parent company.

A more recent picture of Belgian investment abroad is only available for the metal sector (Fabrimetal 1982). To the extent that this sector would be representative for other sectors, it follows from table 3 that developing countries represent a larger share than before. In 1982 one out of four Belgian subsidiaries abroad which were active in the metal sector were located in developing countries. This proportion also applied to the employees of Belgian subsidiaries abroad. Latin America took up about 15 per cent of the total, while Asia surpassed Africa in terms of the number of subsidiaries and total sales.

4. Location Motives and Direct Investment Route of Belgian Multinational Enterprises

4.1 Location Motives

Table 4 presents the foreign investment motives of 33 Belgian MNE, i.e. about one third of the total population. In the first part of the table the motives are grouped, e.g. all market related factors are taken together. In the second part of the table the most important individual factors are listed separately. For almost 2 out of 5 Belgian MNE market related factors have been a relevant part of the decision to invest in foreign countries. Only one out of five companies took cost considerations into account, while about 10 per cent of the foreign subsidiaries have been established while considering the investment climate of the host countries, the advantages of internationalization such as economies of scale and the faster introduction possibility abroad of new products, and the necessity to overcome trade barriers by way of direct investment.

The determining influence of market considerations is most pronounced in industrial countries. The fact that market factors also dominate in developing

Table 4: Location motives of Belgian subsidiaries abroad (1976)

Location motives (N = 33)	Industrial countries		Developing countries		All countries	
	%	Rank	%	Rank	%	Rank
A. Grouped Factors						
Market determinants	42.5	1	31.9	1	38	1
Cost factors	15.5	2	25.9	2	21	2
Investment climate	11.5	4	12.7	4	11	3
Advantages internationalization	13.0	3	9.0	5	11	3
Trade restrictions	5.5	5	14.5	3	10	5
Research experience and know how	5.5	5	1.8	6	4	6
B. Individual factors						
Lower wages	7.0	4	12.0	1	9	1
Lower transport costs	6.5	6	10.8	2	8	2
Higher market share	7.5	3	6.0	4	7	3
Insufficiency of exports to maintain market share	8.0	2	3.0	9	6.5	4
Better knowledge foreign markets	8.5	1	4.2	7	6.5	4
Adaption of products to local consumers	4.5	8	7.8	3	6	6
Challenge competition abroad	5.5	7	4.8	6	5	7
Geographical diversification to spread risks	4.5	8	5.4	5	5	7
Participation in government procurement	4	10	4.2	7	4	9
Nature of product	7	4	1	7	4	9

Source: Haex and Van Den Bulcke (1979, p. 84–91)

countries and are relevant for one out of three MNE is entirely due to the Latin American countries. In Africa and Asia cost factors come out ahead. In one out of four Belgian subsidiaries in developing countries cost aspects had a determining impact. Trade restriction in developing countries were more often a relevant factor than in developed countries.

As the above classification is influenced by the number of factors which belong to each category, the listing of the individual factors is more relevant. Two cost factors, i.e. lower wage levels abroad and the elimination or decrease of transport costs when compared to exporting, take first and second place in this more specific classification. Practically all other factors which are listed among the ten most important investment determinants are market related. Both in industrial and developing countries Belgian MNE have established manufacturing subsidiaries to increase their market share. Location in industrial countries is considered as necessary to get better acquainted with local markets while exports are often considered as insufficient to maintain the existing market share.

The most important marketing incentive to locate in developing countries is the need to adapt the products to the preferences of the local consumers and buyers. The most relevant trade related factor is the tendency of foreign governments to reserve government orders for locally established companies. This factor was quoted by four per cent of the Belgian subsidiaries both in developed and developing countries.

It will be evident that the distinction between industrial and developing countries does not bring out the differences that exist among the regions within these groups. As has already been mentioned market factors play a larger role for Belgian MNE in Latin America, while cost elements dominate in the other developing regions, especially as a favourable investment climate had little effect. Within the group of industrial countries, the marketing related motives dominated in the immediate neighbouring countries. The investment climate exerts more influence in the other further away industrial countries, while the insufficiency of exports to maintain the existing market share, the higher rate of return and the lower transport costs were especially important for the United States and Canada.

4.2 The Direct Investment Route

For 41 manufacturing subsidiaries of Belgian MNE which were established between 1970 and 1976 it was possible to identify the various phases preliminary to their investment decision process. Sixteen of these foreign ventures were established in developing countries, while 25 were located in the industrialized world (15 in the European Communities and 10 in other industrial countries, mainly in the United States).

One out of five of the subsidiaries were established after the parent company had only been engaged in a very limited form of export activity, i.e. direct exporting. In six of the eight cases, this was the first venture abroad. The direct investment decision was considerably influenced by the existing tariff and non-tariff barriers in the host countries, and the belief that the existing or potential possibilities of the internal local market justified the establishment of a production unit of a certain size. Five of the eight subsidiaries which only went through direct exporting before putting up a plant abroad, were located in developing countries (e.g. Brazil) and took the form of a joint-venture with a local partner.

In almost half of the other cases the sequential investment process follows the longest route as it started, with incidental export orders, proceeded to the acquisition of a local agent distributor-importer, then expanded to a directly-owned sales subsidiary or distribution network and finally resulted in the direct ownership of a manufacturing plant (see figure 1). About thirty per cent of the

Figure 1: Preliminary stages to the establishment of a production subsidiary abroad by Belgain multinational enterprises

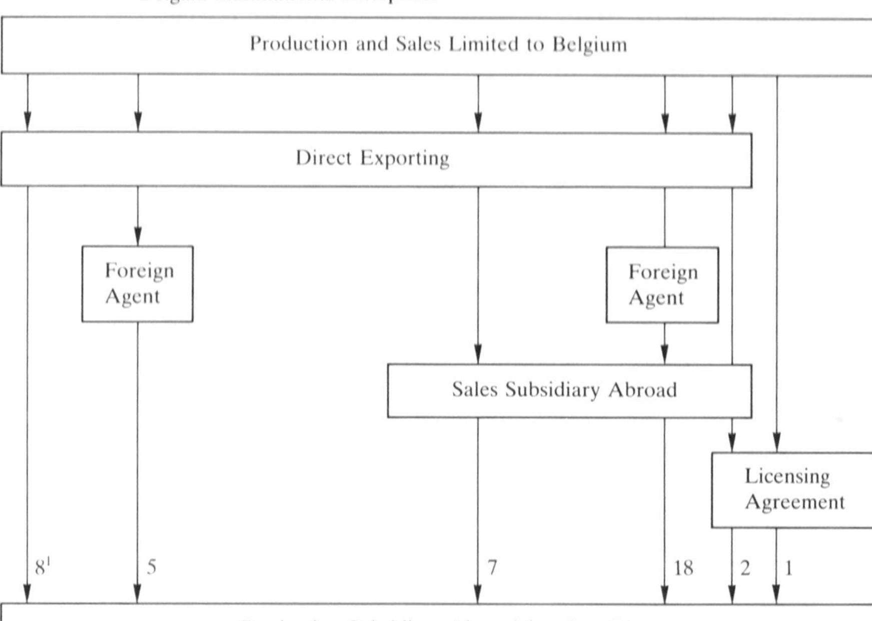

Note: 1. Number of cases
Source: Haex and Van Den Bulcke (1979, p. 63–65). Based on Newbould, Buckley and Thurlwell (1978)

studied manufacturing subsidiaries skipped only one of these stages and gave themselves sufficient time to get gradually acquainted with the foreign market by using either the foreign agent or the sales subsidiary as a sounding board. In a few cases the established subsidiaries resulted from a licensing agreement, although some had been preceded by a commercial sales office.

It will be recalled that the most important advantage of this foreign location chain consists of the possibility for a company to gradually acquire the necessary management expertise to manufacture abroad. It has been shown that for British subsidiaries the longest route generally leads to better results, i.e. less failures and a better "success ratio", a combination of the rate of return on capital, the subjective evaluation of the parent company's general manager, the rate growth, the eventual new projects and the export increase of the parent company (Newbould, Buckley and Thurlwell 1978).

5. Ownership Pattern, Organizational Structure and Control Relationship of Belgian Multinational Enterprises

5.1 Ownership Pattern

In three out of four subsidiaries abroad, the Belgian industrial parent company possessed a majority interest. The Belgian holdings have a majority participation in about 30% of their foreign ventures. MNE in the chemical sector are least inclined to accept a minority position in a foreign venture (table 5).

The ownership pattern differs when it is related to the geographic location of the subsidiary. Belgian firms have accepted a minority position in almost half of their subsidiaries in developing countries. This of course is related to two well known factors. First, the governments of developing countries often insist upon joint-ventures with local partners which have a majority participation. Secondly certain MNE prefer such a joint venture arrangement because they are to same extent a guarantee for good relationships with local governments.

It should also be noted that foreign owned enterprises located in Belgium which themselves control subsidiaries abroad, show a more marked preference than Belgian owned firms, for a higher degree of equity participation, both with respect to the subsidiaries in the industrialized and developing world. Almost two thirds of the foreign subsidiaries of foreign MNE established in Belgium, are wholly owned. Belgian MNE own only half of their foreign subsidiaries for a hundred percent.

5.2 Organizational Structure

In his book about "The European Multinationals" Franko pointed out that the so-called mother-daughter relationship was an important feature of the multinationalization process of European enterprises (Franko 1976). This special

Table 5: Ownership pattern of the subsidiaries of Belgian multinational enterprises (1975)

Degree of ownership	10–49.9%		50–74.9%		75–98.9%		99–100%	
Sectors	N	%	N	%	N	%	N	%
Chemicals and petroleum	12	13	13	15	9	10	55	62
Metals	46	31	25	17	15	10	63	42
Other sectors	27	23	13	12	23	20	52	45
Total	85	24	51	15	47	14	170	48

Source: Haex and Van Den Bulcke (1978, p. 38)

relationship was characterized by the direct contact between the general manager or president of the parent company and the managers of the local subsidiaries. Probably because the Harvard University's Comparative Multinational Enterprise Project did only include MNE which were listed on the Fortune list, the author found no differences between multinationals with many and few subsidiaries.

American MNE only used the mother-daughter or president-to-president relationship in the very first stage of the multinationalization process. Wherever American MNE adopted this form of organization, 60 per cent abandoned it before they had acquired five foreign subsidiaries. All American MNE had taken on other organizational structures before they controlled ten subsidiaries abroad.

These results from the Harvard Study Group on MNE are only partially confirmed with regard to Belgian multinationals (table 6). While practically all the bi-national firms have opted for the mother-daughter relationship, this organizational structure was only used by 2 out of the 22 more globally oriented enterprises. More than one out of three of these multinational oriented companies have a worldwide functional structure. Almost one out of four of the Belgian MNE have chosen the set-up of an international division to control and manage their foreign operations. Only a very limited number of enterprises chose the regional structure or the worldwide product structure. That very few companies belonged to the holding types, is a result from the exclusion of this typical form of Belgian corporate structure in this part of the analysis. No Belgian MNE out of the sample had taken up the more elaborate grid or matrix structure.

Table 6: Organisational structure of Belgian multinational enterprises (1976)

Organisational Structure	Bi–National Enterprises		Multinational Oriented Corporations		All Enterprises	
	N	%	N	%	N	%
Mother-daughter	7	88	2	9	9	30
Worldwide-functional	1	12	8	36	9	30
International division	-	-	5	23	5	17
Regional headquarters	-	-	3	14	3	10
Production division	-	-	2	9	2	6.5
Grid or matrix	-	-	-	-	-	-
Holding	-	-	2	9	2	6.5
Total	8	100	22	100	30	100

Source: Haex and Van Den Bulcke (1979, p. 99)

5.3 Control Relationship

The control relationship between parent company and subsidiary has been studied extensively. The fact that no general model has been developed is not too surprising when one realizes the complexity of this relationship (Van Den Bulcke and Halsberghe 1984). The organizational structure, the nature of the manufactured products, the size of the foreign market, the size of the subsidiary, the number of subsidiaries abroad, the corporate objectives of the parent company and the degree of multinationality of the parent company influence on the choice of a MNE to operate in a centralized or decentralized way.

The decisions themselves and their expected effect on the enterprise as whole also have a large impact on the degree of autonomy of subsidiaries abroad. Because the effect on the total corporate results will be larger for a bi-national enterprise than for a global MNE with very many subsidiaries, one would expect a more closed relationship in the former case. The possibility to standardize certain decision-making procedures or the uniformization of the exchange of information such as reports, visits, etc. have an influence on the decision-making authority of the subsidiary. Standardization initiatives are normally higher in larger MNE because the flow of information tends to expand exponentially with the increase of the overall network.

In general the autonomy of decision-making in Belgian subsidiaries abroad confirms the results of previous studies which were carried out in other parent countries. In matters of personnel policy the subsidiary has much leeway. Half of the about 25 Belgian MNE which provided information on this topic, are able to develop their personnel policy without any interference from the parent company (table 7). In the other cases the subsidiary management is obliged to ask for the advice from corporate headquarters. Only in some particular cases in the personnel decision taken by the parent company after having consulted with the subsidiary, however. Headquarter influence is most pronounced for financial decisions such as the choice of investment projects and the method of financing and also for essential production decisions as the creation of a new department and the determination of the R & D program. For each of these decisions the parent company decides either autonomously or after having consulted with the subsidiary in at least two out of three of the surveyed companies. Although budgeting decisions are prepared by almost half of the subsidiaries it is the parent company which sets the budgeting priorities, the subsidiary is generally consulted. About the same conclusions can be drawn for the determination of the R & D program.

The decision-making authority with respect to marketing is typically less clearcut. That some marketing decisions are more centralized than others might theoretically be explained by the similar or different nature of the foreign

Table 7: Decision-making authority by subsidiaries of Belgian multinational enterprises (1976)

	Decisions	Autonomous decision by parent		Decision by parent after consultation of subsidiary		Autonomous decision by subsidiary		Decision by subsidiary after consultation of parent		Total	
		N	%	N	%	N	%	N	%	N	%
I.	*Marketing and purchasing*										
1.	Product policy	5	19	8	31	4	15	9	35	26	100
1.1.	Design	5	27	4	15	5	19	10	39	26	100
1.2.	Quality level	6	23	8	31	6	23	6	23	26	100
1.3.	Guarantees and services	4	17	6	25	5	21	9	37	24	100
1.4.	Introduction of a new product	6	23	10	39	4	15	6	23	26	100
1.5.	Composition of product range	5	19	11	40	3	11	8	30	27	100
2.	Pricing policy	3	13	7	29	5	21	9	30	27	100
3.	Publicity and promotion policy	2	8.5	7	29	9	37	6	25	24	100
4.	Distribution policy	1	4	6	26	7	31	9	39	23	100
5.	Marketing research policy	3	11	3	11	10	39	10	39	26	100
6.	Selection of clients	1	4	5	20	13	52	6	24	25	100
7.	Selection of suppliers	4	15	5	19	11	43	6	23	26	100
8.	Import decisions	3	13	7	29	6	25	8	33	24	100
9.	Export decisions	4	18	10	45	3	14	5	23	22	100
II.	*Personnel*										
1.	Recruitment and selection	-	-	1	4	16	59	10	37	27	100
2.	Remuneration	-	-	2	7	13	48	12	45	27	100
3.	Attitude to union demands	-	-	1	4	14	51	12	45	27	100
4.	Decisions on collective labour agreements	-	-	2	7	13	48	12	45	27	100
5.	Determination of general policy objectives	1	4	3	11	7	26	16	59	27	100
III.	*Financing*										
1.	Choice of investment projects	5	19	13	48	1	4	8	29	27	100
2.	Choice of method of finance	7	26	13	48	1	4	6	22	27	100
3.	Budgeting	4	15	10	37	1	4	12	45	27	100
IV.	*Production*										
1.	Determination of product volume	3	11	8	29	7	26	9	34	27	100
2.	Determination of productivity standard	3	12	6	23	7	27	10	39	26	100
3.	Establishment of new departments	4	15	15	55	1	4	7	26	27	100
4.	Organisational changes	2	7	10	39	3	12	11	42	26	100
5.	Determination of R & D program	3	13	12	52	2	9	6	26	23	100

markets where the multinational enterprise operates. Following this hypothesis the marketing strategy should be more centralized in countries with comparable market characteristics (consumer tastes, distribution methods, expected quality level, etc.) and implies that within Europe the marketing centralization should be higher than in the rest of the world. That this is partly so can only be seen from the more centralized marketing behaviour of the bi-national companies which are mostly limited to the European market, while the global MNE which scan the world, follow a somewhat more decentralized approach. However, it is quite likely that the effect of the decisions themselves on corporate strategy and results is a more relevant explanatory variable and, as has already been mentioned, this impact will be larger in the emerging MNE. Yet the tendency to centralize the marketing decisions in bi-national firms is – in comparison with the more multinational oriented enterprises – more explicit than for other decisions. This actually means that both market uniformity and the relative importance of the subsidiary for the group as a whole are relevant factors to explain the control relationship for marketing decisions. The least centralized marketing decisions are distribution strategy, marketing research and the choice of buyers and suppliers in the local market. All of these marketing-mix components are oriented towards the local market and have a less direct effect on corporate strategy than other marketing-mix elements such as the introduction of a new product or the composition of the product assortment. Export decisions are also highly centralized. Subsidiaries of bi-national companies have no export decision-making authority, while only 15 per cent of the more globally oriented MNE can decide autonomously with regard to exports. Especially in this latter group of companies some kind of internal division of markets is carried out in order to avoid competition among subsidiaries of the same group or limit transport costs. Import decisions are somewhat more autonomous for local management than export decisions. Price policy, advertising strategy and distribution methods are more strongly controlled in globally oriented MNE than in bi-national enterprises.

The findings of the Comparative Multinational Enterprise Project from Harvard University showed that standardized written reports were only of limited importance to enterprises with a mother-daughter relationship. In Belgian bi-national firms, most of which have a mother-daughter structure, standardized reporting plays a major role in the control relationship, however. Almost nine out of ten bi-national firms have to fill in standard monthly forms provided by the parent company. While fewer multinationally oriented enterprises not only fall under the obligation to report, some also are allowed to transmit their reports on a less frequent basis. The influence of the mother-daughter relationship becomes also apparent for the frequency with which managers visit their subsidiaries. On average the general manager of a bi-national enterprise visits his only subsidiary abroad 7–5 times a year, as compared with 4–3 for the general manager of a more globally oriented company. For this latter group of companies, as might be expected from their organizational set-up, the frequency with which the functional managers visit their local counterparts in the host countries is much higher.

6. Effects of Belgian Foreign Direct Investment Abroad

6.1 Balance of Payment Effects

Although it is not possible to deal with the balance of payments effects of Belgian FDI in a systematic way, a few indications will be given. (Haex and Van Den Bulcke 1979)

Belgian outward direct investment has increased since the beginning of the 1970s. The initial export of investment goods which goes together with the construction of foreign plants was only of a limited importance. This additional export amounted to about 13 per cent of their total investment abroad in 1976 for a sample of 20, i.e. one out of five Belgian MNE. A blow-up of these findings for Belgian exports as a whole showed that this supplementary export represented only 0.15 per cent of total investment abroad.

Direct investment abroad leads to the payment of dividends, interest, royalties and management fees to the parent company. On the basis of detailed information on a sample of 16 Belgian MNE (1976) it was estimated that this came to 2,2 billion Belgian Francs, which represented about 1 per cent to the value of total production abroad.

Imports of finished and semi-finished goods from Belgian subsidiaries abroad were of only marginal importance in 1976. If one excepts raw materials the total import by Belgian MNE into Belgium from their subsidiaries abroad represented 2.5 per cent of their total purchases from foreign countries. An extrapolation of these figures to all Belgian MNE indicates that in 1976 only 0.2 per cent of the total Belgian imports consists of re-exports by Belgian subsidiaries to their parent company.

Exports of manufactured products from the Belgian parents to the foreign subsidiaries are relatively more important than imports. About 14 per cent of the total exports of sample of Belgian MNE had their subsidiaries as a destination. Most of these exports were finished goods and were sold through the subsidiaries without any further transformation. The extrapolation to all Belgian MNE indicates that this export activity would represent 2.5 per cent of total Belgian exports. As the subsidiaries are mainly used as an export platform for products from the parent company, it is quite likely that a certain percentage of these exports would have been realized even without the manufacturing subsidiary.

The effects of foreign direct investment on the total export activity in Belgium can be approached from different angles. First, more than fifty per cent of the managers of Belgian MNE answered to an enquiry that their ventures abroad had not changed their overall export performance. One third of the questioned managers mentioned an increase, while about 10 per cent registered a decline of their exports after having invested abroad. Secondly, there is evidence that the export intensity as a percent of total sales is generally higher for multinational than uni-national enterprises. The average export ratio for Belgian MNE was two thirds compared to only half of uni-national companies. Most of these differences can be explained by the fact that MNE are typically larger than uni-national firms. Thirdly, although one regression analysis study (Jacquemin and Petit 1975), showed that foreign subsidiaries had a positive effect on Belgian exports our own regressions indicated slight negative correlations (Haex and Van Den Bulcke 1979; Van Den Bulcke 1982).

6.2 Employment effects

While Belgian trade unions have claimed that FDI by Belgian companies have negative employment effects, several employer's associations have argued that such investments actually create jobs in Belgium or at least allow the maintenance of the existing employment level. Besides, the government takes the position that FDI result in more exports and thus more employment for the national economy. However, it is extremely hard to carry out a satisfactory evaluation of the employment effects as the analysis is cluttered with a great number of theoretical and material problems. The most serious problem consists of taking into account what would have happened in the absence of this multinational investment, both in the home and host country.

The employment effects of Belgian subsidiaries have been studied using Hawkins' approach for the United States as a model (Hawkins 1972). If one estimates first the job displacement effect of foreign activities of Belgian MNE and assumes that 10 per cent of the Belgian production abroad could have been exported from Belgium, that production in mining could not be substituted and that the import from the foreign subsidiaries of Belgian MNE could have been produced locally, the displacement effect – until 1976 – would have been 12 700 jobs. If one assumes a substitution rate of 30 per cent then a supplementary 39 000 jobs could have been created in Belgium (Van Den Bulcke and Halsberghe 1979).

The second effect, the export stimulation effect, estimates the positive results from the existence of production units abroad through their function as export platforms for goods produced in Belgium. If one accepts as best assumption that at least 20 per cent of the sales and in the worst case 40 per cent of the sales towards the markets served by foreign subsidiaries of Belgian MNE could not have been produced in Belgium, one arrives at a positive employment contribution which varies from 2650 to 5300 jobs.

The third effect, the so-called home office employment effect results from the supervisory and supporting management activities in the home country to service the subsidiaries abroad. As most Belgian MNE are still in the emerging stages of the multinationalization process it was estimated that only 700 managerial jobs in the parent company dealt directly with the foreign subsidiaries.

The fourth effect, the supporting firm employment effect, relates to the employment in firms and institutions which carry out supporting services for the foreign activities of Belgian MNE. Because of a lack of data, it was not possible to estimate this effect.

If one combines the negative job displacement effect with the positive export stimulation and the home office employment effect, one finds a total negative employment of the activities of foreign subsidiaries of Belgian MNE, which varies – according to the assumptions – from 9350 to 33.000 jobs. Of course this analysis not only neglects the supporting employment effect but is purely static and thus ignores the supposedly beneficial dynamic effects on entrepreneurship, profitability and job security in these enterprises which are better able to withstand their international competition in foreign markets. To be complete one should also take into account the positive employment effect of inward foreign direct investment in Belgium, which is quite high.

7. Conclusion

In Belgium, foreign owned subsidiaries represent a larger share of industrial employment than Belgian indigenous MNE. While one out of three of Belgian employees in the manufacturing industry work in a foreign owned company, Belgian MNE provide jobs to only about 15 per cent of Belgian industrial employees. From 1970 to 1978 inward FDI varied between 5 to 8.5 per cent of the gross fixed capital formation, while outward FDI oscillated from 1 to only 3 per cent (UN, CTC 1983 a). Although Belgium originally was one of the more important foreign direct investors, their one sided orientation first on Russia and later on Zaire, resulted in serious setbacks because of the nationalization measures of these countries.

Since the beginning of the seventies Belgian investment abroad not only increased but also became somewhat more diversified as Belgian enterprises started to show more interest in North America and South East Asia. Belgian investment abroad is not very global yet. Very few enterprises can be called fully fledged MNE which operate in a geocentric way. Even Belgium's larger MNE are rather small when compared to the dominating multinationals that are located in the Netherlands, its Northern neighbour. Market share potential was the major determinant for Belgian MNE to locate abroad, while cost factors such as wage levels and transport costs are increasingly taken into account. Unfavourable cost developments in Belgium were largely responsible for this renewed interest in cost conditions abroad. Especially for the North American market Belgian industrialists are convinced that exports are insufficient to maintain one's market share and that the elimination of transport costs and the prospects for a higher net return are positive factors to start production in this region.

That the majority of Belgian MNE have not yet become global MNE is also reflected in the organisational structure with which they link their subsidiaries to the parent company. Most Belgian bi-national enterprises subscribe to the straightforward mother-daughter relationship, while one third of the more multinational oriented firms opt for a worldwide functional structure which is seldom used by American MNE. Almost one out of four of the more multinational oriented firms have set up an international division, a typical mode of organisation by American emerging MNE.

In general the autonomy granted by Belgian parent companies to their subsidiaries abroad is not very different from other investing countries. Personnel policy is most often decided upon by the local subsidiary, while financial and some production decisions are highly centralised and marketing problems are often settled by local management, sometimes after having consulted with headquarters.

Since the beginning of the 1970s the Belgian government has acted upon the belief that outward investment brings benefits to the Belgian economy, especially through increased exports. Although the evidence of the static analysis on the export performance of Belgian MNE is not too convincing, there are sufficient reasons to assume that a small open economy as Belgium needs dynamic and internationally competitive enterprises and that direct investment abroad is necessary to maintain existing market positions abroad and conquer new markets.

Although changing cost conditions push towards location abroad, it may be more interesting from a national point of view, to have the international division of labour carried out by indigenous MNE which will keep part of their operations in the country of origin (Helleiner 1980).

Bibliography

Andersen C./Van Den Bulcke, D.: *Belgian Private Direct Investment Abroad.* UNIDO-UFSIA, Antwerp-Vienna 1982.

Fabrimetal: *Investissements belges de l'industrie des fabrication métalliques à l'étranger.* Brussels 1982.

Franko, L.: *The European Multinationals.* Harper and Row, London 1976.

Haex, F./Van Den Bulcke, D.: *De Belgische industriële investeringen in het buitenland. Een oriëterend onderzoek.* EHL-Schriften, Diepenbeek 1978.

Haex, F./Van Den Bulcke, D.: *Belgische Multinationale Ondernemingen.* LEHOC, Diepenbeek 1979.

Hawkins, R.: *Job Displacement and the Multinational Firm: A Methodological Review.* Center for Multinational Studies, Washington 1972.

Helleiner, G.: *Intra-Firm Trade and the Developing Countries.* MacMillan, London 1980.

Jacquemin, A./Petit, J.: *Les exportations des entreprises belges: Elements d'explications structurelles.* UCL, Working Paper 753, Louvain-la-Neuve 1975.

Newbould, G./Buckley, P./Thurlwell, J.: *Going Internationaal, The Experience of Smaller Companies Overseas.* Associated Business Press, London 1978.

UN, Center on Transnational Corporations, *Salient Features and Trends in Foreign Direct Investment.* New York 1983.

UN, Center on Transnational Corporations, *Transnational Corporations in World Development: Third Survey.* New York 1983 b.

Van Den Bulcke, D.: Export Activities of Multinational Companies in Belgium. In: Czinkota, M./Tesar, G. eds.: *Export Management: An International Context.* Praeger, New York 1982.

Van Den Bulcke, D./Halsberghe, E.: *Employment Effects of Multinational Enterprises: A Belgian Case Study.* International Labour Office, Working Paper 1, Geneva 1979.

Van Den Bulcke, D./Halsberghe, E.: *Employment Decision-making in Multinational Enterprises: Survey Results from Belgium.* International Labour Office, Working Paper 32, Geneva 1984.

Industrial Relations and Europe's Multinationals

Wolfgang H. Staehle

Summary

The internationalization of enterprises has led to a significant shift in power in favour of multinational corporations. The paper uses the concept of Industrial Relations to explain the developments of the three actors, employers, trade unions, and governmental agencies during the rise of multinational corporations in Europe. The responses of trade unions and international organizations to this development are discussed.

1. The Growing Significance of Multinational Corporations

The phenomenon of multinational corporations only began to receive greater attention in Europe in the nineteen sixties. Up to that point in time, in the Federal Republic as in other European industrial countries, exports of goods predominated, aided by low production costs and inflation rates, as well as favourable exchange rates. Then the first marketing problems arose. In 1961 the German mark underwent its first revaluation, making a gradual reorientation from the export of goods to that of capital seem advisable (Perridon and Rössler 1980). This trend is also reflected in the growth in the level of German direct investment abroad (See Table 1).

In the Federal Republic of Germany as in other industrialized countries, expansion in world markets and internationalization of enterprises followed in the wake of goods exports. It was not until the mid-sixties that West German enterprises' investment abroad assumed internationally significant proportions. In 1976 the level of West German direct investment abroad (47 billion DM) for the first time exceeded the level of foreign direct investment in the Federal Republic of Germany (45.5 billion DM). Of this, some 73% of Federal German investment goes to industrialized countries (primarily the USA, France, Switzerland, the Benelux countries) and 27% to developing countries, chiefly threshold countries such as Brazil and Mexico (Kisker et al. 1982).

This trend toward direct investment was assisted by further revaluations of the German mark. As a result it became cheaper to purchase or build factory premises abroad whilst goods exports, on the other hand, became more expensive.

Government economic and financial policies (tax privileges, federal guarantees, capital protection agreements) also promoted German direct investment abroad, and in the process it was accepted consciously or not that the export of capital stimulated in this way would weaken the inclination to invest at home.

The main beneficiaries of government promotion of direct investment and of the government's technology policy are and always have been big enterprises, especially in the growth industries of the day (the chemical industry, electrical engineering, the automobile industry, mechanical engineering). In the course of investing abroad, they became increasingly active internationally, developing into socalled *multinational corporations* (MNC's). Nowadays, the term MNC is

Table 1: Growth in the stock of German direct investment abroad, 1952–1979 (Position at the end of each year)

Year	Assets* (in million DM)	Changes vis-a vis the previous year in million DM	in %
1952–55	421.1		
1956	831.0	409.9	97.3
1957	1 349.2	518.2	62.4
1958	1 858.6	509.4	37.8
1959	2 422.2	563.6	30.3
1960	3 161.8	739.6	30.5
1961	3 842.5	680.7	21.5
1962	4 955.7	1 113.2	29.0
1963	6 070.8	1 115.1	22.5
1964	7 205.1	1 134.3	18.7
1965	8 317.1	1 112.0	15.4
1966	9 995.3	1 678.2	20.2
1967	12 056.8	2 061.5	20.6
1968	14 349.0	2 292.2	19.0
1969	17 618.3	3 269.3	22.8
1970	21 113.2	3 494.2	19.8
1971	23 780.7	2 667.5	12.6
1972	26 596.9	2 816.2	11.8
1973	32 235.0	5 638.1	21.2
1974	36 764.9	4 529.9	14.1
1975	41 991.5	5 226.6	25.4
1976	47 048.4	5 056.9	12.0
1977	52 142.3	5 093.8	10.8
1978	58 192.8	6 050.5	11.6
1979	66 002.0	7 809.2	13.4
1980	83 300.0	17 298.0	26.2
1981	101 200.0	17 900.0	21.5

* These are cumulative transaction values

Source: Kisker et al. (1983, p. 63)

used if an enterprise maintains production plants in more than one country, and these are subject to uniform management (planning and decision-making powers) by the parent company (Lück and Trommsdorf 1982 for the growth and level of internationalization).

According to calculations of the International Labour Office (ILO 1981a, b) in Geneva, MNC's employed 35–40 million workers in industrialized countries (OECD) in the midseventies, and a mere 4 million in developing countries, 60% of them in Latin America alone. These figures make plain that public discussion of MNC's which seizes primarily upon their activities and business practices in developing countries addresses itself to only a minor, albeit important, aspect of the problem.

In addition to being accused of exporting jobs, an accusation which weighs particularly heavily in times of economic recession, criticism is levelled at MNC's above all on the following counts (for example Tudyka 1974; Piehl 1974; Bomers 1976; Krieger 1977; Eichner and Hennig 1979):

- threatening the trade unions that they will transfer production elsewhere
- placing the responsibility for unsocial decisions in the host country on anonymous decisions taken by the company's central management
- obscuring the true earnings and profits position (inter alia by transfer pricing)
- supporting undemocratic regimes (e.g. Chile, the Philippines, South Korea).

Whereas enterprises are controlled at national level by a more or less well functioning industrial relations system, this no longer succeeds to the same degree at international level.

2. Dunlop's Industrial Relations System as a Conceptual Framework

To understand the shifts in power in favour of multinational corporations, it would seem helpful to examine industrial relations at national level first. For this purpose, the model devised by Dunlop (1958) is a simple frame of reference. Dunlop's 'Industrial Relations System' is composed of four basic elements (See Figure 1):

1. Actors
2. Rules
3. The environmental context
4. System of values (ideology)

On 1. Dunlop identifies three groups of actors:

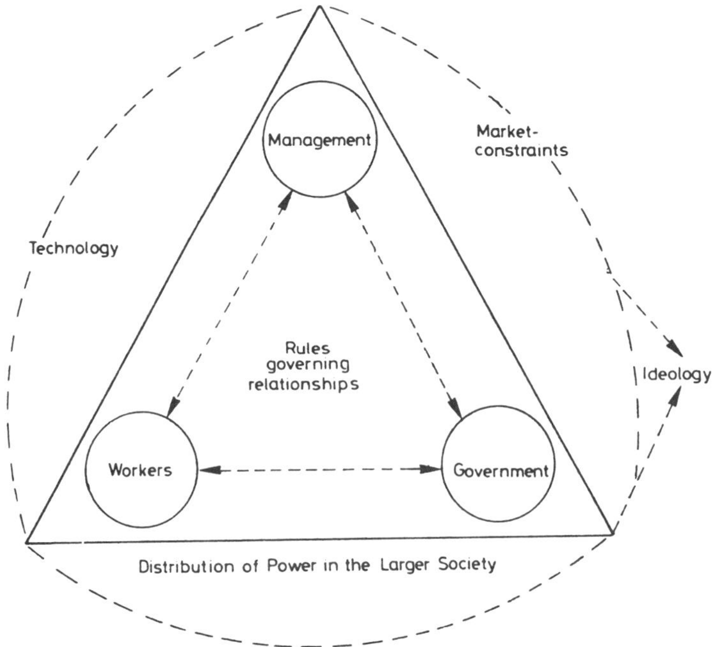

Figure 1: Dunlop's Industrial Relations System
Source: Bomers (1976, p. 5)

a) Managers (employers) and their representative organizations (federations)
b) Workers and their representative organizations (representatives of the work force, trade unions)
c) Governmental agencies concerned with worker/management relations.

On 2. The central function of the actors is to devise universally acceptable rules (rule-making process) that govern the actions and relationships of the actors toward each other.

On 3. The actors interact within an environment of three interrelated contexts:

a) Technology (and its change)
b) Market or budgetary constraints imposed on the actors
c) The distribution of power amongst the actors (social power structures)

On 4. The whole system is integrated and held together by an all-embracing system of values, a set of attitudes, values and ideologies shared by all the actors. This does not mean that no group of actors has his own system of values;

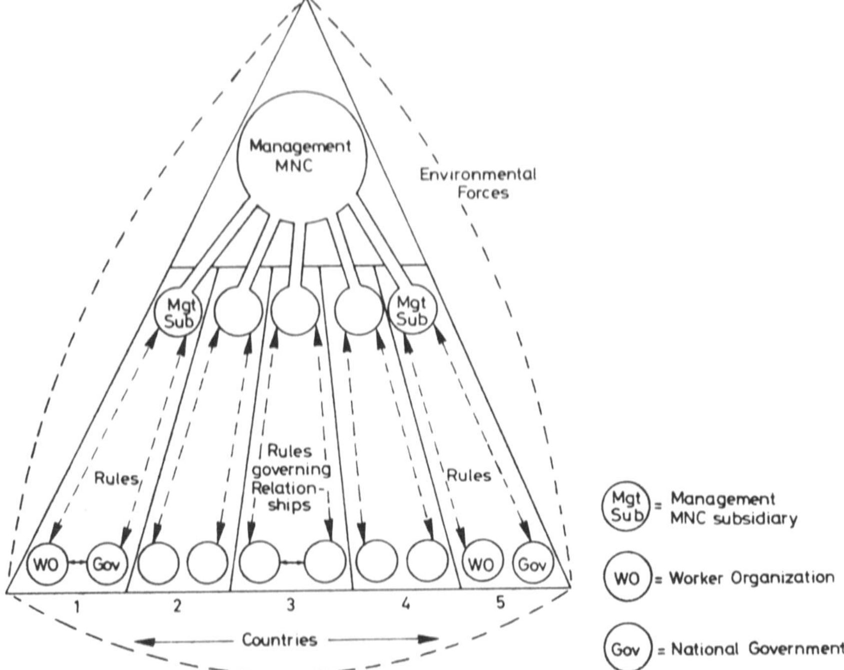

Figure 2: A model depicting a state of unbalanced industrial relations between a MNC and the partners in five industrial relations systems

Source: Bomers (1976, p. 15)

the various ideologies merely have to be sufficiently compatible to allow codes of behaviour acceptable to all sides to form.

To sum up, the following general conclusions can be drawn from Dunlop's model (Dunlop et al. 1975):

1. Each nation develops an industrial relations system.
2. This system is consistent in principle with the fundamental institutions in the surrounding society.
3. As industrialization progresses the system becomes increasingly triangular and comprises the actors government, management and workers.
4. Within this triangular constellation the government becomes progressively more influential.

Now if one of the actors – the MNC in its capacity as employer – becomes active internationally, the result can be a change in the power structures as they developed historically. By no longer being an actor in one country only and becoming instead an actor in all countries simultaneously in which it maintains production plants, the MNC gains a financial, organizational and information lead over the actors at national level – the "workers" and "government" – and can allocate its resources worldwide primarily according to considerations of capital return without any controls to speak of.

The defect of the Dunlop model, in addition to other weaknesses such as failure to take conflicts of interest and industrial disputes into account, is its inability to make theoretical provision for internationalization (Liebhaberg 1980, p. 27). Bomers (1976) developed the model further in an attempt to rectify this (See Fig. 2).

As the subsidiary's local top management (Mgt Sub) is dependent on the top management of the parent company (Mgt MNC) in all major decisions, a fourth actor emerges de facto in the national industrial relations system (countries 1 to n). The imbalance of power already existing in most countries between big enterprises on the one hand and workers and government on the other is increased further by internationalization.

3. Responses to the Development of MNC's in Europe

Given this situation it is natural for the actors remaining at national level to at least press for a restoration of the status quo. Here the notion of forming a countervailing power immediately suggests itself (Galbraith 1952; Liebhaberg 1980), resulting in the

- internationalization of the trade union movement and the
- creation of international organizations.

The development in the case of the third actor – internationalization of the employers' organizations – can be interpreted as a counter-reaction to the internationalization of industrial relations, the object being to prevent any limits whatsoever being imposed on multinational corporations' powers of decision at any level of interaction (company, branch, country, Europe, the world economy) and counter a possible pay increase and an improvement in working conditions, perhaps as a result of international collective agreements.

In this connection mention should be made of the following institutions:

- at EC level: Union des Industries de la Communauté (UNICE)
- at OECD level: Business and Industry Advisory Committee (BIAC)

As these organizations in no way advance the process of internationalizing industrial relations, but instead use every possible means to hinder it, they will not be considered further here (Northrup and Rowan arrived at this same assessment in 1979: Liebhaberg in 1980). The negotiating partners of the international trade union confederations are not, moreover, the international employers' organizations but the multinational corporations themselves.

3.1 Union Responses

The history of the international labour movement and the international trade union movement shows both the strengths and the weaknesses of internationalization as a counterforce (Piehl 1974; Krieger 1977).

In 1913, after lengthy preparatory work above all by the metalworkers' unions (Iron International), the International Confederation of Trade Unions was founded, backed up by international trade union secretariats (ITS) oriented toward particular branches of industry. World War II put an end to all these activities which even then were already directed specifically at international monopolies.

Immediately after the end of World War II, in October 1945, the inaugural congress of the World Federation of Trade Unions (WFTU) was held. Worldwide solidarity amongst workers seemed to have made a fresh start. However, the Cold War, the strictly anti-Communist posture particularly of the American trade unions and the anti-American sentiment of the WFTU majority, which found expression in the rejection of the Marshall Plan amongst other things, soon lead to a split.

In 1949 the "free" democratic trade unions withdrew from the WFTU with headquarters in Prague and founded the International Confederation of Free Trade Unions (ICFTU) with headquarters in Brussels, whereas the more Communist-oriented European trade unions such as the Confederazione Generale Italiana del Lavoro (CGIL) in Italy and the Confédération Générale du Travail (CGT) in France remained in the WFTU. In 1969 the AFL – CIO, the American trade unions' umbrella organization, withdrew from the ICFTU on account of ICFTU members' alleged "Communist contacts" (under Lane Kirkland who succeeded to the presidency on the death of the conservative president George Meany, the AFL – CIO joined the ICFTU again).

In 1969 the trade unions in the countries of the European Community founded the European Confederation of Free Trade Unions. This dissolved in 1973 and became the European Trade Union Confederation (ETUC) which is still in existence today. After long and heated discussion the adjective "free" had been deleted in order for it to be open to Communist trade unions. Then, at the Copenhagen Congress in 1974, the "historical compromise" was reached: the Communist-oriented CGIL was admitted. Incidentally, the German Confederation of Trade Unions and the then ETUC president, Heinz O. Vetter, came out vehemently against the opening up toward the Left. As a compromise it was agreed at the time that membership of the ICFTU must be a prerequisite for membership of the ETUC.

Now the world of labour is split not only along ideological but also along religious lines. From 1920 onwards there existed, for example, an International Federation of Christian Trade Unions which re-emerged after World War II as the World Confederation of Labour (WCL) with headquarters in Brussels, since when it has sought to play the role of Socialist-oriented intermediary between the power blocs.

In 1978 122 national member organizations with some 60 million members were affiliated to the ICFTU, 82 organizations with a membership of 15 million were affiliated to the WCL, and 64 organizations with a membership of 170 million were affiliated to the WFTU.

The work of the international trade union confederations is complemented at industrial branch level by the international trade union secretariats (ITS) which are of particular importance especially in formulating international trade union policy toward multinational corporations. The ITS are autonomous bodies, but maintain close links with the ICFTU. Unlike the international trade union confederations whose function is more the international representation and coordination of trade union strategies toward international organizations such as the UN, OECD and the EC, their concern is the multinational corporations themselves. Recognizing that, a few conglomerates apart, multinational corporations with their programme of products are dominant in one branch of industry, their declared counter-pole is not some international trade union confederation but the respective branch trade union.

Of the 16 branch trade unions affiliated to the ICFTU, three play a special role (these are the branches which feature the most multinational corporations worldwide).

1. The IMF (International Metalworkers' Federation), headquarters Geneva; membership 13.5 million (1977). The IMF, the biggest and most important ITS, counts such powerful single trade unions as the IG Metall, the West German Metalworkers' Union, or the American UAW amongst its members. The most important instrument at the IMF's disposal is the setting up of world company councils. In the automobile industry, for example, there are councils for GM, Ford, Chrysler, VW and Daimler, and in the electrical industry for GE, Westinghouse, ITT and Siemens.

2. ICEF (International Federation of Chemical, Energy and General Workers' Unions), headquarters Geneva; membership 5.5 million (1978).

By contrast to the team-work of the IMF, the work of the ICEF hinges entirely upon the person of the General Secretary, Charles Levinson. Levinson is one of the most ardent critics of multinational corporations and a fervent advocate of the counter-force strategy. The ICEF has come to the attention of the public at large chiefly through its spectacular campaigns against chemical multis. Like the IMF, the ICEF has set up world councils (such as, for example, the permanent world council for AKZO or St. Gobain), in order to be able to counter company policy with a uniform trade union policy. Unlike the other international trade union secretariats, the ICEF declines to co-operate with or even be supported by international organizations such as the UN, ILO or OECD.

3. IUF (International Union of Food and Allied Workers' Association), headquarters Geneva; membership 2 million (1977).

IUF works in the same way as the above two industrial branch trade unions and has also set up company councils for MNC's such as Unilever, Nestlé, BAT and Oetker.

Given its ability to exercise a direct influence on the international transport network which is of such importance for world trade, the ITF (International Transport Workers' Federation), headquarters London, membership 4.4 million (1976) plays a special role within the context of the international trade union secretariats.

In addition to the international trade union secretariats operating world-wide, there are also regional unions at EC level. One such is the EMF (European Metalworkers' Federation) which monitors mainly the European activities of multinational corporations.

The focus of the international trade union secretariats' work is on gathering information (the collection and exchange of all obtainable data on a multinational corporation), and this at company headquarters level.

Both IMF and ICEF are equipped, for example, with computerbased data banks in which all information available worldwide on the enterprises in a branch of industry are stored. Access to this material is intended in particular to prevent local union inexperience from being exploited by the management side in negotiations.

One of the international trade union organizations' most important strategic objectives is to achieve company-wide multinational bargaining arrangements. All the experts are agreed that, given the extreme differences in industrial relations from country to country, in working and living conditions and the peculiarities of the local workers' representatives, an international *tariff policy* in quantitative terms is not feasible. It is conceivable, however, that skeleton international collective agreements laying down minimum hours and conditions of work could be concluded.

Another important ITS strategy toward individual multinational corporations is to call for harmonization of the period for which collective agreements run. If a multinational corporation's collective agreements expire simultaneously in the countries of its main subsidiaries, the workers' negotiating position is greatly enhanced if they proceed with co-ordinated solidarity.

The following further measures to strengthen workers' solidarity at international level are under discussion (Jungnickel and Matthis 1973; Piehl 1974 and 1975; Bomers 1976; Eichner and Hennig 1979):

- Refusal to perform extra work and increase output out of sympathy for colleagues on strike in other company works
- Demonstrations of sympathy, solidarity strikes, works sit-ins
- Publicity campaigns aimed at damaging a company's image, boycotts.

The setting up of *world company councils* or world councils by the ITS owes more to ideas of harmony. In 1964, on the initiative of Walter Reuther, the president of UAW (United Automobile Workers), the IMF (International Metalworkers' Federation) set up the first world councils for the automobile industry. World automobile councils were first set up for General Motors, Ford and Chrysler and later for the European and Japanese automobile companies as well. World company councils also exist in other branches too such as the electrical industry, chemicals and pharmaceuticals, and the food and beverages industry. As a rule half of their complement is made up of full-time trade union secretaries and half of works delegates from an MNC's various subsidiaries. These world councils meet at regular intervals to exchange information and views, to co-ordinate, for instance, collective negotiations or prepare worldwide solidarity campaigns. They make every effort to hold joint meetings with the respective company management without, however, being accepted by the latter as legitimate discussion partners.

3.2 Responses of International Organizations

With the internationalization of economic activity in particular, individual countries set up international organizations at the beginning of this century (especially after the end of World War II) to co-ordinate and harmonize common interests in the field of economic, social and defence policy. In the context of international industrial relations only the International (Inter-)Governmental Organizations are of interest here. These are international institutions under international law which have been established by several countries or governments to solve certain tasks jointly or harmonize individual national measures (Michler and Paesler 1983). Whereas the only means of guidance available to *international* organizations are as a rule recommendations which are not legally binding or conventions requiring ratification by member-countries, *supranational* organizations are vested with national sovereign rights to varying degrees. Of the supranational organizations, the EC is most deserving of the attribute supranational as the direct election of members to the European Parliament, its own budget (income of its own from customs duties, taxes and other dues) and the ability to create Community law lend it a quasi-national character (Möller 1979).

3.2.1 *European Community*

The European Community (EC) is a union of at present twelve European countries bound together by treaty (concluded in Rome 1957). As the European Parliament's competences are decidedly modest, the *Council* of the European Community is considered to be the real lawmaker. The Council is composed of one government representative from each of the member-countries, the choice of minister sent depending on the subject under discussion. The Council has the following statutory provisions at its disposal:

- Ordinances (become law applying in the member-countries direct)
- Directives (minimum requirements which member-countries must meet, possibly by amending their national legislation)
- Recommendations.

In connection with MNC's, a draft Council "Directive on procedures for informing and consulting the employees of undertakings with complex structures, in particular transnational undertakings" (Vredeling proposal) deserves special attention (Kolvenbach 1982). It provides that the management of a controlling enterprise be required to inform the management of its subsidiary in the EC about important data and projects, such as the staffing and financial position, production and investment programmes and rationalization measures at least every six months. For its part the subsidiary's management must then pass this information to the employee representatives without delay. Now the important thing is that this provision is not only to apply to parent companies with headquarters in another country within the EC; it is to apply to those *outside* the EC too.

In October 1982 the European Parliament with its centre-right majority watered down the draft directive in important points. The provision was to apply only to a work force of at least 1000 and the point at which the work force was to be informed was postponed from "before taking the decision" to "before implementing the decision".

3.2.2 *Organization for Economic Cooperation and Development*

The Organization for Economic Cooperation and Development (OECD) was founded in 1961 as the successor organization to the Organization for European Economic Cooperation (OEEC) in Paris. The European Economic Council (founded 1948) comprised the European countries in receipt of Marshall Aid. When this programme came to an end, new fields of activity were sought for the OEEC and, after Europe's economic recovery (amongst other things the setting up of the European Economic Community), these were found in international co-operation between highly developed western industrialized countries to achieve healthy economic growth and social progress. The OECD now has 24 full members who, united by a comparable economic order (rich men's club), defend common economic and political interests primarily for the benefit of member-countries vis-a-vis the rest of the world (Hahn and Weber 1976, Sautter 1981).

The central body in the OECD's organizational structure is the *Council* which as a rule meets once a year at ministerial level and regularly at ambassadorial level. The Council is made up of the permanent representatives from the 24 membercountries, and only governments are members, unlike the tripartite membership structure of the ILO. The Council takes political action in two ways: on the one hand by decisions which are legally binding upon governments, and on the other hand by recommendations, and whilst these are not binding, there is a strong moral obligation to observe them. The work of the Council is prepared by the Executive Committee whose 14 members also coordinate the work of the numerous Specialized Committees.

Compared with governments, member-countries' employers' and workers' organizations have only advisory status at the OECD. The Trade Union Advisory Committee (TUAC) was set up as early as 1948 to ensure that the interests of the European trade unions were taken into account in connection with the management of the Marshall Aid funds. It was officially recognized by the OEEC and has been from 1961 onwards by the OECD as the representative of organized labour. In 1971 a joint TUAC Secretariat was set up, bringing together members of the International Confederation of Free Trade Unions (ICFTU) and the World Federation of Trade Unions (WFTU).

The Business and Industry Advisory Committee (BIAC) was set up in 1962 as an independent employers' organization. It too is officially recognized by the OECD – as the business lobby in the OECD.

The Committee on International Investment and Multinational Enterprises (CIME), which was set up by the Council in 1975, has acquired special importance in the context of international industrial relations. In 21 June 1976 the 'Guidelines for Multinational Enterprises and Labour Relations', which it drew up, were adopted by the Council of Ministers as 'recommendations' (IBFG 1979; Blanpain 1979). This code of behaviour consists of voluntary recommendations, some of which are exceedingly vague, for the management of multinational corporations.

Following publication of the guidelines, the TUAC and individual governments in particular have raised infringements by enterprises at the OECD in recent years. The following two cases attracted particular publicity:

1. Does the parent company have to assume financial responsibility for the subsidiary's commitments, for instance in the case of a factory closure (Badger in Belgium)?
2. Can an MNC order staff from a branch in one country to a branch in another which is currently undergoing strike action (Hertz Rent-a-Car in Denmark)?

The OECD cannot act as a court in such cases. It can only instruct the CIME to bring about clarification of the relevant provisions (Blanpain 1979). It remains to be seen from future practice whether such informel recommendations on behaviour can bring about a lasting change in multinational corporations' company policy and thereby in international industrial relations.

3.2.3 The Council of Europe

The Council of Europe is a union of at present 21 European countries, founded in 1949 to further the economic, social, and cultural progress of its member-countries. In 1976 the Parliamentary Assembly of the Council took up the question of MNC's for the first time. On the basis of a report by the Council's Committee on Economic Affairs and Development (CEAD) the Assembly adopted a resolution which mainly calls for strict observance of the OECD Guidelines for Multinational Enterprises. Nevertheless the Council of Europe considers the existing international guidelines to be insufficient and calls for more binding regulations along lines similar to the Vredeling Proposal of the European Community.

The process of internationalizing industrial relations has taken a very different course where the various actors are concerned. Internationalization of the actors "trade unions" and "countries" has come to a virtual standstill in the course of world-wide recession. For their part, multinational corporations see no cause to be despondent about this for their opportunity lies in the very exploitation of the differences in national industrial relations and not in their harmonization at an international level.

Bibliography

Blanpain, R.: *The OECD Guidelines for Multinational Enterprises and Labour Relations 1976–1979*. Deventer etc. 1979.

Bomers, G. B. J.: *Multinational Corporations and Industrial Relations*. Assen/Amsterdam 1976.

Dunlop, J. T.: *Industrial Relations Systems*. New York 1958.

Dunlop, J. T./Harbinson, F. H./Kerr, C./Myers, Ch. A.: *Industrialism and Industrialized Man Reconsidered.* Some Perspectives on a Study over two Decades of the Labor and Management in Economic Growth. Princeton/N. J. 1975.

Eichner, H./Hennig, L.: *Die sozialen Aspekte der Tätigkeit der Multinationalen Unternehmen.* Berlin 1979.

Galbraith, J. K.: *American Capitalism, The Concept of Countervailing Power.* Boston 1952.

Hahn, H. J./Weber, A.: *Die OECD, Organisation für Wirtschaftliche Zusammenarbeit und Entwicklung.* Baden-Baden 1976.

IBFG (Eds.): *Die Gewerkschaften und die Transnationalen.* Brüssel 1979.

ILO: *Employment Effects of Multinational Enterprises in Industrialized Countries.* Geneva 1981.

ILO: *Employment Effects of Multinational Enterprises in Developing Countries.* Geneva 1981.

Jungnickel, R./Matthies, K.: *Multinationale Unternehmen und Gewerkschaften.* Hamburg 1973.

Kisker, K. P./Heinrich, R./Müller, H.-E./Richter, R./Struve, P.: *Multinationale Konzerne – Ihr Einfluß auf die Lage der Beschäftigten.* Köln 1982.

Kolvenbach, W.: EG-Richtlinie über die Information und Konsultation der Arbeitnehmer (Vredeling-Initiative). *Der Betrieb*, Vol. 28, 1982, pp. 1457–1466.

Krieger, R.: *Der Europäische Gewerkschaftsbund und die europäische Aktiengesellschaft.* Diss., Münster 1977.

Liebhaberg, B.: *Relations Industrielles et Enterprises Multinationales en Europe.* Paris 1980.

Lück, W./Trommsdorf, V. (eds.): *Internationalisierung der Unternehmung als Problem der Betriebswirtschaftslehre.* Berlin 1982.

Michler, G./Paesler, R. (eds.): *Der Fischer Weltalmanach 1983.* Frankfurt/M. 1982.

Möller, H.: Europäische Gemeinschaften. In: *Handwörterbuch der Wirtschaftswissenschaften.* Stuttgart etc. 1979, columns 472–503.

Northrup, H. R./Rowan, R. L.: *Multinational Collective Bargaining Attempts.* Philadelphia 1979.

Perridon, L./Rössler, M.: Die internationale Unternehmung: Entwicklung und Wesen. *Wirtschaftswissenschaftliches Studium*, 1980, pp. 211–216.

Piehl, E.: *Multinationale Konzerne und internationale Gewerkschaftsbewegung.* Frankfurt/M. 1974.

Piehl, E.: Gewerkschaftspolitische Strategien gegenüber den Multinationalen Konzernen. *WSI-Mitteilungen*, April 1975, pp. 145–156.

Sautter, H.: Organisation für Wirtschaftliche Zusammenarbeit und Entwicklung (OEEC, OECD). In: *Handwörterbuch der Wirtschaftswissenschaften*, Bd. 6. Stuttgart etc. 1981, columns 26–33.

Tudyka, K. P. (ed.): *Multinationale Konzerne und Gewerkschaftsstrategie.* Hamburg 1974.

Part 2
State and Future of Europe's Important Industries

introduced by Klaus Macharzina

While Part 1 of this book concentrates on important features of European multinational corporations mainly from a country-specific standpoint Part 2 covers past and future developments of European business from the *industry-specific* perspective. Such an analysis seems to be justified and necessary on two grounds. On the one hand has Europe's future stand in the world economy been accused to be threatened by its maturity of industries and inflexibility to diversify in or concentrate on new relevant and potential industries. On the other hand, relocation of certain industries and assistance in the establishment of industrial capacities in certain regions of this world may contribute to a more rational international division of labour, redeployment and industrialization. The potential of a change in such a direction should, however, be assessed by taking into account certain constraints. Firstly, the different geographic regions may change over time, particularly due to changing technologies. Secondly, protective devices such as host governments' regulatory frameworks influence the flow of investment, the transfer of technology and the exports of goods and services. Thirdly, there is not only a tendency for industry-oriented internalization in international economic transactions rather than corporate internalization by way of combining foreign direct investment, technology and capital transfers, and trade flows in an internationally integrated manner.[1]

As regards the internationalization trend across industries in the period between 1971 and 1980 the share of foreign sales rose considerably in metal, electronics and transportation industries but most importantly in the petroleum industry. Whereas there was only a moderate increase in the construction, textiles, lumber and wood, chemicals, rubber and machinery industries, food and paper industries' share remained constant.[2] As Europe has largely relied on the nonspectacular industries in terms of international growth, and on the other hand lost ground mainly to Japan in growth industries such as electronics and

1 For example the share of British intra-firm trade accounted for about one third of the total of British exports in 1984.
2 Cf. United Nations, Document E/C. (10, 1983, p. 2).

transportation there are industry-specific problems which relate to Europe's competitive edge in the international market place. In certain industries, newly industrializing countries have reached a well established international market position due to comparative advantages such as cheap labour and largely at the cost of European industries. Examples are the manufacturing sector, particularly in the textiles, clothing and shoe industries but also such industries as steel, machinery and transport equipment.

Taking into account these developments the following chapters provide indepth analyses of Europe's troubled industries with a view of suggesting solutions for measures at corporate, industry and public policy level with respect to potential improvements.

The European car industry still occupies a central position within the European economy; it has, however, lost ground opposite world developments recently. Whereas world car production increased by 5% to 42,1 million units in 1984 the European production decreased by 4% to 12,25 million cars. Thereby, the European share in world production decreased from 32 to 29%. The US account for the largest growth and have reached again their 30% share of 1979 in world markets which have been dominated by Japan since 1980. The major problem issues on an international level relate to increased penetration of domestic markets by imports and local manufacture by foreign MNEs, the low commitment to international production and the future of inter-firm collaboration.

The European aerospace industry, inspite of its excellent technological competence, has faced enormous competitive problems, particularly vis-à-vis the US and mainly due to its traditional fragmentation along national lines and customers. Careful attempts to co-operate on a cross-boarder basis may improve the competitive position of a potential truly European aerospace industry. The European petrochemical industry needs a fundamental redesign of its industrial policy. The industry is troubled by the pre-energy crisis problem of overcapacity which was aggravated during the post-energy crisis period. Besides there are pricing problems due to the pricing policies of Eastern Europe, international competitive distortions through price controls and other protectionist measures, and finally the problems which relate to Arabian industrial attitudes and actions. There are calls for sectoral, bilateral and business-specific solutions to tackle these problems but there is a unitary strategy missing.

The European steel industry has suffered from uncoordinated industrial strategies of the various governments which led to a maldistribution of benefits and costs of corporations across Europe. A redesign of industrial strategies should aim at compensating the existing differences of comparative advantages among Europe's steel producers which in turn should improve their world competitive position.

The European textile and clothing industries have certainly faced a damaging crisis in the seventies. This was marked by a rapid decline of industrial performance which resulted in a loss of jobs in the order of one million and the disappearance of over 2500 clothing firms in Europe. The decrease in the rate of population, serious economic problems, changes in materials and in relative material prices, changes in the composition of demand, but also vertical integration and horizontal centralization trends are among major structural features which have to be considered when designing appropriate strategies for adjustment. Yet above all there has been a significant growth in the volume and geographic diversity of trade in textiles and clothing which calls for truly international businesses in this sector.

Europe's position in information technology oriented markets can be summarized by the following data. Nine out of ten video recorders sold in Europe are Japanese, eight out of ten personal computers sold in Europe are American, 80% of Europe's consumption of integrated circuits is imported, the European market share in peripheral equipment has fallen from ⅓ to ¼ over the last ten years. It is obvious, that Europe lags behind the US and Japan considerably in the related industries. As traditional industries will become increasingly dependent upon the microelectronics industry European companies and countries are bound to strenghten their R & D, manufacturing and manpower development in this sector. Also in terms of skill and capability Europe's scientific, economic and social resources have the potential to satisfy the demands in the area of microelectronics and new technologies on a worldwide scale. At the moment, however, these resources seem to be underused as the following figures show. In 1984 the per capita consumption of microelectronic goods in the US was $ 19,5 per year while in Japan it was $ 19,0 and in the European Communities $ 21,0. At the same time, the yearly per capita production of microelectronic goods was $ 23,0 in the US, $ 18,5 in Japan and less than $ 4,0 in the EC. Europe has still to cope with the challenge of the new information technologies; if it would not be able to do so the survival of Europe's industries in toto is at risk.

Also, in the telecommunications industry the traditionally tight network between national carriers and as a rule domestic suppliers which are supported by state-national monopolies undergoes a drastic change towards increasing international competition, following the break up of supplies-dominated monopolies and deregulation in several countries. It is probably to early to assess whether the prevailing trend of the European telecom industry to engage in international link-ups will turn out to be a successful industrial strategy or merely an emergency measure.

On a more general level, future European industrial strategies will increasingly have to take into account factors such as dynamics of the economies and the markets' long-term future orientation, particularly with respect to human resources, socio-economic infrastructure and public policy including the role of the nation states in the international economic development.

European Car Industry

Stephen Young

Summary

Car industry still occupies a central position within the European Economy although the future is very unclear. Despite a general return to profitability, the position of some firms is highly uncertain and dependent on government policies. Problem issues relate to increased penetration of domestic markets (including local manufacture by foreign MNEs), the low commitment to international production, the future of inter-firm collaboration, the financing of new models and investment in innovation, and non-motor industry diversification.

1. The Background of the World and European Industries

In many ways the problems of the European motor industry epitomise those of European industry as a whole. In the motor sector, Europe and European companies lack the low production costs of Japan and the resources of America (which may facilitate the restoration of competitiveness in an era of technological innovation) and, moreover, do not possess the potential for high market growth or the very low labour costs of many developing countries. The industry has, nevertheless, a central position within the European economy and its performance will be a major determinant of the European Continent's prosperity for at least the remainder of this century.

The motor industry in the last decade, arguably, entered a new phase in its international evolution, the final outcome of which is as yet, however, highly uncertain. The dominance of Japan is the most obvious manifestation of this new stage in the industry's history: Japan became the world's principal producer of cars and trucks in 1980 (with a cost advantage over the Americans estimated at between $ 1,200 and $ 2,000 per unit), having one year earlier replaced the European Communities (EC) as the major net exporter of all automotive products. International patterns of production are changing in other ways, as 'new' manufacturing nations doubled their share of world output to almost 20 percent in the decade to 1980. Of special importance are three groups of countries: state trading nations, countries that have applied for membership of the European Communities (Spain & Portugal) and the newly industrialising states. Such changes in the location of production have been accompanied by changes in the levels and patterns of international trade: the share of exports in world production of finished vehicles has risen substantially, with trade in components, equipment and technology also becoming of considerable significance (United Nations Centre on Transnational Corporations 1982).

For some, these trends have been interpreted as a product cycle effect, with the motor industry being seen as a mature oligopoly in the United States and Western Europe. By this reasoning, multinationals (MNEs) especially from Europe and the USA would seek lower cost Third World locations and serve developed country markets by exports from these foreign subsidiaries. Such strategies would be reinforced by demand trends and the low motor vehicle density and high market growth in developing countries. In truth, however, government policies in both the developed and developing world have had at least as important an influence and have substantially distorted the production and trade patterns which might have emerged in a free market situation. These policies include the protectionist stances adopted by Western Europe and US governments against Japanese exports, the positive and negative inducement policies pursued by host developed and developing economies in relation to MNE investment (capital grants and loans, duty exemptions on components and parts, export subsidies, local content requirements, export obligations, foreign exchange contributions etc.), and support policies for indigenous manufacturers.

The restrictions operating against Japanese exports are well-known, and have had the effect in Europe, for example, according to one author (Jones 1981) of keeping out around 500 000 cars a year from Japan – or the equivalent of two assembly plants and one engine plant of minimum efficient scale. The various policies on investment incentives and performance requirements have probably led to a widening of the country sources for multinational-based production in Europe, especially for Ford and General Motors; and a great concentration of MNE investment in various developing countries, especially Mexico and Brazil. Then too, several of the major Western European and US producers have been in receipt of government assistance to help their survival and subsequent restructuring, Chrysler and BL (British Leyland) being the most spectacular but by no means the only examples. Rather than resulting in liquidations or mergers, therefore, producers' problems have led to a spider's web of joint ventures and collaborative agreements, over 200 of which were in existence in 1983 (Automotive Industry Data 1983). Overall, government policies have had the effect of distorting and disguising patterns of international comparative advantage in the industry; while in relation to the product cycle specifically it has been indicated (Lall 1983; Jones 1983) that the recent acceleration in the speed of product innovation may have forced the industry back to an earlier state in its development cycle when close coordination is required among R & D, engineering and marketing activities.

2. The Size, Structure and Performance of the European Industry

2.1 Employment

The motor vehicle industry is a major employer of labour in Western Europe. Taking account of employment in the manufacture of vehicles together with parts and accessories (NACE 35), almost two million people were directly employed in the EC alone in 1980, and the industry was the predominant employer in the four largest Community countries. The significance extends further because of linkage effects and so some 20 percent of all steel and machine tools produced in the Community, together with 5 percent of glass and approximately 15 percent of rubber output are intended for the motor industry. This employment importance extends to other European countries including Sweden and Austria, and especially Spain where 113 000 people were employed in 1982. Despite these facts, the motor industry, especially in the European Communities, is now likely to be facing a period of substantial employment decline; in 1981 alone 157 000 jobs were lost in the industry and total employment in this sector thus declined in a single year to its lowest level since the early 1970s (Commission of the European Communities 1983). Regional effects have been markedly different and so almost half of all job cuts in the Community in 1981 were made in the United Kingdom. Alongside the basic employment changes taking place in Western Europe overall therefore, the distribution of motor industry employment between countries is also changing significantly.

2.2 Industry Structure

Turning to the structure of the industry, the importance of economies of scale in product development, production and marketing are well known and have driven the industry of necessity towards a concentrated structure internationally. Compared with the American industry the European motor vehicle sector industry is more fragmented, although in part this is due to the survival of specialist producers such as BMW, Daimler-Benz and Alfa Romeo which have cornered particular market niches. Four European companies (Volkswagen-Audi, Renault, Peugeot and Fiat) were represented within the top ten automobile manufacturers worldwide in 1982 occupying 5th to 8th positions behind GM, Ford, Toyota and Nissan. But the European groups are much smaller than their US counterparts especially, and some have come into being through mergers where problems of the assimilation of acquisitions exist. As such the groups may lack the cohesiveness of competitors such as General Motors and Ford. Moreover, several of the European companies have interests outside automobiles and uncertainties over their future commitment to the motor industry still exist.

Fragmentation of the industry in Western Europe extends particularly to the components sector. With the high level of bought-in components in cars, the performance of the components industry is important to the competitiveness of the assembly companies. In this respect, it has been indicated that there are five times as many components companies supplying the European as compared with the Japanese automobile manufacturers (Commission of the European Communities 1981).

In the present environment of technological innovation and fierce international competition it is widely accepted that the structure of industry in Western Europe is far from stable. Equally, nevertheless, there is only limited scope for further domestic mergers in the industry (although, for example, the possibilities of a Renault/Peugeot merger have been mooted from time to time, and there have in the past been unsuccessful merger discussions between Volvo and Saab-Scania) and undoubted government barriers in some instances to transnational mergers. The outcome has been a big growth in collaborative agreements between enterprises. These may involve long term research, the development of components and/or new models, the production of components and/or supply purchasing, assembly, distribution, etc.; in some cases, equity linkages are involved, in some cases not; and the agreements may be national (as between Renault and Peugeot for the manufacture of components in France), regional (as between been Fiat and Peugeot for a 1 million unit per annum engine joint venture), or international. In the latter context, particular interest attaches to the cooperation ventures between Japan and European Communities countries including:

– BL's licensing agreement with Honda, the model involved being sold as the Triumph Acclaim in Britain. BL and Honda have also reached agreement on the manufacture of a jointly designed executive car for sale in Europe and Japan;
– the agreement between VW and Nissan to produce the Santana model in Japan;
– the joint venture between Alfa Romeo and Nissan for the production of small cars using Nissan-supplied bodies and Italian engines and other mechanical equipment. Production of this car, which is to be sold in Europe only, commenced in 1983. The structure of the industry is thus highly unstable and there must be serious doubts about the ability of companies to effectively manage the range of agreements in which they are currently involved. In some cases, the present linkages may be the precursors of acquisitions in the future and for example the British Government would probably look favourably upon a full-scale bid by Honda for BL.

2.3 Costs, Productivity and Competitiveness

The period since the oil crisis in the early 1970s, and with it the emergence of Japan, has concentrated the minds of most manufacturers on the issues of costs, productivity and competitiveness. There is little doubt that production costs have been and probably still are much lower in Japan, with figures of a 20–30 percent cost advantage over Germany and France being quoted (Commission of the European Communities 1981.) These cost differentials are a consequence of a variety of factors: the industry's internal organisation, plant size and the efficiency of plant utilisation, hourly wage costs and automation, including within this the more general issue of the application of technical know-how. Appreciation of such problems have led several of the European groups, sometimes under the threat of their actual demise, to embark upon huge reorganisation and restructuring programmes and leading in some cases to quite spectacular improvements. To give just one example, much has been made of the "Miracle at Longbridge", where changes in work practices allied to better production scheduling and control, and heavy investment in robotics have led to dramatic improvements in productivity at BL's Metro plant. Volkswagen and Fiat in particular have been involved in similar programmes, but, while apparently successful, the cost in terms of plant closures and job losses has been equally dramatic. The question still arises as to how the European companies will fare in the late 1980s: whether profits will be sufficient to justify the massive commitment of resources and to finance new models and further efforts at automation.

2.4 Production and Trade

The structural readjustments taking place in the European motor industry are reflected in patterns of production and trade. As Table 1 shows, car production in the European Communities declined at an annual average rate of 0.7 percent, leading to a fall in the Communities share of world output from 41 percent in 1970 to just over 30 percent in 1981. Part of this decline has, however, been taken up by increased production in Spain where car output nearly doubled over this period to 855 000 units; this output level is now rivalling that of the United Kingdom which has seen an almost equally spectacular output decline during these years.

Imports have risen sharply in most countries and by 1982, the Japanese had an 8.1 percent market share of the EC (10) passenger car market, a level of penetration which had increased from 0.6 percent in 1970. This expansion has taken place despite national import restrictions which limited Japanese car market penetration to 0.1 percent (2200 units) in Italy, 2.9 percent in France, 9.8 percent in Germany and 11 percent in the United Kingdom; in Greece by

Table 1: European Community Production and Trade in Passenger Cars, 1970–81

	Annual growth rate (1970–81)	1981 1000 units	1981 Share of world total
Production	– 0.7%	8 695	30.3%
Exports	– 2.5%	1 704	20.1%
Imports	+ 21.4%	1 297	15.5%

Source: Commission of the European Communities (1983)

comparison the Japanese market share was 45 percent. (It should be noted that Japanese imports are also subject to restraint agreements and surveillance at Communities level).

Apart from the competition from imports, indigenous Western European manufacturers also face the challenge of foreign multinationals with production bases on the Continent. Ford and General Motors have, of course, been long established in Europe and in 1982 accounted for 42 percent of sales in the United Kingdom, 29 percent of the market in Germany and 18.5 percent of the Spanish market (in all cases, including captive imports). The reinvestment and restructuring programmes of these US multinationals, which have paralleled but probably surpassed those of their European competitors, have brought an enhanced challenge to the latter. This challenge is all the more real when it is realised that General Motors' expansion plans in the late seventies involved boosting capacity by 29 percent or 300 000 units annually by 1982/3 in a determined bid to catch-up with Ford internationally. Spain has become the key new ingredient in GM's strategy, with the production of the Opel Corsa from a highly automated, 250 000 unit capacity factory at Zaragoza, commencing in 1982; this buildup has been partly offset by a rundown in Britain where Vauxhall is now essentially an assembly company, although even this subsidiary has hopes of new investment following its return to profitability.

For the future, GM and Ford will be joined by production in Europe from Nissan. The joint venture with Alfa Romeo has already been mentioned, but particular interest attaches to the Nissan investment in the wholly-owned facility in the United Kingdom. To begin with at least a very small scale of operation is envisaged: thus a pilot plant producing 24 000 units from imported kits is to be constructed, coming on-stream in 1986. In this is successful the company will move towards a 100 000 unit per annum operation in 1990, and a target 80 percent local content. At 100 000 units, output will be no greater than the present level of Nissan exports to the UK, but the fact that the company is keeping its options for the 1990s is shown in its search for an 800 acre site. The announcement of the Nissan investment, which was made early in 1984, has been long delayed for a variety of reasons, including, apparently, Japanese union opposition to the arrangement; but more probably to the duration of the recession, fears over the return of a Labour Government committed to withdrawal from the EC, the level of locally produced components to be incorporated in Nissan's British cars, and fears that the French and Italians might exclude British-produced Nissan vehicles from their markets. The allegation of the Nissan plant as a "Trojan horse for Europe" has been made frequently, with Fiat and Renault at the forefront of the attack. The EC Commission is attempting to play down the local content issue which is at the heart of the matter, arguing that: "Any efforts to tighten the existing rules could divert Japanese investment projects from the Community to other countries where the rules would be softer, yet still providing access to the Community market. Furthermore, any move towards specific local content requirements could be dangerous, be it under GATT aspects, or by promoting protectionist tendencies in other countries ..." (Commission of the European Communities 1983, p. 46).

For the future, therefore, EC-based production by the Americans and Japanese will cause a major threat to the indigenous European producers. The Italian and French markets would seem to be particularly vulnerable. In the past there seems to have been opposition from the domestic manufacturers to the establishment of Ford or GM plants in France and Italy, and the American MNEs have been unable to penetrate these markets successfully on the basis of exports. (There is a close relationship between the US MNEs' market shares and the countries in which they have manufacturing or assembly facilities in Europe). Supplies from Spain may change this position for the future, while the Nissan/Alfa Romeo linkup will undoubtedly further increase competition in the domestic Italian market.

The other market which is vulnerable for the future is the United Kingdom. Import penetration is already higher than in the other major car markets and domestic production from Nissan will further intensify competition. The further problem is likely to stem from Communities moves to try to harmonise prices for new cars, which are currently between 30 and 50 percent higher in Britain than those in some Continental countries (Crane 1983). The differences are essentially a matter of tradition and cannot be explained away by exchange rate or inflation differentials, divergent tax structures, transport costs or government price regulations, and moves to end the differentials would undoubtedly affect BL.

Another measure of the European competitive performance is given by the companies' market shares in external markets. Taking the position for passenger cars, the Japanese market share in third countries (i.e. excluding the EC and Japan) rose from 5.2 to 18.9 percent between 1970 and 1981 while the EC market share declined from 18.7 to 10.1 percent over the same period. Of course, the EC remains a huge net exporter of automobile products (exports of $ 24 billion and an export: import ratio of 3:1 in 1981). But Japan's trade surplus is almost twice as high as that of the Communities because of the paucity of its imports. The United States had $ 12 billion trade deficit in this sector in 1981.

3. Corporate Strategies and the Internationalization of the European Industry

Because of the limited number of manufacturers in this sector, industry performance is directly related to the corporate policies and performance of the major manufacturers. The major strategy themes for selected European manufacturers are summarised in Figure 1. And these in turn have to be seen

---

France	
Peugeot:	France's largest private company. Grew by government-sponsored takeover of Citroen in 1974 and acquisition of Chrysler Europe in 1978. Problems in integration have led to financial difficulties. Labour troubles in France. Large scale restructuring necessary. Operations and future growth centred on Europe principally, including inter-firm collaboration & licensed production in Eastern Bloc. Outside Europe, significant involvement in Argentina as base for S. American, plus Africa & Asia. Aims to build export market in USA through niche strategy.
Renault:	State-owned group. Substantial government support for investment programme in early 1980s. Focus on production in France, despite labour unrest, plus Belgium and Spain. Expansion into Eastern Bloc. Major strategic move was acquisition of equity stake (now 46.4%) in AMC; latter now linked to facility in Mexico. Other important bases in Latin America. Other developments: minority holding in Volvo; 50% stake in Peugeot's Dodge Trucks; shareholding in US Mack Trucks.
Germany	
Volkswagen-Audi:	Developed through internal growth and acquisition of Audi-NSU Auto Union. Financial rescue in mid-70s and thereafter strategy of restructuring domestically and expansion internationally. Main international developments: assembly in US, components manufacture in Canada; large scale operations in Mexico & Brazil; agreements with Nissan for Japanese market and joint venture in China; link with SEAT in Spain. International thrust may be hampered by problems in USA & Latin America. Apparent attempt to diversify with acquisition of Adler-Triumph (office information equipment), but losses recorded since purchase in 1979.

Italy
Fiat: Italy's largest private company, owned by Agnelli family. Wide spread of interests.
Major restructuring of auto side of business and withdrawal from other peripheral activities. Themes in autos – automation, cost cutting, fewer suppliers fewer car types, simpler cars.
Abandoned many international markets eg. US, Spain (withdrawal from arrangement with SEAT), S. Africa and several Latin American countries. Only large car-making centre outside Italy is Brazil, but active in building up motor industries in Eastern Bloc.
Focus on building up inter-company links to minimise financing costs.
Despite improvements in autos, long-term prospects depend on success of non-car interests.

Spain
SEAT: State-owned enterprise formed in 1949, with Fiat having a minority equity stake in exchange for technical assistance and licensing agreements.
Continuing management and production problems, brought to the fore with gradual liberalisation of Spanish market. Fiat withdrew from commitment to acquire 80% of SEAT by 1981 because of financial difficulties of latter. Subsequently agreement signed with Volkswagen to manufacture in Spain for sale elsewhere in Europe; also SEAT became Spanish agent for VW.

Sweden
Volvo: Development from car, truck & bus manufacture into Swedish conglomerate, after acquisition of Beijerinvest.
Truck and bus businesses significantly internationalised, with purchase of White Motor Co. in US and commencement of manufacture in Brazil.
Car business centred on Europe: acquisition of loss-making Daf in Netherlands followed by financial support from Dutch government (which is now the majority shareholder); Renault became minority shareholder in Volvo in 1979.
Continued speculation about mergers with or takeovers by other enterprises eg. Saab-Scania, Renault; talks with Norwegian government to take 40% holding broke down.

United Kingdom
BL: State-owned after financial rescue in 1975. Since then massive but successful injection of public funds in restructuring, automation, new facilities and new models.
Withdrawal from a number of overseas activities and now developing links with Honda: BL producing Honda Ballade under licence in UK & agreement to build joint-designed executive car for sale in Europe and Japan.
Government committed to privatisation with profit-earning Jaguar as most likely possibility.
Volume car division faces uncertain future because of small size of operation and level of competition in UK market and internationally.

Figure 1: Main Strategy Themes for Selected Manufacturers

Table 2: European Car Producers – Selected Date

	1978	1979 National	1980 currencies	1981	1982	1982 $ US million[a]	1982 Group-employment (000)	Cars, (Cars, cvs, parts etc) as percent of turn-over[b]
France								
Peugeot								
Sales (FFr mill)	65 978	71 034	71 103	72 389	75 263	11 311	208	88.4
Net income (FFr mill)	1 288	1 800	(1 504)	(1 993)	(2 148)	(323)		(88.4)
Renault[c]								
Sales (FFr mill)	34 201	42 363	75 741	81 215	97 126	14 597	217	78.5
Net income (FFr mill)	159	470	638	(607)	1 420	213		(94.5)
Germany								
BMW								
Sales (DM mill)	6 184	6 833	7 261	8 072	9 756	4 021	41	n. a.
Net income (DM mill)	152	177	163	144	189	78		(c 100.0)[d]
Daimler-Benz								
Sales (DM mill)	24 236	27 367	31 053	36 661	38 905	16 037	186	48.1
Net income (DM mill)	591	637	1 098	822	921	380		(c 100.0)[d]
Volkswagen-Audi								
Sales (DM mill)	26 724	30 707	33 288	37 878	37 434	15 430	239	85.3
Net income (DM mill)	553	680	310	224	(233)	(96)		(c 100.0)[e]
Italy								
Alfa Romeo								
Sales (Lire bill)	1 192	1 411	1 701	1 556	2 277	1 684	42	89.7
Net income (Lire bill)	(84)	(55)	1	(97)	(80)	(59)		(c 100.0)

Fiat								
Sales (Lire bill)	4 511	n. a.	n. a.	20 312	20 619	15 251	264	50.6
Net income (lire bill)	74	39	51	90	137	101		(74.7)
Spain								
Seat								
Sales (Pta mill)	95 686	112 805	115 183	102 329	112 184	1 023	25	n. a.
Net income (Pta mill)	(10 358)	(15 090)	(20 544)	(20 169)	(23 665)	(216)		(c100.0)
Sweden								
Saab-Scania								
Sales (SEK mill)	11 642	13 426	13 990	16 188	18 726	2 569	40	52.0
Net income (SEK mill)	198	233	356	398	471	65		(83.3)
Volvo								
Sales (SEK mill)	19 133	23 472	23 803	48 017	75 624	10 374	75	23.9
Net income (SEK mill)	312	416	38	453	496	68		(39.6)[d]
United Kingdom								
British Leyland	3 073	2 990	2 877	2 869	3 072	5 373	108	62.5
Sales (£ mill)	(13.2)	(121.8)	(397.2)	(345.0)	(233.9)	(409)		(c100.0)
Net income (£ mill)								

Notes: [a] Converted on basis of average daily rates for 1982

[b] Percentages are approximate since most companies have minor interests for which data are not shown in accounts.

[c] Data before 1980 relate to parent company only.

[d] BMW includes motor cycles. Includes buses for Volvo & Daimler-Benz; and for Daimler-Benz tractors, cross-country vehicles etc.

[e] Cars as percent of total output in units.

Sources: Extel Statistical Services, Annual Reports.

alongside the sales and profit data in Table 2. Reflecting earlier comments, several of the groups have gone through or are continuing to experience severe financial problems. Peugeot, Alfa Romeo, Fiat and BL fall into the latter category, although BL is about to return to profitability after a decade of losses. The problems of Fiat are disguised by the financial data which refer to group operations as a whole: Fiat Auto has in fact been recording substantial losses, but returned into the black, albeit fairly marginally, in 1983 following its huge restructuring programme.

Volkswagen falls into the category of a more recent loss-maker, a consequence largely of its heavy commitment to overseas operations (curiously, in the light of later comments). The company, which was the first overseas producer to begin assembly in the United States, suffered a slump in sales, first because of the US recession, and then because of some apparent switch in demand back to large cars; problems with the price and quality of American components' supplies and an expensive recall programme all added to the financial pressures. The result was that VW temporarily abandoned their expansion plan in the United States and sold off its second assembly plant at Sterling Heights, Michigan before completion (with closer links with the buyer – Chrysler – a probability for the future). The national economic situation in Mexico and Brazil has caused further problems in markets in which Volkswagen has a heavy commitment, and which have until recently been highly profitable.

The Volkswagen experience is an interesting one. This company has a much heavier commitment to production overseas than any of the other European car producers. Over one-third of its output is overseas compared with under 20 percent for the other three European majors, Renault, Peugeot and Fiat. While the setbacks the company is currently experiencing may yet cause a more fundamental change of direction, to date the company is still committing itself to other growth markets including Japan, China and Spain. The Spanish deal is particularly significant; in return for VW technology, SEAT is to manufacture in Spain 120 000 Volkswagen units per annum for export through the German company's outlets in Europe; conversely, SEAT has become the exclusive agent for the marketing of Volkswagen and Audi models in Spain. This almost costless entry into its Spanish market has been seen as a major coup for VW after the problems faced by Ford and GM in gaining market access in the past. Despite the difficulties with its internationalisation programme, the Volkswagen strategy is probably necessary for any world league manufacturer. Even if the product cycle hypothesis is rejected for this industry, participation in the world's growth markets will require, initially assembly, and then fully integrated manufacture on the spot. And for the future, the possibility of global sourcing in the industry cannot be ruled out.

Of the other European producers, Renault is also expanding overseas, principally into the Americas where its strategy of linking operations in Mexico and the United States is similar to that of the Big Three US auto firms. Its state-owned position may, nevertheless, put a brake on such moves, especially when the French Government is being called upon for substantial investment funds. The principal problem; nevertheless, occur for the companies which have been forced to retrench internationally as the price of short-term profitability. Thus Fiat has been divesting itself of many of its overseas activities and Peugeot is heavily Euro-centred.

Where several of the European producers appear to have an advantage over their Japanese and US rivals, is with their links with Eastern Bloc nations. Fiat, which operated in pre-Communist Eastern Europe, won the contract in 1965 to build Volga Auto Works massive Togliattigrad plant, and discussions regarding new cooperation ventures are under way. Renault too has numerous licensing and joint venture arrangements in Eastern Europe and is currently working with the Soviet Union on a replacement for the Moskvich: in return for technical advice Renault is to receive French Fr. 300 million and French industry about FF one billion in equipment orders. Similar deals exist between Comecon countries and other European auto firms and extend beyond cars to trucks, components and construction equipment. While the Japanese will undoubtedly provide increased competition in these markets in the future, the Americans are likely to continue to be excluded because of political factors.

Some comments have been made earlier about the lack of cohesiveness of a number of the European groups, derived essentially from their merger-oriented development, and the same description could be applied to the overall business strategies of the companies. Thus at Volkswagen, Fiat and Volvo, there are uncertainties over corporate commitment to the motor industry. Diversification moves, moreover, have not always been successful. There are also uncertainties over the way ahead in the automobile sector itself: the degree and form of international expansion is one of these and another, of course, concerns linkages with other manufacturers on R & D, production and marketing.

4. The Future

As the above discussion has indicated, the future seems likely to see increasing pressure on the European producers, both in their domestic and international markets. Some of these pressures within the Western European market are indicated in the projected market shares through to 1988 shown in Figure 2. Share reductions are forecast for all the major indigenous producers at the expense of the Americans and Japanese. This will put a special pressure on

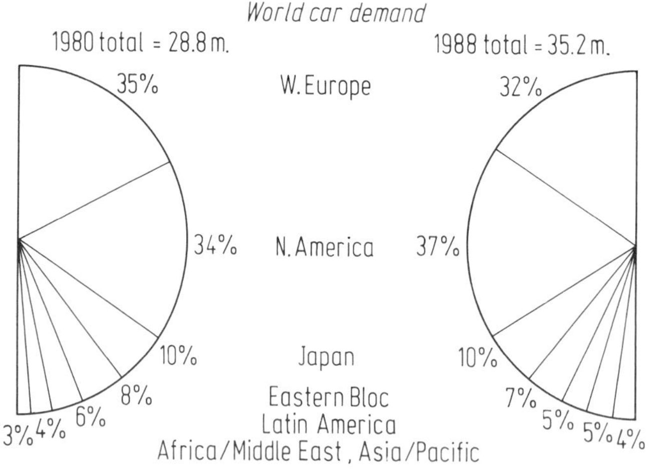

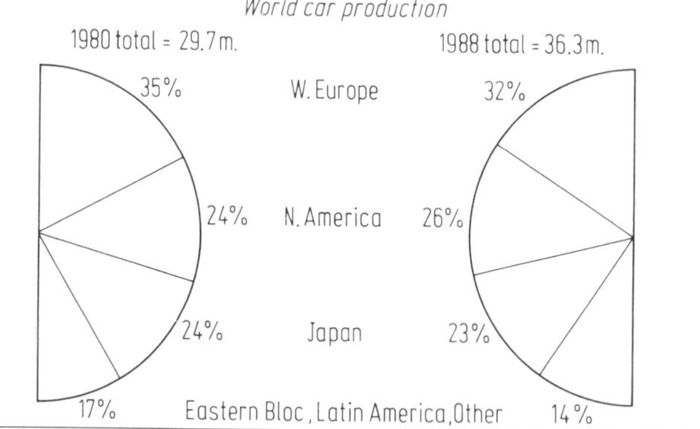

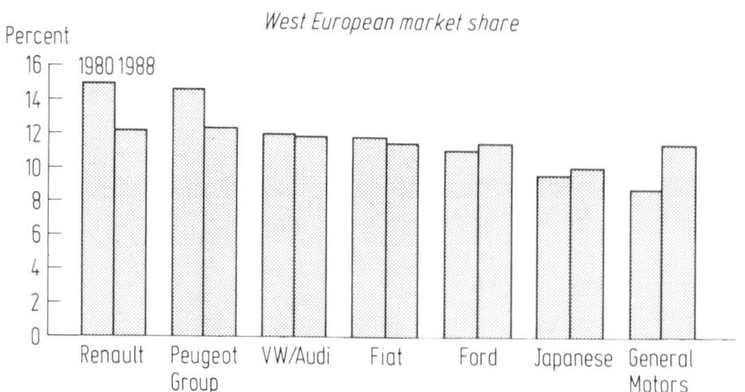

Figure 2
Source: DRI Europe forecasts quoted in The Economist (26 November 1983)

companies or groups such as Peugeot which have yet to restructure; SEAT is in a rather different position in this regard, given that it is state-owned and has been heavily subsidised over the years. For companies emerging successfully from rationalisation programmes, such as Fiat and BL, the difficulty is one of earning a level of profits sufficient to fund new models and further investment in innovation for the late 1980s. Apart from doubts over its profit-earning capability, BL's small size offers further competitive problems, although the company itself has argued that new technology has increased in flexibility of medium-sized manufacturers such as itself. With the British government commitment to privatisation, the extension of collaboration agreements may be followed by an outright takeover. Some of the other small companies, especially BMW and Daimler Benz, have continued to pursue differentiated, upmarket strategies, but while their future may be secure, the betting must be in favour of further structural adaptation of the European industry before the end of the present decade, leading to a reduction in the number of manufacturers.

This expectation that collaboration agreements would be replaced by more formal mergers or takeovers on a transnational basis is very dependent upon government policies. The possession of an indigenous motor industry is still seen by most governments as a necessary component of a developed economy, and protectionist policies appear likely to continue to be a major influence on the development of the sector in Europe and worldwide into the 1990s. The local content issue seems bound to influence the course of events both for European firms investing abroad and, as noted, for Japanese and US investments in Europe. While Japan is the major focus of attention in the latter regard, it is interesting that the British government announced early in 1984 that it was monitoring the progress of Ford and GM towards higher levels of local content in the UK. The scene is set for intra-Europe as well as Europe-Rest of the World difficulties.

Bibliography

Automotive Industry Data, *Joint Ventures*. AID, Lichfield, Staffs. 1983.

Commission of the European Communities: *The European Motor Industry*, Supplement 2/81. Brussels 1981.

Commission of the European Communities: *Commission Activities and EC Rules for the Automobile Industry 1981/83. Progress Report on the Implementation of the Commission's Statement "The European Automobile Industry" of June 1981.* COM (83) 633 final, Brussels, 21 December 1983.

Crane P.: Have you Paid Over the Odds for Your New Car? *Europe 83*, No. 12, 1983, pp. 8–9.

Jones D. T.: *Maturity and Change in the European Car Industry: Structural Change and Public Policy*. Sussex European Papers No. 8, Sussex European Research Centre, 1981.

Jones D. T.: Technology and the UK Automobile Industry. *Lloyds Bank Review*, No. 148, 1983, pp. 14–27.

Lall S.: Prospects for Automotive Transnationals in the Third World. *National Westminster Bank Quarterly Review*, February 1983, pp. 13–20.

United Nations Centre on Transnational Corporations, *Transnational Corporations in the International Auto Industry*, 1982.

Industrial Policy and Industrial Culture: The Case of European Petrochemical

Max Boisot

Summary

The term "Industrial Policy" means different things to different people. This paper presents a conceptual framework within which different types of industrial policies can be evaluated. The framework is applied to an analysis of the European Petrochemical industry the results of which are then briefly discussed.

1. Introduction

The term industrial policy has by now worked its way into the collective unconsciousness of policy makers where it has fallen prey to the psychic forces that shape images and associations. Like the word "sex" in Freud's time, it remains a taboo subject for some and a source of titillation for others. But since a growing number of practioners on both sides of the Atlantic are openly advocating the adoption of an industrial policy as the therapy needed to restore to health our stricken economies, there is a need to free the term from the tangle of associations that still shroud it in order to examine it more closely.

A modest attempt to do so will be made in this chapter. In the next section we briefly discuss some current uses of the term. In section three, we present a conceptual framework that can be used to analyse different types of industrial policy. A particular application of the framework is illustrated in section four where the current and future prospects of the European petrochemical industry are described in a qualitative fashion. In the concluding section, we try to assess what the framework adds to our understanding of industrial policy.

What follows is a thinkpiece illustrated in faint pastel shades. The richer colours of a full empirical exploration can only be painted in when the framework's theoretical contours can be discerned more clearly.

2. The Range and Depth of Industrial Policy

The term Industrial Policy generally refers to government actions designed to bring about needed adjustments at the sectoral level. The tools used can be macroeconomic, microeconomic or a mix of the two. An export industry, for example, can be stimulated by exchange rate manipulations as much as by direct state subsidies, but in the first case the government's involvement in the resource allocation process remains indirect. Exactly where on a continuum linking macroeconomic and microeconomic measures, policy makers wish to pitch their intervention depends on conditions within an industry, on how these translate into political pressure for action, and on how the prevailing political culture can cope with such pressure.

Conditions within an industry may be cyclical or structural, but in either case the complexity of industrial structure can make diagnosis difficult. Unlike microeconomic theory, industrial organization lacks an unambiguous efficiency concept that commands wide assent. Diagnosis will be hesitant and will most likely open the door to political pressures, stemming from the opportunities or threats that confront an industry. Where industry evolution is the source of such pressures one would expect the greatest agitation for an industrial policy to occur in emerging or declining industries. As Tyson and Zysman (1983) note, a government – they cite France as an example – may develop an industrial policy to deflect demands for protectionist measures by firms that face a serious loss of competitiveness in emerging or declining markets. The distribution of power within the political system will also have a bearing on what kind of an industrial policy government decision makers will propose and on how far they can hope to implement it. The EC Commission, for example, has to contend with the countervailing power of its member states in proposing solutions to Europe's industrial problems. It is less likely to provoke them if it adopts with a macroeconomic approach but lacks the means to implement one. A nation state the size of France, on the other hand, can sometimes have its government "pick winners and losers directly without provoking the wrath of overpowerful interest groups" (Saussois 1984). One might argue, therefore, that the larger the political unit relative to industry size, the more likely that a macroeconomic approach to industrial policy will be chosen, and that conversely, the smaller the political unit relative to industry size, the more likely that a microeconomic approach will be prefered.

Consciously or unconsciously, ideological considerations will also influence a government's thinking on industrial policy. They will give more legitimacy to some types and sources of political pressure than to others. They will also sanction the mix of macroeconomic and microeconomic policy instruments selected.

In the US, for instance, the prevailing belief that government should write the rules of the resource allocation game but should not participate as a player translates into a preference for aggregate policies over sectoral ones. Of course, in America as elsewhere, sectoral policies have always existed but they have been tolerated rather than proclaimed. The electorate's traditional distrust of big government, together with the widely held conviction that the state lacks a sufficiently detailed knowledge of firms and markets to outperform them in picking winners and losers, have generally favoured policies aimed at improving the functioning of the market rather than replacing it. Only in clear cases of market failure is a sectoral level intervention required of the State.

France and Japan, by contrast, provide examples of countries where the state has traditionally enjoyed more legitimacy as a player at the sectoral level. Central government bureaucracies, in both countries enjoy a higher degree of prestige than in the US, and are presumed to work in the national interest, broadly defined, and not for narrow sectional ones. A strongly mercantilist tradition in each country has made the electorate tolerant of state power in many areas of the economy where there are numerous issues on which a hierarchically imposed state arbitration is prefered to a market solution.

Further down towards the microeconomic and of the intervention scale one finds the command economies where even the detailed resource allocation process carried out within the firm is subject to state approval. Furthermore the range of industries across which the state is expected to intervene is much broader. Emerging and declining industries then merely become one subcategory among others.

The different types of intervention options so far discussed can be graphically described as in Figure 1. Moving up the vertical scale we find increasing levels of state intervention with macroeconomic solutions at the bottom of the scale and microeconomic solutions at the top. The horizontal scale describes the range of industries across which state intervention can occur with the left hand side of the scale representing a few critical industries – say emerging or

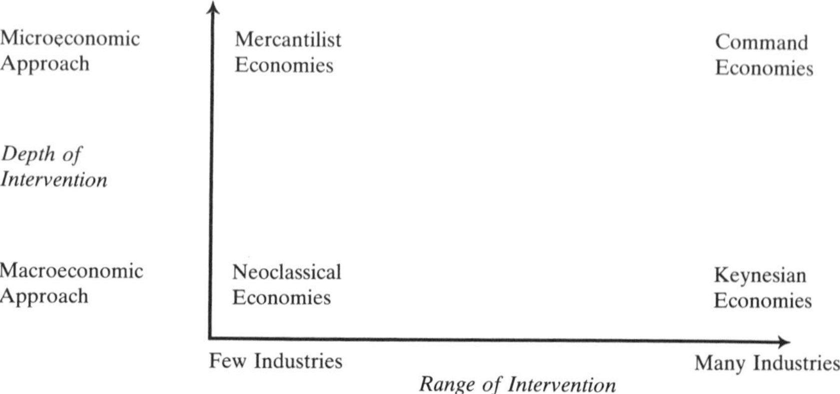

Figure 1: Options for State Interventions

declining ones – and the right hand side covering the economy as a whole. Different types of economic systems can then be positioned in the space, and, as will be clear from our discussion, each will be underpinned by a distinctive approach to industrial policy, with the lower left hand corner describing pure market solutions and the top right hand one describing pure hierarchical ones.

Insofar that a position in the space describes a genuine societal preference, it expresses distinctive cultural values, attitudes, and perceptions. Cultural factors have often been invoked to explain variations in national economic performance and the recent vogue enjoyed by the term "corporate culture" suggests that the firm can function as a culturally autonomous unit at the macroeconomic level. But the nation state and the firm represent levels of analysis rather than real entities. Above the nation state we may select a level of analysis at which we can talk of "Western" or "Asian" culture, and outside the firm we might talk of an industrial culture in which only those values, attitudes and perceptions shared by a particular industry are considered. Students of industrial organization have hitherto regarded such variables as unanalysable, and in looking at industry structure, conduct, and performance, have tended to treat them as "noise", a residual factor (Scherer 1980). If, as we have suggested, the choice of industrial policy instruments is inextricably linked to cultural preferences, then the ability to conceptualize the term culture at the industry level becomes important to any discussion of industrial policy. Such a conceptualization will be briefly attempted in the next section.

3. A Conceptual Framework

In this section we present a conceptual framework for analysing cultural phenomena in general and then apply it at the industry level. In the next section, we shall illustrate a particular use of the framework by applying it to a particular industry – the petrochemical sector. The framework's theoretical underpinnings have been discussed elsewhere (Boisot 1983a and 1983b) so that only its main features will be summarized here.

The framework takes the broadly accepted anthropological definition of culture as a shared system of meanings (Kroeber and Kluckhohn 1952) as its point of departure and then looks at how well such meanings have been articulated and how extensively they are shared. A cultural product is the fruit of two interrelated processes in which experience is first structured – we shall call this *codification* – and then shared – we shall term this *diffusion*. The codification and diffusion of experience is a form of social information processing, in which the first step (i.e. codification) is carried out within individual heads and the second step (i.e. diffusion) is carried out between them. Thus the cultural

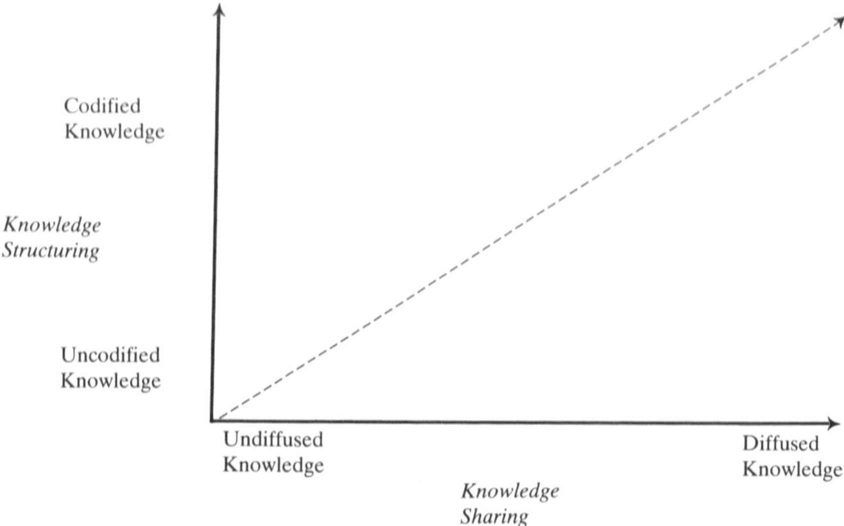

Figure 2: The Codification – Diffusion Concept

product has both a psychological and a sociological component. How are they related?

At the simplest level, the answer is given in Figure 2. It should be intuitively clear that the more an experience has been codified the more easily it can be diffused. Of course this is a purely technical characteristic since it assumes that a recipient has the ability to decode a message upon receiving it. In practice, beyond a certain level of codification, diffusion may well be hindered. An example will make this clear. Much of our knowledge is of a personal, tacit and intuitive kind (Polanyi 1958) that cannot be put into words without distortion or loss of information. Joyce's attempt to fully capture through words twenty four hours in the life of Leopold Bloom was heroic but doomed from the start. Such experiences cannot be put into words, they can only be *shared*. What can be communicated to those not present always involves a process of selection and structuring (i.e. codification) in which features believed to be relevant are highlighted. A talented novelist can evoke a scene for a literate audience but it will never be the scene as he himself sees it. A further process of selection and abstraction is involved when an experience is reduced to a mathematical and quantitative form.

Such information reduction, technically speaking, will increase diffusability but will limit the size of the audience capable of understanding a given message. Think of stock market data that can travel throughout the globe in seconds but

Codified Knowledge	Proprietary Knowledge	Textbook Knowledge
Uncodified Knowledge	Personal Knowledge	Common Sense Knowledge
	Undiffused Knowledge	Diffused Knowledge

Figure 3: Different Types of Knowledge in the C-D Space

that can only be fully interpreted by specialists. We shall not concern ourselves here with the coding skills of the recipient although in some applications of the framework it has considerable relevance.

By simply dichotomizing the two dimensions of our codification-diffusion framework henceforth referred to as the C-D space we can locate different kinds of knowledge in the culture space (Figure 3). Further subdivisions of the two dimensions give us an ordinal scale that can be adapted to a given level of cultural analysis. Figure 4 illustrates an application of the framework at the industry level.

Knowledge is not a static thing. It flows and as it does it undergoes transformations. The stimuli for any given experience are initially picked up from the physical and social environment through a scanning process. Most stimuli, as well as the experiences they provoke remain fleeting and formless, but some will be structured and may then be communicated, diffused, and absorbed.

New knowledge flows clockwise throuth the C-D space as shown in Figure 5. The resulting cycle may take many shapes depending on the barriers encountered, but in each case four phases can be discerned:

Need formulation – Generally available knowledge is scanned on the right hand side of the C-D space and picked up in idiosyncratic ways by individuals on the left. Sometimes this knowledge points to threats and opportunities in the social and physical environments which call for some kind of response.

Problem solving – Herbert Simon once observed that effective problem solving was a process of structuring problem and relating information until the solution became transparent (Simon 1969). Structuring information means codifying it, through an upward movement in the diagram. When the process is carried out on the left hand side of the space, new, and as yet, undiffused information is created. Most problem solving, however, does not involve the creation of new

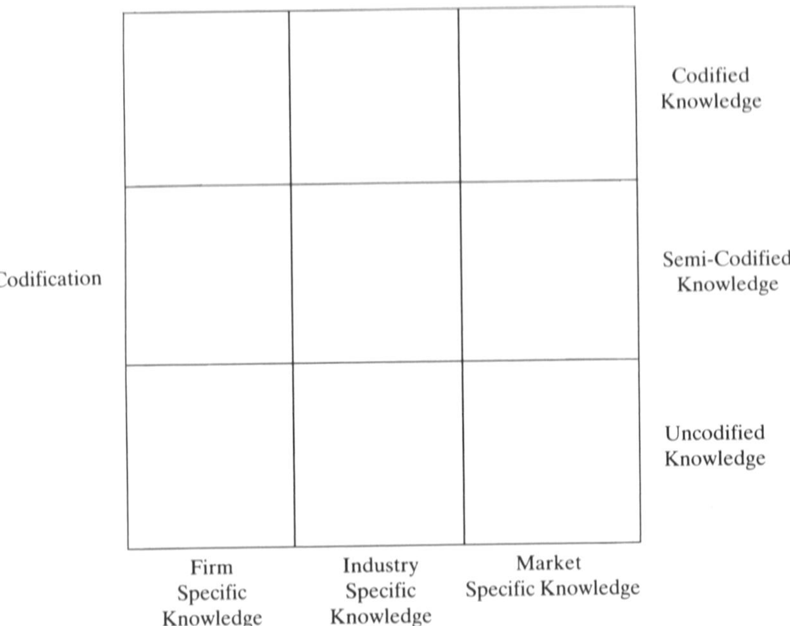

Figure 4: The C-D Space at the Industry Level

Key:
Codification

- Codified knowledge: that can be completely set down on paper and transmitted impersonally.
- Semi-codified knowledge: that can be partly set down on paper but whose transmission requires personal contact.
- Uncodified knowledge: that cannot be set down on paper and can only be transmitted in face to face situations.

Diffusion

- Firm specific knowledge: knowledge available only within or through the firm.
- Industry specific knowledge: knowledge available only to the firm and to its competitors within an industry.
- Market specific knowledge: knowledge available to a firm, its industrial competitors, and industry customers.

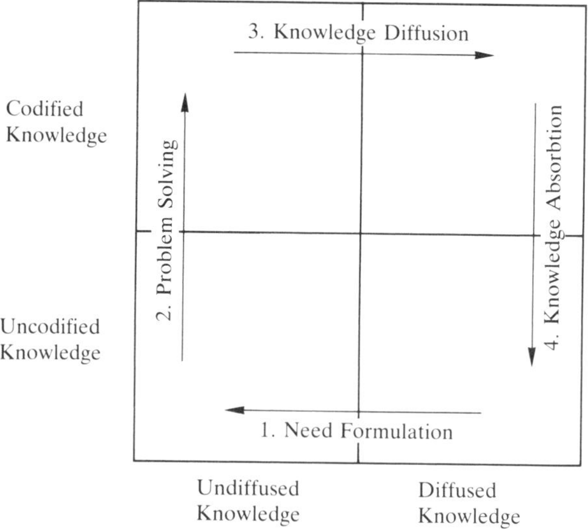

Figure 5: The Knowledge Creation Cycle

knowledge as any schoolboy grappling with Boyle's law or the mysteries of the calculus will testify. In that case it occurs on the right hand side of the space.

Knowledge diffussion – The differential possession of knowledge creates both barriers to, and pressures for diffusion. The more this knowledge has been codified the easier it will be – for better or worse – to respond to the pressures and to overcome the barriers. New knowledge diffuses from left to right in the diagram.

Knowledge absorption – Knowledge is absorbed and inwardly digested by putting it to work and testing it out in new situations. Over time, for example, an engineer develops an intuitive "feel" for how and when to use an engineering formula and his stock of tacit knowledge gradually accumulates, resting on whatever base of codified knowledge he acquired through training or reading. Absorption moves knowledge down the C-D space through a process of learning by doing from which new problems and opportunities may emerge thus reactivating the knowledge creation cycle.

The knowledge creation cycle offers a dynamic representation of the acculturation process through which meanings are created and shared. The shape of the cycle in the C-D space, the speed at which knowledge flows through it, the type of involvement offered to diverse social groups in the production of knowledge, taken together, will give a cultural unit a distinctive configuration within the framework.

	Undiffused Knowledge	Diffused Knowledge
Codified Knowledge	Bureaucratic Hierarchy	Market
Uncodified Knowledge	Feudal Hierarchy	Federation

Figure 6: Transaction Styles in the C-D Space

Key:

Transactional Characteristics	Bureaucratic Hierarchy	Market	Feudal Hierarchy	Federation
1. Is knowledge shared?	No	Yes	No	Yes
2. Are values shared?	No	No	Yes	Yes
3. Are objectives shared?	No	No	No	Yes
4. Are relationships personalized?	No	No	Yes	Yes
5. Is trust important?	No	No	Yes	Yes
6. Is information uncertain?	No	No	Yes	Yes
Examples	– Large firms – Production Department – Govt. departments	– Street markets – Stock markets	– Small firm – R&D Labs – Japanese subcontracts	– Family – Club – Board of directors

But what kinds of behaviour stimulate the flow of knowledge through the cycle? In answering the question we shall use a number of concepts drawn from the literature on institutional economics (Coase 1937; Williamson 1975) whilst maintaining a broader sociological perspective. In particular we shall adopt the transaction as the elementary behavioural unit which involves some manipulation of information whether or not this is central to the exchange process. Transactions may be economically motivated but not exclusively so, and by positioning them in the C-D space according to their information characteristics we obtain the typology of transactional styles shown in Figure 6.

Since transactions incure costs, the institutional form through which they can be accomodated cannot always be freely chosen. A prior institutional investment in market transactions, for example, may lower the marginal cost of transacting in the upper right hand corner of the C-D space relative to competing alternatives. But the decision to invest in a given institutional form in the first place may express unconscious cultural preferences for a particular transactional style (Boisot 1983a). Alternatively it may simply reflect the position of transaction relevant information on a given knowledge creation cycle.

A transaction's position in the C-D space gives us its style, but only very indirectly its institutional form. The assumption encountered in the literature on institutional economics, for example, that transactions conducted inside a firm imply a hierarchical style and that those conducted outside it imply a market oriented style, is misleading. A hierarchical transaction style can be found outside the firm – i.e. in a monopolistic industrial environment – just as a market transaction style can be found within it – i.e. in the multidivisional structure, internal labour markets; etc. The point is perhaps best illustrated by adding a third dimension to our framework that describes the ratio of internal to external transactions conducted by a given social grouping, in this case a firm. In Figure 7, internal transactions (i.e., intrafirm) have been institutionalized into organizational functions each with their own distinctive information environment and management style, and external transactions (i.e. interfirm) have been institutionalized through various contractual arrangements identifiable in the C-D space. A transaction's governance structure (Williamson 1981) then results from:

a) knowledge cycle characteristics,
b) culturally shaped transactional preferences and,
c) prior investments in workable institutional forms.

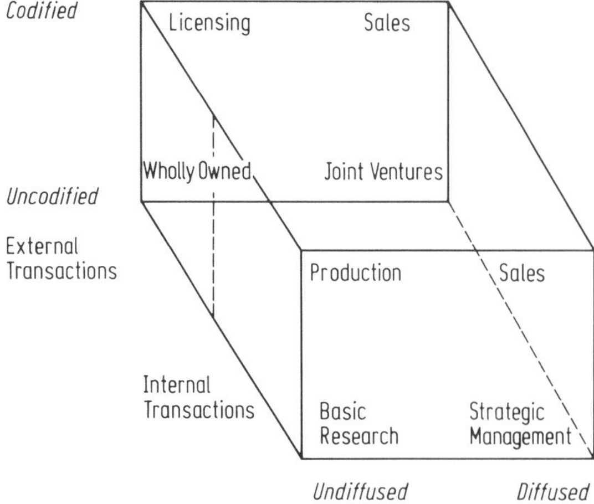

Figure 7: The Relationship Between Internal and External Transactions

This brief presentation of our conceptual framework has given us three variables relevant to any discussion of industrial policy and each locateable in a three dimensional culture space here, we shall only need two of them, since although intra and interfirm transactions are clearly related, our discussion deals only with the latter. To use our framework at the industry level we shall merely aggregate transactions as is implicitly done when working at the level of the individual firm or even at that of its constituent organizational units. We shall now apply our conceptual framework to an analysis of certain issues that confront the European petrochemical industry to see what light it throws on our discussion of industrial policy.

4. An Application of the Conceptual Framework: The European Petrochemical Industry

4.1 General Background

The petrochemical industry converts raw materials of petroleum origin into chemical products. It has been a natural focus for attempts at downstream integration by the oil makors seeking to diversify out of an industry with a limited future, and for efforts at upstream integration by chemical firms unsure about future supply conditions. The industry's core technologies use large scale, highly automated, continuous processes, and are capital intensive. The scale economies achieved in plant construction in the past decades have meant high entry barriers into the industry, and the "transaction specific"* nature of such

Table 1: Capacity Utilization

	1969 (in %)	1972 (in %)	Δ (in %)
Ethylene	84	70	– 14
Vinylchloride Monomer	88	65	– 23
Ethybenzene	85	62	– 23
Styrene	87	68	– 19
Puc	92	75	– 17
Polystyrene	92	70	– 22
High Density Polyethylene	84	68	– 16
Polypropylene	73	67	– 6
Low Density Polyethylene	82	84	+ 2

* The term "transaction specific investment" is used by Williamson (1981) to describe investments that cannot easily be converted to uses other than those for which they were conceived.

capital investments has also created high exit barriers. Thus the structure of the industry is oligopolistic, with a few large producers responsible for the larger part of the output. Yet the need to maintain production in continuous process operations has made price the critical competitive variable, and "lumpy" additions to capacity when the market was growing have resulted in considerable profit fluctuations.

Table 2: Percent of the 1980 Overcapacity Already Present in 1973/1974

Vinyl Chloride	50%	Puc	53%
Ethylene	45%	Polystyrene	71%
Ethylbenzene	55%	High Density Polyethylene	38%
Styrene	45%	Polypropylene	24%
Low Density Polyethylene	36%		

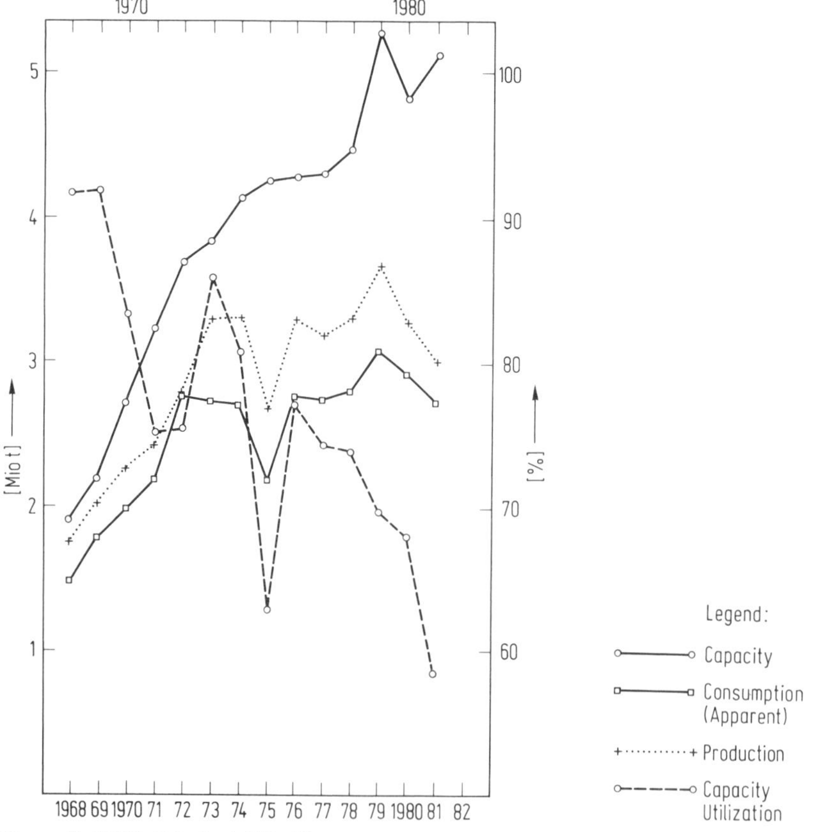

Figure 8: PVC: Polyvinyl Chloride

Any discussion of recent developments in the European petrochemical industry divides naturally into a pre-energy crisis phase and a post-energy crisis phase. As Table 1 indicates, there were additions to capacity before 1973 that led to substantial drops in capacity that plagues the industry today was already present when the 1973/4 energy crisis struck. Table 2 shows what percentage of 1980's overcapacity was already present in 1973 for different petrochemical products. With figures 8–11 we can see how the bulk chemical sector reacted to the 1973 energy crisis. The answer is, it did not. Unlike sectors like oil refining, plastics transformation, and pharmaceuticals, which all adjusted from 1974 onwards, the petrochemical industry went its own way with capacity and demand steadily drifting apart (Figure 12).

It has been argued that firms in the industry were so hypnotized by what their competitors were doing that they became blind to market developments (Davi-

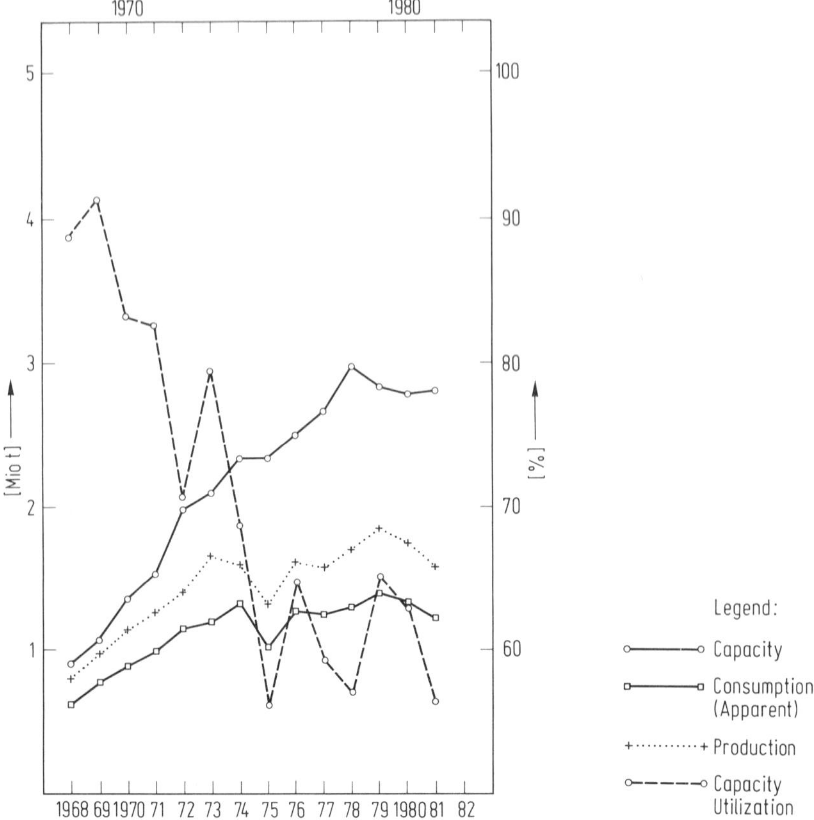

Figure 9: PS: Polystyrene

gnon 1982). After the first energy crisis the industry lived off its oligopolistic fat and the patience of its shareholders. But with the 1980 oil price hike, the recession and the rise of the dollar, chaos and cut throat competition set in. Thermoplastic prices for example dropped between 1981 and 1982 despite a US $ 10 increase in naphta prices (see Table 3). This struggle for market share coincided with a downturn in demand which led firms to look to their short term survival even if this meant allowing plants to become obsolete.

Table 3: Price Decline in Thermoplastics / 1980–81

Low Density Polyethylene	– 230 $ T	Polyvinylchloride	– 150 $ T
High Density Polyethylene	– 260 $ T	Polypropylene	– 180 $ T

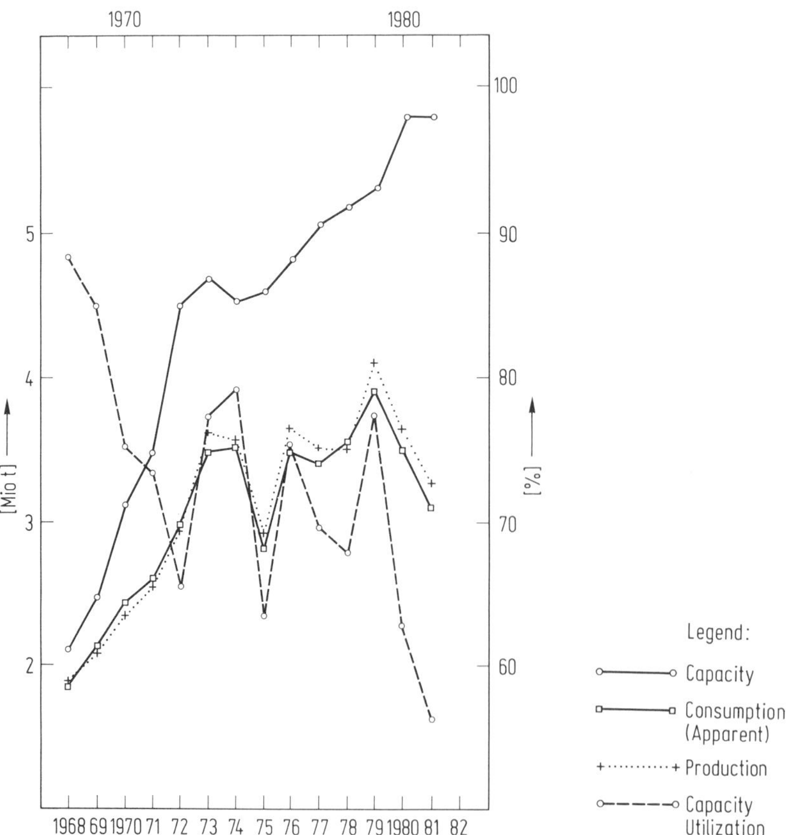

Figure 10: VCM: Vinylchloride Monomer

To the twelve year old internal problems of overcapacity, the West European petrochemical industry faces three external ones:

The pricing policies of East European Countries in the East-West chemical trade. The deficit that the EC chemical and petrochemical trade has run with the outside world (i.e., 50 billion EUA's in 1980) has not helped matters.

International competitive distortions such as price controls in the US, import subsidies on crude oil in Canada, subsidies on petrochemical exports in Brazil, etc.

Arab petrochemical developments. The first petrochemical operation in the Middle East was opened in February 1981 at Umm Saíd in Quatar and others are being set up in Saudi Arabia with Exon, Mobil, and Shell as industrial

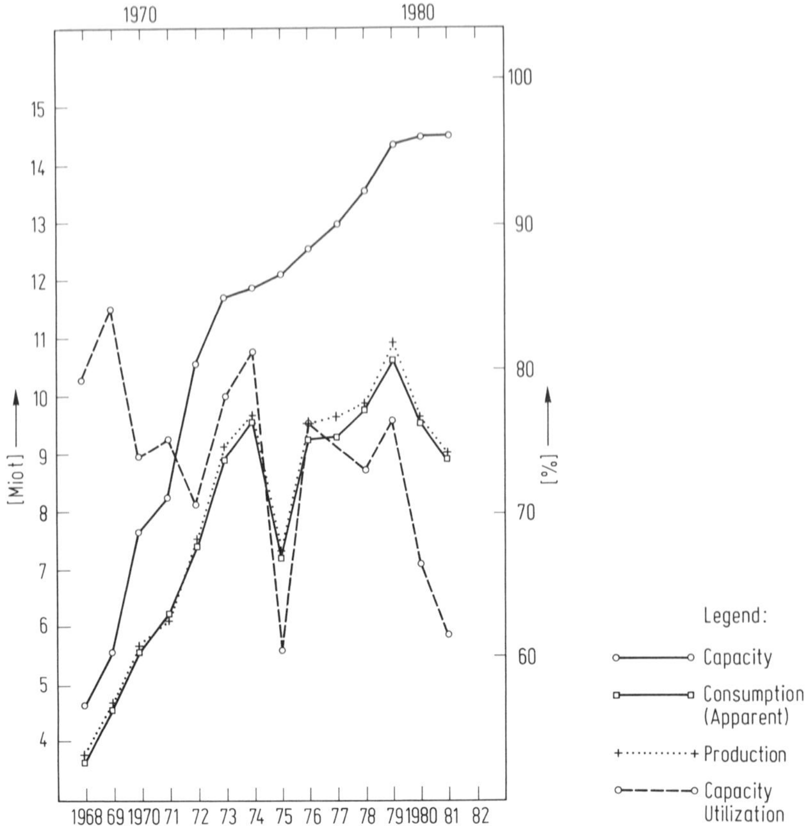

Figure 11: Ethylene

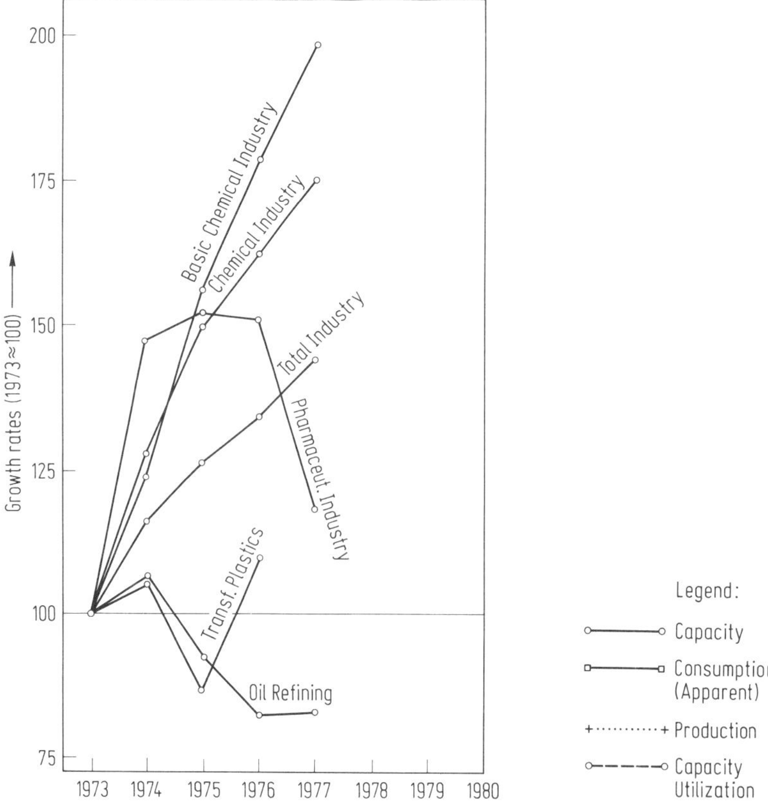

Figure 12: Annual Investment in Fixed Assets (EUROSTAT)

partners. Although the fears of some West European producers verge on the irrational – arab petrochemical producers have thus far shown themselves to be much less agressive on price and volume than other trading partners – the trend towards an internationalization of petrochemical production appears irreversible. Although neither the Middle East countries, Canada, nor the USSR are very visible in the industry for the time being, they all have the oil and the gas necessary to enter the market in a big way by the end of the century.

Nevertheless, the impact of new petrochemical producers calls for less adjustment in Europe, than the structural problems of overcapacity (Schäfer 1983). The price and product linkages that tie the industry to downstream chemical transformations make capacity reductions unusually difficult, so that when they occur, they take place in large chunks. When, for example, Rhône-Poulenc decided to get rid of all its petrochemical interests, it sold them in one job lot to Elf and Total. Yet despite the technical difficulties involved, the social implications of capacity reductions are negligeable compared to other crisis sectors. The industry commissioner, Count Etienne Davignon (1982), has estimated that 10000 jobs at the most are threatened at the community level by a restructuring of the petrochemical sector.

As the EC Commission sees it the industry can tackle its capacity problems in three different ways (Davignon 1982):

- through a sectoral approach that seeks to develop an industry wide consensus;
- through a bilateral approach in which firms seek joint ventures, mergers, or portfolio transfers;
- through an atomistic approach in which companies act on their own and look only to their own salvation.

A sectoral or bilateral approach would have to function within the framework of the EC's competition policy which seeks to prevent measures such as price fixing, quotas, state aids, etc. hindering or delaying the process of industrial adjustment. Paragraph 3 of Article 85 of the Treaty of Rome sets out the conditions under which the EC Commission will be allowed to approve an industrial restructuring operation.

The unitary view of the European Petrochemical industry which is offered sitting in the Commissioner's offices in the top floor of the Beyrlemont in Brussels may be misleading. Domestic political considerations will push member countries to adopt very different approaches to this particular sectoral problem. On past performance, the Germans, for example, are likely to take less time to adjust than the French despite the fact that in France the state owns half of the chemical industry and can act both as shareholder and arbitrator. Problems of overcapacity, notwithstanding, the French petrochemical industry has added 50% to capacity, in recent years (Expansion 1982).

For even in a country, where the dirigiste tradition enjoys considerable legitimacy, a hierarchically imposed technocratic solution to the industry's problems meets impassioned resistance from competitors who heartily dislike each other and between whom mergers have failed far more often than they have succeeded. Many European countries have some way to go before they can match Japan's performance as an industrial adjuster. Today Japan is still the largest chemical exporter to South East Asia, yet under government pressure it is overhauling its industry so that by 1990 it will have become the world's largest petrochemical importer – supplied by Canada and the Middle East.

To sum up, capacity in the bulk chemical sector – which includes petrochemicals – must be reduced by about a third at a time when industrial concentration is increasing. According to a Dow Chemical study, about twenty large firms are likely to divide up the world chemical market between them by the year 2000. The European petrochemical sector appears to have no strategy to cope with this situation. The crisis it faces is very much of its own making as the data presented testify. What light does our conceptual framework throw on the industry's problems? Or on the policy issues they pose? Let us start by locating the industry in the C-D space; we can then look at it dynamically.

4.2 Diagnosis

There is a relationship between the type of technical managerial know-how used by an industry – i.e., its position on the knowledge creation cycle – and its level of development. In the early stages of an industry's life cycle, for example, knowledge is, as yet, poorly structured (uncodified) and available at most to a few firms (undiffused). As the industry grows, the technology used by firms gets standardized (codified) but most of it remains firm specific and proprietary (undiffused). With an industry maturing, its technology becomes widely available, diffusing both to competitors and often to industry customers. It becomes increasingly difficult to differentiate industry products and processes from one another and, with the disappearance of technological barriers to entry, competition intensifies and focuses on price. With the outset of industry decline, some competitors drop out of the market and industrial concentration increases. The remaining firms learn to coexist and implicitly develop a common view (uncodified) of the world and of their industry within it. The resulting consensus may either constitute an obstacle to change, thus further accentuating the decline, or a stimulus for it, thus triggering off a cycle of industrial renewal. This brief idealized sketch of the industry life cycle does not purport to accurately describe any one industry, but if it has any generality, it allows us to position both, the

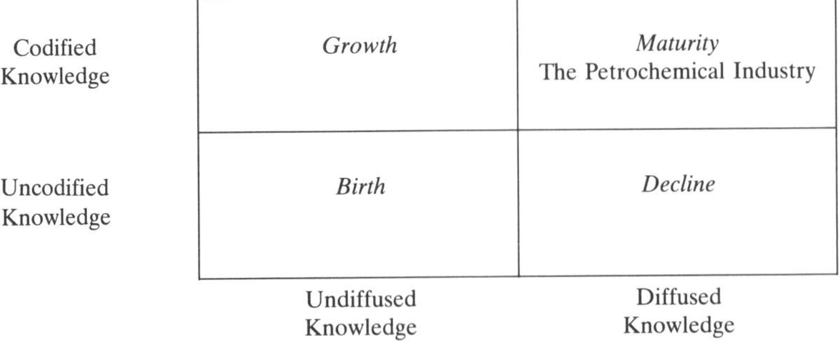

Figure 13: The Petrochemical Industry in the Industry Life Cycle

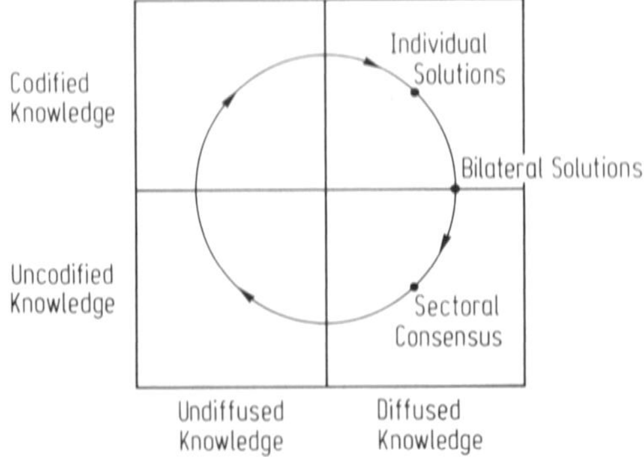

Figure 14: The Petrochemical Industry's Strategic Options

cycle itself and the European petrochemical industry in the C-D space (Figure 13).

In placing the petrochemical industry in the upper right hand quadrant of the C-D space – the one favouring market transactions – we can argue that its core technologies have become for the most part standardized and will established (i.e. codified) and that they are now widely available (i.e. diffused). They can be bought on a turnkey basis either from petrochemical producers themselves or from chemical contractors. Production is being internationalized and, in many countries hitherto serviced by exports, domestic producers are entering the market. They compete on price since petrochemicals, now commodities, do not readily lend themselves to a strategy of differentiation.

Looking now at the industry dynamically we could set out the industry's strategic options as outlined by the EC Commission. On the idealized knowledge creation cycle of Figure 14. The options can then be interpreted as follow:

Sectoral consensus – A move towards federal transactions in the lower right hand quadrant based on objectives and values shared by a limited number of firms and a willingness to pool risks at the industry level. Firms follow the cycle.

Bilateral solutions – A partial move towards federal transactions halfway down the right hand side of the C-D space. The sharing of objectives and values, and the pooling of risks will take place through mergers, joint ventures, or other arrangements between individual firms. The outcome will be fewer and larger firms than in the market quadrant, but more competition and less overall consensus than in the federative one. Firms follow the cycle, but reluctantly.

Individual solutions. A decision to keep a firm in the market quadrant and to enhance its competitiveness through internal measures. Firms resist the cycle.

In both options, sectoral and bilateral, the EC Commission wishes to avoid compromising its competition policy and to maintain a market ethic. In a sense it feels uncomfortable with a federative transaction style, even though it has, often been perceived as a natural remedy – if not the only one – for firms in trouble in the market quadrant. Some countries have shown more aversion to federal arrangements between firms than others. The United States, for example, with a strong instutituonal commitment to making the market quadrant function properly has tended to resist such arrangements more vigorously than, say, Japan which, despite the anti-trust legislation inherited from the US in the post war years, seems to find the corporate atmosphere (Williamson 1975) of the lower quadrants culturally congenial.

But it should not be assumed that if firms are discouraged from following the cycle and moving towards federative solutions, they will necessarily sit in the market quadrant and take their medicine. Much will depend on the level of institutional investments undertaken to keep them there in preference to other parts of the C-D space. The shape of the knowledge creation cycle largely depends on where in the space social institutions – willingly or not – invest in transactions that simulate knowledge flows, and on where they invest in transactions that erect barriers to such flows.

Thus, for instance, with a move into the lower right hand quadrant blocked firms in some countries might look to some central authority rather than to themselves for a way out, being prepared to accept a hierarchically imposed bureaucratic order*. It implies a transactional preference for the top left hand quadrant which, given the petrochemical industry's current location in the C-D space, would result in the flattened knowledge creation cycle of Figure 15.

The type of industrial policy that would emerge on the left of the C-D space from a flat cycle in the upper quadrants would differ substantially from one that followed a full cycle through all quadrants. The case of Japan once more comes to mind where since the war, the government – through the MITI and the Ministry of Finance – has shown great skill in developing industrial policies in the lower left hand quadrant. But their hierarchical nature has been masked by the fact that they complement a sectoral consensus established in the lower right hand quadrant by informal means. They do not substitute for it. By contrast, industrial policies in the upper left hand quadrant will appear as government arbitrations between competing interest groups. Given their position on the knowledge creation cycle, they are likely to lack innovativeness and to be overly cautious. Only command economies have shown a consistent preference for seeing interfirm transactions conducted in this quadrant.

* This was the fear expressed by W. Schäfer of the EC Commission in a 1983 paper. He saw the spectre of a command economy looming up behind failures to achieve urgently needed industrial adjustments.

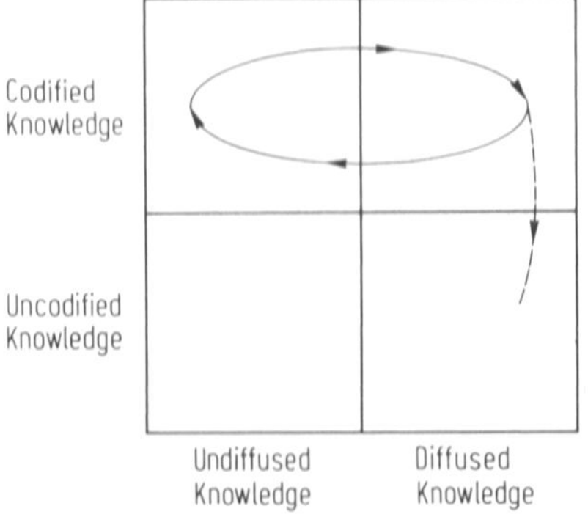

Figure 15: A Flat Knowledge Creation Cycle

5. Conclusion

What does the foregoing analysis add to our understanding of industrial policy. The answer can be summarized under three headings:

Where market failure is the result of industries moving through knowledge creation cycles as they evolve, then, as Schumpeter first observed, for a technologically vigorous industry, it becomes the rule rather than the exception. Furthermore, given the choice of positions in the C-D space and the different shapes of knowledge cycles through which an industry can reach them, it is clear that markets can fail in different ways. In some circumstances, there may be a case for letting them do so where, for example, completing the cycle encourages industrial adjustment and renewal. In fact, it could be argued that only a marked cultural preference for corralling transactions in the market quadrant can justify the expression 'market *failure*'.

Appropriate industrial policies can be developed for any part of the C-D space. Towards the left they will be *dirigiste* and towards the right, *market oriented*. Industrial policies in the upper quadrants will be *impersonal* and *rule based*. In the lower quadrants they will be more *informal* and *personalized* and will produce a negotiated order.

An effective industrial policy must strike a balance between a political unit's cultural and institutional orientation towards a certain transactional style – market, bureaucratic, federal or feudal – and the requirements imposed by an industry's position on a given knowledge creation cycle. The policy must acknowledge the imperatives both of a national and an industry's culture operating at different levels. Each moves cyclically through the C-D space but at its own pace. Over the centuries, historical development will push national culture towards one point in the space and, within a shorter time frame, life cycle characteristics will place an industry's culture in another. At times these two points will coincide. More often they will not. The gap between them is a basic constraint on the design of any successful industrial policy.

We conclude that to present industrial policy as an alternative to market solutions, as is frequently done, is to seriously limit the scope of the expression, and thus to oversimplify the terms of the debate on industrial renewal in Europe.

Bibliography

Boisot, M.: Convergence revisited: the Codification and Diffusion of Knowledge in a British and a Japanese Firm. *Journal of Management Studies*, Vol. 20, No. 2, April 1983.

Boisot, M.: The Shaping of Technological Strategy: European Chemical Firms in South East Asia. *Management International Review*, Vol. 2 No. 3, 1983.

Coase, R.: The Nature of the Firm. *Economica*, (4), 1937.

Davignon, E.: *Restructuring the European Chemical Industry: the Position of the EC Commission*, Annual Meeting of the Society of Chemical Industry. Oct. 1982.

Expansion, *La chimie cherche sa formule*, 18 Juin/1er Juillet 1982.

Kroeber, A. L./Kluckhohn, C.: Culture: a Critical Review of Concepts and Definitions. *Harvard University Peabody Museum of America Archeology and Ethniology Papers*, Vol. 47, No. 1, 1952.

Polanyi, M.: *Personal Knowledge.* Routledge and Kegan Paul, London 1958.

Schäfer, W. A.: *The Need to Integrate Corporate Perspectives into a Chemical Industry Sector Context.* European Chemical Marketing Association, May 1983.

Scherer, F. M.: *Industrial Market Structure and Economic Performance.* Rand McNally, Chicago 1980.

Simon, H. A.: *The Sciences of the Artificial*, MIT Press, Cambridge 1969.

Tyson, L./Zysman, J.: American Industry in International Competition: Government Policies and Corporate Strategies. In: Zysman, J./Tyson, L. eds.: *American Industry in International Competition: Government Policies and Corporate Strategies.* Cornell University Press, 1983.

Williamson, O. E.: *Markets and Hierarchies: Analysis and Antitrust Implications.* The Free Press, New York 1975.

Williamson, O. E.: The Modern Corporation: Origins, Evolution, Attributes. *Journal of Economic Literature*, Vol. XIX, December 1981.

Steel and the European Communities

Bruce Kogut

Summary

The focus of this paper is to describe the historical background of the industry, the strategies of governments and firms and the role of the Commission of the European Communities (EC). The pursued thesis is that the uncoordinated industrial strategies of the diverse European governments led to a maldistribution of benefits and costs across the region. As a result, not only did this maldistribution generate tremendous inter-governmental conflict, but also led to an economic outcome that is decisively sub-optimal at the regional level in terms of differences in comparative advantages among European nations and particularly in the context of world competition.

1. Introduction

European steel has been in crisis for almost a decade. The external factors contributing to the crisis are fairly transparent. Competition on world markets has grown significantly over the years, as Japanese exports have increased and developing nations have begun to create their own steel industries. A second factor has been the poor state of the European economies, resulting in a depressed demand for investment goods, including steel. Coupled with a longterm trend towards the use of nonferrous materials, increasing world competition and slower economic growth translated into a stagnant, if not declining, demand for European steel. None of these factors are policy variables to European governments or firms, but represent complex structural changes.

If the causes of the crisis are outside the control of the European steel industry itself, the process of adjustment is, on the other hand, directly influenced by the policies pursued by national governments and the strategies employed by enterprises. National policies can vary between nationalization, subsidization, and various types of regulation. Firm strategies differ in the choice of final products, technologies, or scale of production. In the context of the European Communities (EC), there is also the participation of a third actor, that is, the Commission which is embodied with certain regulatory powers.

The overall thesis developed in this paper is based on a historical description of the steel industry. The first part explains the institutional structure of the

European Coal and Steel Community as laid out in the Treaty of Paris in 1952. The second part describes the historical developments of the Community up to 1975. Based upon this background, the third section turns to an analysis of government and firm policies during the crisis. The conclusions address the troubling issue of the implications of the steel crisis for the Community at large.

2. Institutional Background

The European Coal and Steel Community was the first major achievement towards the elimination of trade and investment barriers in Western Europe. Within two years of the proposal of the ECSC by the French foreign minister Robert Schuman in 1950, it had been debated, contested, and accepted by the national governments. If the political motives behind the creation of the ECSC have proven successful in contributing to the pacification of Western Europe, the economic contribution is far more problematic. In addition to political motives, Schuman's plan was influenced by the fear of the recartelization of Ruhr industry and the recognition of the benefits flowing from the unification of Ruhr coal with Lorraine iron ore. The irony is, however, that the "natural harmony" of the region was established politically at a time when the economic value of the region's coal and iron ore was no longer viable relative to the international market.

Substantively, the Treaty of Paris which established the ECSC in 1952 can be broken down into four facets: prohibitions on member states' interventions, the anti-trust provisions, supranational powers, and pricing rules. The prohibition on the member states took the expected form of the elimination of all tariffs, of subsidies (except for regional development), of preferential taxation, and of certain kinds of non-tariff barriers (particularly on border crossings). The provision that proved particularly troublesome was that relating to subsidization. The issue has never been resolved satisfactorily in the case of coal, and it has become increasingly sensitive in the present European steel crisis.

The later Treaty of Rome (which established the then European Economic Community, EC) contained a number of anti-trust provisions that were generally stricter than the various national codes, with the exception of that of Germany's. Article 85 made illegal any restraint of trade which may affect trade between member states, except when justified by welfare considerations. Article 86 outlawed the abuse of a dominant position. Of importance is that the treaty of the ECSC stipulates that notivication of and authorization by the High Authority – absorbed eventually in the Commission of the EC – is, by Article 66, a legal prerequisite for any merger or contract which affects control. The High Authority has, therefore, greater power to influence and constrain mergers than that granted to the EC Commission in respect to other industries.

Partly related to the above are the supranational powers granted to the High Authority to fine and subpoena (including violations of Article 66), to tax production, to borrow on international markets, and to grant loans for the purposes of investment or employment relocation. The power to tax has been especially important, as it allowed the ECSC in its early years to build up a sizeable treasury for future loans. A particularly important power, granted by Article 58, is the right to declare a "manifest crisis" by which mandatory reductions in production schedules may be set (Joliet 1979).

The provisions establishing a set of pricing rules proved to be of special importance in influencing the behavior and conduct of the industry in that it reinforced the tendency of an oligopoly inclined, as will be seen, towards collusive behaviour. The history of pricing and production behavior reflects a remarkable stability within national markets (Stegemann 1977, chs. 1 and 2). The pricing mechanism of the ECSC operates on a multiple basing-point system, that is, producers are obligated to publish a list of their mill prices and then charge a buyer a price no lower than listed, plus some standardized amount representing transportation costs as a function of distance. By the word "multiple", it is meant that there exist several possible reference points, one of which each producer is expected to choose for each product. Whereas, for example, a producer of steel plates in the Ruhr might choose Oberhausen as the basing-point for this product, a Lorraine producer might choose a point such as Thionville. The territory between Oberhausen and Thionville would, then, be the natural area of competition for the Lorraine and Ruhr producers. Though, in general, a producer is expected to choose a basing-point within close proximity, this was not always the case; some producers adhered to basing-points hundred of kilometers away. Whereas most of the discussions in favor of the founding of the ECSC took note of the natural harmony of the Saar, Ruhr, and Alsace-Lorraine area, there has, at least up to 1977, been a complete absence of joint basing-points across national borders (Stegemann 1977, p. 39).

Despite justified claims by the High Authority of the early success of the ECSC, industrial behavior was conditioned along national lines due to an explicit set of pricing rules embodied in the Treaty of Paris (Haute Autorité 1963; Diebold 1959; Haas 1959). These rules can be broken down into four primary components:

1. Prices must be published and open.
2. Firms cannot exceed their list prices, including freight, from their basing points.
3. Firms can not undercut their list prices in their own basing-point regions, with certain exceptions.
4. These exceptions fall under what is called the "alignment clause" (Article 60), which permits the matching of prices against third party imports or

against products of competing basing-point regions. In such cases, the producer is allowed to match the competing price (what is commonly called "freight absorption") but may not price under it.

These rules, as described in the next section, were reinforced by minimal transnationality in ownership and intrasectoral specialization.

3. Historical Background to 1975

The history of the ECSC displays three major institutional trends, namely, increasing government ownership and intervention, increasing concentration rates, and transparent collusion between firms. It is not the purpose of this chapter to investigate whether these trends represent attempts to increase efficiency and scale of the operations or to effect market power. Rather, we restrict ourselves to a description of how these trends varied in the different national settings.

As collusion has proven to be of central importance, it is worthwhile, nevertheless, to consider some of the theoretical aspects. Because the production of steel incurs tremendous upfront capital investment, there are significant cooperative incentives to coordinate investment programs and stabilize prices by quantity allocations across firms. If formalized, cooperation may be institutionalized in a formal cartel. Under standard economic assumptions, the optimal cartel rule is to set equal the marginal costs and marginal revenues of all firms in order to achieve maximum profits for the entire group. While the fulfillment of such a rule diminishes profits of inefficient firms and raises profits of others, these distributional effects can be solved, *in theory*, by compensatory transfers. The dilemma facing the cartel is, then, to devise procedures for determining the optimal allocation of production under conditions of uncertainty, as well as for restraining and detecting cheating (Stigler 1963; Osborne 1976). As the requisite knowledge of marginal costs of each plant and the enforcement of disciplinary powers are likely to be flawed, most cartels are imperfect in their strategy and organization.

As commonly witnessed in the steel industry, attempts to make compliance more transparent include the advertising of price lists (which is required by the Treaty of Paris), the announcement of new investments, and joint sales agents. The ability of a cartel to monitor and enforce can be enhanced through crossequity participation or through mergers. In fact, the perfect cartel is the multi-plant monopolist which can enforce the cartel rule without the costs of monitoring and enforcement. Cartelization agreements can vary, therefore, from informal channels of collusion to the extreme solution offered by mergers.

Another form of cartelization is government intervention. Governments can, in a sense, *perfect* the cartel by serving as an enforcer of cooperative rules. It is unlikely, however, that the cooperative rules for the cartel are the same when government is an active player, for governments and firms pursue invariably different objectives. As a normative statement, both governments and firms will seek investment redundancies, the difference lying between the two actors in that firms may seek market power at the expense of consumers in the form of pricing and production agreements, whereas governments may be sensitive to particular political constituencies, such as labor. Despite the perjorative connotation of collusion and cartels, one can posit that all things held equal investment coordination in capital intensive industries may avoid redundancies and operations built at less than optimal scale. In short, collusion can under reasonable assumptions be welfare improving (Dewey 1979; Smith 1983).

In the various national industries, diverse institutional frameworks evolved to solve the cartel problem of investment coordination and redundant capacity. One of the more interesting mechanisms which facilitated coordination are the formal ownership links between the firms. The multiple interests of Société Générale de Belgique, for example, consisted of sizeable holdings of the Luxembourg-based corporation ARBED and of Cockerill-Ougree (13% and 19%, respectively). The Groupe Schneider also was an active participant in many of the Belgian and Luxembourg concerns, as well as in Creusot-Loire in France. Similar sets of relations can be charted for France and, less strikingly, for Germany. In part, these ownership patterns result from the massive size of certain financial groups in Europe and the magnitude of the steel industry, in addition to the pooling of capital for investments in specialized products or in finishing plants.

Furthermore, the interests of the industry and government were often one and the same, as the state held substantial control in most European countries. State ownership resulted not from the aftermath of World War II, but evolved steadily over the thirty year history of the community. British Steel Corporation is the product of government nationalization of a score of smaller firms in 1967 and represents over 90% of British steel. The Italian industry is dominated by state-owned Finsider, though its share of Italian production has fallen under 50% as small private northern firms have grown. Hoogovens, of which the Dutch government and the city of Amsterdam owns 37%, produces over 90% of Dutch steel. The Belgian government was also historically an equity participant, holding in the late 1970s 29% of Cockerill, 10% of Carlam, and 22% of Sidmar. The French government exercised substantial financial control through its state-owned banks and through the administration of its economic plans (Padioleau 1981; MacArthur and Scott 1969). Even the German government, which has been influenced by the free market policy stemming from the Erhard era, owns outright Salzgitter, one of the top five German producers.

In addition to state participation, a second major trend has been the increasing industry concentration resulting from mergers. The immediate impact of the creation of the customs union was a visible increase in the number of mergers in order to achieve defensible scale economies in production. Mergers were particularly notable in Germany, where the steel industry had been fragmented as part of allied policy to break the market power of the historical firms, such as Krupp, Hoesch, and Thyssen. Much of the German mergers in the 1950s were a regrouping of these enterprises according to traditional affiliations.

Moreover, the development of the basic oxygen process and continuous casting mills had increased the minimum efficient scale of steel production. It has been estimated that the minimum efficient scale for a fully integrated steel plant is in the order of at least 6 million tons of annual steel production (Cockerill 1974, pp. 70–73). While few EC plants have achieved more than half of this scale, the trend in new investments had been toward considerably greater scale, thus eliminating the competitiveness of many smaller producers. It is this trend towards greater scale that explains the plant closures and rationalization, for example, following the acquisition of Bochum by Krupp, Dortmunde Hoerde by Hoesch, and Niederrheinische by Thyssen.

Because of the creation of the common market as well as increasing pressure from efficient overseas competitors, the Commission recommended in the early 1970s that further consolidation be encouraged towards the goal of concentrating 90% of production to approximately a dozen firms, with no firm having more than 12% to 13% share (Journal Officiel 1970). By 1974, almost 80% of all crude steel was produced by the ten largest firms, although plant size was still smaller than the estimated minimum efficient scale. The concentration ratios (i.e. the ratio of output of the ten largest firms to total industry output) were, however, all in the range of 90% for finished products, with the exception of wire rod and merchant bars (Stegemann 1977, pp. 256–257).

Despite these high concentration ratios, the Commission encouraged consolidation in the belief that the Community would only be viable if world competitive. Shifting from a relatively strong anti-trust policy in the late 1960s, the Commission was particularly anxious to encourage the development of new coastal plants and transnational cooperative ventures. As the costs of shipping plummeted and iron ore far superior to traditional sources in Europe became available, new steel coastal sites, e.g. Dunkerque and Marseilles in France, Bremen in Germany, Ghent in Belgium, the south of Rome in Italy, and the further development of Ijmuiden, began to displace the competitiveness of the Saar and Lorraine. These coastal developments were completed in the early

1970s, thus greatly expanding European capacity just prior to or concomitant with the fall in steel demand.

The Commission also sought the creation of transnational ventures to bind the Community in interlocking patterns of ownership (Journal Officiel 1971). The most notable ventures have been Solmer at Fos-sur-mer in France, involving originally Usinor, Sacilor, and Thyssen; Sidmar in France, involving ARBED and Cockerill, among others; ARBED's acquisition of Roechling-Burbach in Germany; and ESTEL, which was the most extensive venture, involving Hoesch and Hoogovens. Solmer illustrates most persuasively the desire of the Commission to foster transnational ventures at the expense of competition. Originally planned to produce 12–15 million tons a year, Solmer would have represented just under 10% of total EC crude steel production and a far greater proportion of flat products. It is difficult, to say the least, to reconcile the planned Solmer venture between the two largest French producers and the largest German producers to the anti-trust clauses of the ECSC and EC treaties.

In addition to government ownership and concentration, a third trend consisted of tacit and formal collusion in intra-European sales as well as in exports. Whereas most national markets were dominated by a state-owned firm, the Belgian, French, and German industries consisted of several private firms. The German industry maintained discipline through the creation of joint sales agents that stabilized prices through quantity adjustments of inventories (Stegemann 1977). Four *Walzstahlkontore* or rolled-steel sales associations – were created in 1967 during a major slump in orders, but were prohibited by the Commission in 1971. They were succeeded by so-called "rationalization groups" that were theoretically prohibited from entering into production quotas. Interestingly, recent proposals by the German government to restructure the industry is strongly reminiscent of these earlier groups.

The French industry cooperated at multiple levels ranging from industry associations to participation in the national plans. Investment coordination was facilitated by the *Groupement d'Industrie Siderurgique* which borrowed against the collective creditworthiness of the industry. Furthermore, cooperation was organized through the industry trade association, as well as through the participation of industry leaders in joint government-business planning committees. The *Plan Professionnel* of 1967 is a classic example of this cooperation, whereby the state provided some 2.7 billion francs in financing over five years in return for new investment programs, including the consolidation of smaller units into four principal firms (Padioleau 1981; MacArthur and Scott 1969; Stora 1978).

A major exception to industrial cooperation during this period were the Belgian producers. Having been the most efficient producers of steel in the 1930s, the

Belgian firms suffered from their small scale and outdated equipment. An important market for the Belgian producers were exports outside of the EC, but as world competition increased, their targetted markets shifted increasingly towards the continent. Thus, in order to cover fixed costs, the Belgian producers tended towards aggressive price cutting, particularly on the German market. Price cutting led to competitive responses on the part of German producers, until an uneasy stability again prevailed (Stegemann 1977, chs. 2 and 3).

Thus, by 1974, the European Communities displayed a combination of new and efficient plant installations and of older plants that were maintained for cyclical swings in demand. Production reached a historical peak of 155,000 tons. New coastal plants were on-stream, and Kloeckner's new Bremen facility would soon open. Moreover, interpenetration of trade in steel was significant, partly due to differences in business cycles, partly due to the achievement of a regional basis for trade (Stegemann 1977, pp. 153–160). Although each national market was dominated either by a single national firm or industry cooperation, a number of transnational ventures promised the growth of a steel industry not only European in trade, but also in ownership. Few suspected that neither production nor employment in the steel industry would ever be so high again.

4. Historical Background since 1975

The collapse of the demand for steel in 1975 led, at first, to a number of interim agreements at the regional level designed to respond to a crisis that was not expected to last ten years. That the crisis has indeed endured ten years can be seen from table 1. What is striking from this table is the persistence of the downturn of steel production from its 1974 peak of 154.7 million tons. Accordingly, utilization rates averaged in the low 60 percentile for the period, having fallen from 87% in 1974 to its lowest point of 55.9% in 1982. Yet, despite these low rates, capacity was, in fact, added during this period, rising from 197.4 million tons in 1976 to 202.5 million tons in 1980.

The growth in capacity is the result primarily of the rapid expansion of Italian mini-mills in Brescia. This expansion is reflected not only in the growth of electric arc furnaces (which is the process technology of a mini-mill), but also in a remarkable increase of the Italian share of the European market from 14% in 1974 to 19% in 1983. Since mini-mills produce long products, particularly reinforcing rods for construction, they compete in products which are undifferentiated and price sensitive. Whereas the rest of the EC was trimming workforces and setting capacity idle, steel capacity of electric-arc furnaces in Italy grew from 14.4 million tons in 1974 to 20.1 million tons in 1980, an increase of 40%. By 1980, electric arc furnaces were producing 53% of Italian crude steel.

At the same time that the Bresciani were placing pressure on the lower end of the product line, the new coastal plants of Solmer, Sidmar, and Kloeckner were coming on stream and competing in flat products. The dilemma was straightforward. As outsiders, the Bresciani posed a long term threat in long products by pricing under the umbrella set by the dominant German producers. As new plants came on stream and demand fell, excess capacity in flat products posed the threat of a collapse in industry discipline and incipient competitive price cutting.

The ensuant pressure on prices and national shares of production has led to the intervention of governments and the Commission. The Commission has been particularly activist, serving as a power broker between the various governments while seeking to preempt purely national solutions to the crisis by framing policies of intervention under its own auspices. These policies have been crystallized under two major programs, the first called the Simonet Plan, introduced in 1976, and succeeded by the Davignon Plan in 1977 which has evolved increasingly in its powers and provisions. The thrust of the two programs, which we will treat as one, is based on the simple premise that European steel can only effectively compete when inefficient plants are closed. In the short run, though, the Commission was faced with the safeguarding of European industry against third country imports and with the maintenance of discipline among European firms. Only by regulating import and regional competition, the Commission felt, presumably, could it preempt more massive interventions at the national levels.

But the short-run and long-run policies are, however, at loggerheads with each other, unless there exists a supranational agency endowed with powers to extract capacity concessions in return for pricing stability. In other words, what is required is an agency with the powers to tradeoff its ability to *perfect* the cartel in terms of pricing and quotas in return for extracting concessions on investment and capacity. The original provisions of the Davignon Plan were deficient in these powers. The Commission relied primarily upon its coffers – derived from taxing production – to bargain with ailing firms in return for aid and its right to review all investment programs and potentially influence banks by its non-binding veto and to fine for violations of minimal prices. One reflection of this deficiency is the reliance of the Commission upon an industry cartel, called Eurofer, to negotiate the specifics of its broader policies. Created in 1976, it consists of 12 of the major integrated steel firms in the EC. As Eurofer publishes no record of its activities and grants no interviews, its significance is open to debate. But it has played an important role in negotiating the critical issue of burden sharing.

The initial program established by the Simonet Plan required community and third country steel firms to file a record of their deliveries with the Commission.

Based upon this record, the Commission in 1977 developed two sets of measures to regulate imports and internal competition. The first set consisted of production and price regulations. Initially, the Commission recommended a set of production targets for EC producers. Due to the difficulty of enforcing production targets, the Commission also established a list of "recommended" prices and later fixed minimum prices for certain long products. Not surprisingly, these minimum prices were particularly unpopular among the Bresciani, who were the principal target of the measures. Following the imposition of fines by the Commission on violators on the minimum prices, the Bresciani filed for suit against the Commission at the European Court of Justice. Subsequent to the failure of legal recourse, the Bresciani and smaller firms of the Community established their own association, called the European Independent Steel Association, to represent their interests in Brussels. Competition had shifted from the market place to the halls of policy making.

The second set of measures were designed to regulate import competition. Requiring initially that exporters to the Community acquire an import license, import regulations were expanded subsequently by an aggressive anti-dumping policy and by orderly marketing agreements established with principal exporters to the EC. Having established market shares, the Commission also stipulated that third country imports must also comply with the recommended and minimum prices, thus eliminating the possibility that community producers would align their prices to imports. (For alignment, see the pricing rules outlined in section one above.) Since the late 1970s, imports have fluctuated around 9% of market share as measured in tons.

Ironically, due to the success of the short-term measures, guidelines towards reductions in capacity were uneffective. Though the market rebounded slightly in 1978, excess capacity remained a substantial issue. Due to low utilization rates and excess capacity, a number of governments, particularly the Belgian and French, also increased their subsidies to their national industries. The Commission had hoped that its control over regional aid and its putative influence over bank lending to new investment projects would lead to the scrapping of capacity. National subsidies prevented this result. As a result, the more efficient firms of the community were unable to utilize full capacity.

One solution to this dilemma was to increase exports to third countries, especially to the United States. Two kinds of firms exported. One kind was efficient and turned to export markets as European demand fell. The second was subsidized and turned to export markets to cover some of their fixed costs. But what should not be overlooked is that exports from the first kind of firm were also promoted because subsidies to inefficient firms producing for the community market pushed all firms towards exporting. EC exports to the United States rose from 2694 million tons in 1976 to its peak of 6222 million tons in 1977, consisting of 1867 million tons from Germany, 1020 million tons from Belgium, and 1484 million tons from France. Belgium was, thus, exporting nearly 9% of its total crude steel production to the United States. Despite that the eventual inquiry by the United States found remarkable differences in subsidies and dumping between different national arenas, the EC and the United States reached an accord which did not respond directly to these interfirm differences (Lambert 1982). These accords established in 1978 a trigger price mechanism based on the yen costs of the most efficient Japanese producers. In 1982, as the yen appreciated and European exports to the United States of the previous year remained near the 1977 peak, the trigger price mechanism was replaced by a voluntary export restraint agreement. Thus, by 1982, export growth to the United States as a vehicle to dampen the sharing of burden within Europe was eliminated.

On the other hand, tremendous structural change had already taken place. One dramatic index of the extent of structural adjustment are changes in employment in representative countries given in the table below (Hogan 1983, p. 51):

The magnitudes of these figures express concisely the depth of the steel crisis. Between 1974 and 1981, the United Kingdom shed 56% of its steel labor force; Luxembourg, 41%; France, 33%; Belgium, 31%; Germany, 20%; and the Netherlands, 13%. On the other hand, Italian employment went up 2.1%. (Commission of the EC 1982).

Despite this structural change, the Community had not solved the basic issues of reducing excess capacity. To resolve this issue, the Commission established in 1980 a five year program designed to eliminate all state subsidies by the end of 1985. Declaring a manifest crisis, the Commission broadened its quotas on: 1) imports, 2) exports, 3) intra-European trade and 4) production. Quotas on

Table 1: EC Crude Steel Production (million tons)

	1974	1975	1976	1977	1978	1979	1980	1981	1982	1983
Belgium	16.2	15.5	12.1	11.2	12.6	13.4	12.3	12.2	9.9	9.2
France	27.0	21.5	23.2	22.1	22.8	23.3	23.1	21.2	18.4	16.0
Germany	53.2	40.4	42.2	38.9	41.2	46.0	43.8	41.6	35.8	33.1
Italy	23.8	21.8	23.4	23.3	24.2	24.2	26.5	24.7	24.0	19.1
Luxembourg	6.4	4.6	4.5	4.3	4.7	4.9	4.6	3.7	3.5	2.9
Netherlands	5.8	4.8	5.1	4.9	5.5	5.8	5.2	5.4	4.3	4.0
United Kingdom	22.3	19.7	22.3	20.4	20.3	21.5	11.2	15.5	13.7	13.9
Total	154.7	124.3	132.8	125.1	131.3	139.1	126.7	124.3	109.6	98.2

Source: Merrill Lynch, *Steel Industry Quarterly,* December 1983 and London Financial Times (March 16, 1984)

imports had been established previously. Export quotas were set on finished products. There is also an agreement that transnational shipments are to be set at the July 1981 to June 1982 levels and are to be monitored through the Commission's compulsory record of all steel shipments.

The most controversial quota has been the one set on production and illustrates the fundamental dilemma in resolving economic issues by policy. A production quota poses the problem of designing an enforceable rule of allocation. The Commission decided to permit firms to choose the best month of the period between 1974 and 1977 as the reference point (Hogan 1983). Whereas this rule favors the status quo as of 1975, it penalizes heavily firms whose major expansion came on stream after 1975 and whose production was constrained by the initial agreements. In addition to hurting the Bresciani, the rule also penalized very heavily the German firm Kloeckner whose modern coastal works at Bremen came on-stream in 1975 and was not allowed to be counted towards the quota. Representing one of the most efficient installations in Europe, the Bremen works consist of a production potential of 4 to 5 million crude steel, a continuous casting facility, and a rolling mill for wide strip. Distressed by being required to leave idle their Bremen plant, Kloeckner withdrew from Eurofer – which had been instrumental in allocating production quotas by product at the national level – and from the German industry association – which had allocated the quotas at the firm level. Kloeckner's refusal to abide by the production quotas, which were stipulated by the Commission under the powers of a manifest crisis, led to a levying of some 58 million DM in fines by the start of 1984. In response, Kloeckner has announced its future compliance and has rejoined Eurofer. The Commission has also extended the duration and breadth of minimum prices, as well as required in late 1983 that producers post a bond of 15 ECU on every ton shipped to assure compliance (Official Journal 1983).

The stated target of the Commission is, however, not to regulate competition, but to reduce excess capacity in the steel industry. To accomplish this end, the Commission has negotiated, once again with the assistance of Eurofer, an agreement to reduce capacity at hot rolling mills from 165 to 137 million tons a year (Bulletin 1983). (Capacity was measured for hot wide-rolling mill for the period between 1977 to 1980, as these mills represent the binding constraint on the production of the targetted products.) The national breakdowns are given in table 2. Further reductions are still under negotiations.

The proposed reductions imply dramatic alterations in the structure of European steel and have been anticipated by, or resulted in further consolidation of production under the auspices of the national governments. Following the election of François Mitterand in 1981, the French government ended a long

Table 2: Allocation of Capacity Closures

	Maximum Production Capacity		Closure Commitments since 1980	Contribution Requested by Commission	Total 3 + 4 (% 5/1)
	1000ts	%	1000ts	1000ts	1000ts
Belgium	16 028	10.0	1 705	1 400	3 105 (19.4)
France	26 869	16.0	4 681	630	5 311 (19.7)
West Germany	53 117	32.0	4 810	1 200	6 010 (11.3)
Italy	36 294	22.0	2 374	3 460	5 834 (16.1)
Luxembourg	5 215	3.0	550	410	960 (18.4)
Netherlands	7 297	4.0	250	700	950 (13.0)
United Kingdom	22 840	14.0	4 000	500	4 500 (19.7)
Total	167 660	101.0	18 370	8 300	26 670 (15.9)

Source: Bulletin of the European Communities (June 1983)

process of creeping nationalization and took complete ownership over the major steel firms – Sacilor, located primarily in the Lorraine and producing long products and Usinor, located primarily in the North and producing flat products. It established a coordinating committee for the two major steel firms plus the firm Normandie, creating, thereby, the largest steel producing group in the Community. In compliance with the proposed capacity reductions, the French government has announced the elimination of some 25 000 to 35 000 further jobs in steel, which will bring employment down from 157 000 in 1974 to around 50 000 in 1985.

Similar measures have been announced by other governments. Given the size of their national industries, the further closures required by the Commission are particularly problematic for Belgium and Italy, the former facing the prospects of closing capacity in distressed Walloon, the latter being asked to close the Bagnoli plant south of Rome after having modernized it. Belgium is particularly troubled by the closures. Having merged Cockerill and Sambre-Hainaut in 1982, the government must now move past administrative changes to actual capacity reductions that tradeoff issues of equity and efficiency in the context of the Walloon and Flander dispute. The Italian government is caught between the choices of closing the state-owned and labor-intensive plants in the south or forcing several smaller and often efficient mini-mills to close in the north. On behalf of the Bresciani, EISA has filed suit against the latest price measures of the Commission and is not anxious to cooperate on capacity reductions.

The Dutch case is complicated by the dissolution of Estel into the constituent parts of the Dutch Hoogovens and the German Hoesch. Hoogovens is in the peculiar position of having lost a substantial part of its rolling mills and thereby, a portion of its share of production quotas. (Oddly, though, it slips under the export quotas by shipping semi-finished steel which is not covered by the Community agreement.) It also faces further capacity reductions, while negotiating for new mills and for new downstream partners. One likely candidate is Valfil in the French-speaking part of Belgium, which could use Hoogovens high quality steel for producing wire. But one obstacle are linguistic differences – which had troubled the Estel merger –, and it is likely that Valfil and ARBED will enter into a formal agreement, even though ARBED already has modern wire facilities.

The United Kingdom may be in the best position in the Community. Having targetted in the early 1970s a production of over 30 million tons, the United Kingdom responded dramatically after 1979 in cutting capacity and production. Whereas the United Kingdom cut some 40% of its steel employment between 1979 and 1982, Belgium shed only 2% of its workers. Though BSC is still subsidized, the United Kingdom has now the lowest per capita steel production of traditional producers in the Community.

The German producers, on the other hand, are confronted with the politics of having to allocate plant closings among five major steel producers. Partly to arrive at an equitable and efficient solution, the German government established a commission (the so-called "Moderatoren") to investigate possible avenues of consolidation and rationalization (Bierich, Herrhausen and Vogelsang 1983). The commission recommended in 1982 that German production be consolidated in two major holdings. Hoesch, Kloeckner, and Salzgitter would merge into one group, whereas Thyssen and Krupp would join their steel facilities. Moreover, sales would be made through four associations, which, as noted before, resemble the earlier sales associations. If enacted, the reorganization would have created two groupings roughly equal in size and balanced in product mixes. The plan failed on a disagreement between Thyssen and Krupp regarding the valuation of the latter's assets. Despite promising some 3.2 billion Deutsche Mark in aid between 1983 and 1985, the German government refused to make up the difference.

Given the highly politicized environment, corporate strategies have to be designed within these broader constraints, as well as directed to influence the nature of policy interventions. The primary trend has been further merger activity, either by choice or by government fiat. With the exception of the Italian and German markets, each national industry is dominated currently by a single firm or coordinated group. Moreover, the Italian Finsider is one of the largest steel firms in the world, and if the report of the "Moderatoren" had been accepted, German industry – which produces about one-third of EC steel – would have been organized around two groups.

Despite the growth in concentration, it is yet to be seen whether the increase in administrative size translates into more efficient productive units. Usinor and Sacilor, for example, produce generally in different regions and different products. Much of their current competition is directed towards shifting the burden of plant closures on the other (Le Monde 1983). Nor is the Cockerill-Sambre merger likely to generate the sought efficiencies without resolving conflict over the rules for allocating plant closures and compensation between the Walloon and Flander operations. The situation of Belgium is the microcosm of Europe.

Other firms are better positioned than those located in the Lorraine or in Belgium. Thyssen, for example, has pursued for a number of years both a policy of diversification and development of steel products of high value-added. Thyssen has traditionally benefited from being situated in a region where 50% of its buyers are within 100 kilometers. With the purchase of Rheinstahl in 1974, Thyssen acquired substantial capabilities in specialty steel, which proved to be a significant contributor to profits. Its diversification policy proved less successful, as its acquisition of the American Budd Company – a producer of auto parts and metropolitan trains – has drained substantial financial resources. Like Krupp and Kloeckner, Thyssen also integrated over the past ten years further downstream, including shipbuilding and machine tools. Given the general political climate of European steel, Thyssen has, therefore, announced a reduction of its steel production from 16 thousand tons to 11 thousand tons, concentrating its efforts in the area of flat products to meet the needs of German customers.

Unlike Thyssen, ARBED is banking primarily on long products. ARBED controls one of the most advanced integrated plants in Sidmar, located in Flanders, which produces flat products for export and for the German market. Its works in Luxembourg are, however, less favorably situated and are dedicated to long products, which are generally lower value-added products. It faces considerable competition from the Bresciani in these products. Its competitiveness will depend partly on its ability to streamline production, partly on the price of scrap which is the major input for mini-mills. (To encourage this trend, there is some discussion that firms are withholding scrap from the market.)

The success of these corporate strategies depends not only on conditions of future demand, but also on the success of the Davignon Plan itself. No firm can tolerate successive years of losses as experienced by the main integrated producers. Finsider, for example, reported losses of $ 1300 million; Sacilor and Usinor, over $ 1100; Thyssen's steel operations, lost over $ 200 million; and

British Steel, near $ 300 million (London Financial Times 1984). As a result, government subsidies have been flowing rapidly. By the agreement established under the "Codes of Aids", national subsidy programs must be submitted to the Commission and approved if in concordance with Community objectives on capacity reduction. By 1983, some 9032 ECUs of aid had been approved, with 16 747 ECUs still being examined. France is responsible for some 40% of the subsidies; another 23% is earmarked for the British Steel Corporation. Given the magnitude of the aid, it is unlikely that subsidies will indeed be phased out entirely by the 1986 deadline (Europe 1983).

5. Conclusions

That the European steel industry has undergone tremendous structural change is not open to question due to the massive changes in employment and shrinkage of activity in traditional but dated regions. Nor has the costs of worker displacement and regional dislocation been achieved without remarkable accomplishments. In 1972, 18.5% of crude steel was produced in open hearths. By 1983, all open hearths were out of production. (Even in the strong year of 1979, only 5.4% of crude steel was produced by open hearths.) Another strong indication of the strengthening of the industry is the increase of continuously cast steel from 7.1% in 1972 to 53.2% in 1982. It is not unlikely, therefore, that subsidies may be minimal, certainly not by 1986, but by the close of decade.

On the other hand, the lowering of subsidies is a poor index of the success of the restructuring unless placed in the larger context of the degree of insularity of the European market. For the steel crisis is currently being resolved in terms of a regional problem when, in fact, the issue is structural change in world competition. Here, in fact, lies the irony. The solution sought to the steel crisis has been predicated upon the reallocation of *intra-sectoral* activity within the protected borders of the common market. The Community was not able to solve the crisis as an issue of *inter-sectoral* allocations at the regional level, not to mention at the global level.

The result of the present agreements is easy to forecast. Every European nation with a historical tradition in steel-making will maintain a national producer. This outcome not only defies the benefits of specialization of the Community. It also raises the troubling question whether European steel must forever remain behind a wall of import quotas in order to survive internationally. Proposals to reorient corporate strategies to specially steels and other high-value added products avoid, undoubtedly, the corrolary implied by this kind of capital and technology intensive production, namely, that these products do not require anywhere near the present labor force or crude steel capacity of the European producers. If crude steel production and labor are to be maintained, then, the implications are quite clear. Europe must maintain its share of production of low-value added products and basic steel facilities. In other words, it must operate behind tariff walls, especially given its inability to transfer resources to regions and firms where the competitive advantage is the greatest.

It can be reasonably argued that given the political sensitivity of the steel industry, the EC has displayed significant resilience in responding to the crisis and has achieved a fundamental objective, that is, the preservation of the Community itself. But there are two objections to this argument. The first is that the behaviour of the industry and Commission over the history of the steel and coal agreement displayed a sort of cognitive dissonance. On the one hand, the Treaties of Paris and, even more so, of Rome embraced market competition. On the other, industry agreements and government interventions have historically prevented the emergence of a European market. This conflict raises the perplexing, though mute, question: what would be the result today if competition had been more bold? Indeed, at present, the only competitive market in European steel is the trading of production quotas.

The second objection rests on the current status of the Community, a status best illustrated by the fate of transnational ventures upon which the Commission had once banked its hopes. Thyssen withdrew from the Solmer venture in 1975, citing, among other factors, difficulties with government intervention. Sidmar is no longer a joint venture between European firms, but between ARBED and the Belgian government. Estel dissolved officially in 1982. Hoesch is seeking a German partner, while Hoogovens is troubled by its loss of a foothold in the German market.

The frustration of the German producers, who possess among the most efficient integrated steelworks in Europe, over their loss of export markets and inability to seize, if not defend market share against more heavily subsidized European firms has led to certain proposals for a concerted German effort. As one executive of a leading German firm explained: “The present crisis can be resolved in three ways for German producers. Close the borders, close the plants, and open the coffers.” Though an extreme position, there exists a sentiment that access to the German market may no longer be as easy as in the past. No better example of this is available than ARBED’s desire to retain 25% of its ownership in Saarstahl, which is highly unprofitable and represents redundant capacity to ARBED, in order to maintain a German presence.

The exact conditions of negotiation and trade in the steel industry are not presently known. The role of associations such as Eurofer is not specified in law and is not open to public scrutiny. Without knowledge of these negotiations, it is difficult to answer the fundamental question over the extent to which agreements over the intra-European allocation of steelmaking activity will generate a Europe that survives only behind protective walls in other sectors. But the crisis in the steel industry presents, nevertheless, an intriguing, if not troubling hypothesis on European cooperation. For perhaps the misfortune of the steel industry is that the national character of steel production prevented the entry of firms by third countries. The resulting irony is not lost on the designers of the Davignon Plan. In advancing towards the rationalization of the industry on a regional basis, the achievement of a more fundamental goal has been bypassed: the creation of a European steel industry competitive on world markets.

Bibliography

Bierich, M./Herrhausen, A./Vogelsang, G.: *Stahlgespräche – Presseinformation, Bericht der Moderatoren.* 23 January 1983.

Bulletin of the European Communities. June 1983, pp. 7–11.

Cockerill, A.: *The Steel Industry.* Cambridge University Press, Cambridge 1974.

Commission of the EC: *La Position de Cockerill-Sambre dans la Siderurgie européenne.* February 1982.

Dewey, D.: Information, Entry, and Welfare: The Case for Collusion. *American Economic Review*, Vol. 69, September 1979, pp. 587–594.

Diebold, W.: *The Schuman Plan: A Study of Economic Cooperation 1950–1959.* Praeger, New York 1959.

Europe, Agence Internationale d'Information Pour la Presse, *Steel: Aids Notified to European Commission in Favour of Community Steel Industry Total some 26 Billion ECUs.* No. 3603, 6 May 1983.

Haas, E.: *The Uniting of Europe: Political, Social, and Economic Forces 1950–1957.* Stanford Press, Stanford 1958.

Haute Autorité, *La CECA 1952–1962: Les Premières 10 Années d'un Integration Partielle.* Bulletin de la Communauté Européenne du Charbon et de l'Acier. ECSC, Luxembourg 1963.

Joliet, R.: *Fixation des Prix, Cartels de Crise et le Régime de Concurrence dans la Communauté Européenne.* Paper presented at the seminar of the Commission Droit et Vie des Affaires, Liege, October 18–20, 1979.

Journal Officiel des Communautés Européennes Vol. 13, 30 January 1970.

Journal Officiel des Communautés Européennes Vol. 14, 29 September 1971.

Lamberg, R.: Why is the United States Fighting Back. In: *London Financial Times*, 10 June 1982.

MacArthur, J./Scott, B.: *Industrial Planning in France.* Graduate School of Business Administration, Harvard University, Boston 1969.

Official Journal of the European Communities. Vol. 25, 23 December 1983.

Osborne, D. K.: Cartel Problems. *American Economic Review*, Vol. 66, December 1976, pp. 835–844.

Padioleau, J. G.: *Quand la France s'enferre.* Presses Universitaires de France, Paris 1981.

Smith, R.: Efficiency Gains from Strategic Investment. *The Journal of Industrial Economics*, Vol. 30, September 1981, pp. 1–23.

Stegemann, K.: *Price Competition and Output Adjustment in the European Steel Market.* J. C. B. Mohr, Tübingen 1977.

Stigler, G. J.: A Theory of Oligopoly. *Journal of Political Economy*, Vol. 72, February 1964, pp. 44–61.

Stora, B.: *Crise, Puissance, Perspectives de la Siderurgie Mondiale.* Economica, Paris 1978.

Without author, La revision du Plan Acier. *Le Monde*, 21 December 1983.

Without author, EEC Sees Light at the End of the Tunnel. *London Financial Times*, 20 February 1984.

The European Aerospace Industry

Milton S. Hochmuth

Summary

After a view on the historical development of the aerospace industry the different parts of this industry and its importance for the economic well-being in the present time are shown. The situation of the European aerospace industry is discussed in the awareness of the dominating competition of the U.S. industry.

1. Introduction

Aerospace, more than any other industrial sector, typifies on one hand the hopes and on the other the challenges facing European industry at the mid-1980s. In an era where world-wide competitiveness in advanced technology is considered a sine qua non to the economic well-being of an industrialized nation, aerospace incorporates the fruits of almost every high technology sector. As a result a strong aerospace industry is an index of international prestige. Moreover, aerospace is also essential to national defense and sovereignty. Yet *Europe's aerospace industry*, despite a technological competence second to none, *must struggle to compete successfully against a U.S. industry that dominates the "free world" market*. The basic reason is that the European industry has long been fragmented along national lines as have been its European customers, government and civil, as opposed to the huge homogeneous U.S. market enjoyed by the U.S. industry.

But the U.S. industry was not always dominant. Though the Americans rightfully pride themselves on ushering in the age of flight with the Wright brothers in 1903, Europe quickly became the center of aviation progress. France, Britain, Germany, Holland, Italy and Russia soon made significant contributions and by the first World War Europe dwarfed the American effort. Not until the close of the second World War did the U.S. industry gain ascendency. And even today's key "inventions" of modern aerospace are of European origin. The cantilevered wing introduced by the Dutch and Germans, the use of aluminium alloys by the Germans, the jet engine perfected by Whittle in Britain and successfully reduced to practice by the German industry during World War II; and of course the development and production of large rockets, which ushered in the space age, by Werner von Braun and his team, are examples. More recently Europeans have demonstrated their technical capabilities with the only supersonic commercial transport, the Franco-British CONCORDE, and the only production model of a vertical take-off fighter, the successful British HARRIER.

We can therefore understand European dissatisfaction when in 1971, 26 years after World War II, 75 percent of the world's commercial aircraft on a numerical basis (excluding the USSR and China) were of U.S. manufacture. On a value the basis figure was 90 percent. In 1982 72 percent by value of the Common Market based airliners were of United State manufacture. This was despite the success of the Airbus, Fokker, and other smaller European planes. In the military field, where national industries are favored, and notwithstanding the striking success of the French Mirage, a large British, and important German and Italian industries, 43 percent by value of all EC member countries' military aircraft were of U.S. design in 1982. The trend is shifting, but the question remains: can the European industry compete meaningfully in the world market place vis à vis the United States?

Before attempting to answer the question it is important to place aerospace in the overall economic and industrial context. As a percentage of gross domestic product aerospace turnover in Europe is small, ranging from a low of 0.35 percent in the Netherlands to 1.82 percent in the United Kingdom (1981 in ECUs.) (Commission of the European Communities 1984, p. 84). This compares to 1.82 percent in the United States and a mere 0.12 percent in Japan. A more meaningful statistic is aerospace turnover as a percentage of all manufacturing industries. Here we have (Commission of the European Communities, 1984)

United Kingdom	6%
France	4.7%
Federal Republic of Germany	1.6%
Netherlands	1%
United States	7.5%

A still more meaningful set of statistics are the following employment comparisons (Commission of the European Communities 1984; U.S. Bureau of Labor Statistics 1983):

Here we begin to see that aerospace is indeed important to the advanced industrialized countries (Japan excepted) for economic reasons.

But it is in examining international balance of trade accounts that we see the true economic importance of aerospace. For France, net 1982 aerospace exports of 4.46 billion European Currency Units (ECUs) to the other EC nations and customers outside the EC resulted in an overall positive trade balance in manufactured goods of ECU 3.2 billion. Without her aerospace

Table 1: Employments

	Employments (thousands)			
	1975		1982	
	Motor Vehicles & Accessories	Aerospace	Motor Vehicles & Accessories	Aerospace
United Kingdom	478	234	308	250
France	447	109	423	114
West Germany	592	52	679	69
United States	792	941	784	1207

industry's positive contribution France's overall 1982 negative balance of merchandise trade (ECU 14.5 billion) and negative current account balance (ECU 12.2 billion) would have been significantly worse. For West Germany and the United Kingdom whose current account balances were both positive (ECU 3.3 billion and ECU 7.1 billion respectively) the net balances in aerospace trade were equally important – a negative ECU 3.6 billion for Germany and a positive ECU 0.41 billion for the U.K. West Germany is far less dependent on aerospace than the other European countries since she enjoys an overall favorable balance of trade in manufactured goods – ECU 68.9 billion in 1982 compared to France's positive ECU 3.2 billion, the Netherlands' negative ECU 0.1 billion and the United Kingdom's positive ECU 0.41 billion. Only Italy, with an overall positive balance in manufactured goods of ECU 24.6 billion and Japan with a similar positive balance of ECU 106 billion can "ignore" their overall negative aerospace trade balances (U.S. Department of Commerce 1983). It is important to note that if aerospace is in the fore front of French exports, aerospace is also the single largest manufactures export of the United States. The latter experienced an overall $ 35 billion deficit in manufactured goods in 1983 whereas the U.S. aerospace industry contributed a positive $ 13 billion balance for that year.

2. What is Aerospace?

Until World War II the aerospace industry consisted of two subsectors – an airframe subsector that built the entire aircraft, buying the engines from the engine sub-sector and a minor amount of electrical and other equipment primarily from the automotive parts sector. Today the industry is vastly more complex. The roles of the airframe and engine sub-sectors are relatively unchanged. But the use of complex electronic systems for control, navigation and communication in all aircraft and for fire control in military aircraft and missiles; the introduction of highly specialized mechanical and hydro-pneumatic components, the use of exotic metals and materials, the advent of guided missiles, longrange rockets, and of satellites for a host of civil and military uses has changed the industry structure considerably.

The EC divides the industry into four product sub-sectors for statistical purposes: *Airframes* (includes military and missiles), *engines, equipment* (includes all aerospace specific equipment such as electronics, brakes, communications, radars, etc.) and *space* (includes launchers and satellites including their electronic components and the largely electronic ground stations). The EC also maintains statistics according to customer categories: civil (including transports and light aircraft in various sub-categories), and military aircraft in various categories, etc. (Commission of the European Communities 1984).

A better grasp of the industry's importance is obtained from the following market estimates (Commission of the European Communities 1984; Flight International; Financial Times 1982 and 1983).

Engines (including spares and parts) account for about 40 percent of commercial transport aircraft turnover, about 27 percent of military aircraft and about 22 percent of general aviation (small) aircraft. Equipment accounts for about one-third of commercial transport turnover, at least one-half of military aircraft turnover, and 50 percent to 60 percent and more of missile turnover.

The market for aircraft, then, is very large. By comparison, in 1982 about 37 million cars were manufactured in the non-communist world. At an average wholesale price of about $ 5500 per car this amounted to over $ 200 billion, approximately three times the market value of aerospace sales.

But there are vast differences between the two industries. To begin with there are the prices.

Table 2: Estimated Sales 1983–1993

	billions 1982 dollars
Total World Sales	555–785
Commercial Air Transports	130–170
Military Aircraft	200–300
General Aviation (Small)	60– 70
Missiles	150–225
Satellites (Military & Civilian)	15– 20
Helicopters	
Civilian (included in General Aviation)	12– 14
Military (included in Military Aircraft)	18– 21

Table 3: Approximate Prices for New Jet Airliners

Airliner	Seating Capacity	Prices millions $ 1982–1983
British Aerospace 146	(90–105)	12
Fokker 100	(107; new, available in 1986)	14–15
Boeing 737–200	(110–120)	16–20
McDonnel-Douglas MD–80	(150–172)	18
Boeing 737–300	(128–140; new engine)	21–23
Airbus A-320	(150–179; new, available in 1988)	24
Lockheed L-1011	(250–385; discontinued in 1981)	40–50
McDonnell-Douglas DC-10	(250–375; only 1 sold in '82–'83)	40–50
Airbus Industrie A-310	(200–250)	47
Boeing 767	(204–250)	47
Airbus Industrie A-300	(250–300)	52
Boeing 747	(up to 650)	85–99

Source: Flight International (October 15, 1983, p. 1042) and press reports.

Table 4: Approximate 1982–1983 Prices for Military Aircraft millions of mid-1983 U.S. dollars

German UBB BO105 Helicopter	$ 0.75–0.8
U.S. General Dynamics F-16 Fighter	25–30
French Dassault Mirage III Fighter	6–7
French Dassault Mirage F-1 Fighter	9–11
French Dassault Mirage 2000 Fighter	25
British-German-Italian Panavia Tornado Fighter	24
U.S. Grumman F-14 Tomcat Fighter	35
U.S. Rockwell B-1 Bomber	200 +

Source: Press reports and EC Document (III/202/84-EN, January 11, 1984, p. 38)

Table 3 shows the *approximate* prices for new aircraft. It should be noted that aircraft prices are the result of extensive haggling and negotiating and are always part of a complex financial package.

Market: The industry serves two distinct markets – military and civil. This is not the same distinction as state and non-state, for in many countries the state purchases non-military products, e.g., commercial aircraft, space material, etc. not to speak of nationalized airlines which purchase civil products. The importance of the military/civil market distinction is that the domestic military market in every country is usually a percentage of the nation's gross national product that changes only slowly over time, barring major international incidents.

Similarly, the state-financed portion of the civil space market also seems to be a slowly changing percentage of a nation's GNP. Curiously, the military and space portion of United States and West European aerospace industries' total sales (including exports) appears to have hovered in the narrow range of 65–75 percent for many decades. This is one major reason why the industry is so fundamentally politically oriented.

The aircraft part of the civil market consists of general aviation – small light planes, business aircraft and helicopters, small commuter planes – and the far more important market segment of large commercial passenger and cargo planes. Because the battle for world market share of large commercial transports has become the most visible cockpit for the competition between U.S. and European manufacturers the bulk of this essay will concern this segment of the market.

3. Large Airliners

There is no widely accepted definition of what is "large" but most observers would agree on a minimum seating capacity of about 100 in a typical mixed class seating configuration or cargo planes of the same size. This corresponds to a payload of about 14 tons over a "normal" range of about 2500 kilometers.

3.1 Market

The market for these planes – the airlines – in turn depends on the market for air transportation. This latter market is driven by a complex host of factors chief among which are the world economy (and its growth) in general and the relative cost of air transportation in particular. In the two decades from 1964 to 1984 the gross domestic product per capita of the average West European rose some 20 percent in real terms. During the same period the cost of the least expensive economy transatlantic fare, say Paris – New York and return, actually fell in term of 1984 dollars from $ 950 to $ 600. Under these circumstances it is clear that the growth in the market for air transportation would exceed overall economic growth. The underlying reason for this difference is the amazing advance in aeronautical technology.

The markets for transport planes can be measured in a number of different ways: passengers, passenger-kilometers, seat-kilometers offered, ton-kilometers of freight, mail, or passengers or total, etc. Table 5 shows the evolution of the passenger market (the largest).

Obviously, the growth rate of air travel has been phenomenal, especially if one would add the growth of non-scheduled travel (as much as 20 percent across the

Table 5: Average Annual rate of growth (%)

	Air passenger-kilometers (world scheduled airlines)[1]	Real gross domestic product of developed countries[2] (excluding Soviet bloc)
1958–1965	13	
1965–1969	16	
1969–1971	7	5.1
1971–1973	12	
1973–1977	7	
1977–1979	13	2.7
1979–1981	6	
1981–1982	2	0.9

Sources: 1 Annual reports of International Civil Aviation Organization (includes Soviet Union after 1971)
2 OECD and U.S. Bureau of Labor Statistics

Table 6: Total Ton-Kilometers Carried on Sheduled Services of All National Companies (millions)[1]

	1965		1970		1982	
	Domestic	Total	Domestic	Total	Domestic	Total
United States	9183	13112	20398	26537	35710	47150
Japan	229	492	756	1731	2540	7310
United Kingdom	160	1467	196	2293	240	6660
France	87	894	275	1754	1040	5660
West Germany	42	520	122	1284	220	2585
TOTAL WORLD	11922	23404	25645	47773	50123	118690

1 Excluding USSR, China and Eastern Europe . Source: ICAO. Annual reports.

From the above we get the following percentages of the *total* world traffic (less USSR, etc.) carried by U.S. national airlines:

	Within U.S.	International	Total
1965	39%	17%	56%
1970	43	13	56
1982	30	10	40

Atlantic in the late 1970s). Amore detailed breakdown of the total market gives a clue to the problem facing Western European manufacturers – the enormous U.S. market.

It should be pointed out that while the U.S. carriers' share of the international market was only 10 percent in 1982, approximately one-third of the total international market involved aircraft departing or arriving in the United States. All in all, the U.S. airline industry's dominant share of the "free world" market appears to be shrinking.

To share this market there were, in 1984, some 650 "scheduled" airlines (USSR, China, and Eastern Europe excluded). However, of these less than thirty maintained fleets of 50 or more large airlines and could be considered as significant potential customers for the world aerospace industry, the launching of a proposed new airliner development required a substantial number of orders before the manufacturer and his bankers could risk the huge financial investment involved. And only the largest airlines could place enough orders (and make the necessary initial and progress payments) to insure such a launch. This does not apply in Europe where the governments have been willing to make the necessary initial "up-front" investments. Boeing did not launch the 747 until Pan American ordered 25 planes in April 1966 *and* until several major subcontractors agreed to share the start-up costs (and risks). Boeing did not firmly launch the 757 until firm orders were received from British Airways for 19 planes and from Eastern Airlines for 21 in March of 1979. By way of contrast the first real challenge to American supremacy in the airliner market since World War II – the Airbus A-300 – was launched by formal agreement between the French and German governments (with firm state financial backing) in 1967 *without any real orders*. Five years later, by the beginning of 1972, only Air France had ordered six aircraft and by the end of 1973 firm orders for the A-300 still amounted to only 17 (Hochmuth 1974a and 1984).

We see that despite a basic market that far outpaced general economic growth the aircraft manufacturers have had to proceed warily. How warily can be seen from the following:

Table 7: Number of Major Aircraft Manufacturers (Number Developing and Constructing Large Airliners in Parentheses)

	1955	1965	1975	1983
US	12(6)	10(4)	9(4)	9(2)
UK	14(5)	4(3)	3(3)	1(1)
France	5(3)	4(3)	2(1)	1(1)
Germany	0(0)	4(1)	3(2)	2(1)
Netherlands	(1)	1(1)	1(1)	1(1)

Moreover in 1984 there were only *three* market economy firms, world-wide, manufacturing and marketing trunk-line (110 seat and larger) airliners – the Franco-German-British Airbus Industrie, U.S. Boeing and U.S. McDonnell Douglas companies.

Obviously, there must be strong economic factors to create a shrinking world-wide oligopoly in the face of a mushrooming market that even in periods of recession has outpaced world economic growth.

3.2 Development Times and Costs

In the early 1930s the development of the 25 seat DC-3 required three years and $ 1.5 million (current) to develop (excluding the engine) (Hochmuth 1974a, pp. 149–152 and Hochmuth 1984). The Franco-British supersonic CONCORDE cost some $ 3 billion to develop and prepare for production and required 14 years from the time a formal agreement launched full scale development in 1962 until the first commercial flight. Moreover, preliminary design work had been going on in France and Britain since 1958 (Hochmuth 1974b, pp. 126–156). A more representative plane would be Boeing's 727 which has been the world's largest selling transport. 1832 of these tri-jets were built when the last one was delivered in September 1984. The time required from the launch of full-scale development in December 1960 to entry into service of the first plane in February 1964 was three years and two months. But preliminary design work began in mid-1956, four years before the formal 1960 launch was triggered by orders for 80 planes from United Airlines and Eastern. This preliminary work included 150 different design studies of which 68 were wind tunnel tested. Aircraft manufacturers are constantly investing in such design studies, covering a wide range of candidates, which they discuss with potential customers, probing for a "launch window" and sufficient orders for a launch. A "launch window" occurs when a sufficient number of the world's larger airlines need to replace a significant portion of their fleet because of age or technological obsolescence. This does not mean that the airlines can afford to buy new planes. The 727's non-recurring costs – which include preliminary design work, full design and laboratory work (including wind tunnel tests etc.) and production tooling and special facilities probably cost Boeing on the order of $ 750 million (current) not counting know-how and tooling available from the 707 program.

There was a time, in the 1950's, when lower development costs and mushrooming demand allowed a successful manufacturer (and they have been very few in either Europe or the United States) to recover their investment after selling 300–350 planes under then normal competitive conditions. This magic "break-even point" usually required about five years to reach. More recently, with much higher development costs, cut-throat price competition among the remaining few competitors and slower demand, the time required to reach break-even can be twenty or more years (Newhouse 1983, pp. 144–160). Figure 1 gives an estimate for the European Airbus A-300 whose true development costs have been authoritatively estimated from between a low of $ 1 billion (current between 1969 and 1974) to as much as $ 1.5 billion and even much more (Assemblé Nationale 1976; The Economist 1980, p. 17; Süddeutsche Zeitung 1984). The 210 seat Airbus A-310, a *derivative* of the larger A-300, cost from between $ 850 million to $ 1.2 billion in nonrecurring costs between 1978 and 1983 (in current dollars). A derivative is an improvement of an existing successful aircraft incorporating some newer technology, usually more efficient and more powerful engines, improved aerodynamics, or improved controls, but keeping much of the existing design and production tooling. A "stretched" aircraft permitting more seats is a typical derivative. The A-300 is termed a "new/new" aircraft since it had no precedent. A derivative usually costs much less to develop. The break-even point for the A-300/A-310 has been estimated by Airbus Industrie to be about 860 aircraft. But this depends much on what will happen in the world economy and competitively by 1995.

Obviously with "up-front" investments of this nature and pay-back times of 10 to 20 years it is small wonder that only one U.S. firm has shown any profit in this sector since the advent of the jet. And it is equally obvious why European firms cannot undertake the development of large airliners without massive

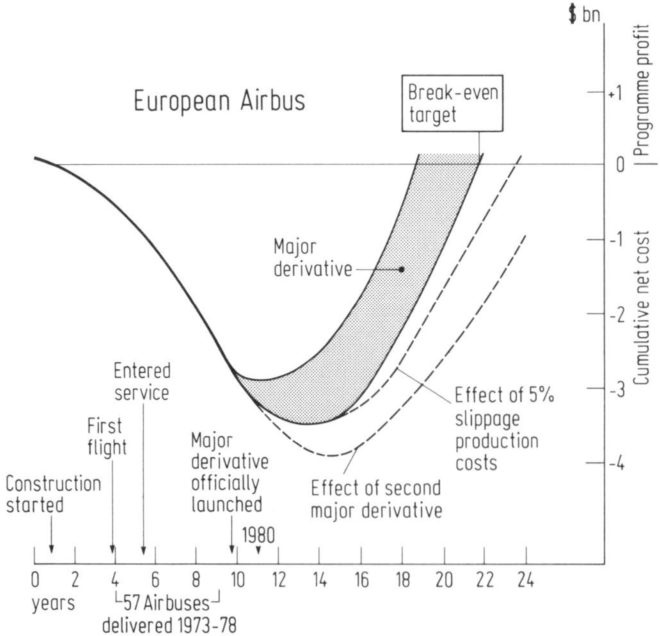

Figure 1: European Airbus

Source: The Economist (30 August 1980, p. 11)

government financial support. But even with such financial support the separate national European markets are too small to provide a domestic launching base. Inevitably co-national ventures such as the CONCORDE and Airbus arose to spread the investment and enlarge market opportunities. But the awkwardness of managing such ad hoc, co-national ventures led to a search for a more efficient and permanent solution.

3.3 An Attempt at a Truly European Marriage

In 1967 when discussions between the several European governments and their industries leading to the Airbus A-300 were hot and heavy, the situations of the Dutch and German industries were quite different from those of Britain and France.

The Netherlands possessed a relatively small aircraft company of unique international stature. Not only was Fokker privately owned, it required a minimum of state support. As early 1960 it had already established itself in a market niche with what was to become one of the world's finest small civil transports – the turbo-propeller, 30–50 seat F-27, of which derivatives are still in production. Based on the success of the F-27 the Dutch firm launched a larger turbo-jet in 1962 the F-28, which has also enjoyed respectable sales. On the military side, Fokker had been given a strong boost as a major participant in the European manufacture of the U.S. F-104 G fighter at about the same time. But this program was coming to an end. To insure a continued military aircraft capability (and industry employment) the Dutch government had participated as one of the original partners in what became the co-national Multiple Role Combat Aircraft (MRCA)/Tornado program (together with Britain, Germany and Italy).

In July 1969 the Netherlands withdrew from the MRCA fighter program. The evidence suggests that the main reason was that the degree of expensive technical sophistication desired by Britain and Germany was too rich for the parsimonius Dutch. At the same time they were reluctant to see their efficient and unique firm swallowed up in the joint Airbus venture where the larger countries and their industries would hold technical and production sway. Still, the economic and technical forces discussed earlier would inevitably require a firm much larger than Holland alone could support. Though well established in a particular niche, and doing very well, what Fokker needed was a partner that could help widen its foothold in the civil market, and more importantly, provide a significantly greater base of military support than could be obtained from the limited Dutch requirements. In scanning the industrial and political environment it appeared that joining with a German partner would be the best solution.

Meanwhile in Germany, the wave of mergers that began in the early 1960's under government pressure to rationalize the aerospace sector had resulted in two major firms – Messerschmitt-Bölkow-Blohm (MBB) and the Vereinigte Flugtechnische Werke (VFW). The former was engaged in both the MRCA and the Airbus, as a major partner, while the latter was only a junior partner in the Airbus program and had managed to capture only a minor share of the German military market, though it was strong in the satellite sector. VFW thought it saw a "window" in the civil field for a small, 40 seat twin jet – the VFW 614 – aimed at feeder routes and developing countries. Smaller and more modern than the turbo-prop Fokker F-27 and half the capacity of the F-28, there seemed to be a complementarity with Fokker.

Acting under the economic and political pressures of the day, the two firms agreed in 1968 to discuss a merger. Having seen the problems of co-national marriage in the CONCORDE and Airbus programs, a great deal of thought was given to insure a workable management structure. It would have to be centralized for strategic purposes, decentralized for operating purposes to avoid jeopardizing the vitality of Fokker and VFW, and to insure "national identities" in order to attract home nation military development and production contracts.

There were inumerable legal, financial and personnel problems to overcome, but at the end of 1969 the co-national marriage was consummated. The

Group Structure:

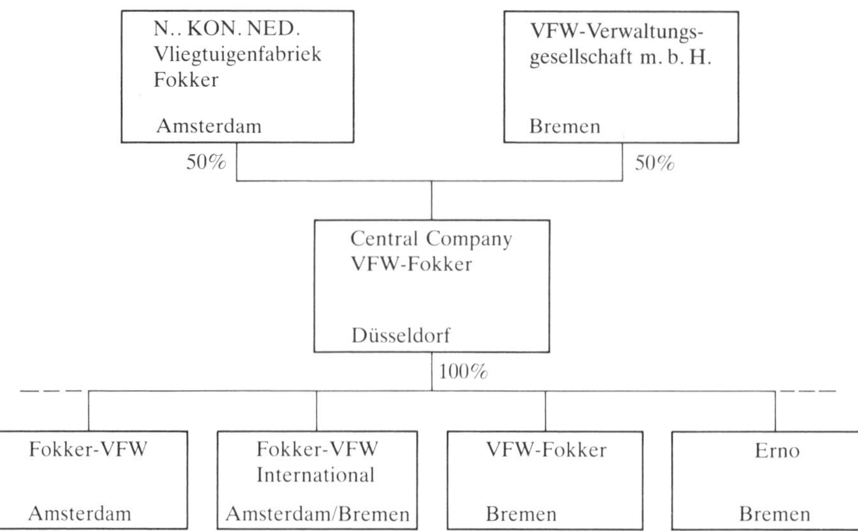

headquarters – the intended strategic center – was located in Düsseldorf, halfway between the location of Fokker in Amsterdam and VFW in Bremen. A German corporate seat made more sense because the location and legal nationality of the company was important for military business – and Germany was by far the larger potential military customer. Nationality was less important for civil aircraft business. The organization looked as follows (see p. 216).

The years following the marriage were marred by the inability of either partner to obtain the results they had counted on. VFW was unable to find customers for its VFW-614 for which the German government had provided heavy financial support. Was the experienced Fokker marketing organization deliberately neglecting the plane in favor of its F-28? On the Fokker side, there was disappointment that major German military programs and helicopters remained in MBB's domain and VFW was getting only some of the space effort (satellites within European co-national consortia and 'space-lab' within the European Space Agency/NASA structure). Meanwhile Fokker had obtained substantial non-German military work when the Netherlands government joined in the European production of the U.S. F-16 fighter program.

Thus, despite a potentially workable management structure, the organization began to disintegrate. The original goals of the two partners were simply not being met. Only drastic integration of the functional sub-units would have created a viable whole, and then only after several years. Such a reorganization implied a change that the Fokker team could not accept. Moreover, the German government began to believe that a meaningful (and less expensive German presence in aerospace required a *single* national champion. This could only mean building up MBB at VFW's expense. By late 1978 there was open talk of "divorce" and a subsequent merger of VFW and MBB. The VFW-614 was then terminated and the divorce became final in February of 1980. In the spring of 1982 MBB and VFW were in the first stages of their merger and it was decided that the name VFW would disappear after mid-1983. An ideal European marriage had failed.

3.4 The Search for a "Window"

If the VFW-614 had been a successful airplane VFW-Fokker might well have become a meaningful international competitor. What factors must be considered by a manufacturer in determining whether or not to launch so expensive a venture? Economic forecasts, forecasts of airline traffic growth, the need of airlines to replace ammortized (but still useful) aircraft, the need to replace overage/worn-out aircraft, to replace aircraft that do not meet new severe noise regulations, and the advent of more efficient planes that reduce operating costs (that a competitor may have bought) are some of the key considerations. To these must be added the financial health – or lack of it – of the airline.

A well maintained airline can last twenty years or more. In October 1977 840 of the pure jet Boeing 707/720s were still in service. Of these 310 were over fifteen years old and five had more than 60 000 hours of flying time, the equivalent of 20 years at an average *heavy* use of 3000 hours per year. However U.S. tax laws, for example, allow an airliner to be fully depreciated to residual value in 12 years or less. Therefore for tax purposes an airline would like to have a fleet with an average age of 6 years or so.

When an airline decides to purchase a new model it generally purchases as large a block as it can in order to facilitate maintenance, crew training, and to replace a complete block of existing planes for some of the reasons previously mentioned. For example, in November 1980 Delta Airlines placed an order for 60 Boeing 757s at a cost of $ 3 billion including spares, etc. ($ 25 million 1982 dollars per plane). In February 1984 American Airlines ordered 67 McDonnell Douglas MD-80 planes, a derivative of the DC-9, at a cost of about $ 1.35 billion to be delivered at a rate of 25 per year beginning in 1985. At the same time the airline placed option orders for an additional 100! The volatility of the market is evidenced by the fact that in 1981 so few orders were received for the MD-80 that production was slowly being phased out and only an agreement by American Airlines in October 1982 to lease 20 planes and a large order for 30 planes in January 1983 by Airitalia breathed life into the program. The development of the MD-80 consisted of stretching the DC-9-50 fuselage to accomodate 142 mixed class seats, using more powerful, more efficient derivative motors, increasing the wing size, and – most importantly – designing the cockpit for a crew of two, eliminating the need for a flight engineer. Originally the development was to have cost a mere $ 110 million and may well have cost three times that.

When in 1983 McDonnell Douglas tried to repeat the MD-80 experience by offering a more efficient derivative of the larger 270–300 seat DC-10 (with a new two-man cockpit) a "window" was there but the airlines could not afford to buy.

The proposed $ 800 million to $ 1 billion development was cancelled, leading industry observers to wonder whether a manufacturer with only one plane in his product line – and a ninth generation derivative of that – could remain a viable factor in the industry.

The purchase of planes is therefore cyclical and "lumpy". Since the development cycle is three to five years, the launch window must be based on a projected "need". But if a competitor comes up with an almost as good and cheaper derivative, or a cheaper equivalent, or if the economic cycle plunges in an unforeseen manner as it did after 1973 or in 1979 reducing traffic demand, then a billion dollar gamble can put a company out of the airliner business. To the above unknowns must be added the uncertainty of successful development as planned. Technical miscalculations concerning its RB-211 engine for the Lockheed Tristar forced Rolls-Royce into bankruptcy and would have forced Lockheed into bankruptcy had the U.S. government not come to the rescue. In fact Lockheed in 1984 is no longer in the airliner business, having opted for the more profitable and secure military market. If to all these unknowns and uncertainties are added the vagaries of government policies – as they must be for European manufacturers who depend on their governments for launch financing – the plight of the European manufacturer is glaringly clear. This combination is what ultimately reduced Britain's aircraft industry from near parity with the United States at the end of World War II to its present position of being overshadowed by the French industry. On the other hand, the steadfast and unwavering goal of French political leadership since DeGaulle to regain a leading place in the world aeronautical industry (ably assisted by the remarkable Marcel Dassault and his Mirages) in the face of losses and uncertainties has made France the leading Western aerospace power after the United States. The February/March 1984 announcements by Germany and Britain that they would join France in supporting the development of Airbus Industrie's "new/new", 150 seat A-320 plane is an instructive case in point.

4. A-320

The British government's announcement of 2 March that it would provide "loans" of £ 250 million to the British Aerospace Corporation (BAe) fell far short of the "minimum essential" £ 437 million BAe had requested. But by having the aid scheduled early in the program and by arbitrarily reducing the projected inflation rate during the development period, the reduced sum was sufficient to trigger an informal but full scale launch of the long discussed and long-delayed A-320. What nudged a reluctant Mrs. Thatcher to give her approval was no doubt an equally reluctant but wealthier German government's decision two weeks earlier to provide a subsidy of DM 1.5 billion to cover 90 percent of Deutsche Airbus' share of the overall $ 1.8 billion development costs. The allocation of financial responsibility and work-sharing was as follows (Flight International 1984, p. 738):

	Funding share	*Work share*
Germany	37.6%	31.0%
France	37.6%	36.0%
Britain	20.0%	27.0%
Spain	4.8%	6. %

The work share above shows the allocation of work to the three major national firms. But because these firms must in turn sub-contract some 20 percent of the total work for equipment (avionics, power supplies, brakes, controls, etc.) some hard negotiations would be required before a memorandum of understanding would be signed in June 1984. In the Airbus A-300 and A-310 French firms had received about 50 to 60 percent of the equipment orders, U.S. firms about 20-30 percent and British firms only about 8 percent. In engines for the A-300/310 the French portion was about 27 percent to U.S. General Electric's 63 percent. For the A-320 the only available engine choice was the 50-50 French SNECMA/U.S. General Electric CFM 56-4.

The expected June 1984 memorandum would bring to a formal close but the latest round in a long series of negotiations and agreements for co-national aircraft ventures that began in the late 1950s. Such agreements have led to the CONCORDE and Airbus on the civil side and the Jaguar and MRCA on the military side. These seemingly endless negotiations between the Europeans, with the Americans occasionally involved, have been variously described by observers as a complex international ballet, a frantic scurrying about helterskelter, bitter dog-fights, and more elegantly as stately mating dances. Be that as it may, Europe has thrown the gauntlet down at the U.S. industry and specifically at Boeing, the U.S. (and world) champion.

The A-320 saga traces its roots to the mid 1960s as the second wave of jet transports entered service. The first wave, which entered service in the late 1950s, consisted largely of Boeing 707s and Douglas DC-8s and, to a lesser extent, of the smaller Sud-Aviation Caravelles. The second wave, consisting entirely of more modern, short/medium range jets carrying (initially) 70–100 passengers was launched in the 1959–1963 period. By the time they entered service in 1964–1966, the 707s and DC-8s had been "stretched" to carry as many as 200 or more passengers over large distances. As traffic demand continued to increase at the 16 percent rate, Boeing launched the 747 in 1966, and Douglas and Lockheed launched their large tri-motors in 1968. It seemed to Marcel Dassault that a "gap" had opened up between the smaller existing jets that could be stretched with increasing difficulty and the larger jets including those under development. Heady with the large sales of his Mirage military aircraft and small Falcon business jets, he was sure he could repeat this success in the commercial airliner field. In this belief he received the enthusiastic support of DeGaulle. Identifying the 150 seat, short-range plane as the ideal candidate, he invested some FF 600 million of his own money and FF 700 million of government and other funds in the MERCURE-100, as the plane was called. Full scale development began in 1969. But the program ended in 1973, a year before its first commercial flight, with only 10 planes sold, all of which were forced on France's Air-Inter airline. Sabena airline's 1973 comment explaining its preference for the latest model Boeing 737 – that the slightly smaller 737 had half the operating costs, two-thirds the price and almost twice the range of the MERCURE – was hardly an exaggeration. Moreover in 1973 Boeing's larger 727 was selling for as low as $ 6–7 million compared to the smaller and less efficient MERCURE's $ 8 million bottom price. Meanwhile another competitor, Douglas, had stretched its DC-9 series to seat as many as 139 passengers in the $ 5.2 million DC-9-50. The 727 went on to become the most successful airliner in history, with 1832 sold. This demonstrates that the existence of a "window" does not alone insure success.

It was against this background in the mid-1970s, that the world's few manufacturers eyed the market. The Airbus A-300 had already began flight tests in late 1972 but only 13 firms orders were received by mid-1973. Meanwhile Boeing was riding the crest of its success with the derivative 727-200, and Boeing's 737 and 747 were increasingly successful. At the same time Lockheed and Douglas were destroying each other with the almost identical L-1011 and DC-10. Bitter over the lack of Airbus' success, CONCORDE's lack of promise, the MERCURE'S failure, and the continuing overwhelming dominance of the world airliner market by U.S. manufacturers, the Europeans debated whether cooperation between themselves would ever succeed. Would they have to start cooperative ventures with the U.S. industry as "junior partners", forever giving up hope of becoming a major player in the game? The Americans encouraged the transatlantic advances of the Europeans and there were numerous flirtations but no meaningful relationships.

By the end of 1975 there seemed to be industry-wide agreement that despite the world recession induced by the 1973 oil crisis and price rise, there was still a need for a new transport and that it would be a short-to-medium range 200 seat plane. Such a plane, it was thought, would be needed beginning around 1980 to replace the aging Boeing 707s, Douglas DC-8s and older 727s equipped with early, inefficient jet engines. A market of 1200 such planes was foreseen between 1980 and 1985 (Business week 1976, p. 62). Boeing had for some time been sounding out the airlines with a series of design studies – 7X7, 7N7, and 7S7 while McDonnell Douglas was touting a scaled-down DC-10. Airbus Industrie was attempting to get European support, especially British, to launch the derivative 210 seat A-300 B10, later to become the A-310. Unfortunately the British industry was then in the final throes of nationalization and consolidation of the two remaining major aircraft firms, British Aircraft Corporation and Hawker – Siddeley, into BAe. Traffic growth seemed to be recovering and the world airline industry appeared on the verge of profitability (ICAO). Despite unsatisfactory sales of the Airbus, gloomy prospects for the CONCORDE and turmoil in Britain, the French were determined not to cede the potential market to the U.S. manufacturers. But how to prevent it?

The period from late 1975 to mid-1977 may have looked like a complex international ballet to some within the aerospace industry. But it is best described as a mad, helter-skelter jumble of stately mating dances between all the players concerned – European and American. Four main themes characterize this period.

a) French determination, to proceed including collaboration with the U.S. if necessary
b) German lukewarm support
c) British paralysis due to the 1975-1977 debate ending in the nationalization and consolidation of her airframe industry into the British Aerospace Corporation, and British vaccilation on whether to turn to Europe or the U.S.
d) not least important, the efforts of American manufacturers to simultaneously prevent creation of a purely European competitor (that could have access to fat government subsidies) while obtaining some of these subsidies for their own projects.

When hot and heavy negotiations between the French government, Dassault and McDonnell Douglas on a joint 150 seat, advanced MERCURE 200 development collapsed in May 1977, the French took the lead in re-starting European negotiations. It had now been 8 years since either a major "new/new" or derivative airliner had been launched in Europe or the United States. The ballet resumed, this time centering on the 210 seat A-310 derivative and on a "new/new" 150 seater. Germany, faced with the impending failure of the VFW-Fokker mariage was as usual lukewarm, but tending toward the less expensive A-310. Britain faced with a realization that France was becoming the indisputable European leader in large airliners wanted to regain a place in the sun by getting program leadership of a collaborative 150 seat project based on the almost successful BAC 111 (which had entered service in 1965). But Britain wanted the project *outside* of Airbus Industrie which was French dominated. This France – and Germany – would not agree to. So in November 1978 Britain re-entered Airbus Industrie as a 20 percent partner on the just launched, $ 900 million A-310 project. Meanwhile a few weeks earlier McDonnell Douglas had announced the formal launching of the Super 80, or MD-80 as the stretched 140 seater derivative of the old DC-9 series is known.

Despite occasional statements from various airliners that there was a need for a new short range 150 seater, the manufacturers had their hands full. Boeing had simultaneously launched its 767 with the A-310 in July 1978 and, even more, had also launched the 757 a 180 seat replacement for the 727 at the same time in what was sure to be at least a $ 1.5 to $ 2.5 billion development.

1978 had been a banner year for the world's airlines. Travel had jumped and profits had even jumped further, which explains the launch orders for Boeing. The A-310 was launched without firm orders, although there was a Lufthansa "promise". A sign of Boeing's strength was that as it became evident that there was not only a window, but an airline willingness to renew their medium/short range fleet, Boeing launched a major derivative of its 737 in 1980, a 135 seat "stretch", powered with the Franco-American CFM-56 motors.

Major improvements in airliners depend largely on major improvements in motors. A truly new aircraft must have a significantly improved motor if it is to be successful. (More air seat-kilometers per liter of fuel consumed). What had happened in the motor sector is that the big three – Pratt & Whitney, Rolls-Royce and General Electric had been battling it out for supremacy on the larger airliners – the 747, then the McDonnell Douglas DC-10, Lockheed L-1011, Airbus A-300/310 and later for dominance on the Boeing 757 and 767. These were 15 to 25 ton thrust motors. The only new motor in the ten metric ton class under development was the General Electric – SNECMA CFM-56, whose development was begun in December 1971. And only such a new motor could be the basis for a truly efficient "150 seater". Though the CFM-56 was the only "new" engines available in 1983/1984 it is still based on technology developed by General Electric for the U.S. B-1 bomber in the late 1960s.

Was it too late for Europe to compete across the whole product line? Airbus Industrie took the lead, encouraged by a late-blooming success in the sales of A-300/A-310 planes in 1978 and 1979. Finally, after years of famine, almost 200 had been sold in two years, almost four times as many as all previous sales combined (since 1969)! Unfortunately traffic growth plumetted to 2.6 percent in 1980 and stayed there. As a result airline profits dropped, and beginning in 1980 the airlines were flying in a cloud of red ink. The usual mating dances took place but the key to a European 150 seater was Britain's willingness to share the risk. Germany could always be persuaded, albeit grudgingly.

In an effort to force the British and German governments' hand Bernard Lathière, Airbus Industrie's French president, announced the "launch" of the A-320 at the June 1981 Paris Air Show. He was later chastised for this premature statement. At the same time Air France announced its "intention" to order 25. A month earlier, a key potential customer, Reinhardt Abraham, president of German Lufthansa, had publicly stated that his airline would not order the A-320 because it would be scarcely more economical than the 737. (Lufthansa had just ordered a large number of late model 737s). Nevertheless BAe immediately announced it would seek British government support for the $ 1.5 billion or more project.

5. The International Ballet Resumed Again

Boeing began its usual mating dances with British industry probably to fend off an A-320 launch. It also released such statements as "the market is not ready" and that until a truly new motor was available there should be no launch. Much of this was aimed at the British government.

Throughout the rest of 1981, 1982, and into 1983 the ballet continued. What was different now was that Airbus Industrie was a seasoned, agressive competitor and political actor. Preliminary design work went on, even in England. Then in October 1983 British Caledonian Airways signed a (no doubt provisional) contract with Airbus Industrie for 7 A-320s at a cost of $ 32.3 million each (1988–1989 dollars) including spares. This probably represented a 1983 price of less than $ 20 million, but the details of a purchase contract are seldom made public (Newhouse 1983, note 10). This set the stage for events leading to the German and British go ahead described earlier.

Will the A-320 succeed? It is difficult to say. Airbus Industrie estimates a total market for the 150 seater as 2500 by the end of the century, of which they conservatively expect 750–800 sales. This implies a break-even point of some 600 or so which would not be reached for at least a dozen years or more. Given the existence of a redoubtable competitor such as Boeing, break-even may not be reached until the year 2000, if ever. But one thing is certain. Europe is here to stay in the large commercial airliner business, mostly due to France's stubborn insistence.

With regard to commercial exploitation of space, the picture is remarkably similar.

Bibliography

Assemblé Nationale: *Rapport No. 2525, 1ère session, 1976–1977.* 10 October 1976.

Business Week. 12 April 1976.

Commission of the European Communities: *The European Aerospace Industry – Trading Position and Figures.* Document III/202/84-EN (final), (Commission Staff Working Paper), Brussels, 11 January 1984.

Financial Times. London, 23 August 1982.

Financial Times. London, 23 May 1983.

Flight International. 24 March 1984.

Hochmuth, M. S.: Aerospace. In: Vernon, R. ed.: *Big Business and the State.* Harvard University Press, Cambridge/Mass. 1974 (a).

Hochmuth, M. S.: *Organizing the Transnational.* Sijthoff, Leiden 1974 (b).

Hochmuth, M. S.: The Aerospace Industry. In: Hochmuth, M. S. ed.: *Revitalizing American Industry.* Ballinger, Cambridge/Mass. 1984.

ICAO, *Annual Reports.*

Newhouse, J.: *The Sporty Game*. Alfred Knopf, New York 1983.
Süddeutsche Zeitung. 25 February 1984.
The Economist. 30 August 1980.
U.S. Bureau of Labor Statistics: *Labstat series*. 1983.
U.S. Department of Commerce: *International Economic Indicators*. December 1983.

Corporate Adjustment Strategies in the European Clothing Industry

José de la Torre

Summary

This paper draws heavily from a long-term study of private and public strategies for adjustment in the clothing industries of eight major industrial economies prepared for the Trade Policy Research Centre, London. The larger study extends the present analysis by a detailed examination of the public policy approaches undertaken by six European nations – Belgium, France, the Federal Republic of Germany, Italy, the Netherlands and the United Kingdom – Japan and the United States in order to deal with the crisis facing their respective industries. The conclusions presented here are partly based on this aspect of the study which attempted to relate various public adjustment strategies to their relative success and cost.

1. The Forces of Change

The most commonly used measures of industrial performance – growth, employment, balance of trade, investment, price stability, profitability, etc. – when applied to the clothing sector of most OECD countries invariably show a record of marked decline in recent years. Between 1973 and 1980, the OECD countries suffered a loss of over 500 000 jobs in the clothing industry alone, in addition to losses of approximately one million in the various textile and fibre sectors. Taken together these losses represent nearly 25% of the net increase in unemployment in the region. Parallel to these developments, production declined or remained stagnant in most industrial countries and the OECD's trade balance in clothing with the rest of the world deteriorated from a modest deficit of US $ 900 million in 1970 to over US $ 12.5 billion in 1979 and US $ 15.1 billion in 1980. These competitive pressures and the serious economic conditions prevailing during the last decade resulted in the net disappearance of over 2500 clothing firms in the European Community and of nearly 3200 in the United States.

Factors pressuring the clothing industries of the industrialized countries to adjust have varied but none perhaps has had such a widespread influence as the stagnant demand conditions prevailing since the early 1970s. The marked decrease in the rate of population increase in the industrial world, the low income elasticity of demand for clothing and the cyclical economic conditions prevailing since 1974 have had a major impact on both disposable income and consumer expenditures on clothing.

Changes in materials and in relative material prices have also had a considerable effect on the industry. While the growth and popularity of synthetic and other man-made fibres afforded the industrialized countries a period of competitive advantage during the 1960s, by the early 1970s the fibre industry had matured and spread worldwide, eliminating this edge. The decline in man-made fibre prices, while benefitting the industry, also caused a realignment of the total cost structure, increasing the importance of labour costs as a competitive component.

The industry was also affected by a significant shift in the composition of demand for clothing, away from labour-intensive traditional suits and dresses to more simply constructed casual wear. The result has been lower unit costs contributing to a drop in relative prices and to increases in productivity shown in some countries. The opportunities for increased market segmentation have had important implications for manufacturing flexibility, distribution channels, product range, etc.

The increased importance of large chain and discount stores with centralized buying departments on one side and the development of the large synthetic fibre producing chemical firms on the other has resulted in diminished bargaining power for clothing manufacturers. The impact of this trend, however, has varied by product group, once again increasing the scope for segmentation and differentiation.

Technology is, of course, of great importance in shaping potential response strategies but the scope for innovation and process improvements in the clothing industry is limited. In an industry where labour costs represent 25–30% of factory prices, it is clear that in order for the industrialized countries to remain competitive they must maintain a ratio of productivity advantage which approaches the inverse of their wage ratio disadvantage vis-a-vis the NICs and LDCs. However, this is extremely difficult to achieve in a sector which is characterized by standardized production processes, readily available technology and relatively high inputs of low-skill labour. The persistent wage escalation in the industrialized countries, occuring simultaneously with the loss of relative productivity advantages in industries such as textiles and clothing, is one of the major causes of the adjustment problem.

The last major force for change, both a contributing factor and a result of the others discussed above, has been the significant growth in the volume and geographic diversity of trade in textiles and clothing products in the last 20 years. Since 1963, the volume of world trade in textiles and clothing has increased by nearly 300% while worldwide production has risen by only 79%. This rapid increase in the proportion of world textile markets open to international competition has accelerated the adjustment required of firms in all countries and segments of the industry.

A major shift of employment in the textile and clothing industries – both nationally (inter-industry) and internationally (intra-industry) – has been underway since the 1960s and has been moving considerably faster since the 1974–75 crisis. To the extent that other sectors in the economy were expanding and able to absorb these labour resources, the process could take place at a relatively smooth pace. However, this was not the case after 1974 and pressures mounted to accord protection or other forms of relief to the industry. The pace of the growth of government intervention accelerated dramatically after 1975. But in all cases, except for the U.S., a rise in the import penetration of clothing products was partially offset by large increases in export production, indicating a relative success in shifting resources to those lines of clothing where some international competitive advantage is enjoyed.

2. Elements of an Adjustment Strategy

There are a number of responses open to any clothing firm facing international competitive pressures. Six major sets of possible actions are discussed here: they concern technology and investment, size and concentration, wage policies, market segmentation manufacturing abroad for the domestic market and foreign direct investment. A seventh and highly rewarding strategy not considered here is in the non-economic field and consists of pressuring governments for higher levels of protection and for public assistance.

2.1 Limits to Technical Development

The advocates of a technological solution are not calling for the acceleration of the process of gradual technological improvement, but rather a radical transformation of the industry through massive investments in new technology. Some of the necessary pre-conditional elements for this transformation are already in place. For the last decade the United States has been the centre of new developments in automating equipment for the clothing industry. Using their experience in electronics and automation processes, industrial machinery companies with no relation to the textile or clothing industries, such as CAMSCO, Hughes Aircraft, Gerber Scientific *et cetera,* have led the field in innovations of this sort.

One major issue that deserves attention is the tremendous variability in capital/output ratios among segments of the industry (for example, underwear *versus* ladies' dresses) and between one process (for example, cutting) and another (for example, assembly). The implications of this variable capital/output ratio are two-fold. First, research resources could be applied to those areas and problems which are both significant bottlenecks in production and amenable to automation. Second, however, it also implies that to the extent that various processes are discrete, firms could choose between automation and relocation (to low-wage areas) for *every* step in the manufacturing process according to the economics in question. To the degree that this latter alternative is viable, innovations in automation will have to be justified not only on how many highly paid, industrial-country workers they replace, but on a similar comparison based on the option to execute that particular process using cheaper labour abroad. Furthermore, the fact that most new technology is immediately available to producers in the developing countries (witness the high degree of automation of Hong Kong's industry) reduces the advantages to be gained by following such a strategy.

The future for technological change is clouded by uncertainty. Japanese machinery companies, spurred on by the Agency of Industrial Science and Technology, affiliated to the Ministry of International Trade and Industry (MITI), are committing large amounts of R & D resources to automate clothing manufacturing at all stages, through the use of flexible manufacturing systems. Their 1982 project to promote the development of "automatic sewing systems" is geared at four problem areas identified as critical bottlenecks: pre-sewing processes, sewing assembly, cloth handling and production control. Others are experimenting with three-dimensional forming and bonding techniques that may drastically alter the way garments are made. A recent study for the Commission of the European Communities by the industrial consultants, Kurt Salmon Associates (Salmon Associates 1979), analyzed the potential impact of these new technologies on the operations of a 'typical apparel manufacturer'. The optimal investment level appeared to be in the order of ten to twelve times current levels. On this basis, if current production in the European Community, the United States and Japan were to be modernized to this level, it would entail the loss of 1.2–1.5 million operator jobs and an investment in the order of 25 billion.

2.2 Size and Scale of Individual Companies

In spite of whatever pressures technology has imposed on the minimum corporate size required for survival, the evidence to date shows very little increase in the levels of industry concentration or average firm size. Vertical integration (that is, control of production processes from raw material stage to finished product) is also a rare phenomenon in the clothing industry, with a few notorious exceptions such as Courtaulds in the United Kingdom and Prouvost in France. In this, the most fragmented of all industries (over 50 000 firms operate in the eight countries under study), the disadvantages of scale appear to have prevailed.

Our analysis of value added per manufacturing man-hour in the American industry in the late 1960s and early 1970s, showed that large plant size could have a negative effect on economic efficiency. In fact, some segments of the industry appeared to experience significant diseconomies of scale in factories with more than 250 employees. Firms which operated a number of manufacturing plants, however, could benefit from the scale advantages inherent in centralised administrative, design, cutting and information systems without incurring the penalties associated with large size. By organizing production in a series of small manufacturing establishments, each with no more than 250–300 employees, in rural areas located in a circle around a centralized warehouse and distribution centre, the firm could organize its various functions in terms of their respective sensitivity to scale effects. In this 'spokes-and-wheel' system, the manufacturing facilities would remain manageable and perform those processes (essentially assembly) not amenable to automation.

A similar, more recent analysis of the clothing industry in Italy shows that the relationship between size and efficiency is the same there. Significant cost economies were possible by transferring sewing and pressing operations to specialized plants. Unit costs were found to drop by 5 per cent as volume increased from 100 000 to 500 000 units per annum, but by less than 1 per cent if volume increased to 1 500 000 units. The analysis established that 24 firms operating 72 plants of the minimum optimal scale (600 000 units) would be required to supply the total Italian market. Instead, Italy had 470 companies engaged in this one sector, an indication of the potential gains in efficiency which could be obtained from a more rational structure of firms operating several plants. Of course, issues such as flexibility, independence, avoiding union pressures and diversified production may account for the continued resistance of the industry to the benefits that could be derived from rationalization.

The evidence from various countries indicates that there is plenty of scope for rationalization and concentration across all product groups and all countries. Size alone is clearly not a solution to the competitive problems the industry is facing, but the current state of the industry's structure in all the countries studied does not allow for even the most basic investments either in technology or in product design and administrative support systems for the vast majority of firms in each country. Unfortunately, the family-owned nature of most firms and the fierce sense of independence that characterizes most of their management is a major obstacle to concentration in the industry.

2.3 Wage Adjustment

A preferred and time-honoured response of textile and clothing companies to cost competition has been to seek the lowest possible wage. They have attempted this by avoiding highly industrialized areas where alternative employment opportunities would push up wage costs, employing large proportions of low-cost labour such as women, immigrants or low-skilled workers, and by fighting unions with all available means. In most OECD countries the labour force has absorbed a large proportion of the adjustment burden, not only by seeking jobs elsewhere as part of inter-industry shifts of resources, but also by reducing their relative earning power. The weighted average wage in the clothing industry went from 73 per cent of the average manufacturing wage in 1967, in the countries listed in the table, to 68.5 per cent in 1978. Exceptions to this general rule were countries where the level of contraction in the industry had been the highest (for example, Switzerland, the Netherlands and Sweden) or where it was expanding the fastest (for example, Italy). The textile industry, on the other hand, seems to have fared better in these terms since, it has succeeded in greatly enhancing its competitiveness through investment and modernization.

One major means of achieving wage reduction has been domestic migration. The experience of the United Kingdom during the first half of this century (Miles 1968) was later put into practice by its American and West European counterparts. Hence, the concentration of clothing industry employment in the northern states of the United States dropped from nearly 80 per cent immediately after the war to 51 per cent in 1970 and 42 per cent in 1976. A similar situation prevailed in other countries where the Dutch industry moved to Belgium in the 1960s in search of lower wages, Italian companies moved to the South and West German firms moved both within the Federal Republic and to countries in Southern and Eastern Europe.

The evidence from some countries is also fairly clear in terms of the employment of lower-wage workers in the industry. The high proportion of women, immigrants, older and poorly educated workers allowed the industry to keep its average wage at a fraction of the overall manufacturing wage in the country and to widen this gap over the years. The price of these actions was high employment turnover and resistance to change. As the industry contracts further and begins to require higher skills in keeping with the progressive modernization of its manufacturing processes, a key social and corporate problem will be one of training.

2.4 Product and Market Shifts

Probably one of the most successful adjustment strategies utilized by industrial-country producers is to move up-market and incorporate better product design, higher quality, more elaborate materials and accessories, or – perhaps more important than all others – to improve the distribution network and services provided to retailers. The philosophy behind such moves stems from a conviction that there is little the clothing manufacturer in a high-wage country can do to meet the price competition of developing-country producers. Given the wage-rate differentials, no amount of investment and automation can close the gap in the short to medium term. Thus, the solution lies in shifting the competitive struggle to non-price factors where, so the theory goes, advanced-country producers have a comparative advantage.

In general, an international market appears to be rapidly developing for well-designed, high-quality clothes, which are priced relatively high and are sold in exclusive and high-quality department stores and in significant volumes. Not all of the OECD's clothing industry can gain access to this market, but those who succeed are guaranteed relative immunity from developing-country competition. It remains to be seen whether production of these lines will remain in the industrial countries or whether the succesful international houses that pioneered them will also move abroad for their labour-intensive processes.

Evidence of the effects of these strategies can be gleaned from the continued importance of clothing exports from most industrial countries. An obstacle to this international specialization, however, is the continued protection given by most developing countries to their own domestic industry. Except for two notable exceptions, Hong Kong and Singapore, most major producers of clothing in developing countries are also heavily involved in protecting and supporting their native firms. While perhaps justifiable in terms of the level of economic development and their need to conserve foreign exchange, this attitude hands over to would-be protectionists in the industrial nations one of their most formidable political arguments to resist further liberalization in their own markets (Curzon 1981).

2.5 Foreign Assembly and Sub-contracting

Foreign assembly (known as 'off-shore manufacturing' in North America and 'outward processing' in European economic jargon) is the practice followed by many manufacturers in high-wage countries whereby home-designed and home-cut pieces of clothing are sent to foreign (low-wage) locations for assembly and then re-imported into the home country. In most, but not all, cases and with subtle variations in their application, most governments of the originating country will exempt the domestic content from import duties and tax only the foreign value added at the appropriate rate.

Not all is rosy in this business, however, as many companies attempting to set up assembly operations abroad have run into problems caused by low productivity, high employee turnover, over-zealous government bureaucrats, delivery delays and bad quality control.

West Germany and the Netherlands are the two West-European countries that have made the widest use of outward processing provisions in their customs regulations. Historical data show that roughly 12–15 per cent of clothing imports into West Germany benefit from special value-added duty provisions and that foreign value added is roughly similar to that in the American case. The total, however, represents about five per cent of West German clothing consumption *versus* one per cent in the United States. Although no breakdown is available for country of origin, various estimates are that in 1972, 59 per cent came from Eastern Europe and Yugoslavia and 28 per cent from Mediterranean countries. Similarly, it has been estimated that 68 per cent of all East European clothing exports to West Germany and 90 per cent of those from Yugoslavia consist of outward processing activities conducted by West German firms. In fact, West German manufacturers, through their foreign assembly, sub-contracting and direct investment activity are supposedly responsible for 40 per cent of all clothing imports.

The perils of processing abroad can also be seen in the experience of a French shirt manufacturer, Sunay-Fortier, a company that had sales in 1977 of 109 million French francs and employed 1000 people. The company used to produce low-cost shirts for large department stores. From 1973, when it began to feel the impact of low-cost competition from Asia it took three steps. First, it moved its entire production 'up-market' to 'fantaisie' shirts and sportswear. Second, it restructured its four plants into two (without shedding labour) and introduced modern automated equipment designed to increase productivity. Third, it began to import through both outward processing activities and by subcontracting the lower end of its product range. By 1977, one third of its volume was produced abroad. Following the renegotiation of the MFA and France's tough new policy on imports, the company found itself cut off from this source of low-cost supplies. After scrambling unsuccessfully for eight months to replace the lost sources, the company had to close its doors.

For the rest of the OECD countries, foreign processing arrangements are practically non-existent. Switzerland, the United Kingdom and Japan have rather strict eligibility rules and the Italien industry does not appear interested. They have their own low-wage suppliers either in the labour black market or in the Mezzogiorno.

The developing countries, on the other hand, can see major advantages in this direction. As a measure of their interest, nine countries had eleven export-processing zones (EPZ) in 1970. A decade later, the list had expanded to thirtyfour countries managing a total of ninety-six EPZs. The potential impact on jobs for some of these countries is significant (Basile and Germidis 1982).

Regulating foreign processing in clothing has been a hot political issue within the European Community for some time. Given that most such source communities benefit from preferential access to the Community markets (they are either associated members or belong to one or another preferential agreement), the Community has no legal right or power to control this traffic. In order to do so, the Community had to offer the Mediterranean countries reasonably generous outward processing quotas in addition to those of general applicability, which had been previously negotiated through a series of 'voluntary' export-restraint agreements (VERS) with most of these countries. The United Kingdom refused to accept these additional volumes and with French support asked for the drafting of a regulation. This process took nearly three years until the Council of Ministers approved it in February 1982. The Regulation reserves outward processing quotas for clothing manufacturers and imposes severe limitations on the use of materials not of Community origin. But the issue as to whether such quotas would be in addition to or part of other quantitative restrictions (MFA or VER quotes) has not been resolved with France and the United Kingdom who are taking the lead in promoting the narrowest interpretation possible (Woolcock 1982).

2.6 Direct Foreign Investment

Whether in support of their foreign processing activities or as a way to enter and aggressively exploit market opportunities worldwide, direct foreign investments by clothing manufacturers could provide another dimension to the adjustment process. The reality is that the level of investment in foreign subsidiaries is extremely low in general for all countries, particularly when compared to the size of the industry and the average propensity to invest abroad of most OECD countries.

West German investment in foreign production of clothing is mainly confined to foreign processing of clothes for the West German market. As for the French, investment abroad met both local production and re-import objectives, but in different markets. The Dutch industry's investment in foreign supply facilities seems also to be made mainly with a view to re-importing to the home market and only partially as a way of gaining access to foreign markets.

Other countries have much less in the form of foreign investments. American companies in the jeans sector have set up facilities in Western Europe and Asia but, other than a few assembly plants sprinkled around the Caribbean, there is no evidence of significant use of foreign direct investment as a way to enter foreign markets. Nor are the Western Europeans, other than those discussed above, very active in this sense. As the upper end of the market becomes more of a global business, investment abroad in key markets will become an essential requirement for survival in that product group.

2.7 Exit and Diversification

When all else fails and there is little chance left of adjusting to new competitive conditions, then the market may reassign the resources thus released to other more profitable activities. The French industry has lost an estimated 25 000 jobs per year since 1973 in both clothing and textiles and saw a yearly average of nearly a hundred companies disappear. In 1981–82, the American industry was shrinking at a rate of two to three hundred companies per annum. Some were relatively large companies with well-known brand names. In some cases, an option remains to apply the same technology to other markets. Thus one troubled French clothing manufacturer is now making seat belts for cars and other industrial textile products where the competitive storms are somewhat less turbulent.

2.8 Ability to Adjust

There are indicators that the industry's plight is not common to all its members. There are, and will continue to be, a number of firms that cannot cope with the intensive price competition that low-cost foreign producers can mount on a wide range of product lines. But case studies show (de la Torre et al. 1976) that domestic firms can adjust successfully to the challenge, or avert it altogether, by pursuing aggressive policies aimed at both the internal (productivity) and external (sales) sides of their business.

Manufacturing costs are a critical area for control regardless of the companies' strategy on other fronts. Successful firms devote considerable resources and effort to keep costs down and productivity up. The spokes-and-wheel concept, high capital-investment ratios, foreign processing facilities, large industrial engineering staffs and extensive efforts aimed at training and motivating personnel are prevalent among these firms. Size is clearly important, not because it allows for larger plants, but because it permits the firm to centralize a number of production services that it could provide to its various plants at significant savings. The chances for survival in the contract manufacturing business, however, appear to be severely limited, even when a successful costcontrol effort is in effect.

A second necessary condition for success appears to be a product-marketing strategy aimed at the leading edge of the fashion market. By investing heavily in a product-differentiation strategy that includes a fashionable branded product line and dependable delivery schedules, the firm can compete successfully at premium prices.

In the final analysis, management remains the key to success. The small family-oriented firm pursuing unchanging policies in the midst of rapid environmental change is not likely to survive unscathed. But if these firms were to incorporate external managerial resources attuned to the market-place and capable of formulating and implementing rapid adjustments in corporate policies as competitive trends develop, their performance could be extremely successful. Unfortunately, the industry, partly through its own attitudes and traditions, partly because of the 'bad press' which has been directed at it on many occasions and partly due to the sheer limitations of smallness and fragmentation, has never succeeded in attracting talented professional management to the extent necessary.

3. Future Developments

Projections are inherently risky. The last decade has shown both the folly of extrapolation and the economic value of flexibility. But decisions cannot be postponed simply because the world has become less predictable; moreover, there are many basic trends that can be extrapolated with some degree of certainty. It is unlikely, for example, that real demand growth for clothing in the industrial countries will exceed 2% per annum over the next ten years, irrespective of economic conditions. Significant growth in demand will, however, occur in most of the developing world, where population growth continues to exceed 3% per annum and income growth is also putting more and more people into the cash economy. Thus, the shifts of world production and consumption of clothing towards the third world which characterized the past 15 years are almost certain to continue in the future.

Most important, perhaps, for the industrial countries is the continued pressure that developing country producers will exert on world markets. Barring a near-magical discovery that drastically alters the manufacturing process (or indeed the nature of the garments themselves), the economies of clothing production will continue to favour producers in low-wage countries. The industrial countries' share of world employment and exports in the industry will, therefore, probably follow the decline in their share of production and consumption, but at a faster rate. The loss of competitiveness in export markets, combined with the productivity gains induced by continued competitive pressures will tend to ensure these results.

The prognosis would be rather gloomy, if it were not for one other trend of capital importance to the industry: the emergence in the 1970s of a global consumer for clothes with a high fashion content. Design, style and colour, as well as selective distribution, are the hallmarks of this market. Market strategies of product value and differentiation aim at a narrow segment of the market for clothing, i.e. the relatively affluent consumer who is willing to pay for the intangible qualities of excellence in design and a limited degree of exclusivity. Thus one can distinguish two broad segments with differing international competitive conditions. One is the relatively more functional end of the market, which accounts for the bulk of sales in the industrialized countries and an overwhelming proportion in the developing world. These are the price sensitive, low demand growth, and extensive distribution product groups where import competition has been felt most severely. Firms still operating in these areas in high-wage countries are likely to see their competitive position erode irrevocably over the next decade. Some will, of course, survive as they will provide insurance against the vagaries of international supply and owing to the difficulties inherent in serving a very large market at a considerable distance. But, import penetration in these product segments could reach (or even exceed) 50% under free trade conditions in most industrial countries.

The keys to success are very different in the second segment of the market and are only partially related to cost. Quickness of reaction, the ability to incorporate new trends and designs into production schedules, flexibility in operations, relatively good access to quality fabric suppliers, proximity to major centres of demand, and intimate and service-intensive relationships with distribution channels are the factors that determine success in these product markets. Location near the principal and wealthier consumer markets is essential, therefore, even though some of the manufacturing and assembly may in fact be carried out in low-wage countries. For these product lines, the bulk of the added value, from fibre production to final sale, will accrue to citizens of the developed countries. As this segment of the industry is growing rapidly and is also expanding into the middle-income developing countries, the opportunities for successful adjustment strategies in this direction would seem to be plentiful.

The successful clothing companies of the next decade will have to become truly international in order to achieve the customer base necessary to capitalize on investments in design and product image. Thus the establishment of international distribution and marketing operations are a prerequisite for assuring domestic success. In addition, manufacturing operations will tend to reflect conflicting requirements for scale, proximity of market and fabric suppliers, and competitive labour costs. How best to balance these claims will be a function of the product and market circumstances of each firm.

4. Protection as a Policy

The implication of these trends for employment in the industrial countries are unequivocal: the number of jobs in the industry will continue to contract. To the extent that a broader distribution of the costs of adjustment is deemed desirable, the state will intervene to assure it. How then can such intervention be made compatible with the inevitable long-term evolution of the industry?

The most widely used approach has been to tighteen the provisions of existing trading arrangements. Advantages of this strategy are, for one, that the effective level of protection can be manipulated to sustain only those firms with some chance of success in the long-term, while letting the marginal ones disappear. Protection is also relatively easy to implement, enjoys a clear and vociferous constituency, and the costs associated with it are widespread, difficult to evaluate and of not immediate consequence to policy makers.

But the costs associated with protection are present and real. For one, protection delays inevitable adjustments to the point where their magnitude makes them far more difficult to absorb. Secondly, it diverts the energies of the good firms in the industry form the necessary transformation toward global market segments, by encouraging them instead to serve the vulnerable domestic markets now under protection. Thirdly, the costs of providing special measures of protection to the industry will grow as more and more low-cost producers try to enter but are excluded from the market. Finally, and most importantly, protection tends to extend its lease on life unchallenged once initiated. Expectations of automatic renewal of quota restrictions are self-fulfilling in the sense that they remove the incentive to design and implement an appropriate adjustment programme and so establish the basis for further renewals of the arrangements.

Bibliography

Basile, A./Germidis, D: *Politiques d'attraction des investissements étrangers orientés vers l'exportation: le rôle des zones franches industrielles d'exportation.* OECD Development Centre, Paris 1982.

De la Torre, J./Stobaugh, R. B.: *Nine Investments Abroad and their Impact at Home.* Harvard University Press, Boston 1976.

Kurt Salmon Associates ed.: *The 1980s: The Decade for Technology, a Report prepared for the Commission of the European Community.* December 1979.

Miles, C.: *Lancashire Textiles: A Case Study of Industrial Change.* Cambridge University Press, Cambridge 1968.

Woolcock, S.: Textiles and Clothing. In: Turner, L./McMullen, N. eds.: *The Newly Industrializing Countries, Trade and Adjustment.* George Allen & Unwin, London 1982.

The European Microelectronics Industry and New Technologies

Klaus Macharzina

Summary

Analysis of the position of information technology oriented markets reveals that European industries are forced to take into account the challenge of these technologies. The paper elaborates on the development and structure of the European industries in microelectronics and new technologies. The sectors using the new technologies are investigated with regard to the importance of microelectronic components. Also the design of appropriate industrial strategies and the types of public policies employed by the governments are discussed.

1. Europe's Market Position

Europe's position in information technology oriented markets can be summarized by the following data. Nine out of ten video recorders sold in Europe are Japanese, eight out of ten personal computers sold in Europe are American, 80% of Europe's consumption of integrated circuits is imported, the European market share in peripheral equipment has fallen from ⅓ to ¼ over the last ten years. It is obvious, that Europe lags behind the US and Japan considerably in the related industries. As traditional industries will become increasingly dependent upon the microelectronics industry European companies and countries are bound to strenghten their R & D, manufacturing and manpower development in this sector. Also in terms of skill and capability Europe's scientific, economic and social resources have the potential to satisfy the demands in the area of microelectronics and new technologies on a worldwide scale. At the moment, however, these resources seem to be underused as the following figures show. In 1984 the per capita consumption of microelectronic goods in the US was $ 19,5 per year while in Japan it was $ 19,0 and in the European Communities $ 21,0. At the same time, the yearly per capita production of microelectronic goods was $ 23,0 in the US, $ 18,5 in Japan and less than $ 4,0 in the EC (n. a. 1984). This shows that Europe has still to cope with the challenge of the new information technologies; if it would not be able to do so the survival of Europe's industries in toto is at risk.

Table 1: Relative competitive position of microelectronics related world exports

Product no.	EUR 4* (% of world total exports 1980)	Major producer in EUR	Evident losses in EUR	Best potential worldwide	Promising growth	"Battlefields" (winner//loser); (/ = undecided)
1	39.0	FRG	UK	FRG/JAP	/	JAP//US
2	40.6	FRG	UK	FRG/JAP	I	JAP//US
3	28.6	FRG	I/UK	US/JAP	/	JAP + US//EUR
4	60.2	FRG	UK	FRG	I	EUR + JAP//US
5	57.9	FRG	UK	FRG	/	EUR//US
6	37.6	FRG/F	UK	FRG/JAP	I	EUR + JAP//US
7	43.5	FRG/F	UK	/	F	JAP//US + EUR
8	50.5	FRG	UK	/	F	/
9	46.9	FRG	/	/	F/I	EUR + JAP//US
10	42.8	FRG	UK	/	F	/
11	49.7	FRG	UK	/	/	JAP//US
12	26.8	FRG	UK	JAP	/	JAP//US
13	57.9	FRG/I	UK	FRG/I	/	EUR + JAP//US
14	19.9	/	/	US	/	/
15	39.3	FRG	/	/	F	EUR//US
16	37.0	FRG/F	UK	JAP	/	JAP//EUR + US
17	42.5	FRG	UK	FRG/JAP	/	JAP//US
18	42.5	FRG	UK	FRG	/	EUR//US
19	53.8	FRG	UK	FRG	I	/
20	21.9	FRG/UK	F	US	/	US//EUR + JAP
21	18.1	/	FRG	JAP	/	JAP//EUR + US

* France, FRG, Italy, UK (adapted from Battele-Institut 1982, p. 51)

Key to products:

1 International combustion engines, 2 Agricultural machinery, 3 Office machinery, 4 Metal working machinery, 5 Textile and leather machinery, 6 Construction machinery, 7 Heating and cooling equipment pumps, 8 Pumps, 9 Mechanical handling equipment, 10 Electric power machinery, 11 Electrical distribution equipment, 12 TV sets and radios, 13 Domestic appliances, 14 Transistors, 15 Electrical measuring equipment, 16 Private cars, 17 Busses and trucks, 18 Car bodies and chassis, 19 Road vehicles, 20 Aircraft and parts, 21 Ships and boats.

Looking at Europe's export performance puts machinery, electrical engineering and vehicles into first place. These on the other hand represent products which will probably benefit most from information technological innovations. Table 1 reveals the competitive posture of microelectronis related world exports with respect to the range of products which fall under this category. Whereas the

Table 2: Ranking of Europe's position in microelectronics related commodity trade (adapted from v. Gyzicky, Schubert 1984, p. 36)

Products	Shares in world total exports		Foreign trade indicators		Europe's position
	1980	1990	1980	1990	
Aircraft engines	12	10	17	11	weak
Internal combustion engines	14	14	6	8	-
Agricultural machinery	11	12	7	7	-
Office machines	16	17	19	18	weak
Computer and related equipment	5	3	4	12	strong
Metal working machinery	1	1	3	4	strong
Textile machinery	2	2	5	5	strong
Printing machines	9	11	13	-	-
Mechanical handling equipment	8	6	15	2	strong
All other non-electrical equipment	4	5	2	6	strong
Equipment for distributing electricity	6	7	8	3	strong
TV sets and radios	18	18	16	14	weak
Domestic appliances	3	4	9	10	strong
Medical electrical appliances	17	19	-	-	weak
Electrical measuring equipment	13	13	14	16	weak
Other electrical equipment	7	8	10	9	strong
Private cars	15	15	11	13	weak
Buses and trucks	10	9	1	1	-
Aircraft and parts	19	16	18	17	weak
Scientific medical instruments	-	-	12	15	weak

Legend: Europe represented by France, FRG, Italy, UK

European development in this sector seems to be difficult to forecast – apart from the dominant position of West Germany in terms of its export shares in this product group and also its overall economic performance – there is some indication that Europe may have a chance to recover if it would manage to gear its technological development towards the microelectronics potential inherent in these products.

Analyzing Table 2 allows for some conclusions which point at the importance of measurement, regulation and control techniques (MRCT) which seem to have a high synergetic, standardizing and integrating effect. Consequently, the development and international competitiveness of Europe's microelectronics and new technologies industries will largely depend upon achievements in this area, particularly sensors, activitors, MRCT software and network technology (v. Gizycki, Schubert 1984, p. 37).

2. European Developments in Microelectronics and New Technologies

2.1 Integrated Circuits

The world market for information technology related products has grown to about $ 230 billion and therewith multiplied by five in the period from 1974 to 1983. A good indicator for the technological capability in the area of microelectronics is the integrated circuits market. About $ 17 billion out of the above amount account for semi-conductors and their components. In 1984 this market grew by 38% and it will reach a world volume of $ 1 trillion over the next decade. In 1983 the US share of the semi-conductors market was 43%, followed by Japan with 37% and Western Europe with 20%. Also with respect to the production of microelectronic goods the US take the biggest share with about 65% of the world production, followed by Japan with about 25% and Western Europe with about 10%. North America and Japan thus control about 90% of the market. Whereas roughly 50% of the world demand for semi-conductors arises in the US, Japan accounts for about 30% and Western Europe for about 20%. In other words, while Europe's semi-conductor production only satisfies about 10% of the world demand there are about 20% of the world production consumed in Europe. While in the US domestic corporations cover 90% of the American demand for semi-conductors and in Japan 80%, Western Europe must go to corporations outside Europe to satisfy 70% of its own demand (n. a. 1984).

Table 3: Leading manufacturers of integrated circuits in the US, Japan and European (adapted from Battele-Institut 1982, p. 23)

USA Company	Production Value ($ M)
Texas Instruments	610
Motorola	365
National	310
Intel	300
Fairchild	285
Signetics	205
Mostek	130
AMD	130
RCA	130
Harris	86
Total	2556

Company	*Japan*	Production Value ($ M)
NEC		280
Hitachi		200
Toshiba		180
Mitsubishi		90
Matsushita		85
Fujitsu		80
Tokyo Sanyo		60
Sharp		40
Oki		25
Sony		20
Total		1060

Company	*Europe*	Production Value ($ M)
Philips		160
Siemens		80
ITT		75
SGS-ATES		55
Thomson-CSF		30
Plessey		20
Ferranti		12
Total		432

In the line-up of leading manufacturers such as Texas Instruments, Motorola, Nippon Electric, Hitachi, Toshiba, and National Semiconductor, there is no significant European company. For the time being, Europe plays the role of the consumer in this market despite its good reputation in the microelectronic field which can be attributed mainly to the efforts made by the individual countries in R & D, production, and in customer relations.

For example, the Federal Republic of Germany (FRG) enjoys a leading position in x-ray lithography due to joint research efforts made by Siemens, AEG, Volvo, Eurosil and the Fraunhofer Institute. It is expected that these efforts will have a great impact on the manufacture of highly integrated chips in the future. Another example is Standard Telephone Laboratories in Britain which have achieved world recognition for successes in the development of gallium arsenid technology which is said to be *the* semi-conductor technology of the future.

A closer look at the sectors in which microelectronics have had a strong impact will illustrate where successes have been achieved, and where the Europeans must gain ground.

2.2 Information and Communications Technology

The fastest growing market in the area of microelectronics is data processing. The expected growth of this industry in the eighties is about 10% p.a.

The German Nixdorf group, for example, has shown which opportunities there are for growth and profit in this area; by constant expansion of about 20% per year over the last 5 years it managed to gain a reputable market share. Nixdorf recognized the growth potential of the microcomputer market early enough. Its success was, however, limited to this and did not apply to mainframes. At present only the US and Japan have significant computer industries on an international scale. The latter is expected to catch up with the Americans in the next computer generation. The US account for half of the world production and further 30% is accounted for by American based subsidiaries in other countries. The reverse is true of communications technology, where Europe has a strong international position, based on a high net density, a powerful supply capability, and a highly developed telex and data transfer net.

Only in Sweden and the FRG, in addition to the business sector over 90% of private households are connected to the telephone network. The European telex net has the highest density in the world and is three times as dense as the one in the US. This position can be attributed to the determined policy of the European postal administrations which set precisely defined technological objectives in the past.

Europe is the world-leader in digital exchanges mainly due to the efforts of West Germany which gained a significant position not only in domestic but also in export markets.

In the optoelectronics industry where there are ambitious developmental projects there have already been achieved noticeable advances by companies of the highly industrialized European countries. Outstanding results have led to the introduction of high quality products on the world markets not only in fibers and diodes, but also in optoelectronic subscriber systems. In the optical singlemode-fiber field, the British companies STC, British Telecom and York Technology are world leaders. A visible result of the technological standard will be the transatlantic glassfiber cable which will be established in 1987. From a more general standpoint, companies in France such as Thomson-Brandt, and in Germany ANT, Siemens and SEL have achieved highly developed glassfiber landline and submarine systems. Siemens has a leading position in shortwave laser diodes. British and French companies such as Plessey and STC, and

Thomson-Brandt, respectively manufacture high quality laser diodes, and manage to successfully market them. ANT, Siemens, SEL and Plessey claim to posses the most highly advanced know-how in the production of photodiodes. Technological developments in this area are the basis of efficient communication structures (Ohmann 1985).

A good example is the development of the local and trunk net in the FRG. Here the logical steps from analog to narrow band digital, and then to broad band digital technology were consistently followed. In a number of concentrated test series (BIGFON) with the transfer-medium glassfiber, the German Federal Post Office has tested the potential of the broadband integrated fiberglass local telephone net in seven major cities from 1984 onwards. After the successful completion of these tests, broadband services such as video-phone, data services and improved radio and TV quality will be offered in the Federal Republic in addition to the existing narrow-band integrated services digital network (ISDN). According to the present technical and economic planning, a glassfiber net permitting teleconferences, video-phone and interactive broadband services should be available by the early nineties. All existing services are expected to be integrated and connected to the user by a single glassfiber cable. Still in 1985 glassfiber facilities with transfer rates of 565 Megabits per second will be installed. To complete the planned development of a technically challenging communcation and information net which is to link up West Germany's regions with a high industrial concentration by 1995, about 1,6 million miles of glassfiber are to be laid. A stretch with a 140 Megabits per second transfer rate is presently under construction between Hamburg and Hannover (Arnold 1984). Apart from the German efforts there are attempts to research the potential of glassfiber broadband technology in France, Spain and Norway. These European technological achievements may well serve as an excellent starting position for world market activities. In order to speed up the development in information and communications technology and to assist the electronics industry in achieving a promising outlet in the international arena, the Federal German government alone intends to make research funds available to the amount of about DM 3 billion between 1984 and 1988 (Regierungsbericht 1984).

The development and marketing of a new fully digitalised mobile radio system represents another technically and economically balanced move in the area of European cooperation. This new broadband transmission system, designed for a high number of subscribers, will be developed by a Franco-German consortium including SEL, AEG-Telefunken and Société Anonyme de Telecommunication. The technology involved are cellular radio sets which bring about a fundamental change of mobile radio transmission. This technology makes it possible to design long-range mobile communication systems for data transfer using freely transportable, lightweight communication terminals which allow for high-quality voice reproduction and which are highly resistent to interference.

Finally, based on developed microelectronics technology, a whole series of modern communication services has been installed particularly in Great Britain and in the FRG. Prestel (formerly Viewdata) is the name given to the Vtx system developed in Great Britain for the transfer of texts or graphics using the existing telephone network. A similar communication system exists in the FRG, called "Bildschirmtext" (Btx). Subscribers to this system can use the telephone net to reach the nearest postal Bildschirmtext-Center and gain access to graphic or text information. The institutions which offer this kind of information are connected to the center by the Datex-net. The user spectrum of this communication service ranges from accessing current general information to home-banking. The "European compatibility" in this field is ensured by the standards agrees upon by CEPT, the European Conference of Postal and Telecommunications Administrations.

2.3 Consumer Electronics and NC Machinery

At present Japan's ten major exporters cover about 90% of the world but also the European videorecorder market and 75% of the European hi-fi market. The Japanese market share of numerically controlled machinery and robots is more than 50%. This remarkable success seems to be less due to technological superiority; rather it was the aggressively marketed and market potential-oriented products (Beckurts, Hoefle 1984) which proved the critical key to success, and less technical superiority. Restructuring measures which were undertaken by European brown goods manufacturers such as Philips, Thomson-Brandt, and ITT which among others rely on larger units and trends towards increased automation which are designed to strengthen European competitiveness on the international markets. Looking at the Japanese comparative advantages particularly with respect to the cost and public policy dimension it remains doubtful as to whether these measures will be apt enough to challenge the Japanese predominance.

The developments in information technology which are accelerated by microelectronics strongly affect the powerful European machine construction industry. At present, Europe is leading the NC machine production which accounts for over 200 000 jobs in the European Communities. Because of its great economic and technical potential for automation numerically controlled machines are of special interest to Europe's competitors, especially Japan; therefore, European companies are put under increasing pressure in the area of advanced numerically controlled systems. The enormous efforts which Japan has invested in this area are documented by the impressive growth rates of the past few years. These again are mainly due to the advantages of about 40% lower wages compared to Europe, nation-wide cooperation, and the availability of advanced microelectronic developments. The Japanese target to dominate the NC-machine market has not been achieved yet; rather they often miss the mark particularly on the European market mainly because of the medium-sized companies in Europe which are more flexible in fulfilling customers' wishes while at the same time offering more comprehensive systems.

2.4 Industrial Structure

The European microelectronics and information technology industry is highly concentrated. There are few vertically integrated producers manufacturing components and final products which mainly serve the domestic or even regional markets. Besides there is a large network of US and Japanese multinational business operations in which also European companies, particularly German and French ones, are involved by joint ventures. Transnational, let alone genuine European co-operation, however, is largely missing. Only a handful of equipment manufacturers possess a wide spread of development, production and marketing facilities outside their own country while transmission and services remain the province of nationally based carriers. National markets have been effectively closed to outside manufacturers by tightly-knit relationships between these carriers and their favored local suppliers. Traditionally these barriers have been underpinned by statutory monopolies conferred to state-owned telecommunication authorities, the so-called PTTs. In this framework of nationally segmented markets Germany holds the largest share of more than ⅓ of the European integrated circuits market while the remainder is split into segments of around 10% including France, Italy and Scandinavia, apart from the UK which occupies about 20% of the entire market. There is also a large concentration of the entire range of information technologies with respect to single producers which tend to cover the whole range from communication, consumer and domestic appliances to vehicle electric systems and data processing equipment. The same is true of the tendency to internalize application of memories and microcomputers within each particular company.

When looked at the production value of leading manufacturers of integrated circuits in the US, Japan and Europe (Table 3) there is a remarkable discrepancy which leaves Europe behind. This gap is expected to continue to widen in the future (LLT-Report 1981) which may lead to Europe's loosing ground on one of the fastest growing product markets of the world with a growth rate of about 25% p.a. worldwide and more than 30% p.a. in Europe itself.

The major problems which have caused this situation are inferiority in the production of high-performing integrated circuits and a low degree of independence in integrated circuits production (Friebe, Gerybadze 1984).

Also the structure of trade reveals a considerable disparity between Europe's performance in the markets for electronics based goods when compared with all engineering products with a particularly weak position at the high technology end of the electronics product range (OECD 1981). The result of this development led to the prominent negative trend of the balance of trade of information technologies with high integrated circuit contents (telecommunications, electronic office equipment, computer hardware and software) of all European countries since the introduction of microcomputers (NEDO 1983; v. Gyzicki, Schubert 1984; Sharp 1985).

3. Industrial Strategies and Public Policies

On an overall scale the industrial strategies and governmental policies of Europe's semi-conductor industry and national governments are said to have had causal effects for Europe's mal-performance in microelectronics and new technologies. The recent FAST-Report of the European Communities (Battelle-Institute 1982) relates four major strategies with the European performance in this area, R & D strategies, manpower strategies, market and production strategies, and technology transfer strategies. The findings of this analysis are summarized below. With respect to *R & D strategies* three strategic alternatives are discriminated as is shown in Exhibit 1: the leading edge strategy, the

Figure 1: Possible R & D strategies to remain in front in RAM production (adapted from Battele-Institut 1982, p. 68)

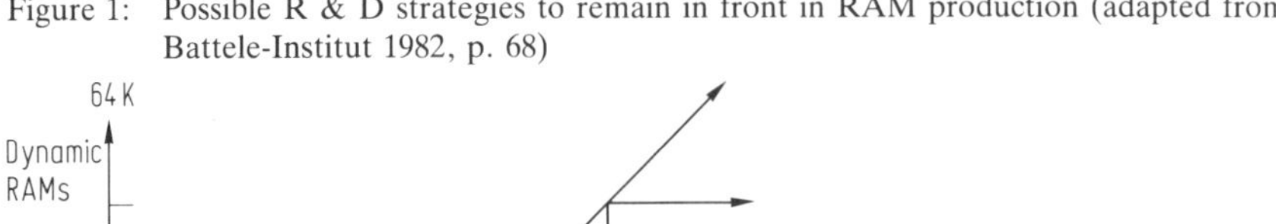

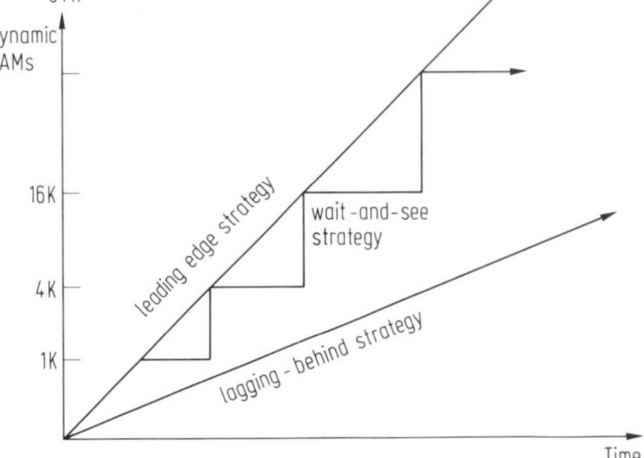

wait-and-see strategy, and the lagging-behind strategy. The strategic choice of the small, high-tech North American companies is certainly related to the first among these as is the second one to large capital US producers such as IBM. The third strategy represents the type of company which despite heavy and continous R & D investment does not manage to provide a sufficient competitive edge in the respective markets. This type of strategy seems to be representative of European R & D efforts which lack of application orientation and have a slow innovation rate. Specific R & D efforts of European companies are oriented towards integration with respect to increasing circuit density on the chip, the integration of the chip into its technological environment, and integration of lower level into higher level systems. There are several problems related to these integrative approaches which European semiconductor firms are confronted with: the problem of developing an integrated computer-aided design (CAD) philosophy; the necessity for these firms to develop much of the complex equipment needed on their own; the problem of interaction and cooperation between researchers on the one hand and end-users on the other, including the various intermediaries; and finally the inter-system oriented integration.

With respect to *manpower strategies* it appears that there is a shortage in European engineering skills which is caused by structural reasons and which was made worse by company specific devices to cope with the problem of qualified skill shortage. The shortage of semi-conductor engineering skills is certainly there but will become a serious problem only during the nineties because of the expected decrease of student population. On the other hand, there are qualifications missing which are related to electronics processes and application, and which are not appropriately covered yet by university curricula and/or company training programs. While national governments try to update university education in this respect the European semi-conductor industry has been reluctant to directly influence university training or to supply the technological equipment necessary for high standard and application oriented training. Instead industry has shown preference for expansion of their intra-company training and development programs in information technologies, and for adaptation of the technology to existing skill levels. While the first strategy seems to be a rather short-term measure incapable of curing long-term problems the latter raises the impression of a defensive type of emergency solution which may well lead to a slowdown of innovative processes.

The development of new technologies has brought about a challenge for corporate *production and marketing strategies* including the major problem of appropriate end-user fits and related test programs on the one hand, and the problem of occupying significant market segments on the other. The first relates to the problem of high volume standard integrated circuits markets versus unique customer integrated circuits production which does seem to be the typical feature of the European semi-conductor industry. Among the three existing strategies of a "combination type, specialization type and ULA-type (uncommitted logic array)" does the latter seem to solve Europe's problems best. Under this strategy chip production concentrates on digital problems and provides structures of prearranged logic cells leaving them uncommitted with respect to the customer specific desires. This strategy is also called semi-customized because after having specified the devised function in close cooperation with the customer the final layout-work is done to commit the array. In standard integrated circuits European microelectronic firms seem to rely on a limited number of computing circuits. This is because huge manufacturing capacities for advanced integrated circuits such as metaloxyd on silicon (MOS) devices are largely missing. These capacities include highly sophisticated process equipment for the design, production and testing of advanced integrated circuits. There are no synergetic effects between European integrated circuit equipment producers and users which results in a strategy where European leading companies do not attempt to challenge their major overseas competitors on conventional high-tech standard integrated circuit markets rather than specialize in leading edge concepts. This net oriented strategy may well lead to Europe's ranking on the extreme low and high ends of the microelectronics technology scale both of which lack of opportunities for a profitable or indeed intensive high volume market breakthrough. Other problems in this area include the necessity to develop a European market for automatic test equipment. With respect to application strategies Europe has largely withdrawn from the consumer markets and concentrates instead upon telecommunications. Also Europe seems to have been caught right in the middle of pull and push oriented application strategies. While the former puts priorities on market needs and application know-how which should determine R & D and manufacturing activities, the latter concentrates on advanced standard technology and innovative products which would then lead to adequate applications. Following the pull approch may lead to Europe's being unable to successfully enter the standard integrated circuit markets; the drawback of the push strategy, however, is the necessity of importing American and Japanese front-edge technology. Therefore, international attractiveness in terms of licensing and other cooperative agreements seems to be a precondition for Europe's future success in the high volume standard integrated circuit production on the low or very low scale integration level.

Europe's major trade in semi-conductor technology consists of imports from the US while the *transfer strategy* is effected through licensing, joint ventures, and mutual direct investments. In recent years there has been a slow but increasing technology transfer also from Japan. Europe's technology transfer balance opposite the US and Japan, needless to say, is negative in microelectronics. There are, however, signs of an improvement through increasing cross licensing, joint venture operations, increasing export shares of integrated circuits production, R & D effects of foreign direct investment in Europe and a reduction of the time-span between the licensing agreement and the marketing of the licenced product. Besides the approach of importing overseas technology, the intra-European technology transfer and the transfer to developing and industrializing countries may be in support of these trends.

Table 4: European R & D-Programmes in Information Technologies (adaptes from LLT-Report 1981)

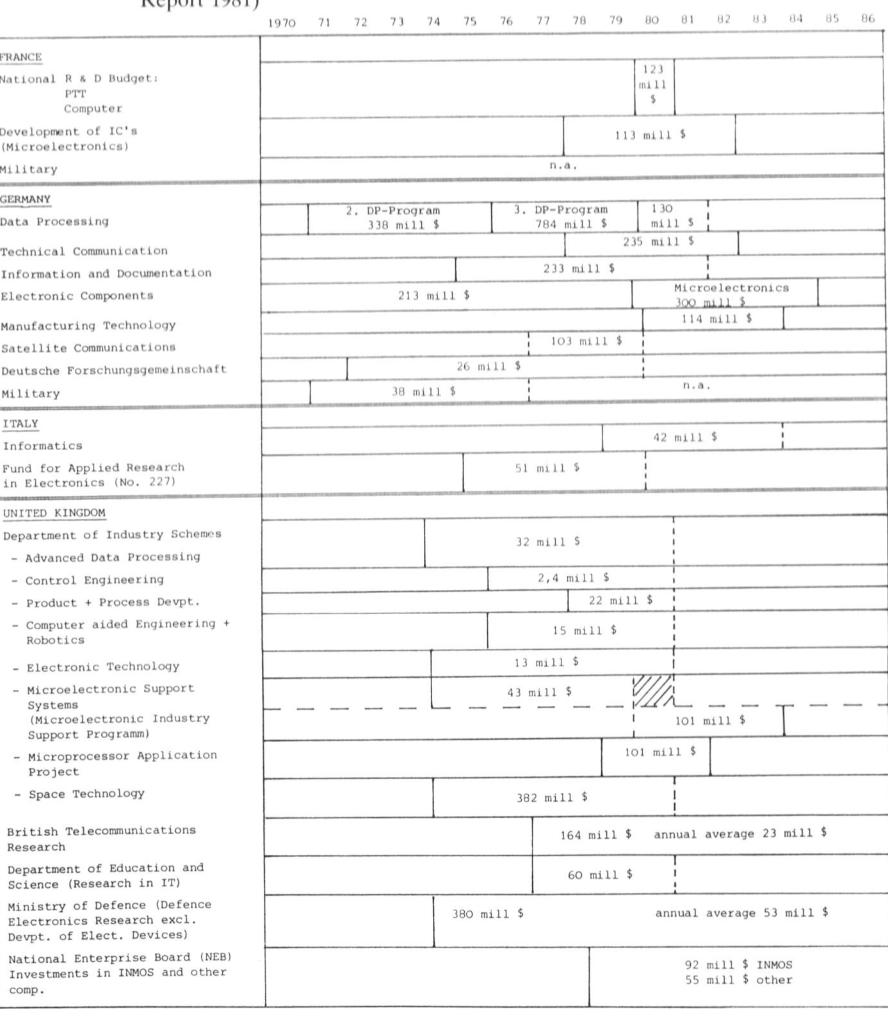

Programme	1970 – 86
FRANCE	
National R & D Budget: PTT, Computer	123 mill $
Development of IC's (Microelectronics)	113 mill $
Military	n.a.
GERMANY	
Data Processing	2. DP-Program 338 mill $; 3. DP-Program 784 mill $; 130 mill $
Technical Communication	235 mill $
Information and Documentation	233 mill $
Electronic Components	213 mill $; Microelectronics 300 mill $
Manufacturing Technology	114 mill $
Satellite Communications	103 mill $
Deutsche Forschungsgemeinschaft	26 mill $
Military	38 mill $; n.a.
ITALY	
Informatics	42 mill $
Fund for Applied Research in Electronics (No. 227)	51 mill $
UNITED KINGDOM	
Department of Industry Schemes	
- Advanced Data Processing	32 mill $
- Control Engineering	2,4 mill $
- Product + Process Devpt.	22 mill $
- Computer aided Engineering + Robotics	15 mill $
- Electronic Technology	13 mill $
- Microelectronic Support Systems (Microelectronic Industry Support Programm)	43 mill $; 101 mill $
- Microprocessor Application Project	101 mill $
- Space Technology	382 mill $
British Telecommunications Research	164 mill $; annual average 23 mill $
Department of Education and Science (Research in IT)	60 mill $
Ministry of Defence (Defence Electronics Research excl. Devpt. of Elect. Devices)	380 mill $; annual average 53 mill $
National Enterprise Board (NEB) Investments in INMOS and other comp.	92 mill $ INMOS; 55 mill $ other

The major problem with *public policies* at governmental level seems to be a defensive type of reaction which were not restricted to protective trade and tariff measures but mainly concentrated on subsidising and supporting the respective national microelectronic industries. The only common feature of European governments' policies seems to be a shared attitude to defend themselves against the US and the Japanese threat to their domestic industries. Table 4 illustrates time scale and scope of European national R & D programs which have been complemented by protectionist trade and tariff policies. These, however, could not prove successful to date. Moreover, there is a danger that the restrictionist stance of European governments is inhibiting industrial renewal and re-investment towards technological innovation.

4. Conclusions and Outlook

It can be expected that countries and regions which today are technologically, economically and socially dominant in microelectronics will also dominate national and international markets in the foreseeable future. Competition for the control of this key industry is, however, still in its initial stages.

Technological progress in Europe has been partly hindered by an estrangement of technology and by public negative attitudes with respect to microelectronics as a major job-killer. In the past, progress has often been hampered by a fear of technology; opportunities were not taken, and eventually there has been a European inferiority complex in that area.

Instead of taking risks and displaying entrepreneurial activities in nursing promising technologies, perhaps too much effort was spent on the maturing and declining industries. This prevented a necessary change in structure and weakened the innovative spirit. It is imperative for Europe to catch up with the latest technological developments, and to implement structural changes in order to resharpen the ancient Continent's competitive edge in this sector.

There are signs of innovative efforts, particularly numerous establishments of new companies and cooperative agreements. For example in Scotland, a new center for microelectronics has been set up jointly by American and Japanese companies such as National Semiconductor Corporation, Motorola, Hewlett Packard, IBM and Nippon Electric Corporation, respectively.

Moreover, technological advisory centers and technology parks are signs of a forthcoming European "technological spring". The closeness to universities of these operations is important because of the improvement of their interaction with industry and the possibility of an immediate transfer of research results to the locus of their application.

Microelectronics require an integrated strategy for the optimal allocation of existing financial and manpower resources, especially in research and development. There are a number of programs at the European level which support and promote research and development in information technology, for example the "Microelectronics Program", the "European Strategic Program for Research and Development in Information Technologies (ESPRIT)", for which the European Council of Ministers granted $ 650 million in 1984, and the "Forecasting and Assessment in Science and Technology (FAST)" program. There are further concerted actions launched without public financial support. All of these are first steps on the way to a meaningful European R & D strategy in the area of microelectronics, and towards a unified European technological and economic policy in this sector, as can be envisaged by the EUREKA initiative. There is a good chance that by way of such joint efforts the relatively abundant European resources of academic and intellectual capability, engineering skills and abilities of skilled workers will be put to best possible use under a new integral strategy. In case Europe will not follow such a strategy it is in danger to miss out on the potential offered by microelectronics and new technologies. Joint private and public action is necessary to gain technological and market control over the future of microelectronics.

There are many market opportunities available in the range between the microelectronic component and the complete system product. Hopefully, Europe will seize these opportunities and make significant contributions to technological progress. However, Europe's corporations and public policy makers who tend to implement short-term action too rapidly and hastily are to be warned that this may well end up in a failure. Rather a fundamental structural change of the industry should be followed module by module in an evolutionary manner in which case a more solid long-term international market position may be achieved.

Bibliography

Arnold, F.: Die künftige Entwicklung der öffentlichen Fernmeldenetze in der Bundesrepublik Deutschland und ihre Auswirkungen auf die Benutzer. SCS-Studien, Hamburg 1984.

Battele-Institut: Microelectronic Innovations in the Context of the International Division of Labour. Final Report for the Commission of the European Communities, Frankfurt 1982.

Beckurts, K. H., Hoefle, M.: Innovationsstärke und Wettbewerbsfähigkeit. Siemens-Zeitschrift, 58. Jg., 5, 1984, S. 2–7.

Deutsche Management-Gesellschaft: Kommunikationstechnologie im Wandel, Sindelfingen 1985.

Friebe, K. P., Gerybadze, A. (eds.): Microelectronics in Western Europe, The Medium Term Perspective 1983–1987, Berlin 1984.
Gizycki, R. v., Schubert I.: Microelectronics: A Challenge for Europe's Industrial Survival. München/Wien 1984.
LLT-Report: Long-lead Time R & D in Information Technologies. Brussels 1981.
NEDO (National Economic Development Office): A Policy for the UK Information Technology Industry. London 1983.
n. a.: Halbleiter-Markt wächst in Billionen. Süddeutsche Zeitung, Nr. 211, 12. 09. 1984, S. 27.
OECD: Microelectronics, Productivity and Employment. Paris 1981.
Ohmann, F.: Neue Kommunikationstechniken zur Unterstützung von Management-Funktionen. In: Deutsche Management-Gesellschaft, Kommunikationstechnologie, a.a.O., S. 55–57.
Regierungsbericht Informationstechnik, Bonn, März 1984.
Sharp, M. (ed.): Europe and the New Technologies. London 1985.

Part 3
European Concepts of the Managerial, Financial, and Personnel Function

introduced by Wolfgang H. Staehle

Every enterprise in a competitive society is faced with the problem of securing its long term inflow of resources. This pertains to the strategic behavior of organizations, ie. the system sustaining interaction between the organization and its environment. *Strategic Management* is concerned not only with external changes, but also with the preconditions for internal changes.

In Europe the fiscal science, with its emphasis on budgets and directive standards which are followed by control processes, may be considered the predecessor of business related administrative planning. As of 1918, inspired by a renaissance of the fiscal science budget orientation and an increase of controlled economic policies, planning concepts which focussed on financial and managerial accounting and on goal oriented business policies were developed in Europe.

Along with growing market instability the retrospective forms of analysis were replaced by a stronger utilization of forecasted developments. As of 1970, however it has hardly been possible to determine trends which lend themselves to extrapolary techniques, since virtually all typical environmental developments discontinued (eg. new types of governmental, union and consumer behavior). The environment could no longer be considered stabile. Market saturation, political and societal changes obstruct the possibilities of organizational planning in Europe. Hardly foreseeable events, suddenly developing threats, but also new opportunities are constantly responsible for surprises in organizations (eg. oilcrises, microprocessors, ecological problems). Such developments cannot be anticipated in time through classical scanning techniques, which rely on strong signals within and outside the organization. For these reasons it is necessary to research weak signals, a concept which has been made popular in Europe by Igor Ansoff.

While growth strategies were clearly emphasized until the late 1970's, it appears that survival strategies have gained importance in an economic situation in which there have been declining growth rates, market saturation, underemployment of capacities, structural problems (eg. coal, steel, shipping), mass unemployment and bankruptcies. This does not, however, mean that growth strategies are no longer applicable to growing industries (eg. microelectronics).

The central requirement for the survival of an enterprise is the continual cash inflow. Financing and investment as areas in the field of *financial management* are particularly important in expanding as well as threatened enterprises. Every measure in an enterprise has financial effects and is limited by the financial possibilities of the enterprise. The great importance of financial management also becomes apparent through the fact that enterprises which are not in the position to meet their financial committments at any time, must withdraw from the market (illiquidity or insolvency as a reason for bankruptcy). Strategic financial decisions pertain to such aspects as long term investment programs as well as the formation of assett structure which are adequate for the enterprise's development.

The choice of financing instruments and investment projects can only be made sensibly, if preceded by an extensive financial analysis. The objective of this analysis is to ascertain the determinants relevant to financial decisions, to arrange these systematically and to weight them according to the extent of their influence on the entire enterprise. A first approximate basis for the systematic arrangement may be given through the differentiation between external (eg. banking system, tax laws, capital supply, monetary value) and internal determinants (eg. assetts, liabilities, investment programs).

The fact that human input is fundamentally different from other input factors, accounts for the significance of *personnel management.* In contrast to objects like materials, capital goods, finance and information, which are employed towards the entrepreneur's goals, humans have goals, wishes and needs of their own and can therefore not simply be "used" as means or instruments by other humans or by organizations. In order to liberate human work from being equated with other input factors, which implies its exploitation, governments and unions in Europe saw themselves forced to make aware of the particular needs of dependently working individuals. While the state took measures by means of legislation (regulation of codetermination, job security and safety) the unions and works councils as representatives of the employees did so through tariff and shop agreements. This codification of industrial relations as well as the constant personnel cost increases (work time decreases, wage and salary increases and most of all increase in side payments) have lead to a situation in which management more thoroughly plans, coordinates and executes decisions in the personnel field. Beyond this, there has also been a greater emphasis on scientific approaches to business management in Europe. Thus employees moving into managerial positions can no longer meet the demands of such positions merely through experience and intuition. On the basis of management education at the unversities, management training, as the medeation of specific knowledge required by the present position, and management development as the advancement and further education of employees for future positions, have evolved.

Strategic Planning and Structuring of Organization

Michael Gaitanides

Summary

In this paper I attempt to prove that strategy and structure may be interrelated in various patterns. Structural implications of strategies are to be expected, whenever a paradigm shift of strategic planning occurs. However, a change in strategy content just by itself does not necessarily induce structural changes. Much more, the options for structural change are subject to the managers. Their ideas together with structurel constraints influence the choice of strategy. It will be shown, that conceptional differences between the Thesis of Integration and the Thesis of Segregation are responsible for the contradictory findings elaborated in the US and Europe.

1. Introduction to the Problem

Searching for the determinants of organizational structure, Chandler was the first in 1962, who brought strategy into discussion as an essential variable of influence. Since, not only in the US but also in Europe and Japan, numerous studies have been concipated and executed, which – from todays perspective – are related to this tradition. All of them follow the basic assumption that the interaction of strategy and structure is correlating with the success of a company.

Although, there is agreement in the basic assumptions of the studies, there are distinct differences in the resulting hypothesis and empirical results. They cover the whole spectrum from "Strategy follows Structure" to "Structure follows Strategy".

This paper attempts to sort the various contradictory statements and results. The search of the theoretical framework is guided by the idea to draw differences between the American and European studies.

2. Theoretical Framework

In order to sort the various studies I suggest a twodimensional frame of reference. One dimension is to show the degree of dependence between organizational structure and strategy planning. The second dimension is to show respective views of strategic thinking.

2.1 Categories of Determination (Between Structure and Strategy)

The first dimension can be divided into two basic models of thought.

2.1.1 The Integration-Model

The Integration-Model largely follows Chandler's view (Structure Follows Strategy), which states, that the organizational design is strictly dependent on the strategy chosen. According to this model the successfull company is the one which adjusts its structure in respect to the requirements of its strategy. While the succesful implementation of the strategy is verified by the operative actions.

2.1.2 The Segregation-Model

The Segregation-Model assumes only a minor correlation between strategy and structure. Here, the structures of the operative units often serve purposes different than those of the long term strategy. The structures of the operative unites are aimed to solve the administrative tasks, and have to ensure the continuity and stability of efficient performance. Therefore, the respective processes have to be shielded from external turbulences.

2.2 Developments in the Basic Assumptions of Strategic Thinking

Regarding the second dimension it seems to be appropriate to differentiate between three concepts of strategic thinking.

The origins of the concepts have been distinctively successive in time. Hence, they can be seen as "Generations". For the following we will concentrate on strategic planning, since all concepts are centered around this element of strategic thinking.

2.2.1 Strategic Planning of the First Generation

These approaches highlight the decisions on means and actions developed from well-defined, given objectives. Strategies are defined to optimize the allocation of resources. Strategic decisions are restricted to choose projects with consideration of financial outcomes. Thus, corporate planning is primarily financial planning. Forecasting future revenue, cost and capital needs are the main tools. Occasionally, sophisticated instruments such as trend analysis, regression- und simulation models are utilized.

The organizational model of the first generation can be called (in reference to Barney) Organization-Strategy-Organization-(OSO) model. Underlying variables of the development of strategy are information about resources, abilities and characteristics of the organization. "A firm applying the OSO-model begins strategizing by focusing inwardly, by collecting information about its own organization assets" (Barney 1983, p. 8). In the first phase (Organization – Strategy), organizational maximes for the development of strategy are core of research. In the second phase (Strategy – Organization), the essential assets for the realization of strategy are dispersed; if necessary, organizational changes are implemented.

External structure as well as organizational structure is conceptually excluded. They are not shaping elements from the dynamic process of strategic adjustment.

Hence, the possibilities of taking influence on the environmental variables are insufficiently developed, since traditional forecasting models are incapable to detect signs of approaching changes in market structures (see Gluck/Walleck 1980, p. 155). Thus, planning models of such kind will fail continuously, when encountering discontinuities. Organizational structures are excluded from strategic perception, because the system of planning is built as a "Bottom-up-System". That is, strategies for the achievement of given objectives are developed, implemented and controlled from the bottom to the top.

Without question, this generation of strategic planning currently prevails in Europe. However, numerous corporations show effort to supplement strategic planning with an enforced environmental orientation.

2.2.2 *Strategic Planning of the Second Generation*

The approaches of the second generation broaden the strategic context by incorporating the environment of the organization. They are labeled with terms like "Open-System-Model" or "Management of Adaptive Change" (Kirsch/Esser/Gabele 1978, p. 456).

In contrast to the first generation there is a shift perspective. The efficiency of an organization is seen through the eyes of an objective, external observer. Due to the "Outside-in-Orientation", the strategic planning process has an expanded frame of reference. Objectives are not any longer generally given. In order to set the maximes of planning, it becomes necessary for the planning system to overlay the "Bottom-up-System" with a "Top-down-system".

Strategic planning of the second generation can also be illustrated using the Environment-Strategy-Organization-(ESO) Model (Barney 1983, p. 5). In this model strategy planning starts by collecting information about all relevant environmental areas, namely, suppliers, competitors, and customers. This information of opportunities and threats constitutes a strategic challenge and demands strategic responses. The implementation of the chosen strategy requires organizational changes in the event that the existing organization cannot furnish the necessary changes.

Thus, the environmental orientation of strategic planning requires that organizational structure is an object of planning.

The allocation of resources is now a question of setting objectives, and no longer restricted to the selection of means. Consequently, harmonizing of strategic objectives and existing organizational structures becomes a subject of discussion. The conceptional flexibility of the system exposes the organizational structure to various influences. A contingency concept of structuring is necessary.

2.2.3 Strategic Planning of the Third Generation

Here, adaptive change is replaced by applying innovative and flexible strategies. This approach is also called Strategic Management. The fields of strategic action are extended beyond the boundaries of the organization, to customers, to competitors, and to resources.

The strategic planning of the third generation attempts a synthesis of OSO-and-ESO-models, where organizational potentials as well as environmental developments are made "Focus of Control". By means of a Top-down-Process, strategies are differentiated in respect to the prevailing Product-Market-Situation. Additionally, it is decided on the course of action and the resource allocation within the same process. Accordingly, there are differentiated demands on the development of organizational structure.

	1st Generation: Strategic Plng. as resource allocation	2nd Generation: Strategic Plng. as open-system-approach	3rd Generation: Strategic Plng. inbedded in Strategic Mgnt.
Integration Concept	Determination Approach 1. A	Adaptive Organization 2. A	One-House-Model 3. A
Segregation Concept	Learning Approach 1. B	Contingent Organization 2. B	Dual Organization 3. B

Figure 1. Types and Models of the Strategy/Structure Relations

2.3 Six-Field-Matrix

To illustrate the aforementioned dimensions in the proposed frame of reference, we chose a Six-Field-Matrix:

3. Types and models of the Strategy/Structure Relations

When classifying the existing studies according to the proposed pattern, the following aspects of the studies have to be clarified:

- What are the underlying assumptions of strategic thinking?
- What kind of dependencies are seen between strategic planning and organizational structuring?

3.1 Models of the First Generation

Model 1.A describes Chandler's thesis: the direct determination of structure by strategy. Corporations first search for strategies in order to solve oncomming problems and/or to utilize arising opportunities. Then, they develop a course of action (e.g. Diversification) to finally shape the appropriate organizational structure for implementation (e.g. Divisionalization). This almost classical thesis can be attributed to e.g. Chandler (1962), Wrigley (1970), Channon (1973), Dyas (1972), Pooley (1972), Thanheiser (1972), Pavan (1972), Rumelt (1974), Suzuki (1980), Caves (1980) or Chamberlain (1982). This core thesis slightly varied by the above authors, succeeded in the US, Europe and Japan.

Model 1.B comprises cases in which the decision upon structure is independent from decision upon strategy. Organizational structure results from a learning process (Ansoff 1983, p. 77). The learning process is initiated by e.g. imitation, fashion, cultural and national idiosyncrasies, tangible and intangible assets, etc. Sometimes, structure alters without a change in strategy. Furthermore, strategy is occasionally influenced by structure. Structure acts as filter, transforming information, indicating possible ways of action, developing solutions, presenting solutions, allocating resources implementing internal and external diversification. The relationship between structure and strategy is seen as a mutual matching process, rather than a sequential one. Models of this genre are suggested by Rumelt (1974), Mussche (1974), Pavan (1972), Channon (1973), Franko (1974), Galbraith/Nathanson (1978), Hall/Saias (1980).

Notable is that the European followers of this thesis do not principally reject the model 1.A. However, they engage more heavily in the discussion about the autonomy of model 1.B.

3.2 Models of the Second Generation

Models of the second generation, compared to the model 1.A, are more specific. They draw a more detailed picture of the relationship between diversification as an initiating factor and divisionalization as a resulting structural change. For this purpose strategy is differentiated. Additional variables influencing structure are emphasized. Strategy is regarded as a context variable which is confronted with structure as dependent variable. Both models (2.A/2.B) recommend a contingent approach, for organizational structuring when the choice of strategy is concerned.

The model 2.A does not constitute a correlation between strategy and structure per se. Rather, the authors in question designed a typology of strategic context (see especially Miles/Snow 1978; Miller 1979). This opens a wide spectrum of possible constellations concerning environmental settings, strategy, and structure. Simultaneously the authors make clear recommendations to the extent of decentralization, innovation, control. etc. necessary in certain situations and under specific strategies.

Followers of the model 2.B reject any automatism among strategy and structure. Their view is based on numerous empirical research, which uncovered many variables influencing structure by, or without, strategy. Fundamental for all of them are the studies of Lawrence/Lorsch (1969), Burns/Stalker (1961), Woodward (1965), and members of the Aston Group, who stress the influence of technology, size, and environment for organizational structure. Others (Child 1972; Khandwalla 1976; Paine/Anderson 1977; Miller 1979; Kreder 1983; etc.) reduced the directness of the influence by recognizing that every organization in its specific situation commands strategic choices for altering its structure (strategy as intervening variable).

Coexisting are a series of findings, in which strategy is not an intervening variable. But it is competing with other conditions influencing structure. It is indicated that especially Market-Structure (namely competition and financial power) is able to determine internal structure (Galbraith/Nathanson 1978, with reference to Williamson 1970, 1975). These authors stress, that the uncertainty caused by the environment influences internal structuring through the transaction costs. Seen under this perspective the influence of strategy is clearly reduced.

In West Germany, Gabele (1981) particularly recognized the initiating function strategy has as a competing variable for the process or reorganization.

The competing variables are:

- Insufficiencies of managerial behavior
- Environmental- and strategical changes

- Insufficiencies of managerial structure
- Outside information

Among these, environmental- and strategic changes play a dominant role, whenever new organizational structures are drafted and initiated. Here, without doubt, growth is a vital underlying factor but not solely responsible for structural change.

Weighting the findings of the base model 2, it is evident that in Europe differences between integrative and segregative views of strategy and structure are much more discussed, than in the US.

3.3 Models of the Third Generation

The models of the third generation differ among themselves by the principles of grouping they use. Strategic structuring (dependent on strategic planning) relies on the differentiated criteria of the Product-Market-Situation. Whereas, the operative structuring requires only simpler (functional and divisional) criteria. Therefore, the "One-House-Model" (3.A) demands according to the thesis of integration, an equality of strategic business units (SBU's) and operative units. For both of them, the same principles of structure have to be applied. This is achieved by adjusting the operative line-structure to the SBU-structure.

The advantage of this model lies in the fact, that each singular SBU-strategy can be executed within one area of responsibility. However, there are difficulties to enforce structural changes along with every change in strategy, since this would enhance an unwanted independence of the SBU's (Henzler 1978).

Not at last because of this possible unwanted outcome, Szyperski/Winand (1979) propose a seperation between strategic and operative tasks. They call it "Dual Organization" (3.B) when the existing operative attribution of tasks (primary organization) is overlayed by a strategic one (secondary organization). The following combinations are possible:

- primary and secondary organization are identical
- a secondary unit controls several primary units
- a primary unit encloses several secondary units
- a SBU encloses subareas of several operating units

With respect to the twofold task diverging, respectively conflicting areas of responsibility, between strategic and operative structure exist. Strictly following this principle of duality it asks for dual job assignments.

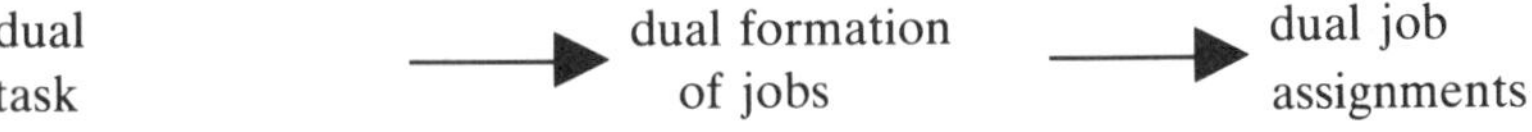

The clear advantage achieved by the assignment of tasks is opposed by several disadvantages; e.g. tedious processes of adjustment, higher labor costs. As a result, team-approaches are prefered in practice (Lessing/Groeger 1983; Schmidt-Offhaus 1983). The SBU's are represented by Task Forces with staff-functions and/or by representatives of the operative units. They perform their strategic tasks using a matrix-like structure (Graf von Faber-Castell/Steinmann 1983, p. 1072). In both cases the dual grouping is supposed to underline the strategic aspect. The operative unites are invited to a dialog about strategic perspectives, in order to widen their short-term-success-orientation.

4. Types of Strategy Change and Resulting Consequences for Organizational Structuring

In the first step we succeeded in sorting out the numerous findings concerning the relationship between strategy and structure, by the means of the Six-Field-Matrix. The question, how the contradictions between integration- and segregation-concepts can be solved, remains to be answered.

First, these contradictions can be seen with respect to the underlying assumptions of strategic planning, and second with respect to the content of the strategic plan.

One way of altering strategy is done by choosing a new angle of perception, meaning the shift from one generation of strategic planning to another. By doing so a paradigm shift of strategic thinking is marked. This shift is not necessarily accompanied by a change of strategic content.

Another way ist to change the focus. This means the choice between different strategic actions, while staying in the given paradigm. This spectrum of strategic alternatives can be described as follows (Rowe/Mason/Dickel 1982, pp. 35):

- Status quo
- Concentration
- Horizontal } Integration
- Vertical }
- Diversification
- Joint ventures
- Retrenchment
- Divestiture
- Liquidation
- Innovation

Switching from one of the above alternatives to another therefore constitutes a change of strategy too. For example, assuming that objectives were not accomplished by the chosen strategy, one would substitute one alternative by another. The other way around is possible as well. For example, the implementation of diversification can be a result of an OSO- as well as an ESO-orientation. Initiating factors could be underemployed overhead capacities in the first case and unutilized markets or competitive pressure in the second case.

To sum up, a change of strategy can be understood as follows:

- Changing the angle of perspective, while maintaining the focus (a switch from one generation to another)
- Changing the focus, while maintaining the angle of perspective (staying within the paradigm given by one generation)
- Changing the angle of perspective along with the focus

It is mostly held that a change of the strategic planning system (change of generation) is accompanied by a specific change in the content of strategy (change in focus).

Facing this fundamental differentiation between angle of perspective on one side and content of strategy on the other, we can evaluate the above mentioned thesises:

4.1 Thesis of Integration (Structure follows Strategy)

Change of structure is strategically implied only if a change in strategy is accompanied by an alteration of strategic thinking (change in generation of the strategic planning). Hence, the thesis of integration is valid whenever a change in the angle of perspective takes place. This thesis is to be reasoned by the activities during the implementation and performance of strategic givens.

Fundamental changes in the premises of the strategic planning system principally demand changes in the potentials of the organization. Whereas here, organizational potentials are objects of strategic changes, they are subjects of the altering process in the case of focal changes. The organizational potentials are supporters of strategic change.

For example, if there is a shift from OSO- to ESO-orientation, then, in most cases, a change in the basis of grouping is required. It could be a shift from "Grouping by Work Process and Function" to "Grouping by Output" or "Grouping by Client".

In the event of a change in the strategic angle of perspective, planning and performing units are objects of planning themselves. Planning has the qualities of metaplanning, since the premises of strategic planning are planned. These changes have a guiding function for focal decisions, because they imply severe consequences for developing and implementing strategies. The rather funda-

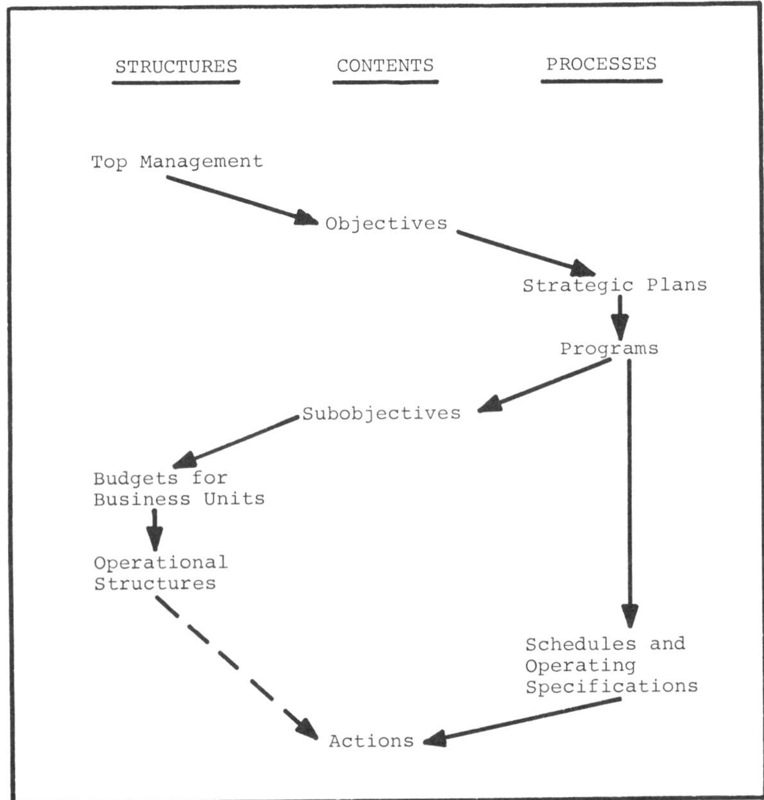

Figure 2: Change of Strategic Generation

mental quality of the change of generations (in comparison to the consequences of the focal change), becomes more apparent when on compares the respective illustrations (Fig. 2, Fig. 3). They show the different sequences of the changing processes.

A change in the angle of perspective is only realized efficiently, if the strategic objective is manifested in programs and action which are implemented from top to bottom. Job formation and job grouping cannot be decided on before tasks and programs are decomposed. Requirements on, contents of, and number of jobs within the areas of strategic plans are found with the help of operative tasks, which have been set to implement the new concepts of strategic planning. The planning sequence is the following:

Strategy ▶ Programs ▶ Structures

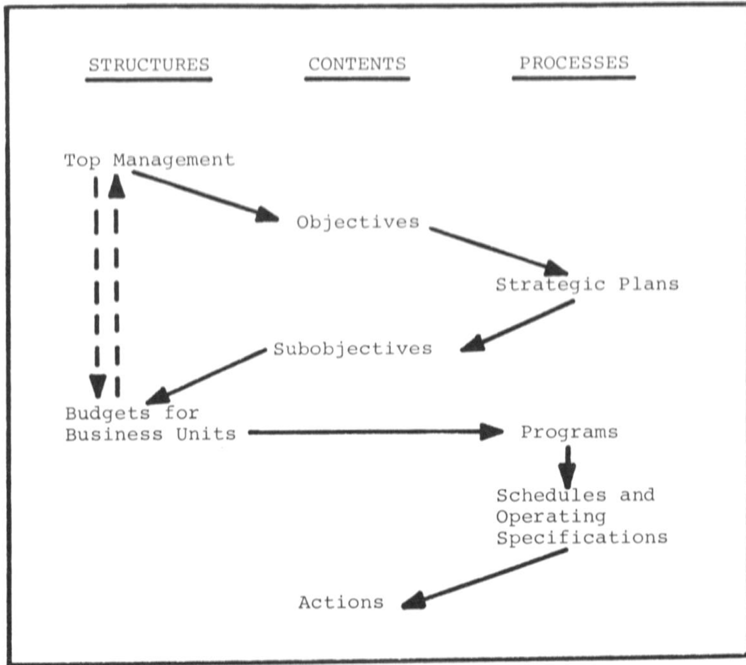

Figure 3: Change of Strategic Focus

------- Processes of Information and Control

——— Processes of Decomposition

Normally, a change of strategy implies, eventually with concurrent focal change, structural changes according to the discussed thesis of integration.

4.2 Thesis of Segregation

Decisions on structure occure quite independently from decisions on strategy. Structural conditions may influence the choice of strategy; in other words, mutual adaption of strategy and structure are mandatory for efficiency.

In the area of focal strategy changes a rather reversed relationship can be assumed.

The planning sequence here is as follows:

Strategy ▶ Structure ▶ Programs

Supports of strategy development and implementation are the respective organizational units themselves. Decisions on strategies and actions are delegated to them. The managers are responsible for design and execution of the strategic alternatives; they are especially responsible for its success.

The delegation of decisions as well as the evaluation of success requires existing structures. If the strategic focus is not altered structural conditions may constitute premises for strategic decision making. These structural implications influencing the development of strategies indicate the validity of the thesis of integration. Other factors of influence such as environment, size of company, and/or technology can dominate the impact of strategy on structure.

Not quite as obvious is the connection between strategy and structure when switching from an ESO-model to a combined ESO-/OSO-model, in the event, that the combination is to be implemented under the rules of the strategic management of the 3rd generation. In this constellation the different SBU's pursue different substrategies in the attempt to utilize various market potentials. Thus, these changes in strategy are restricted timewise as well as in content to singular product-market-fields. Consequently, structural changes, caused by altering the strategic angle of perspective, are often resulting (according to the Thesis of Integration) in adaptive processes of the operative work process. To avoid this outcome, mutual adjustment of structure and strategy is necessary, to enhance flexibility. Flexibility is crucial for the organization to implement a change of strategy with a minimum need for structural changes. This brings us to the conclusion, that organizational potentials ought to be dimensioned in a way, that changes in the orientation of the planning system only exceptionally result in a change of structure.

This is different to the cases where the focus of strategy is changed. Here, the need for change can be absorbed by the flexibility of the "secondary organization". Composition and targets of teams and/or task forces can be changed according to strategic requirements without interference in operative work processes.

5. Summary and Prospects

I attempted to prove that strategy and structure may be interrelated in various patterns. Structural implications of strategies are to be expected, whenever a paradigm shift of strategic planning occurs. However, a change in strategy content just by itself does not necessarily induce structural changes. Much more, the options for structural change are subject to the managers. Their ideas together with structural constraints influence the choice of strategy. As shown, conceptional differences between the Thesis of Integration and the Thesis of Segregation are responsible for the contradictory findings elaborated in the US and Europe.

Bibliography

Ansoff, I.: Methoden zur Verwirklichung strategischer Änderungen. In: Jacob, H.: *Strategisches Management 1.* Schriften zur Unternehmensführung, Bd. 29, Wiesbaden 1983, pp. 73–87.

Barney, J. B.: *Strategy and Organization.* Working Paper, Los Angeles 1983.

Burns, T./Stalker, G. M.: *The Management of Innovation,* London 1981.

Caves, R. E.: Industrial Organization, Corporate Strategy and Structure. *Journal of Economic Literature,* 18, 1980, pp. 64–92.

Chamberlain, N. W.: *Social Strategy and Corporate Structure,* New York 1982.

Chandler, A. D.: *Strategy and Structure.* Chapters in the History of Industrial Enterprises. Cambridge/London 1962.

Channong, D. F.: *The Strategy and Structure of British Enterprise,* London/Basingstoke 1973.

Child, J.: Organizational Structure, Environment and Performance: The Role of Strategic Choice. *Sociology,* 6, 1972, pp. 1–22.

Dyas, G.: *The Strategy and Structure of French Industrial Enterprise.* Unpublished D. B. A. Thesis, Harvard Business School Boston 1972.

Faber-Castell, A. Graf von/Steinmann, H.: Probleme strategischer Unternehmensführung in einem Mittelbetrieb – Ein Erfahrungsbericht. In: *Zeitschrift für Betriebswirtschaft,* 53, 1983, pp. 1066–1075.

Franko, L. G.: The Move toward a Multidivisional Structure in European organizations. *Administrative Science Quarterly,* 19, 1974, pp. 493–506.

Gabele, E.: *Einführung von Geschäftsbereichsorganisationen,* Tübingen 1981.

Galbraith, J. R./Nathanson, D. A.: *Strategy Implementation: The Role of Structure and Process,* St. Paul 1978.

Gluck, S. P./Kaufmann, S. P./Walleck, A. S.: Strategic Management for Competitive Advantage. *Harvard Business Review,* July–Aug. 1980, pp. 154–161.

Hall, D. J./Saias, M. A.: Strategy follows Structure. *Strategic Management Journal,* 1, 1980, pp. 149–163.

Henzler, H.: Strategische Geschäftseinheiten (SGE): Das Umsetzen von strategischer Planung in Organisationen. *Zeitschrift für Betriebswirtschaft,* 48, 1978, pp. 912-919.

Khandwalla, P. N.: The Techno-economic Ecology of Coporate Strategy. *The Journal of Management Studies,* 13, 1976, pp. 62–75.

Kirsch, W./Esser, W.-M./Gabele, E.: *Reorganisation.* München 1978.

Kreder, M.: *Situation–Struktur–Erfolg,* eine Analyse des Erfolgsbeitrags situationsadäquater Strukturformen. München 1983.

Lawrence, P. R./Lorsch, J. W.: *Organization and Environment.* Homewood, Ill. 1969.

Lessing, R./Groeger, H.: Führen mit strategischen Geschäftseinheiten (SGE). *Zeitschrift für Organisation,* 52, 1983, pp. 148–152.

Miles, R. E./Snow, Ch. C.: *Organizational Strategy, Structure and Process.* New York et. al. 1978.

Miller, D.: Strategy, Structure and Environment: Context Influences upon some Bivariate Associations. *The Journal of Management Studies,* 16, 1979. pp. 294–316.

Mussche, G.: Les relations entre strategies et structures dans l'entreprise. *Revue Economique,* 25, 1974, pp. 30–48.

Paine, F. T./Anderson, C. R.: Contingencies affecting Strategy Formulation and Effectiveness: An Empirical Study. *The Journal of Management Studies,* 14, 1977, pp. 147–158.

Pavan, R.: *The Strategy and Structure of Italian Enterprise.* Unpublished D. B. A. Thesis, Harvard Business School, Boston 1972.

Pooley, G.: *Strategy and Structure of French Enterprise.* Unpublished D. B. A. Thesis, Harvard Business School, Boston 1972.

Rowe, A. J./Mason, R. O./Dickel, K.: *Strategic Management and Business Policy – A Methodological Approach,* Reading (Mass.) et. al. 1982.

Rumelt, R. P.: *Strategy, Structure and Economic Performance.* Boston 1974.

Schmidt-Offhaus, E.: Führen mit strategischen Geschäftseinheiten bei Billstein. *Zeitschrift für Organisation,* 52, 1983, pp. 153–156.

Suzuki, Y.: The Strategy and Structure of Top 100 Japanese Industrial Enterprise. *Strategic Management Journal,* 1, 1980, pp. 266–291.

Suyperski, N./Winand, U.: Duale Organisation – Ein Konzept zur organisatorischen Integration der strategischen Geschäftsplanung. *Zeitschrift für betriebswirtschaftliche Forschung,* 31, 1979, pp. 195–205.

Thanheiser, H. T.: *The Strategy and Structure of German Enterprise.* Unpublished D. B. A. Thesis, Harvard Business School, Boston 1972.

Williamson, O. E.: *Corporate Control and Business Behavior.* Englewood Cliffs, N. Y. 1970.

Williamson, O. E.: *Markets and Hierarchies. Analysis and Antitrust Implications.* New York/London 1975.

Woodward, J.: *Industrial Organization: Theory and Practice.* London 1965.

Wrigley, L.: *Divisional Autonomy and Diversification.* Unpublished Ph. D. dissertation, Harvard Graduate School of Business 1970.

Strategic Resource Management: Securing International Competitiveness through Competitive Resources

Werner A. Borrmann

Summary

Traditional strategy concepts like the 'Product Portfolio' or the 'Product Experience Curve' no longer match the realities of today's business environment. However fruitful they were for the late 60's and the 70's, recent experience has shown that these concepts are too general to provide the detailed answers needed for the specific problems of the 80's. Strategic Resource Management is a new approach that combines both the strategic insights and the operational requirements necessary to gain and maintain superior competitive advantages for international markets.

1. The Situation

1.1 The Competitive Game has Changed

Although the slight economic recovery is currently giving some relief to a number of industries, the competitive game has changed dramatically for many European corporations:

- In the past managers could mostly survive all economic downturns and calculate on the next "century year" with its further increased profit throw-offs. In the 80's, however, they can no longer rely on the hope that strong recoveries will more than compensate for their losses incurred in past recession periods.
- Even core products suffer increasingly from the steady decline of traditional market growth rates. While in the past economic recessions have typically only led to temporary underutilization of capacities, companies more and more suffer from structural overcapacities.
- These structural overcapacities combined with steadily increasing factor costs for energy, environmental safety, and labor as well as fiercer international competition erode the earning power of companies.
- Temporary loss periods have forced management in recent years to prune their product portfolios to the extent necessary and to cut down cost, whereever possible. It appears there is not much leverage left in continuing

this particular path in order to increase profitability today: Buyers for unprofitable divisions are difficult to find. 'Friendly liquidation' is too costly. Massive employee layoffs may also be too expensive or even are legally or politically restricted in certain countries.

- Dwindling cashflows and interest rates that are still too high, on the one hand, and scarcity of basic innovative ideas and huge capital requirements for so-called hightech markets on the other, leave today's companies – in particular in traditional industries – little leverage to rechannel their cashflows into areas of higher growth.
- Thus, companies often find themselves in a position where the majority of corporate resources is tied to low growth, stagnant or even declining product markets. And they are stuck to it.

1.2 Consequences for International Corporations

The major consequences of the changed business framework experienced by many corporations today are threefold:

- Drastic differences between the cost structures of individual competitors have developed.
- In spite of these cost differences companies are often forced to compete on price in international markets.
- If companies try to survive in spite of an inferior cost position they often find that the well-known traditional strategy concepts do not match the new realities of today's competitive environment.

1.2.1 Drastic Differences Between Individual Cost Structures

Companies have reacted differently to the changed business conditions and have thus produced widening gaps between their individual cost positions. The following examples show these gaps within several industries.

Exhibit 1 compares two international truck manufacturers. While the European producer suffers a loss of 4.3% on sales, his Japanese competitor makes a profit of 2.7% on sales even though he sells his truck at a much lower price (−21.8%) to the final customer.

Exhibit 2 shows two manufacturers of surgical face masks. The first one suffers a massive loss of 30% on sales on the basis of his detailed but outdated standard costing system. An analysis of the actual cost position even reveals a loss of 60% on sales. His major competitor, however, shows a healthy profit of 15% on sales with a comparable product in the same market.

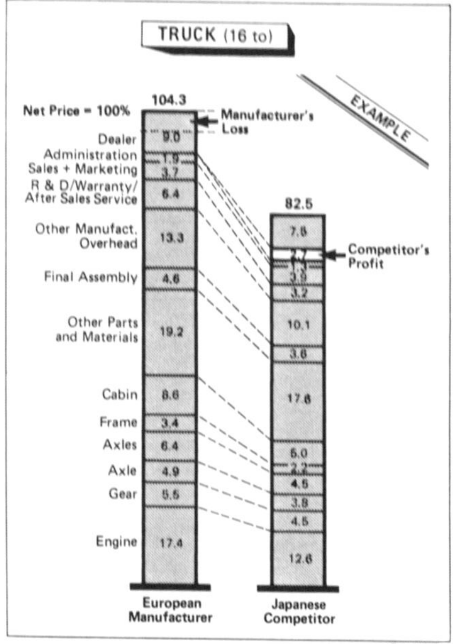

EXHIBIT 1

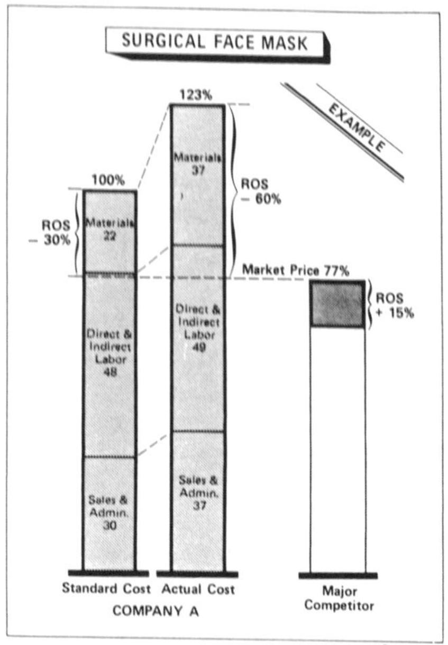

EXHIBIT 2

Exhibit 3 shows a cost gap of 34% between two manufacturers of extruded aluminium profiles for windows. The analysis of the various cost structures shows the major areas of cost differences in all three examples.

1.2.2 Necessity to Compete on Price

In most countries the traditional industries, where the conditions stated in paragraph 1.1 apply, represent far more than 50% of national industrial production and frequently an even larger scare of national exports. For those countries national prosperity depends to a large degree on the ability of corporate managements to develop and maintain superior competitive advantages on an international scale. The basic question, of course, is "how"?

In our work with clients in Industry, Trade, and Services we have found two crucial categories of competitive advantages:

- advantages in terms of user economics
- advantages in terms of price.

In the case of a paper manufacturer, user economics would override a higher unit price if the quality of the paper generated a better runnability, better

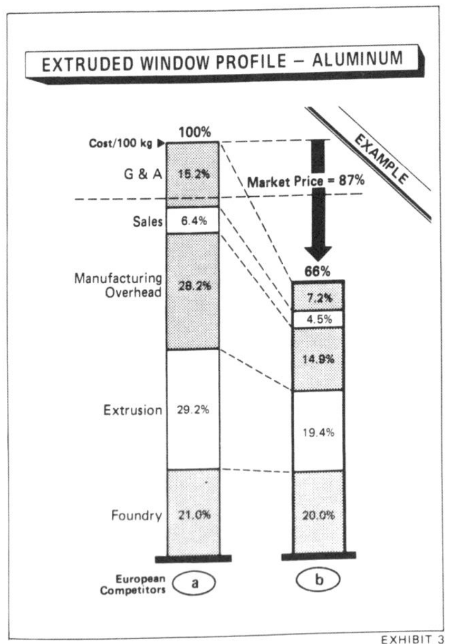

EXHIBIT 3

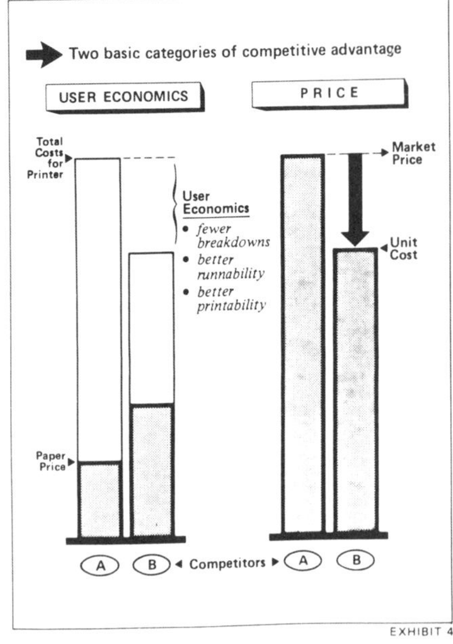

EXHIBIT 4

printability or fewer machine breakdowns for the printer, thus reducing his total cost (Exhibit 4). If, however, all manufacturers can provide the same level of user economics to their customers, or if the product has no definable user economics at all, unit price is the key factor for competitive success.

For most traditional industries it is the price that has become the major purchasing criterion. Profitable corporate survival, therefore, depends on management's ability to be or to become the lowest cost producer in the industry.

1.2.3 Traditional Rules don't Match Today's Reality

Well known strategy concepts, developed in past times of "go-go-growth", low interest rates, abundant resources and wide-spread diversification are no longer useful to serve as an analytical framework today for becoming the lowest cost producer. The experience of those times focussed management's attention mainly on products and markets. Customer needs were researched and, as long as a significant growth potential was suspected, this determined the necessary resources for developing, producing, selling and servicing the product. The rule, as so many strategy gurus told us, was to generate the corporate cashflow by simply chasing the products through the product portfolio matrix and by rapidly sliding them down the experience curve.

Those simple portfolio rules, however, no longer match our current business reality:

- Most products no longer show enough growth to profit significantly from the experience effect.
- New competitors which have far less accumulated production experience than traditional market leaders, enter our markets and sell their products at unit prices that sometimes are below our direct cost.
- Many of our "cash-cows" produce only 'sour-milk' or have dried up completely.
- After all the product pruning of recent years we no longer seem to be able even to divest our current lossmakers because we either do not find a buyer or cannot afford the redundancy payment, provided that government regulations allow heavy lay-offs at all. Or we may find that our loss-makers share the same resources with our profitable products and help to fully utilize the common capacities.

2. The Concept

2.1 Resource Management is the Key

Each business period not only creates new competitive requirements. Sooner or later it also induces the development of those analytical tools that are necessary to cope with the new requirements. In order to secure profitable survival in today's times of scarce resources, we must turn our way of strategic thinking through 180°. Rather than starting with dreaming up new product ideas, we must start with analyzing our current resources (e.g. machines, knowhow, systems, cash) that determine the cost of our products. We must identify their specific strengths and determine which cost-driving factors influence their cost levels. This allows us to reveal the hidden cash-throwoff potential in our resource base and identify those resources where we can be most competitive. And our most competitive resources then determine what products and markets we should concentrate on. In other words, our competitive success depends on our ability to identify and operate the most competitive resources.

If our products are not price/(cost) competitive in world markets we have to reconstruct their cost structure by reconstructing our resource structure. For this we have to close the gap which often exists between strategy and operations. Strategic Resource Management combines both the strategic insights and the operational requirements necessary to gain and maintain superior competitive advantages for international markets.

2.2 Seven Steps for Gaining International Competitiveness

Experience has shown that the following major steps lead to an effective and efficient restructuring of the resource base:

Step 1: Generate the total value added chain

A value added chain should be constructed for major products in order to identify the most important contributing resources. This value added chain should also comprise those value added portions that currently are not under our own control, no matter whether they be upstream (suppliers) or downstream, i.e. all manufacturing and trading stages between ourselves and the final user of the product. Exhibit 5 shows the value added chain of an aluminium framed replacement window. In this case the extruded metals producer contributes only 18% to the total value added process and thus has only a minor influence on reducing significantly the cost for the homeowner.

Step 2: Define the shared resource base

This step portrays the value added shares of all resources across the board and the extent to which they are shared by the various products. Thus we can get a first-cut understanding of those resources that have the highest leverage effect for possible cost reductions. Further analysis should then be concentrated on these resources.

One of the greatest difficulties often encountered in these first two steps is the inability of the current cost accounting system to supply accurate cost. In this case overheads especially have to be reallocated in order to create a realistic data base for the analysis.

Step 3: Define the major cost driving factors

This is a core analysis because it gives vital insights into the cost mechanics of our resources. Many possible factors must be analysed with regard to their leverage for driving the cost down in each major resource area. These factors could be technological, organizational, systems or qualification based. Cost driving factor analysis is a most creative process that requires highly trained and experienced specialists.

Step 4: Build up a resource portfolio

For all major value added contributors a resource portfolio should be constructed in order to visualize the competitive position of our resources. It is important that this analysis not only includes our direct product related competitors but also all companies that are major users of the same resource no matter what industry they belong to. In addition, technological development and substitution trends must be analyzed to identify requirements and timing of structural changes as well as their impact on cost.

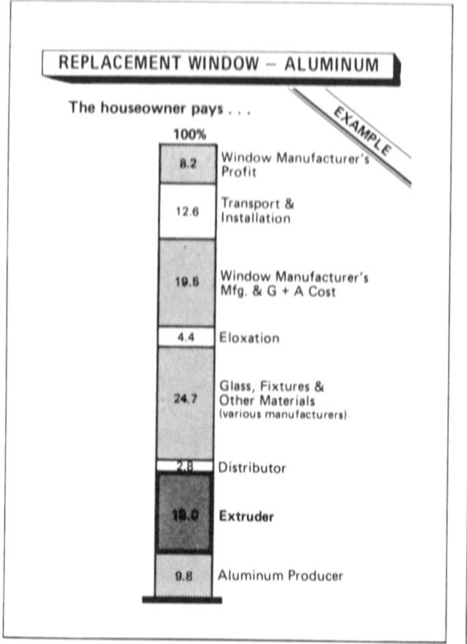

EXHIBIT 5

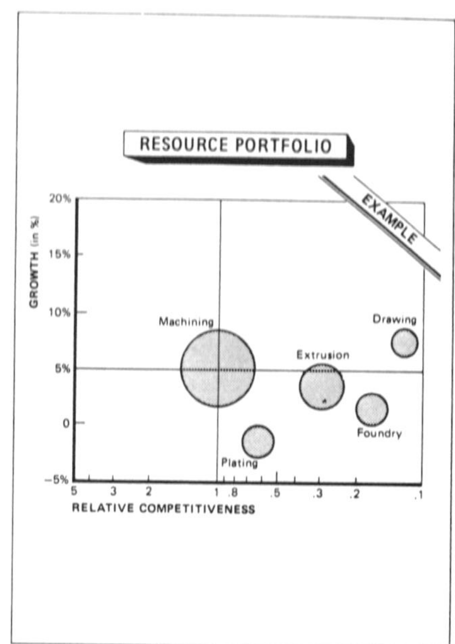

EXHIBIT 6

Exhibit 6 shows the simplified Resource Portfolio of a fittings manufacturer. He is least competitive in his foundry and drawing resources where semifinished products manufacturers have established more economic capacities.

Step 5: Construct comparative value added chains for major competitors

The preceeding two steps provide the basis for a direct comparison of competitive cost structures. They can be built up synthetically and provide a further basis for analyzing areas and reasons of competitive differences. Exhibit 7 reveals some of the differences between several European manufacturers of newsprint.

Step 6: Identify the cash-throwoff potential

Now we are in a position to identify the cash-throwoff potential inherent in our current resource base. Exhibit 8 indicates for a manufacturer of printing and writing paper that the cash-throwoff can be derived from either volume related or non-volume related actions. The volume related moves, of course, have to be justified by appropriate detailed market and competitive research. We also can see – for the first time in competitive analysis – whether we have realistic chances to match or overtake the leading competitor.

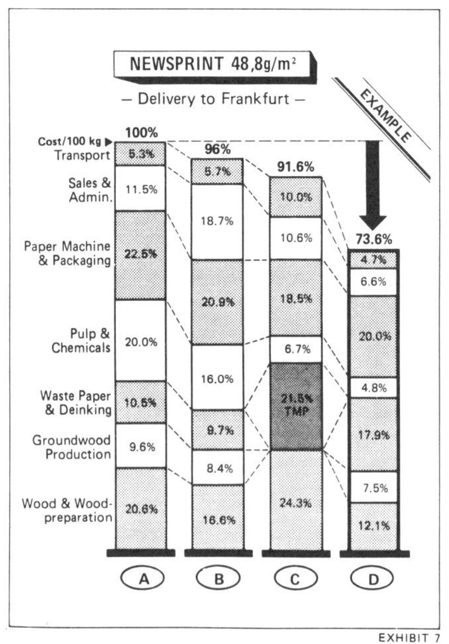

EXHIBIT 7

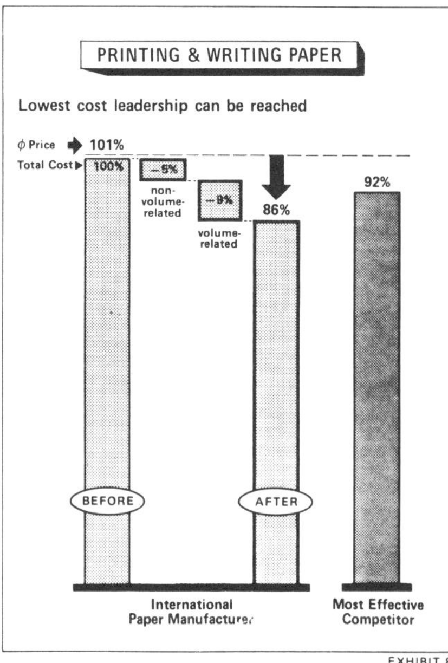

EXHIBIT 8

Step 7: Develop and implement the action programs

Due to the analyse outlined above, these action programs for realizing the cash-throwoff potential are much more detailed and realistic than so-called strategic action programs of past times. Thus they can bridge the gap between intent and implementation successfully – and results of strategic moves begin to show up in next year's balance sheet already.

3. The Results

Traditional cost accounting systems are usually not designed to identify the cost driving factors of the firm's resources and their cost dynamics. The identification of cash-throwoff potentials, therefore, is very time consuming. But without this time investment, there ist no reward.

Strategic Resource Management is the key to remould and redirect traditional thinking and behavior patterns. Rigorous resource analysis provides management with the competitive benefit of focussing all rationalization attempts on those resources, that are critical for winning the competitive game. A company currently suffering from high unit cost can realistically assess its chances to reach or overtake today's low cost producer. And today's low cost leader can design a concrete action path for maintaining his leadership position in the years to come. Strategic Resource Management gives a clear indication about which resources the firm should concentrate on and which one(s) it should divest. This sheds new light on the make-or-buy decision as well as on the strategic requirements of forward or backward integration. The more cash-throwoffs are identified, the more a new "financial freedom" ist reached and management can redirect the cash squeezed out of current resources to build up reliable competitive advantages for the future.

In today's business environment there are not many chances left. Therefore, it is vitally important to be faster than competition. Experience shows also that the process of restructuring the resource base needs fundamental changes in order to show results quickly and permanently. A strategy of many small steps that don't hurt anybody seldom bring the necessary rewards. He who first reaches the lowest cost position in low growth markets can usually stabilize this advantage for a longer period. Time, therefore, tends to be a particular scarce resource.

Future international competition will be won by those firms which win the competition of resources.

Success Factors in International Management: The "Turnaround" Case of a Multinational's European Subsidiary

Hellmut K. Albrecht

Summary

The case study analyzes the unexpected occurrence of major problems in the interactive process between a U.S. parent and its largest European subsidiary during a critical period of change: The daughter company's strategic environment turns from a seller's to a buyer's market while at the same time its formerly uncontested technological and experience curve leadership is disappearing. Strained communication between headquarters and subsidiary only improve when new objectives and strategies as well as a new organization structure, both oriented at the changed environment and competitive situation, are implemented.

1. Introduction

The following article represents the actual case study of a German subsidiary of a Fortune 100 American multinational. The author became associated with the American parent in the early seventies and worked in the U.S. headquarters in a planning, budgeting and control function oriented towards its foreign subsidiaries. Subsequently, he held the function of Vice President Finance, Planning and Administration in the European headquarters and eventually, in the late seventies, moved to the position of President and General Manager of the multinational's largest European subsidiary company.

Purpose of the article is to analyze the interactive management processes of communications and controls between the parent and the overseas unit as they affected the performance of the subsidiary company.

Obviously, the study benefits from the perspective of "hindsight". While this is something all case studies have in common, it is important to state that in the actual decision making process the element of uncertainty prevailed to a much larger degree than the "ex post" analysis would suggest. With regard to all success factors of management, concepts evolve, get changed and are influenced by important, unforeseeable event either in the market place (competitive environment) or within the company itself.

Another observation is appropriate: An analysis of management processes in their impact on a business organization's performance is naturally restricted to the objective, "outside" factors and events. The subjective, people and personality oriented factors are either left out completely or can only be hinted at in circumstances of particular importance. However, the author's experience suggests that such factors as the personality of key executives, their removal, retirement or advent on the scene; personal relationships between executives in the parent and subsidiary organizations; the often quoted "chemistry" between staff and line managers, are often as important to success or failure as willful structuring of organizations or processes as the result of thorough analysis.

For understandable reasons, case studies cannot deal with such subjective and psychological elements; however, it is by no means suggested that their positive or negative influences on a particular organization are just coincidental. Putting "the right man in the right job" (and removing the wrong one at the right moment), i.e. executive staffing, is very importantly based on such intuitive factors as "feel for a fit", the personality factors of a relationship between two key managers. etc.

2. Company Background: The Situation at the Outset

Both the American parent and the European subsidiaries are principally engaged in the manufacture of an industrial component supplied to the food and chemical industries. They are relatively old companies, established before World War I. While the German subsidiary is clearly the market leader in its territory, the American home market, the principal source of revenues of the parent, is characterized by an oligopolistic structure.

The process of internationalization of the U.S. parent is very typical and follows the classical stages widely described in the literature on the evolution of the international corporation:

- At the outset, strong position in the home market, based on superior technology incorporated in the manufacturing machinery.
- First steps outside home territory are to market strongly patent based manufacturing technology; establishment of a network of licencees; supply of standard manufacturing equipment to licencees.
- Since direct exports to foreign markets are uneconomical because of prohibitive transportation costs of the commodity products, the first direct foot abroad is set by taking minority ownership positions in the equity of foreign licencees.
- After World War II, European licencees lack the cash to pay royalties; this results in important increases of shareholding positions by the American

parent. Eventually, majority and 100% ownership of European subsidiaries is achieved.

- European headquarters is established with a "President Europe" who in turn reports to the U.S. based chief operating officer.

3. Strategic Position of German Subsidiary: Analysis of Strengths and Weaknesses

At the beginning of the 1970s, the German subsidiary company has sales of about 1 billion DM, 12,000 employees and is quite profitable, both in terms of return on sales as well as return on equity. Due to a market share of overall around 50% it enjoys strong competitive advantage, derived from its advanced position on the "experience curve". Its size is five to six times that of the next largest competitor.

The markets in the '50s and '60s had grown at a rate of between 1 and 5% above German G&P growth. Share of exports, again due to transportation economics, is negligible. The company had grown to its size through a series of acquisitions of competitors, and as a result has about 25 manufacturing plants which report into divisions organized along the lines of main materials used in the manufacturing process.

The overall organization is "functional", i.e. members of the executive management are in charge of manufacturing, sales, finance and administration, personnel, etc. All decisions, including many of an operating nature, are taken by the central management board.

In some cases this leads to extremely long lines of decision making, also in cases of conflict between functions at the operating level, mostly sales and manufacturing. As can be observed quite often in functional organizations, conflicts are often not resolved; but the operating level, frustrated of not receiving clear direction, turns to "sub-optimizing" in the direction of its own best interest.

Due to the strong growth mode of the market and the company's price leadership, emphasis on costs is not strong. In as much as it exists, cost management focusses on direct manufacturing costs at plant level. The company enjoys strong technical leadership; important process and product improvements lead to constant innovative cost reductions which make meticulous control of ongoing manufacturing and overhead cost not really necessary.

Another one of the widespread features of profitable companies that are leaders in growth markets is the build-up of overhead at practically all levels. Although they should have a clearly defined role limited to the manufacture at lowest cost of the respective product line, the plants are run by their general managers more like small companies in themselves. The accounting and control system highlights plant *income* performance while, within an overall functional organization, their accountability should have stopped at total *cost*. And as long as plant managers are able to "boast" about their profit contribution, the staff overhead which they have built around them is not challenged.

Central management at the same time felt the need to support technical and market development and also built up central staff groups. In addition, a new accounting and manufacturing cost control system had been introduced, based on the direct costing concept. While this in itself was appropriate and improved a firmer grip on cost management, it led to significant build-up of accounting and EDP systems staff at the central level. Faced with new reporting requirements the plant and division management added to the staff in order to comply with the new, more sophisticated requests by the central head office.

By the mid-seventies, important changes in the market had taken place:

- The strong growth of the fifties and sixties did not exist any more. Markets were partly maturing or already saturated.
- In view of the pricing policy which was not oriented at lowest manufacturing cost, competition had found shelter under the "umbrella" of the market leader and strengthened its position.
- As a complement to market maturity, technical innovation had slowed down and break-throughs in terms of new products, processes or in manufacturing costs occurred more seldom and were smaller in scale.

Against this background the major strategic weaknesses of the German subsidiary at that time can be summarized as follows:

- Executive management was not sufficiently aware of the change in market conditions which had occurred by the mid-seventies. Overall and business segment strategies were still oriented as the assumption of continued market growth and achievement of technological innovations.
- The functional organization structure contributed to shielding-off executive management from the actual dynamics of the market place. Overall size of market share was considered as the foundation of success also in the business sub-segments.
- Business segments and manufacturing units were allowed to "sub-optimize".
- Moreover, the functional organization had resulted in overcharging the communication process, both in the "bottoms-up" information flow to top management as well as the "top-down" decision making.
- While market and technology leadership was still accepted by customers and competitors, the image of the company had become that of a rather immobile

"giant" (in its industry) who, in comparison with competitors, had difficulties to react.

During the second half of the seventies, profits had started to decline which led to increasing frictions with the U.S. parent represented by the management in the European headquarters. Legitimate concerns and questions about profitability and strategic direction of the subsidiary were perceived by local management as undue involvement in the company's affairs. Answers had a tendency to be defensive. Major efforts were invested by local management in order to demonstrate that questions asked by the parent people were inappropriate because of a lack familiarity with and understanding of the local business and economic scene. Interestingly, subsidiary executives grew to become a closer team; but not because of a common analysis to the strategic questions; rather by setting up a common defense line in jointly rejecting the involvement of the shareholder.

As an interesting side observation psychological resistance towards this "mixing into the internal affairs" was even greater because it came from the never accepted European headquarters rather than directly from the executive level in the U.S. headquarters. A syndrome of "us, the frontline that knows" vs. "they, the ivory tower people" prevailed.

Looking at this confrontation, both sides were right, at least from a close day-to-day point of view. Questions asked and reports requested by staff representatives of the parent did indeed often lack understanding of the environment, business culture, markets and marketing habits. On the other hand, local management failed to provide answers to the strategic concerns while being heavily preoccupied with rebutting supposedly inappropriate questions. As long as top management of the parent was not satisfied with answers to the subsidiary's strategic direction, it very naturally spurred the involvement of corporate staff with a general "get involved", rather than a structured strategic dialogue at executive level.

4. Putting Management Concepts to Work: The "Turnaround" Strategies

In 1978, as the result of a loss of one geographic market segment, the subsidiary's financial performance dropped to break-even. Interestingly, the loss of this market came as a result of unforeseeable foreign government involvement and management could not be blamed for it.

The change in direction which is described in the following paragraph did not come as the result of a strategic study alone or the ideas of a particular executive, but evolved over a span of several months and took about two years to be implemented.

4.1 Business and Market Philosophy

The fundamental piece of analysis was a solid market segmentation. Up to them, the market was distinguished only through the different materials used to manufacture the products (metal, plastics, fibre/paper etc.). The segmentation highlighted growth vs. stagnation patterns, the competitive situation, product life-cyles, etc. It resulted in a comprehensive analysis of strengths and weaknesses by product or groups of products.

For each of these segments a matrix chart was designed outlining the position with regard to market growth and relative competitive position. In some cases this led to the recommendation of divestments of segments or phase-out of certain products. In other cases expansion of market shares or penetration into neighbouring segments were suggested. For each of the newly created strategic business units a comprehensive plan was developed, based on the analysis of strengths and weaknesses, market development and competition. In projected risks and opportunities associated with a strategy for capital spending alternatives as well as forecast of sales and income, resource requirements and segment employed capital returns.

4.2 Organizational Changes: Decentralization

The subsidiary company's functional organization was fundamentally changed in order to encourage decentralization of authority and responsibility. "Profit Centers" were established, generally along the lines of market oriented strategic business units. The unit general manager was given full responsibility for sales and manufacturing as well as all other decisions of an operational nature. One of the problems that occurred was to divide plants which, due to their manufacturing technology, and for reasons of economics, could not be split up in such a way that they would serve just one profit center. In order to avoid confusion of authority, each plant manager reported strictly only into one profit center, but had a service obligation towards others. The accounting was adjusted to include a transfer price system between profit center units based on total manufacturing costs plus a profit incentive. While at the outset this seemed to be rather complex and cumbersome, practical use, after some time, became rather smooth and unbureaucratic.

The profit center general managers were given relatively small but highly qualified staff support in the fields of marketing, controlling, manufacturing and technical who provided the liaison with the plants and the sales organizations.

In accordance with the new decentralization philosophy the role of central service departments was redefined. Functions such as accounting, personnel, administration, legal and public affairs remained centralized. This was done mostly for reasons of economy, i.e. it would have been more costly to divide the central service functions among the divisions.

It did not take very long until the profit centers had developed a distinct identity of their own and sense of direction, fostered by strong market orientation and the establishment of clear objectives.

4.3 Overhead Reductions

Along with the formation of profit centers went the reduction of staff overhead at all levels; starting with the central staff whose real support functions were more critically analyzed, the reductions affected the intermediate technical and financial staff in the divisions and finally the plant level overhead. The whole communication process in the company got streamlined and unnecessary reporting eliminated. In the course of three years the overhead personnel was reduced by almost 25%.

This was made possible because the top management's information requirements from the self-sufficient units became clearly defined and results-oriented. This was a major shift away from the earlier practice of central staff groups "wanting to know more or less everything that might have been of importance".

The emphasis of senior mangement's attention shifted from the details of day-to-day operational controls to issues of a strategic nature. This greatly enhanced the motivation of the operational managers and their staffs; their work became more meaningful as a result of greater decision making authority.

4.4 Communication with the Parent

At the time when financial results had reached break-even, U.S. parent involvement, directly or via the European headquarters, had become more and more massive. This reflected the parent management's effort to enforce new direction and have local management show a way out of the dilemma of declining profits and weakening of the unit's strategic position. While this direct interference appeared to be totally unproductive, at least in the eyes of local management, it was indeed unavoidable.

As soon as the subsidiary's new strategic direction and organizational change became visible, interference by the parent started decreasing. The communication process which had been overburdened with monthly, sometimes weekly reports on a variety of financial information as well as product cost changes, sales price implementation, material cost changes etc., got reorganized. Meaningful information summaries only on major operational events and an organized exchange of strategic issues were established.

In as much as decentralization became visible in the subsidiary company, it was possible to reestablish the same philosophy with regard to the interaction between the U.S. parent and the German subsidiary.

During the "problem years" the European headquarters staff had almost doubled; it did not take very long after fundamental change had been implemented in the subsidiary for the intermediate headquarters staff to be reduced to below the original level. Later on its function was reduced to mere accounting and technical coordination.

As could be expected, the atmosphere between parent and subsidiary improved greatly. Trust and mutual respect gradually took the place of accusations and defensiveness. During the period of decline capital controls were applied very tightly, and quite often local management did not even submit proposals for necessary capital spending because it was afraid of the difficult justification and approval process.

After only a number of years capital spending in the subsidiary increased; proposals for diversification were submitted and approved; in general, a more forward oriented entrepreneurial spirit with regard to the allocation of financial funds was encouraged. Financial results had improved significantly with the consequence of more attractive dividends paid to the parent. While earlier all surplus cash flow was immediately transmitted to the parent, funds were now left in the subsidiary in order to strengthen its financial position and provide the basis for its long-term future.

5. Conclusion

It is dangerous to generalize since each individual case has a different frame of circumstances, and the driving forces vary a great deal. Nevertheless, a number of conclusions may be drawn from the case study described above:

- In an international company, strains in the parent – subsidiary relationship will start to occur not only when profits and returns are actually declining, but already when a lack of strategic direction in the subsidiary company becomes apparent.
- The same local management that successfully directed the subsidiary company during an era of growth and prosperity may not be able to manage successfully during a period of declining market growth and increased competition. Very often there are psychological barriers, such as the pride of

local management which has difficulties to admit and openly communicate about a decline in its performance and success.

- Intermediary units in the communication between parent and subsidiary are often a disadvantage, in particular at times of needed change in strategic direction. Too much staff involvement tends to overcloud long-term issues and leads to preoccupation with detail as well as an attitude of defensiveness and irritation.
- Only the executive management of parent and subsidiary together can ultimately redesign and agree upon a new strategic course. During times of change solid management by objectives is more critical than at times of growth and prosperity.
- While there is no general pattern for "the best" organization structure of an international company, fundamental change appears to be easier in a divisionalized, profit center-type organization than in a functional set-up. The objective orientation of all management units will make it easier to converge these new trends to an overall company strategy.

Finally, some practical observations on U.S.-European management relationships: European managers of U.S. subsidiaries often complain about the lack of familiarity with the European environment and business basis on the part of their U.S. superior. While this is often true, it is indeed more important that the European managements be thoroughly familiar with the culture and style of the U.S. parent organization and its senior executives. What sometimes appears to be a lack of sensitivity and understanding back in the U.S. headquarters is often enough poor communication and interpretation of local strategies and important business trends by the subsidiary managers. Being a skillful interpreter of his own environment and actions has to be one of the prime success factors of a subsidiary executive. But in the process it is very important not to try and demonstrate "how difficult the job is" in view of the challenges of the local environment. The American top manager does not really want to know how much time and effort the head of their German subsidiary spends on co-determination issues, meetings with works councils, etc. What he wants to see is that in spite of all these hurdles local management sets clear objectives and implements the appropriate plans to reach them.

Financing Corporations in Major European Capital Markets

Otto L. Adelberger

Summary

Based on OECD-statistics, patterns and trends in financing corporations of major European countries are briefly outlined. Tax systems and regulations of personal investment incentives highlight some details of the institutional background of capital markets. Also a case report on financial innovation in West Germany (participation rights certificates) is presented.

1. OECD Financial Statistics on Non-financial Enterprises: France, West Germany, Italy, United Kingdom and the United States of America

Despite the fact that "... International comparisons are particularly difficult ... due to the vast differences in both volume and quality of the basic material available and methods employed for calculation and valuation ..."[1+2], the official OECD material published is the most comprehensive source of information on the financial positions and current transactions of non-financial corporations in a sectorwide perspective for all OECD-countries.

The following tables 1.1 to 5.2 provide an overview of some basic structural data of four major European countries and the US (for the purpose of comparison) by presenting sectorally aggregated balance sheet and flow of funds variables of non-financial enterprises in recent years.

1 Organisation for Economic Co-operation and Development (OECD), Nonfinancial Enterprises Financial Statements 1983, Paris 1984, p. 5.

2 Reference is thus made to the Methodological Supplements (also published by the OECD) "in order to judge the precautions to be taken in establishing international comparisons" (ibid.)
For more detailed and up-to-date material on aggregate corporate financial stocks and flows the official publications of the central banks of the OECD-countries should be consulted, such as Deutsche Bundesbank, Frankfurt, Bulletin; these publications are the European counterparts to the Federal Bulletin in the United States.

Table 1.1: Balance-Sheet of Non-Financial Corporations/France
Monetary unit: million francs.

	1976		1981	
	Industrial enterprises	Commercial enterprises	Industrial enterprises	Commercial enterprises
Number of enterprises	577	112	577	112
Assets	**163 869**	**16 051**	**304 959**	**31 936**
1. Non-financial assets	**89 844**	**8 059**	**158 197**	**14 469**
1.1. Net fixed tangible assets	33 627	3 417	46 981	6 255
1.1.1. net reproducible fixed assets	*31 538*	*2 982*	*40 773*	*5 283*
1.1.2. net non-reproducible fixed assets	*2 089*	*435*	*6 208*	*972*
1.2. Stocks	54 468	4 314	108 447	7 754
1.3. Net intangible assets	1 749	328	2 769	460
2. Short-term financial assets	**58 368**	**6 131**	**112 534**	**12 662**
2.1. Cash and transferable deposits 2.2. Other deposits	5 633	1 793	6 931	3 561
2.4. Short-term loans, n.e.c. 2.6. Other accounts receivable	8 889	1 980	19 220	4 440
2.5. Trade credits extended	43 846	2 358	86 383	4 661
3. Long-term financial assets	**15 657**	**1 861**	**34 228**	**4 805**
• Portfolio investments	140	56	1 060	354
• Trade investments	11 427	1 339	25 886	3 707
3.3. Long-term loans, n.e.c.	4 090	466	7 282	744
Liabilities	**163 869**	**16 051**	**304 959**	**31 936**
4. Equity	**46 217**	**4 058**	**86 206**	**9 163**
4.1. Share capital	21 175	1 841	30 237	2 713
4.2. Reserves and provisions	25 042	2 217	55 969	6 450
5. Short-term liabilities	**87 890**	**9 656**	**171 668**	**19 348**
5.2. Short-term borrowed funds, n.e.c. 5.4. Other accounts payable	38 079	3 204	73 526	6 772
of which: 5.2.2. loans from banks	*15 627*	*745*	*33 487*	*1 263*
5.3. Trade credits received	*49 811*	*6 452*	*98 142*	*12 576*
Long-term liabilities	**29 762**	**2 337**	**47 085**	**3 425**
6.1. Long-term bonds	2 427	593	4 483	658
6.3. Long-term borrowed funds, n.e.c.	27 335	1 744	42 602	2 767
Memorandum items:				
a) amortization of reproducible fixed assets	48 163	2 702	94 020	6 511
b) amortization of non-reproducible fixed assets	88	7	70	6
c) amortization of intangible assets	786	62	1 347	95

Table 1.2: Sources and Uses of Funds of Non-financial Corporations/France

	1981	
	Industrial enterprises	Commercial enterprises
Number of enterprises	577	112
Sources	**39 072**	**5 404**
1. Non-financial sources	*12 904*	*1 976*
1.1. Gross income finance (retained income before depreciation and provisions)	11 102	1 771
1.2. Net capital transfers received	184	7
• Transfers of fixed assets	1 618	198
2. Financial sources	*26 168*	*3 428*
2.1. Increase in short-term debt	**16 549**	**2 928**
2.1.3. Increase in trade credits received	4 825	1 959
2.1.2. Increase in short-term borrowing, n.e.c. 2.1.4. Increase in other accounts payable	11 724	969
of which: 2.1.2.2. borrowing from banks	*6 335*	*221*
2.2. Increase in long-term debt	**9 619**	**500**
2.2.1. Issues of long-term bonds	896	− 19
2.2.2. Issues of shares	1 470	103
2.2.3. Increase in long-term borrowing, n.e.c.	7 253	416
Uses	**39 072**	**5 404**
3. Investment in non-financial assets	*22 945*	*2 650*
3.1. Investment in tangible fixed assets	**12 117**	**1 674**
3.1.1. + 3.1.2. Reproducible fixed assets	11 998	1 631
3.1.3. Purchases of non-reproducible fixed assets	119	43
3.2. Increase in stocks	**10 160**	**905**
3.3. Increase in intangible non-financial assets	**668**	**71**
4. Investment in financial assets	*16 127*	*2 754*
4.1. Increase in short-term claims	**12 532**	**1 898**
4.1.1. Cash and deposits	− 3 813	160
4.1.2. Other short-term claims	16 345	1 738
4.1.2.3. increase in trade credits extended	*12 583*	*1 033*
4.1.2.2. increase in short-term loans, n.e.c. *4.1.2.4. increase in other accounts receivable*	*3 762*	*705*
4.2. Increase in long-term claims	**3 595**	**856**
• Increase in portfolio investments	128	206
• Increase in trade investments	2 469	519
4.2.3. Increase in long-term loans, n.e.c.	998	131

Table 2.1: Balance-Sheet of Non-financial Enterprises/Germany
Monetary unit: billion DM.

	1976	*1981*
Assets	**1 330.1**	**1 819.5**
1. Non-financial assets	**755.0**	**998.9**
1.1. Net fixed tangible assets[2]	478.6	584.7
1.2. Stocks	276.4	414.2
1.3. Intangible assets[3]	. . .	. . .
2. Short-term financial assets	**442.5**	**617.0**
2.1. Cash and transferable deposits	55.8	64.7
2.2. Other deposits 2.3. Short-term bills and bonds 2.4. Short-term loans, n.e.c. 2.5. Trade credits extended 2.6. Other accounts receivable	386.7	552.3
3. Long-term financial assets	**102.2**	**139.4**
3.1. Long-term bonds 3.2. Shares	14.8	19.9
3.3. Long-term loans, n.e.c.	22.2	28.3
• Trade investments	65.2	91.2
• Other assets	**30.5**	**64.2**
Liabilities	**1 330.1**	**1 819.5**
4. Equity	**467.3**	**610.4**
4.1. Share capital	213.7	250.6
4.2.1. Reserves	95.7	118.5
4.2.2. Provisions	157.9	241.4
• Accumulated depreciation reserves	**80.6**	**99.8**
5. Short-term liabilities	**505.1**	**790.1**
6. Long-term liabilities	**250.5**	**313.3**
• Other liabilities	**26.5**	**5.9**

Table 2.2: Sources and Uses of Funds of Non-financial Enterprises/Germany

	1981
Sources	**149.0**
1. Non-financial sources	*93.7*
1.1 + 2.2.2. Gross income finance and issues of shares	102.9
of which: – depreciation	*90.9*
– provisions	*8.3*
• Transfers to reserves	– 9.2
Financial sources	*55.2*
2.1 + 2.2.1 + 2.2.3. Increase in debt (excluding shares)	55.2

Uses	**149.0**
3. Investments in non-financial assets	*121.2*
3.1 + 3.3. Increase in fixed assets (gross)	**106.0**
– Net increase in fixed assets	15.1
– Depreciation	90.9
3.2. Increase in stocks	**15.2**
4. Investments in financial assets	*27.8*
4.1.1. Change in cash	– 2.3
4.1.2.1 + 4.2.1 + 4.2.2. Acquisition of securities	2.9
Of which:	
4.2.2.2 + 4.2.2.3. Trade investments	*4.8*
• Others	27.1

Table 3.1: Balance Sheet of Non-Financial Corporations/Italy
Monetary unit: billion lire.

	1976	1981
Assets	**47 127.1**	**103 086.9**
1. Non-financial assets	**27 495.6**	**51 035.3**
1.1 + 1.3. Net fixed tangible and intangible assets	16 582.1	25 909.7
1.2. Stocks	10 913.5	25 125.6
2. Short-term financial assets	**13 928.8**	**38 613.4**
2.1. Cash and transferable deposits 2.2. Other deposits	943.7	2 400.2
2.4. Short-term loans, n.e.c. 2.6. Other accounts receivable	3 583.0	6 257.8
2.5. Trade credits extended	9 402.1	29 955.4
Long-term financial assets	**5 702.7**	**13 438.2**
3.1. Long-term bonds 3.2. Shares	2 870.0	7 194.9
3.3. Long-term loans, n.e.c.	2 832.7	6 243.3
3.3.1. claims on affiliates	*2 828.5*	*6 243.3*
3.3.2. others (ENEL claims only)	*4.2*	–
Liabilities	**47 127.1**	**103 086.9**
4. Equity	**13 578.7**	**27 366.1**
4.1. Share capital	4 055.5	10 224.6
4.2. Reserves and provisions	9 523.2	17 141.5
5. Short-term liabilities	**22 180.1**	**50 138.4**
5.2. Short-term borrowed funds, n.e.c. 5.4. Other accounts payable	15 107.9	25 670.6
of which:		
5.2.2. loans from banks	*8 481.8*	*12 075.6*
5.3. Trade credits received	7 072.2	24 467.8

Liabilities	**47 127.1**	**103 086.9**
Long-term liabilities	**11 368.3**	**25 582.4**
6.1. Long-term bonds	258.9	932.5
6.2. Long-term borrowed funds, n.e.c.	11 109.4	24 649.9
6.2.1. owed to affiliates	*3 340.0*	*8 619.6*
6.2.3. owed to banks *6.2.4. others*	*7 769.4*	*16 030.3*

Table 3.2: Sources and Uses of Non-Financial Corporations/Italy

	1981
Sources	**22 124.6**
1. Non-financial sources	**2 982.4**
1.1. Gross income finance (retained income before depreciation and provisions) 1.2. Net capital transfers received	2 982.4 . . .
2. Financial sources	**19 142.2**
2.1. Increase in short-term debt	8 412.4
2.1.1. to banks	*321.8*
2.1.2. others	*8 090.6*
2.2. Issues of bonds	443.5
2.3. Issues of shares	3 158.6
2.4. Other long-term external sources of finance	7 127.7
Uses	**22 124.6**
3. Investment in non-financial assets	**7 862.8**
3.1 + 3.3. Investment in tangible fixed assets and increase in intangible non-financial assets	5 322.7
3.2. Increase in stocks	2 540.1
4. Investment in financial assets	**14 261.8**
4.1. Increase in cash and deposits	588.8
4.2. Increase in other short-term claims	10 272.5
4.3. Net purchases of long-term financial assets	3 400.5

Table 4.1: Balance Sheet of Non-Financial Corporations/United Kingdom
Monetary unit: million pounds sterling.

	Large companies: all industries	
	1977	1981
Number of companies	1 524	. . .
Assets	**146 216**	**235 913**
1. Non-financial assets	**92 716**	**151 518**
1.1. Net fixed tangible assets	52 017	96 154
1.1.1. Net reproducible fixed assets	*26 607*	*52 096*
1.1.2. Non-reproducible fixed assets	*25 410*	*44 058*
1.2. Stocks	37 463	52 851
1.3. Intangible assets	3 236	2 513
2. Short-term financial assets	**42 025**	**64 339**
2.1 + 2.2. Cash and other deposits	8 857	13 775
2.3. Short-term bills and bonds	205	264
2.4. Short-term loans, n.e.c. 2.5. Trade credits extended 2.6. Other accounts receivable	} 32 963	50 300
3. Long-term financial assets	**11 474**	**20 056**
Of which:		
3.1.2. long-term bonds of others than affiliates	*435*	*488*
3.2.1. shares of affiliates	*302*	*735*
Liabilities	**146 216**	**235 913**
4. Equity	**68 016**	**113 703**
4.1. Share capital	13 539	18 710
4.2. Reserves and provisions	54 477	94 993
Short-term liabilities[2]	**60 636**	**96 300**
Of which:		
5.2.2 + 6.3.3. loans from banks	*14 566*	*23 377*
5.2.3. other short-term borrowed funds	*5 197*	*7 817*
5.4.2. accounts payable to others than affiliates	*4 861*	*9 033*
6. Long-term liabilities[3]	**17 564**	**25 910**
6.1 + 6.2.1 + 6.2.4. Long-term bonds and other long-term borrowed funds	14 145	18 402
6.2.2. Minority shareholders' interests in subsidiaries	3 419	7 508
6.2.3. Long-term funds borrowed from banks[4]	. . .	. . .
Memorandum items:		
a) Completed depreciation and amortization of reproducible fixed assets	26 286	40 536
Of which: buildings (included in 1.1.2)	*3 086*	*4 708*
b) Amortization of intangible assets	. . .	. . .
c) For unconsolidated accounts of subsidiary corporations: minority shareholders' interests	. . .	. . .

Table 4.2: Sources and Uses of Funds of Non-Financial Corporations/United Kingdom

Large companies: all industries	1981
Sources	**36 534**
1. Non-financial sources	*18 552*
1.1. Gross income finance (retained income before depreciation and provisions)	15 251
1.2. Net capital transfers received	3 301
2. Financial sources	*17 982*
2.1. Increase in short-term debt[2]	**13 320**
Of which:	
2.1.2.2 + 2.2.4.2. borrowing from banks	*3 883*
2.1.2.3. other short-term borrowed funds	*616*
2.1.4.2. accounts payable to others than affiliates	*644*
2.2. Increase in long-term debt[3]	**4 662**
2.2.1 + 2.2.3. Issues of long-term bonds and increase in long-term borrowing[3]	1 691
Of which: issues made in acquiring other companies	*7*
2.2.2. Issues of shares	2 971
Of which: issues made in acquiring other companies	*274*
Uses	**36 534**
3. Investment in non-financial assets	*21 729*
3.1. Investment in tangible fixed assets	18 086
3.2. Increase in stocks	3 100
3.3. Increase in intangible non-financial assets	543
4. Investment in financial assets	*14 805*
4.1. Increase in short-term claims	**10 101**
4.1.1. Cash and deposits	2 498
4.1.2. Other short-term claims	7 603
Of which:	
4.1.2.1. increase in holdings of short-term bills and bonds	*– 37*
4.2. Increase in long-term claims	**4 704**
Of which:	
4.2.2.4 + 4.2.2.5. Increase in holdings of shares of others than affiliates (excluding trade investments)	2 885
Of which: cash expenditure in acquiring other companies	*2 604*

Table 5.1: Balance-Sheet of Non-Financial Corporations[1]/United States
Monetary unit: billion dollars.

Assets	1976 **2 273.9**	1981 **4 012.3**
1. Non-financial assets	**1 662.0**	**2 949.5**
1.1. Net fixed tangible assets	1 275.8	2 254.8
1.1.1. net reproducible fixed assets	*1 089.6*	*1 946.6*
1.1.2. non-reproducible fixed assets	*186.2*	*308.2*
1.2. Stocks	386.2	694.7
1.3. Intangible assets	–	–
2. Short-term financial assets[2]	**465.5**	**835.8**
2.2. Cash and transferable deposits	56.4	78.6
2.2.1. Large time deposits	24.4	54.8
2.2.2. Security repurchase agreements	7.0	22.9
2.2.3. Foreign deposits	7.4	14.5
2.3.2. Short-term private securities	24.7	29.6
2.4. Short-term loans, n.e.c.	24.9	31.9
2.5. Trade credits extended	268.1	504.3
2.6. Other accounts receivable	52.6	99.2
• Central Government securities	**14.3**	**– 0.7**
3. Long-term financial assets[2]	**132.2**	**227.8**
3.1. Long-term bonds[2]	5.6	5.2
3.1.1. claims on affiliates	–	–
3.1.2. others	*5.6*	*5.2*
– State and Local Government	*(3.4)*	*(3.5)*
– Central Government lending agencies	*(2.2)*	*(1.8)*
3.2. Shares	126.6	222.5
3.2.1. claims on affiliates	*126.6*	*222.5*
3.3. Long-term loans, n.e.c.	–	–
Liabilities	**2 273.9**	**4 012.3**
4. Equity	**1 439.1**	**2 506.0**
5. Short-term liabilities	**395.5**	**776.9**
5.1. Short-term bills and bonds	16.1	51.8
5.2. Short-term borrowed funds, n.e.c.	166.9	319.9
5.2.1. loans from affiliates	–	–
5.2.2. loans from banks	*126.6*	*232.7*
5.2.3. others	*40.3*	*87.2*
5.3. Trade credits received	190.7	386.7
5.4. Other accounts payable	21.8	18.5
6. Long-term liabilities	**439.2**	**729.5**
6.1. Long-term bonds	286.3	446.5
6.2. Long-term borrowed funds, n.e.c.	152.9	283.0
6.2.1. owed to affiliates	*30.8*	*90.4*
6.2.3. owed to banks	*49.7*	*109.2*
6.2.2 + 6.2.4. others	*72.4*	*83.3*

Table 5.2: Sources and Uses of Funds of Non-Financial Corporations/United States

Sources	1981 **365.8**
1. Non-financial sources	*230.6*
1.1. Gross income finance (retained income before depreciation and provisions)	230.6
2. Financial sources	*135.2*
2.1. Increase in short-term debt	**67.6**
2.1.1. Issues of short-term bills and bonds	16.9
2.1.2. Increase in short-term borrowing, n.e.c.	29.7
2.1.2.2. from banks	*21.1*
2.1.2.3. others	*8.7*
2.1.3. Increase in trade credits received	27.8
2.1.4. Increase in other accounts payable	– 6.8
2.2. Increase in long-term debt	**67.6**
2.2.1. Issues of long-term bonds	35.5
2.2.2. Issues of shares	10.5
2.2.2.1. placed with affiliates (parent corporations)	*22.0*
2.2.2.2 + 2.2.2.3. others	*– 11.5*
2.2.3. Increase in long-term borrowing, n.e.c.	21.5
2.2.3.2. from banks	*21.8*
2.2.3.3. others	*– 0.3*
Uses	**365.8**
3. Investment in non-financial assets	*261.6*
3.1. Investment in tangible fixed assets	247.1
3.2. Increase in stocks	9.7
3.3. Mineral rights	4.8
4. Investment in financial assets	*62.7*
4.1. Increase in short-term claims[2]	**51.3**
4.1.1. Cash and deposits	14.8
4.1.1.1. cash and transferable deposits	*– 0.6*
4.1.1.2.1. large time deposits	*14.9*
4.1.1.2.2. security repurchase agreements	*
4.1.1.2.3. foreign deposits	*0.5*
4.1.2. Other short-term claims[2]	36.5
4.1.2.1.2. short-term private securities	*2.0*
4.1.2.2. increase in short-term loans, n.e.c.	*2.1*
4.1.2.3. increase in trade credits extended	*23.6*
4.1.2.4. increase in other accounts receivable	*8.9*
• Central Government securities	**– 1.4**
4.2. Increase in long-term claims[2]	**12.8**
4.2.1. Increase in holdings of long-term bonds[2]	*
– State and Local Government	*
– Central Government lending agencies	*
4.2.2. Increase in holdings of shares	12.8
• Discrepancy	*41.6*

2. Patterns and Trends in Financing West European Corporations

The basic structural data in the preceding tables can only convey a rather rough image of the (public and) private non-financial enterprise sector in four major European OECD countries and the US. They should be used and interpreted with caution (or even reservation) for the purpose of cross-sectional analysis because of major methodological deficiencies, mainly affecting the comparability of the reported data regarding the definition of economic units within the sectors and of financial instruments, national accounting principles, and levels

Table 6: An Overview of Financial Market Characteristics of Major European Economies as of 1982/83 (US Data for Comparison)
Figures in (. . .) are US$-equivalents, computed at year-end 1982 exchange rates (line (1))

Item / Country Code / Country / Currency	F France (ffr)	D F. R. of Germany (DM)	I Italy (Lit)	GB United Kingdom (£Stg)	US USA (US$)
General Economic Data (year-end) 1982					
(1) US $ parity at year-end 1982 (1 US = ... units national currency)	6.73	2.38	1,370	0.62	1.00
(2) Population (mill)	54.0	61.7	57.2	56.0	229.8
(3) Gross domestic product (bill)	3,588 (533)	1,548 (650)	466,752 (341)	289 (466)	3,068 (3,068)
(4) Gross fixed capital formation (bill)	750 (111)	317 (133)	88,842 (65)	45 (73)	523 (523)
Private Sector (F, US) or Non-Financial Enterprises (D, I, GB) Financial Data (year-end/year 1982)					
Outstanding shares[1]					
(5) Nominal value (bill)	73.52 (10.92)	97.94 (41.19)	83,720 (61.11)	121.56 (196.06)	1,720.5[2] (1,720.5)
Outstanding corporate bonds[3]					
(6) Nominal value (bill)	116.58[4] (20.27)	32.27[5] (13.56)	21,110 (15.40)	7.62[6] (12.29)	553.43[7] (553.43)
New security issues 1982 (bill)					
(7) Shares (market value)	28.84[8] (4.29)	4.77[9] (2.00)	6,892[10] (5.03)	1.03 (1.66)	22.5 (22.5)
(8) Bonds (par of face value)	29.88 (4.44)	6.55[4] (2.75)	4,415[11] (3.22)	.38) (.61)	33.5 (33.5)

Item / Country Code / Country / Currency	F France (ffr)	D F. R. of Germany (DM)	I Italy (Lit)	GB United Kingdom (£Stg)	US USA (US$)
Sector Balance Sheet and Flow of Funds Financial Ratios[12; 13]					
Percentage of total capital (assets)					
(9) Equity (1976 or 1977: GB)	27.94	41.19[14 15]	28.81	46.52	63.29
(1981)	28.30	39.03	26.55	48.20	62.46
(10) Long term debt (1976/77)	17.84	18.83	24.12	12.01	19.32
(1981)	15.00	17.22	24.81	10.98	18.18
(11) Short term debt (1976/77)	54.22	37.98	47.06	41.47	17.39
(1981)	56.70	43.42	48.64	40.82	19.36
Percentage of uses of funds (1981)					
(12) Non financial assets	57.55	81.34	35.54	59.48	71.51[5]
(13) Financial assets	42.45	18.66	64.46	40.52	17.14
Percentage of uses of funds (1981)					
(14) Internal sources (retained income + depreciation + provisions)	33.46	62.89	13.48	50.78	63.04
(15) External: long term debt + shares	22.75	37.05 (15 and 16 combined)	48.50	12.76	18.48
(16) External: short term debt	43.79		38.02	36.46	18.48

Notes:
1 Financial institutions and non-financial enterprises.
2 Domestic and foreign shares issued (outstanding).
3 Not including financial institutions, if not noted otherwise.
4 1981; including bonds of financial institutions (total of private sector).
5 Including public non-financial enterprises (e.g. post office and railroad companies in Germany; nationalized companies in France and Great Britain).
6 Market value.
7 Domestic private and foreign.
8 Non-financial enterprises, including nationalized enterprises from August 1982.
9 Private non-financial enterprises.
10 Including state-controlled corporations (source: ref. (2)).
11 Firms and public agencies (source: ref. (2)).
12 Computed from tables 1.1 to 5.2 on pages 296 to 304.
13 France: industrial and commercial enterprises combined.
14 Equity including accumulated depreciation reserves.
15 Adjustments through including other liabilities and discrepancies.

of aggregation. However, some intra-sectoral ratios and other characteristics of financial stock and flow variables may at least indicate some relative positions of these major European industrial countries, and in comparison to the US. The following table 6 contains a compilation of some other pertinent macro-economic data, information on outstanding securities, and various ratios based on tables 1.1 to 5.2.

Table 6 lends itself to make at least three basic observations:
1. European countries (except, to some extent, for Great Britain) appear to be rather obviously "undercapitalized" in terms of the value of outstanding corporate shares and bonds relative to the volume of the gross domestic product in 1982; a similar pattern (except for France and Italy) is observable also for the new securities issues in 1982 and 1983 as a percentage of the gross domestic product in 1982.

Rather than reflecting an inferior level of employment of capital in the public and private sectors, this can be attributed to different industrial structures (e.g. company sizes and legal forms of organizations) and capital market characteristics.

Table 7

Percent of the 1982 gross domestic product	F	D	I	GB	US
Nominal value of outstanding shares	6.50[1)]	6.12	17.93	42.06	56.09
Face value (market GB) of outstanding shares	3.25[1)]	2.08	4.5	2.63	18.03
New issue of shares					
1982	0.83	0.31	1.47	0.35	0.73
1983	1.12	0.42	. .	0.64	1.27
New issue of bonds					
1982	0.83	0.42	0.95	0.13	1.09
1983	0.95	0.00	. .	0.05	1.39

1 1981 securities in % of 1982 gross domestic product.

Table 8

	F	D	I	GB	US
short term debt/total debt (%)					
– balance sheets 1976/77	75	67	66	77	47
– balance sheets 1981	79	72	66	79	52
– sources of funds 1981	66	52	44	74	50

Source: Deutsche Bundesbank, Monatsberichte, Vol. 36, No. 5 (May 1984, p. 16)

2. The proportion of equity finance of total capital employed in the US is by far greater than in major European countries, of which Great Britain retains a clearly leading position in this respect. Several conditions, as the functionalism and efficiency of capital markets, institutional regulations, such as tax systems, and management and shareholder's objectives are considered to be the main reasons for this pattern.

3. Non-financial corporations in major European industrial countries tend to employ a much larger proportion of short term debt in financing their assets, both judged by aggregate stock and flow variables. Based on the figures in lines (10) to (16) in table 6 one can imply in general that the share of short term financial instruments in total debt is considerably higher than this ratio in the US, as can be seen from table 8 (page 307).

This pattern again reflects fundamental differences in the capital market structure affecting corporate debt policies, and certainly also shows reactions to the level and term structure of interest rates as well as experiences and expectations about inflation in these countries.

3. Corporate Tax Systems and Financing Behavior of European Corporations

Corporate substance (wealth, trade capital) and income taxation (trade income, retained earnings and dividends) as well as personal wealth, income and capital gains taxation of dividends received are bound to exert considerable influence on the financial structure and financing behavior of corporations. This may be recognized in two dimensions:

- The absolute levels of taxes or relative tax burdens (all taxes paid in relation to corporate pre-tax profits)
- The degree of discrimination of equity financing against long, medium and short term debt.

The following table 9 puts together some basic information on corporate and personal tax system characteristics. It may be of some use for the evaluation of corporate financing behavior in the light of past and presently operative fiscal regimes. Tax systems data may, on the other hand, of course serve only as rough indicators of actual ensuing tax effects: Differences (and partly vast differences) in accounting and tax accounting principles (methods of assessment and accruing of wealth and income, regulations for defining and measuring tax bases), tax thresholds, free quotas, exemptions and preferential rate structures as well as recently wide-spread investment incentive and tax credit regulations (based also on a variety of extra tax depreciation allowances) play a major role

Table 9: Tax Systems and Tax Parameters (Tax Rates in %)

Tax Item	Tax Base		F	D	I	GB	USA
	1. Corporate Taxes						
(1)	Trade (Commercial) Capital			net capital 0,8			"some assets" 0,178
(2)	Trade (Commercial) Earnings		value added + depreciation 3	profits bef. tax and ½ long term interest 13,5		profits bef. tax 8	
(3)	Wealth Tax			"tax equity" 0,6			
(4)		Period's to Carry	0	1	0	1	3
(5)		Back/Forward	5	5	5	indef.	15
(6)	Corporate	Losses					
(6)	Income	Tax System	part. imp.	full imp.	part. imp.	part. imp.	class.
(7)	Tax	tR (gross)[1]	50	56	43,3	52	49,5
(8)		tD (gross)	50	36	43,3	52	49,5
(9)	Tax Cred. (% of TD)		50	100	43,6	39,6	
	2. Shareholders' Taxes						
(10)			1	1	1	1	
(11)	Wealth Tax		0,5	0,5			
(12)	Income	Federal	60	46,5	55	60	24,7
(13)	Tax	State + Local[2]					17,7
(14)	Capital Gains Tax		30			20 (to scale)	17 (to scale)
(15)	Church Taxes May be Levied in Germany			7–9% of personal income tax			

Notes: 1. R = retained earnings; D = dividends; t = tax rate. 2. rates based on an amount of taxable dividend income of DM 100000 p. a. or the equivalent in other currencies (no tax allowances, free quotas etc. operative) in the determination of nominal and effective tax burdens of corporations and shareholders. Of special interest in this respect are the various corporate income tax systems (lines (6) to (9) in table 9): Whereas the US apply the traditional (classical) uniform tax rate system (no differentiation between retained and paid out earnings; no tax credit extended to dividend recipients for income tax already paid at the corporate level), many European countries have adopted some form of imputation (tax credit) system. "part. imp." indicates a system where at least part of the corporate dividend tax is recognized as tax already paid at the individual income tax level (see percentages in line (9)), and

Table 10: Effects of a Full Imputation Tax System (D)

gross corporate profits (before tax)	200	
gross retained earnings (gross dividends)	100	100
56% (36%) corporate income tax	− 56	− 36
net retained earnings (dividends)	44	64
personal income tax base (net dividends plus tax)		100
personal income tax (e. g. 40% tax rate)		− 40
dividend tax already paid by corporation		+ 36
(additional) tax levied from shareholder		− 4
net income after all taxes	44	60

Table 11: Simulfin (Simultax) – relative tax burden of corporations and shareholders (tax rates 1983)

Country	F		D		I		GB		US	
Target ratio of gross earnings retention (percent of total gross profits)	30	70	30	70	30	70	30	70	30	70
corporate substance (wealth etc.) and income tax in % of gross profits	63.6	63.5	70.2	72.5	45.6	45.9	53.5	53.6	51.5	52.6
personal wealth, capital gains and income taxes in % of dividends paid	54.9	111.0	32.7	56.2	48.3	47.2	48.4	78.2	44.3	69.6
total corporate and shareholders' tax burden in percent of gross profits	85.2	81.9	79.9	79.6	72.2	56.4	74.2	67.7	71.0	65.2

"full imp." (West Germany as of 1977) designates a framework in which all of corporate dividend taxes paid are credited towards personal income taxes. A brief example may illustrate the computational procedure (see table 10).

In this example, the overall relative tax burden amounts to 96/200, i.e. 48%. It should be noted that also retained earnings (which had been taxed at 56% in the year of profit generation) will be treated in the same way as dividend payments as soon as they are being paid out (ex-post relief) in later periods.

Using the corporate financial (and taxation) simulation model SIMULFIN (ref. (1)) computational experiments were performed to quantify absolute and relative tax burdens of a hypothetical corporation and its shareholders; the results may be summarized as follows:

Wealth and capital gains taxes play a significant part in these simulated tax assessment cases at the shareholders' taxation level so that relative tax burdens (related to dividends paid) vary distinctly among countries, and depending on corporate earnings distribution policies. Corporate equity capital financing through retained net earnings and/or paid back capital depends on both the relative tax burden under alternative dividend strategies and on the relative tax components in the costs of equity capital vs. debt capital. The comparative disadvantage of equity financing especially in France and Germany is evident. It should be noted, however, that present-day capital structure is the result of a long process of capital formation under specific (historical) tax scenarios.

4. Incentives for Personal Investing in New-issue Stocks and Investment Company Shares

The long recognized (and, for economic policy reasons, deplored) shortcomings in volume and variety of corporate equity financing or personal investing in stocks and investment company shares in all European countries (except for Great Britain) have led to some recent initiatives to boost the issuing of new shares through direct or indirect tax incentives at the personal investors' level and through tax reform at the corporate level (improvement of after tax equity yields). France had already introduced in 1978 the "Lex Monory", allowing for income tax deductions of the purchase value of newly issued corporate or investment company shares up to 5000 ffrs (plus family allowance); this regulation has been prolonged and modified in 1983 to a somewhat reduced level, but still provides strong incentives for improving capital structure and enhancing share ownership by building securities portfolios in large segments of the investing public. Similar regulations were introduced 1982 in Norway and Belgium. Sweden has considerably reduced the tax burden on dividends and capital gains for low-income investors in 1981; West Germany makes progress in alleviating corporate wealth and trade income tax in order to improve after-tax equity return and thus at least partly remedy the discrimination of equity financing against all forms of debt; Great Britain has eased capital gains taxation by allowing tax free gains up to 5000 £ Stg in 1982 from 3000 previously.

5. Potential for Financial Innovations

Many of the great variety of financing instruments used in European corporations as well as in small and medium size business finance have long tradition; some have been developed centuries ago and have been used ever since (e.g. trade bills, negotiable credit, promissory notes, bonds and stocks, international trade financing instruments). Other instruments, such as leasing, factoring, forfeiting, convertible or preferential securities etc. were almost all known in principle and basically well defined in terms of their legal and institutional prerequisites, but emerged only in recent times as important and widely professionally managed credit instruments, as may be seen from the historic records of the European financial markets. Instead of trying to present a catalog and discuss the institutional detail of all the financing instruments currently used to finance business in the different countries in Europe, one single case of financial innovation in West Germany's post war economic history is being set forth and briefly explained in some detail: the Bertelsmann Aktiengesellschaft, Gütersloh, West Germany.

Bertelsmann today is a multi-billion DM publishing and communications media corporation (revenues over 6.5 billion in 1983) which was founded 150 years ago; Reinhard Mohn, successor to the founders in the fifth generation of the family enterprise, presently chairman of the board, took over full responsibility after World War II. Outside equity capital financing of this family owned personal partnership was practically not available at that time, and rather scarce later on. In order to finance the extremely rapid expansion of the firm (sales doubled f.i. each year in five consecutive years in the 1950ies) Bertelsmann was incorporated as an "Aktiengesellschaft" (stock company, without going public) and at the same time the so-called "Bertelsmann-Modell" was conceived and translated into reality.

Two basic features are instrumental to the Bertelsmann model:

- An 'enterprise constitution' which provides a form of profit sharing for the vast majority of employees, and other "social partnership" elements, subject to detailed regulations or agreements between original ownership representatives, management and employees.

- Financing instruments which facilitate the use of corporate earnings before taxes as self financing source by means of formally distributing contractually defined parts of value added to the beneficiaries (where they are subject to comparatively low personal income taxation) and at the same time retaining these funds materially in the firm. This was achieved by creating and issuing Genußscheine ('participation right certificates') as securities in lieu of genuine equity capital, and through extensive pension plans with considerable dotation of tax-exempt provisions for retirement payments to employees. Both financing instruments did in no way impair management or ownership control which still rests in the hands of the original shareholders of the AG.

The acquisition of Genußscheine requires a 25% down payment from the subscriber out of his or her own funds; they yield in the average returns on investment between 12 and 15% p.a. They also have priority before common stocks as regards claims to corporate earnings.

Corporate earnings, defined for the purpose of computing the rate of return of the Genußscheine, are based on total capital returns, i.e. returns before deduction of interest to be paid on debt capital or to holders of certificates, and also include to some extent the capitalization of royalties from publishing rights and of returns from long term contracts with customers and clients. Bertelsmann issues the certificates with the commitment to the subscribers not to dispose of these rights during a certain period of time; after this restrictive period the certificates can be offered and traded at a Bertelsmann in-house market or exchange; plans are being made to open up this market also for third parties (kind of over-the-counter trading). Prices of the certificates are quoted between 90 and 110% of their par value. Frequently rights are being acquired at the margin, especially by middle and higher management, thus taking advantage of leveraged personal portfolios.

Bertelsmann follows strictly some fundamental balance sheet orientated financing and capital structure guidelines. One is a constant relation of genuine equity capital of shareholders to Genußschein-capital; another is to observe a minimum 25% equity and Genußscheine to total capital ratio which is considered to fully meet the necessary leverage-risk-limiting standards of the firm in view of large amounts of pension plan provisions and rather substantial hidden reserves in some typical immaterial asset positions of this publishing and media concern. Dynamic debt servicing capacity (cash flow after tax in relation to debt outstanding) should not fall below a ratio of 3:2; leasing and factoring are limited to certain proportions of balance sheet or flow of funds accounts positions. Within this framework, an average rate of expansion of Bertelsmann activities, specifically a rate of sales growth of 15% p.a., can be maintained in the future, according to medium term budget plans.

As of June 30, 1983, the consolidated balance sheet of the Bertelsmann group shows total assets of 3.1339 billion DM. Capital positions are as follows:[1]

	million DM	
– nominal share capital		
○ ordinary	210.45	
○ preferred (no voting rights)	24.15	
– participation right certificates (nominal)	239.0	
– equity capital surplus (open reserves)	26.27	
– profit brought forward in 1982/83	66.5	
– equity capital equivalents of shares owned by third parties (resulting form balance sheet consolidation; »Anteile im Fremdbesitz«)	206.1	772.47
– provisions (»Rückstellungen«)		
○ employee retirement (pension) plan	596.9	
○ taxes	108.3	
○ other purposes (operating)	499.9	
– long term debt	119.7	
– short term debt	979.7	
– sundry capital items	56.93	2,361.43

For the year ending June 1983, original shareholders and partners of Bertelsmann grossed DM 111.5 million profits of which 54.8 were paid for personal income and wealth taxes (relative tax burden of 49.2%). Bearers of participation rights cerfiticats obtained 47.8 million and payed 10.4 in income taxes (21.1%) so that Genußschein capital holdings yielded (based on nominal or book values) 20% before and 15.6% after personal income tax.

Reinhard Mohn stresses in a recent report on the Bertelsmann-Modell (Mohn, p. 12) the fact that "the personell-orientated (social) and financial arrangements and regulations led to an understanding of the firm which ensues in cooperation, working commitment and creativity. Stability and evolutionary abilities of our firm are influenced decisively by this motivation." The Bertelsmann case thus demonstrates convincingly that financial innovation, based primarily on the ingenuity of management and on available financing techniques or capital market instruments, may play a significant role in the advancement of highly developed, modern economic systems.

1 The equity to total capital relation amounts to less than 25% in the AG – balance sheet; it is maintained, however, throughout the whole Bertelsmann group (consolidated statements).

Bibliography

Adelberger, Otto L.: SIMULFIN. *Die Finanzwirtschaft der Unternehmung als Simulationsexperiment,* Vol. I: Modelldokumentation, XVIII, 227 pp. Vol. II: EDV-Materialien, 405 pp. S. Toesche-Mittler-Verlag, Darmstadt 1976.

Banca d'italia: *Abridged Version of the REPORT for the year 1982.* Presented by the Governor to the Ordinary General Meeting of Shareholders. Rome 1983.

Bertelsmann AG (ed.), *Geschäftsbericht und Sozialbilanz 1982/83.* Gütersloh 1984.

Deutsche Bundesbank, *Monatsberichte der Deutschen Bundesbank,* Vol. 36, No. 5, May 1984.

Mohn, Reinhard: *Alternative Finanzierungsmöglichkeiten einer Unternehmensexpansion.* In: Bertelsmann Briefe 114, January 1984, pp. 8–12.

OECD, *Financial Accounts of OECD Countries,* Vol. 1–3, Paris 1983.

OECD, *Non-Financial Enterprises Financial Statements,* Paris 1983.

Price Waterhouse Inc. (ed.): *Informations Guide: Doing business in France, Germany, Italy, U.S.* United Kingdom, various locations and years.

Margin and Risk Management in International Credit Transactions Undertaken by Banks

Manfred Steiner

Summary

International credit transactions have been signified in recent years by a reduced interest margin, sometimes not even high enough to cover the costs, accompanied by increasing risk. This has been accepted by the banks as a market development and has not influenced their level of lending. The extremely different costs involved with refinancing and the technical organization require quite different cost and risk analysis than have been applied by banks active in the international field. These include a determination of a standard margin contribution, a controlling of risk involved from interest-rate changes by means of the duration index and an analysis of borrower and country specific risks.

1. Current Discussion

International credit transactions by banks have recently become the centre of attention in public and scientific discussion. The reason for this has been political changes and payment difficulties on the part of some important borrowers such as Iran and Poland. The example of these countries shows quite clearly that the frequently used saying – 'The banks are similar to the lenders of umbrellas in that they hire them out when the sun is shining but demand them back as soon as it starts to rain' – is no longer absolutely true as far as international credit transactions are concerned. This is because the sale of the security as a means of enforcing the repayment of credits is no longer usually possible. The experience made in recent times has thus led to a recognition of the inherant political and economic risks involved in the mediation of international credit to individual countries.

For some time specialists have been concerned with different aspects of risk handling inherent in international credit. For example, after the bankruptcy of the bank I. D. Herstatt, the Federal German Bureau of Banking Control (Bundesaufsichtsamt für das Kreditwesen) introduced a new restriction, from the point of view of the credit institutions, regarding the equity and liquidity of these institutions. This new restriction limited the amount of uncovered foreign currency items of 30% of the liable equity of a particular credit institution (restriction Ia). This new regulation is supposed to reduce the exchange rate risks involved in international transactions.

The West German "Commission for Studies Relating to Fundamental Questions in Banking" ("Studienkommission für Grundsatzfragen der Kreditwirtschaft") has also investigated the effects of a limitation of risk taking as being dependent on the magnitude of equity. According to the commission, the proportion of equity to the volume of credit has, in particular due to international transactions, become too small. By means of subsidiaries and participation in foreign credit institutions, credit pyramids have been dormed using the original equity as a basis. German Banks have thus been able to create large volumes of credit on the international market through their subsidiaries in Luxemburg. The commission, therefore, recommended legislation to introduce a method of quota consolidation under bank supervision for participation in domestic and foreign credit institutions (Studienkommission 1979). This would result in taking into account the credits of subsidiaries and banks which are participated in when establishing the liable equity of the parent company. Restriction I of the Federal German Bureau of Banking Control limits the volume of credit of West German banks to a level eighteen times that of the liable equity. The application of the participation consolidation would mean that, in the case of numerous credit institutions, there is not the level of equity as prescribed by the "Credit System Law" (Kreditwesengesetz KWG): This introduction of consolidation could, in turn, force credit repayments of approximately 70–90 billion DM for the West German credit institutions (Kretschmer, Preusche 1981). In contrast to the efforts to limit the risk involved in international transactions, West German banks are demanding that restrictive legislation be slackened in order to increase the international competitiveness of the German credit system. It is proposed, for example, that the permissible volume of credit should be increased from an eighteen-fold level of the liable equity to its previous twenty-fold value in order not to loose the "bread and butter business" of international credit. A compromise to this problem is a gradual grading of taking into account of the credits given by the subsidiaries and participating institutions as part of the credit which the parent company can create. This method of grading will depend on the risks involved in specific countries and, furthermore, the restrictions which apply for domestic transactions will be able to be exceeded. The risks relating to specific countries available at the united bank (world concern) are to be reported to the Federal German Control Commission for Credit within the framework of a gentleman's agreement.

This introduction has shown that international credit transactions, and especially the related risks resulting from them, are the centre of a discussion involving numerous different aspects. The following is an attempt to throw a light on the main aspects of international credit transactions with respect to success and risk.

2. Definition of International Credit

To begin with, it will prove useful to describe what is to be understood under international credit since there is no common use of the expression in the specialist literature. International credit is used most commonly to describe credit transactions which cross national borders. If the aspect of legal property is emphasised credits from foreign subsidiaries and affiliates to domestic borrowers measured in respective national currencies have to be also included. Howeever, these credits are usually excluded in cases of economic analysis. If, however, refinancing takes place using the currency basis of the parent company, then this exclusion is not appropriate for investigations into the risks involved in international credit transactions. International credit transactions by European Banks can be divided on the one hand into Euro-credits which are usually guaranteed in the form of non-allocated financial credits, and on the other hand, into traditional foreign credits which are granted to foreign customers in the form of allocated financial credits. These are related to the financing of foreign trade. However, not every Euro-credit or foreign credit need necessarily be an international credit.

Today, the majority of Euro-credits are characterized by the transaction conditions, in particular:

- Transactions at the centres of the Euro-market (London, Luxemburg) in a Euro-currency;
- Size, usually greater than 1 million DM;

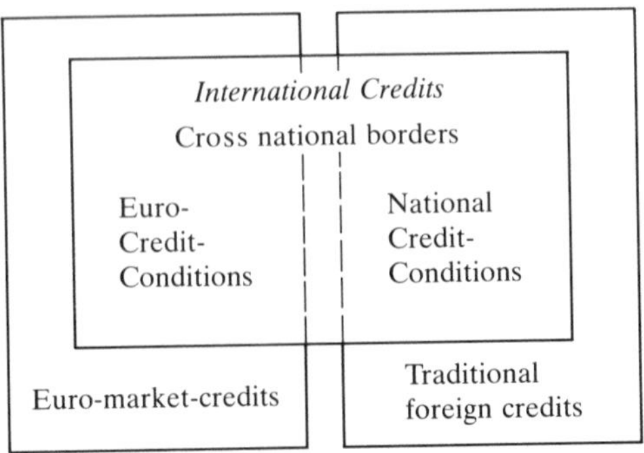

Figure 1: International Credits and their Connection with Euromarket and Foreign Credits

- Inter bank rates at different European locations as the basis for determining the rate of interest;
- Collateral, either none (or a negative clause) or personal security.

An example of a non-international credit would be a national credit (a German bank to a German borrower in Germany) at the Euro-mark terms. The same applies for the case of foreign trade credit to a domestic customer. In both cases, the risk-specific aspects, especially the risk related to a particular country, characterizing international credit transactions no longer applies. The majority of Euro-credits can be classed as international credit. In particular import credits form the largest part of international credit transactions for the case of foreign trade credits.

3. The Development of International Credit Transactions

International credit transactions on the part of banks belonging to the western industrialized nations have increased considerably in the last decade. According to the Bank for International Settlements BIS, the volume of foreign credit granted by banks belonging to the Group of Ten, as well as Switzerland, Danmark, Ireland, Austria and branches of US banks to off-shore financing locations grew by 24% = $ 218 billion in 1979 to $ 1,111 billion. The following illustration shows that such increases have been no exception in the years since 1970.

The international credit market is thus characterized by high rates of expansion which have usually been well above those of domestic credit transactions. The rates of expansion have, however, varied considerably according to a bank's

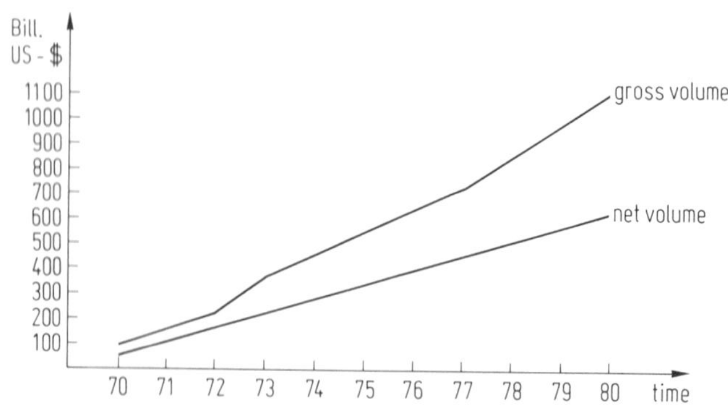

Figure 2: Expansion of the volume of international credit of the commercial banks of the western industrialized nations (Llewellyn 1979)

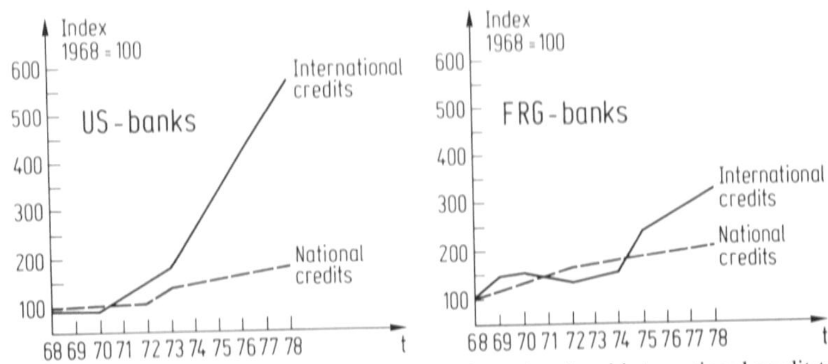

Figure 3: Comparison of the rates of growth in national and international credit transactions for commercial banks in the FRG and USA (Llewellyn 1979)

particular country of residence. For example, German credit institutes had quite different rates of growth to US banks for the period 1968 to 1977.

The lower rates of growth for US banks at the beginning of the 1970's compared to the European credit institutes can be attributed to regulation Q. The abolishment of this restriction then led to an over-proportional increase in US banks' share of international credit. Today, German banking circles thus speak of US banks having a competitive advantage since they are not subject to strict restriction which for instance are imposed on German banks by the Federal German Control Commission. The US banks are, therefore, in a position to follow a more expansive, but at the same time riskier, credit policy. On the other hand, it seems that the rates of growth shown in the past, for German banks have been too low as they did not include the transactions carried out by subsidiaries based in Luxemburg.

The higher rates of growth of the international credit market can, in general, be attributed to the competitive advantage it enjoys over the national credit markets, a fact which especially applies for the case of the Euro-dollar market. Investors can obtain higher interest on desposits, whilst on the other hand borrowers having firstclass standing are able to obtain credits at lowerer rates of interest than those ruling in the domestic credit market. The growth of the international credit market can, of course, also be attributed to economic aspects, such as the recycling of OPEC surpluses and the financing of deficit balances of payment. These aspects will, however not be considered in detail here.

If investors and borrowers are to be able to realize interest advantages, then the margin between creditor and debtor interest rates, and hence the bank profit rates relevant for the credit calculation, are smaller than those in domestic credit transactions with respect to the same prescribed period. This is also

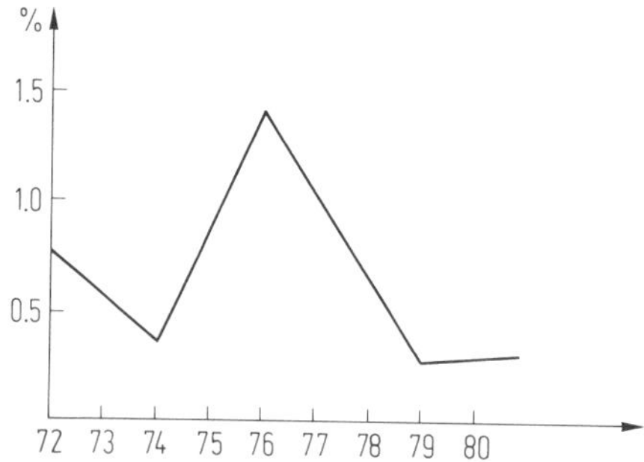

Figure 4: Development of the spreads on the Euro-credit market. (Cramer 1981)

confirmed by statements made by credit institutes and comparisons of bank profit margins. In order to testimate the margin, the spread over and above LIBOR (London Interbank Offerred Rate) is usually used for credits in US Dollars and the spread over and above LUXIBOR (Luxemburg Interbank Offerred Rate) is usually used for DM credits.

The expansion of the market volume was, up to 1974, continually accompanied by a downward trend in the spreads, the lowest margin being ⅜%. After the Herstatt crisis, there was an increase to a peak of 1¼% for industrial countries and 2¼% for developing countries (Guth 1980). The margins fall, however, after 1976 to a level of ⅜% (an average of 0.49% for industrial countries and 0.68% for developing countries) and only after 1980 where there small increases of up to ⅛%.

Parallel to the decline in the spreads, the durations have increased from an average of 6 years in 1976 to 9 years in 1980. The expansion of the international credit volume thus had to be paid for by the credit institutes through a reduction in their margins and at the same time an increase in the duration of repayment. If one assumes that an extension of the durations in credit transactions means a general increase in the risk involved due to increased incertainty with respect to prospective returns, then the banks had to accept a reduction in the expected value of the returns for an accompanying increase in the variance on standard deviation for the case of their international credit portfolios.

Furthermore, this is supported if the other risks involved in international credit transactions are taken into account.

These are: Risks due to changes in interest rates
Risks involved in refinancing currency risks
Credit solvency risks (term and default risks)

- Borrower risk
- Country risk (political and economic)
- Group risk.

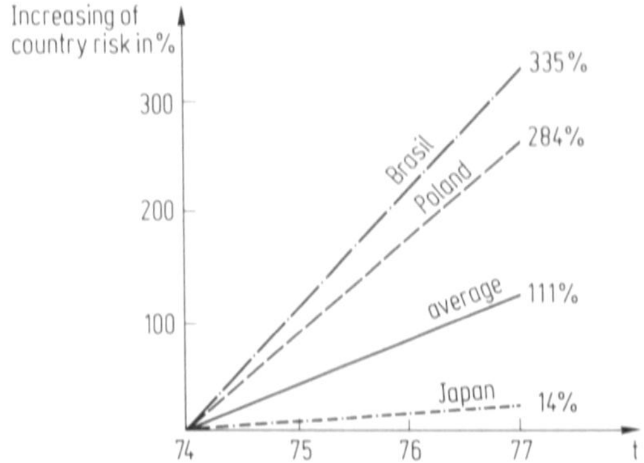

Figure 5: Change in country related risks (BIS, Annual Reports 1974–78)

The normal index analysis and calculations show increasing static and dynamic debt-ratios in the field of credit solvency risks, and in particular increased political and economic risks relating to different countries. This is confirmed in the annual report of the Bank for International Settlement which shows an average increase in country-related risks of 111% for dhe period 1974 to 1977.

What is the reason for banks' behaviour in accepting a reduction in margins for increased risks in international credit transactions?

4. An Explanation of the Behavior of Credit Institutes in International Credit Transactions

The credit sector generally provides the explanation that the international credit market has developed into a buyers' market and in doing so has dictated, via the market, the maximum interest margins which can be obtained. Causes of this development are seen as an abundant supply of liquidity in recent years, a frequent lack of domestic demand and an increasing competitive situation resulting from new sources of supply (Guth 1980). It was only possible for these new suppliers of international credit to enter the market because of a more favourable structuring of conditions whereby the market price fell. The development of the conditions can thus be formerly explained as dependent on supply and corresponding to the shape of the classical price-quantity function. The question to be answered, however, is why are the credit institutes so active in this market. Risk indices such as the BERI (Business Environment Risk Index) show that, from the point of view of investment and credit risk, the Federal Republic is in a more favourable position than most other borrowing countries. This means that an explanation is necessary for the expansion of German but also other European banks in credit markets where demand is accompanied by an apparently higher risk and lower profit margins.

A significant aspect mentioned by credit institutes is often that of diversification. Reductions in domestic profits can be offset by profits obtained abroad and vice versa. According to the portfolio theory, an increase in credit dispersion (naive diversification) cannot alone cause a reduction in the portfolio risk. On the contrary, the risk correlation between different types of credits and hence the change of the total porfolio risk should be taken into account.

One of the prerequisites for a positive diversification aspect in international credit transactions would be in general that business cycles vary for different countries. If this were the case, then the credit institutes could produce a smaller or even negative correlation between their return on equity and the market return on investment by means of international credit activities. A certain phase difference in the business cycles of the western industrialized nations can be observed, but there also seems to be a considerable degree of correlation.

Every diversification in the service sector of a firm can, however, also be substituted by a corresponding diversification in an individuals investment portfolio. From a capital theory point of view, diversification by means of international credit transactions is only of advantage for the shareholders of credit institutes when real economic synergetic effect takes place and/or the danger of bankruptcy is reduced.

If one assumes, however, that the capital market can be split into segments and that the international credit market is such a segmented market in which not all investors can enter, then the standard deviation of the distribution of the business assets becomes more significant than the covariance risk in the latest capital-theory approaches which consider the segmentation hypothesis (Rudolph 1979a). The assumption of the segmentation hypothesis places significance on the diversification aspect, i.e. the risk involved in individual credit transactions is more important than the portfolio risk.

After the risk aspect, the level of interest rates and prospective returns are the central determinants of the flow of international capital.

$\triangle C = f(\triangle i, \triangle r)$
C = Volume of credit
i = Interest rate
r = Risk

According to this functional relationship, a change in the structure of interest or risk should lead to a redistribution of the credit positions. An empirical investigation carried out by Kleinewefers (1972) into the foreign transactions of Swiss banks used regression analysis based on the following estimation function for the period 1959 to 1969:

$\triangle C = ka + kbi_t + kcr_t - kC_{t-1}$
($\triangle C$ = Change in credit volume; k = Rate of adaption; i_1 = Interest rate in period t; r_t = Risk in period t)

The results show that the interest variable only play a secondary role in estimating the changes in international credit transactions. Moreover, the externaly recognizable gross interest margins do not correlate with the allotment of the passive resources to the active credit transactions. The validity of the pure portfolio approach could not be confirmed for the case of the international credit transactions of the Swiss banks and, in particular there were no equilibrium credit positions. The theory of arbitrage was the best explanation for the behaviour of Swiss banks in carrying out foreign transactions. The banks obtain money from abroad and use this for international credit transactions as long as there is a positive margin between creditor and debitor interest rates. The means of raising the credit in this transitory business takes place partially through the active raising of credit by the banks and partially through the money flowing autonomously from abroad which is then automatically invested abroad. In international credit transactions, lending is continued as long as there is a positive interest margin and as long as money flows in from abroad. Arbitrage transactions offer an explanation for the expansion of credit volume in the case of sinking spreads.

Kleinwefer's investigations have, however, made it quite clear that the conditions necessary to obtain an arbitrage profit for the credit institutes vary according to the country of residence. For example, for the analyzed period, the number of foreign creditors of Swiss banks grew considerably even through the gross interest difference between Switzerland and other countries was always negative for the cases investigated. Furthermore, the net interest difference vis-à-vis the Euro-dollar market and German credit market was at all times negative and with respect to other countries was for part of the time negative, i.e. investors could have obtained higher interest rates abroad. It is because of these market imperfections that it is possible for Swiss banks to obtain interest margins in foreign transactions which are higher than those obtainable by German banks. In addition to the uniform classification of first-class standing in the Euro-market, for instance, granting of credit at LIBOR, there thus exists an extremely divers basis of refinancing in the field of the autonomous flow of foreign money. The internationally active credit institutions are assigned different degrees of risk by investors even though the lending to borrowers falls into the same risk category.

5. Cost and Profit Analysis

It is imperative that those banks involved in international credit transactions carry out cost and success analysis due to the different refinancing costs. Only a limited number of institutions apply various forms of analysis to determine lowest possible prices. Wilfried Guth, speaker for the board of directors of Deutsche Bank, thus surmises that the decline of the Euro-margin could be due to unsatisfactory branch accounting of this sector by those credit institutions active in the international field.

The German credit sector offers quite different average minimum margins from ¾% to 1.5% (Reinhardt 1979; Kippenberger 1979). They do, however, have one thing in common, namely they are all above the average spreads of recent years. If the refinancing costs are subject to LIBOR or LUXIBOR then it has to be assumed that international credit transactions, at least in the field of Euro-credit, is not always carried out to cover costs. Statements made in German banking circles support this assumption in that they interpret international credit transactions as a marginal contribution business for unused capacity and in the absence of bottle necks. All credit granted which covers the variable costs brings about a positive margin over direct costs and thus contributes to increasing the total profit. The remaining business sectors are operated so that costs are fully covered and have to bear the running operation costs, i.e. fixed overhead costs such as personnel, EDP and general administration costs.

Since international credit transactions and in particular Euro-credit transactions are counted as "wholesale banking", it is assumed by credit institutions that the personnel and administrative costs are much lower than those in national credit transactions and thus also justify a lower margin. A sensible way of judging the costs involved in international credit transactions would require a splitting up of the block of fixed costs and a definition of the variable costs. This is, however, something not usually practised by European banks. The required transparancy with respect to the costs would be achieved by means of a "fixed cost covering analysis" done in stages (Fixkostendeckungsrechnung; Agthe 1959; Mellerowicz 1961) or by means of determining the "relative direct costs" (Relative Einzelkostenrechnung; Riebel 1972). Furthermore, the slashing of certain fixed costs within longer periods of time should be taken into account. It is, therefore, questionable if a personnel surcharge of 0.2%, as sometimes applied by German banks, is adequate for credits which are granted for periods of up to 15 years. The fixed costs have to be divided according to the particular business branch and benefits sizes (e.g. time reference) and then the standard-margin-contribution have to be determined taking into account the fundamental business policy related to particular credit transactions.

Moreover, the determination of the variable costs is, to a certain degree, due for reform. In the case of Euro-credit, these costs are usually estimated by simply using LIBOR. In doing so, it is overlooked that the risks resulting from an individual credit, represent variable costs which are to be covered. The minimum price is thus determined from the refinancing costs attribution plus the borrower and countryspecific additional risk charge. If the spreads are considered from the point of view of a credit insurance premium, then they are below the lowest value that professional credit insurance would require. This, therefore, confirms that banks only give risk a minor role in international credit transactions. Since only borrowers of first-class standing were allowed to trade on the Euro-market, the risk of default was indexed, on average, lower than for national credit transactions. This does, however, hide the fact that some banks were subject to quite extensive defaults, e.g. 25 million DM in the case of Bankhaus Hill Samuel resulting from the Herstatt crisis. On the other hand, the question remains open whether the defaults in international credit transactions represent an adequate basis for the calculation of future risks. Indices of borrowers and country-specific risks show that the tendency is increasing.

In order to recognize and estimate borrower and country-specific risks, multivariate classification methods, in particular linear discriminance analysis, should be applied. These methods could be used to recognize risky credits in advance and hence avoid such transactions. On the other hand, the risk involved in the current credit portfolio could be estimated and the necessary risk premium calculated. This second case is also possible if the method is not too accurate. The investigations carried out up to now, e.g. Fisk and Rimlinger (1979) as well as Mayo and Barrett (1977), have not produced satisfactory results due to the fact that the obtained indicators cannot stand up to a statistical significance test with respect to reclassification and forecasting. The main reason for this is that, up to now, there have not been adequate number of cases in which country-specific risks actually became effective. The spectrum of different methods of classification used for investigations into national credit transactions in the USA and Europe has not been completely taken advantage of for the case of international credit. There are, admittedly limitations as far as costs are concerned in obtaining data and evaluation for the Credit Scoring System, at least with respect to the field of Euro-credit, if competitiveness should continue. Another disadvantage is that there is no international credit information system as there is at present in W. Germany for large credits.

Apart from the determination of the risk premium it is absolutely necessary for success management that the refinancing costs are established since these can differ enormously for different credit institutions. The assignment of refinancing resources to certain borrowings is no new problem in bank operations and cannot be fully solved. Only transitary resources can be directly accounted for.

The majority have to be assigned by means of artificial relationships, liabilities and equity on the one hand and assets on the other hand. In Germany, the rules laid down by the Federal Bureau of Banking Control regarding equity and the liquidity of the credit institutions are often applied. These restrictions link the volume of credit (restriction I) and the open currency positions (restriction Ia) to the magnitude of the equity. Moreover, the volume of the long-term bound assets is limited to the magnitude of the long-term equity and liabilities (restriction II) and the short and medium-term claims are limited to the magnitude of the short and medium-term financial resources (restriction III). The equity and hence its costs can be accounted for in the different types of credits by means of the various percentage charges of restriction I. In addition, it is also possible to assign the long-term capital to the long-term credits in accordance with restriction II. There remains, however, a margin of latitude for internally controlled assignment so that the determination of the minimum prices already includes fundamental business policy decisions in the case of credit institutions. Some authors are of the opinion that it is not possible to determine the minimum prices in credit transactions and that only minimum total proceeds exist (Krümmel 1964). The minimum total proceeds is given at the point where the block of fixed capacity costs equals the interest margin plus proceeds arising from commissions and charges.

In Euro-credit, there are a relatively large number of resources which can be directly converted into borrowings and which are lent at inter-bank rates within the framework of active transitary transactions. The tolerance for the determination of the minimum prices is hence limited. For those types of credits which cannot be directly related to deposits average rates of interests have to be determined, due to fictive assignments, based on volumes and periods. If there are no regulations relating to the magnitude of credit and the liable equity as is

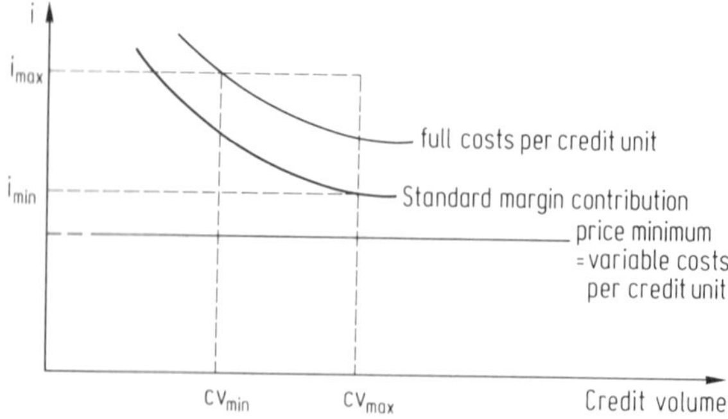

Figure 6: Standard margin contribution as a function of the volume of credit.

the case for example for the credit institutions in Luxemburg, then a small equity is capable of creating a large volume of credit. A lack of legal reserves requirements also reduces the refinancing costs. Credits thus obtained at subsidiaries in Luxemburg are, therefore, more favourable from the cost point of view, than those from the German parent bank.

A fixing of a standard margin contribution which contains those fixed costs directly related to international credit transactions, enables a limitation of the latitude of negotiation needed in decisions concerning interest rates for credits, and nevertheless is still flexible to react in accordance with the negotiation authority of the borrower.

Transactions capable of realizing interest higher than the required margin contribution should be pushed, whilst on the other hand those which do not fetch the required margin should be cut back on. Different standard margin contributions according to the risk classes of the borrowers could also find an application.

6. Expansion in International Credit Transaction and Cost Functions

As far as costs are concerned, American credit institutions are in a more favourable situation because of their dollar basis, then certain European competitors lacking such a basis. The First National City Bank, which already used the concept of setting a required minimum margin, did not have to go below the minimum price for an interest margin of ¾% (Preisig 1976). Furthermore, those banks having large flows of low interest primary deposits from abroad, have great advantages. This is true for the Swiss banks and those credit institutions located in tax havens.

The interest margin which can be obtained is dependent on the chosen strategy for penetrating the market, i.e. whether expansion in international credit transactions takes place by means of subsidiaries, branches or partnerships. The essential point is how much extra investment abroad is necessary to achieve a certain volume of credit. Empirical investigations into the effect of costs and proceeds of a business expansion on the part of credit institutions show that expansion by means of setting up new branches or subsidiaries results in an increase in costs for the technical-administrative sector which are greater than the advantages obtained from the only slightly reduced refinancing costs (Franke 1978). The average profit per unit of borrowed and lent money sinks (Figure 7).

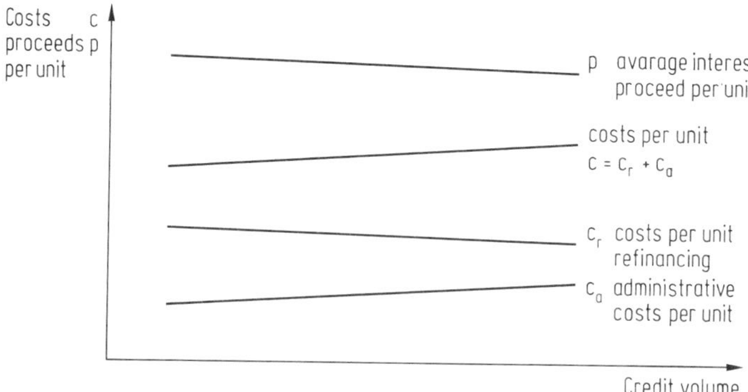

Figure 7: Development of costs and proceeds resulting from an expansion of the volume of credit by means of new subsidiaries etc.

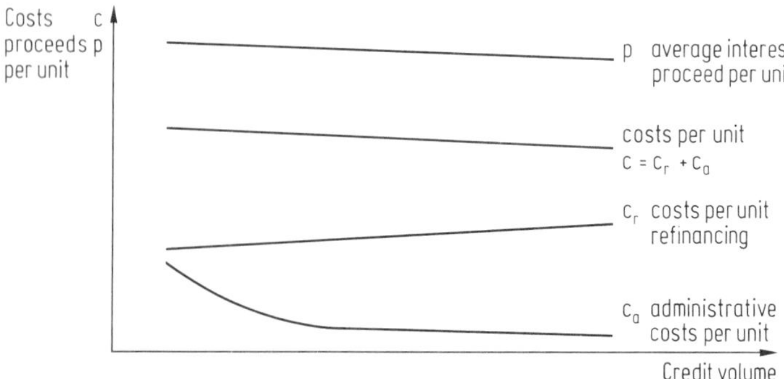

Figure 8: Development of costs and proceeds for an expansion of the volume of credit without additional subsidiaries etc.

As opposed to this, it can be observed that the refinancing costs increase for the case of expansion without the use of subsidiaries etc. This development is, however, more than compensated for by a large reduction in the average costs in the technical sector thus resulting in increasing average profits with an increasing volume of credit (Figure 8).

For those banks already having possible access to the Euro-market and world financial centres, an expansion in international credit transactions can be carried out without or with at the most, a minimum increase in fixed costs. For those credit institutions which are not already represented at these markets, there will, however, be an initial cost development corresponding to that experienced through expansion by means of additional subsidiaries. It should, however, be mentioned that changes are constantly taking place on the international credit market such as, in particular, decentralization attempts which require additional investments. An example of this is the introduction of the IBF dollar (International Banking Facilities) in December 1981 which led to a relocation of Euro-market transactions from London to New York.

Credit institutions and large-scale banks which were active in international credit transactions at a very early stage also enjoy competitive advantage which can be traced back to the fixed cost degression effect in the technical sector on the one hand, and numerous years of experience on the other hand. There is thus a certain tendency for the development of the costs to correspond to the experience curve effect, i.e. sinking average cost per unit of money lent out related to the cumulated credit turnover. This situation is further strengthened if the development of the proceeds is considered. Here market leaders receive one-off management-fees and front-and-fees for syndicating credits so that the interest margin is increased. This shift from interest to fees, achievable only by certain market participants, can lead to a reduction of the number of market participants and hence to a club-like situation (club-deals). It can be observed that such a strategy aimed at removing other market participants, leads to the risk being carried on fewer shoulders.

7. The Risk of a Change in Interest Rates

The risk of a change in interest rates is another aspect of risk involved in international credit transactions. This is generally known for the case of fixed-interest credits, whereas credits on a roll-over basis at variable interest rates are assumed to exclude risk. Risks related to changing interest rates can, however, also occure with roll-over credits, for example in the form of a refinancing risk if the credit institution has to pay an additional premium over and above the interbank rate whilst this rate is fixed as the basis for the borrower's calculation. This risk of interest change has gained significance for small credit institutions in connection with the crisis caused by the Herstatt Bank.

Mauclay's duration ratio can be used as an index for judgement of the risk involved in a change in interest rate:

$$\text{Duration D} = \frac{\sum_{t=a}^{n} \frac{C_t}{(1+r)^t} \cdot t}{\sum_{t=a}^{n} \frac{C_t}{(1+r)^t}}$$

whereby: c = cash return
r = market rate of return
a = first point in time of returns
n = last point in time of returns

The solvency effect of a prospective interest change or one that actually occurs on the total active and passive fixed interest rates positions of a credit institution can be estimated with the aid of the following formula (Rudolph 1976c; Schmidt 1981):

$$\Delta V_r = - \frac{A}{1 + r_A} D_A \Delta r_A + \frac{P}{1 + r_P} D_P \Delta r_P$$

ΔV_R = change in value due to a change in interest rate
Δr = expected or realized change of interest rate
A = present cash value of the fixed interest assets
P = present cash value of the fixed interest liabilities
D_A = active duration
D_P = passive duration
r_A = market rate of return assets
r_P = market rate of return liabilities

The equity at the disposal of a credit institution can serve as a measure for risk limitation as in the maximum risk bearing theory (Stützel 1964). Solvency effects which take place or which are to be expected are examined to see if the equity capital is capable of off-setting any calculated reduction in value. Apart from the risk involved in interest changes, precautionary rates of depreciation can be determined for risk arising from standing and currency changes. The sum of the negative effects on the value, whereby positive effects can off-set negative ones, should not be greater than the value of the liable equity.

If the equity proves to be inadequate, then no further risks should be undertaken. The calculation of the maximum risk bearing theory thus serves as a business policy for limiting risk.

8. Conclusion

Summing up it can be emphasized that efficient international credit management requires calculations of plan success for different interest and credit volume scenarios. In addition, risk analyses are applied, using the instruments of statistical classification analysis, to new engagements and for the current amount of credit to determine allowances for the case of prospective losses. Required standard margin contributions depending on different risk classes, can be used for the decision relating to the granting of credit. The necessity of using planning and controlling instruments for limiting risk does, however, vary for the different European banks. For example, Swiss banks, which are the largest supplier of credit on the international market, provide a half of its foreign credit from trust deposits and the risk thus lies with the investors and not with the banks.

Bibliography

Agthe, K.: Stufenweise Fixkostendeckung im System des Direct Costing. *Zeitschrift für Betriebswirtschaft* (ZfB) 1959, pp. 404–418.

Cramer, M.: *Das internationale Kreditgeschäft der Banken.* Wiesbaden 1981.

Fisk, Ch./Rimlinger, F.: Nonparametric Estimates of LDC Repayment Prospects. *The Journal of Finance,* Vo. XXXIV, No. 2, March 1979, pp. 429–438.

Franke, K.-H.: *Wachstumsplanung in Kreditinstituten.* Berlin 1978.

Guth, W.: Das internationale Kreditgeschäft der Banken und seine Probleme: *Die Bank,* 7, 1980, pp. 308–316.

Kippenberger, H.: Die geltenden Margen decken nicht die Kosten, sie sind bewußte oder unbewußte Rechenfehler. *Handelsblatt,* Nr. 60, 26. 3. 1979, supplement: Banken International, pp. 40–41.

Kleinewefers, H.: *Das Auslandsgeschäft der Schweizer Banken.* Zürich 1972.

Kretschmer, A./Preusche, R.: KWG-Novelle: Nachdenklich, *Die Bank,* 5, 1981, pp. 208–210.

Krümmel, H.-J.: Ansätze zu einer Theorie der Bankpreispolitik. In: Bank für Gemeinwirtschaft, ed.: *Zeitfragen der Kreditwirtschaft.* Frankfurt a.M. 1964, pp. 79–116.

Krümmer, H.-J.: Liquiditätssicherung im Bankwesen. *Kredit und Kapital.* Part one: 1968, pp. 247–307; Part two: 1969, pp. 60–110.

Llewellyn, D. T.: International banking in the 1970's: an overview. In: Frowen, S. F., ed.: *A Framework of International Banking.* Würzburg – Wien 1979, pp. 25–54.

Mayo, A. L./Barrett, A. G.: An Early Warning Model for Assessing Developing Country Risk. In: Goodman, St. H., ed.: *Financing and Risk in Developing Countries.* Washington D.C. 1977 (Export-Import-Bank), pp. 81–87.

Mellerowicz, K.: *Planung und Plankostenrechnung.* Bd. I, Betriebliche Planung, Freiburg 1961.

Preisig, K. W.: *Roll-Over-Eurokredit.* Bern 1976.

Reinhardt, H.: *Die Risiken am Eurokreditmarkt.* Mitteilungen aus dem Institut für das Spar-, Giro- und Kreditwesen an der Universität zu Bonn, Nr. 3, Bonn 1979.

Riebel, P.: *Einzelkosten- und Deckungsbeitragsrechnung.* Opladen 1972.

Rudolph, B.: *Kapitalkosten bei unsicheren Erwartungen.* Berlin – Heidelberg – New York, 1979 (a):

Rudolph, B.: Zur Theorie des Kapitalmarktes. *Zeitschrift für Betriebswirtschaft* (ZfB), 11, 1979 (b), pp. 1034–1067.

Rudolph, B.: Zinsänderungsrisiken und die Strategie der durchschnittlichen Selbstliquidationsperiode. *Kredit und Kapital,* 1979 (c), pp. 181–206.

Schmidt, H.: Wege zur Ermittlung und Beurteilung der Marktzinsrisiken von Banken. *Kredit und Kapital,* 1981, pp. 249–286.

Studienkommission Grundsatzfragen der Kreditwirtschaft. Bericht, Bonn 1979.

Stützel, W.: *Bankpolitik – heute und morgen.* Frankfurt 1964, pp. 41–48.

European Financial Reporting: Standards and Efficiency Problems

Klaus Macharzina

> Accounting must necessarily
> differ from case to case
> if it is to retain the sharp
> cutting edge of social utility.
> (Choi and Mueller 1978)

Summary

Diverse financial reporting standards and requirements in Europe have initiated harmonization programmes particularly on the level of the European Communities. There are also guidelines for financial disclosure of multinationals issued by the OECD. While the latter are not very effective because of their loose and recommendatory nature the former are largely a result of political compromise and not very efficient because of conceptual deficiences. The paper looks at the important requirements of European accounting laws and regulations, and attempts at proposing a new concept based on a critical analysis of the state of the art.

1. European Financial Reporting Revisited

Financial reporting in Europe has been extremely diverse despite the economic integration of this region, and in spite of increasing attempts to harmonize the practices of financial measurement and reporting, European accounting is still national in scope. Except for a few activities this is also true of the related academic discipline. Cognizant of the necessity of an internationalization of accounting standards which is mainly based on the world-wide expansion of trade and investment flows, the present paper attempts to assess this process with respect to Europe's role in it. The way in which international standards have developed to date, and the reflection which they have found in Europe justify such an assessment of the state of this process. It is suggested to examine the relevance for national or even regional differences which are reflected in national laws and professional standards or regional coordinative regulations such as the Fourth European Directive and OECD guidelines not to forget about the early activities of the Union Européene des Experts Comptables Economiques et Financieres (UEC), an organization to which Louis Perridon has been linked in a leading capacity and guiding rôle towards harmonization for many years (Perridon 1975).

The existing diversity of accounting practices is certainly not accidental. Rather it is borne by particular historical roots and specific contextual influences due to different developmental systems. These reflect not only different local information demands of users and measurement requirements of preparers of financial reports rather than also different authorities which have been acting as major driving forces towards the development of accounting requirements at national level. Should international differences of these requirements remain to be relevant – and there is a number of reasons that they are important – then changes brought about by harmonized standards would endanger the efficiency of financial reporting at national level.

As the forerunners of a harmonization of European standards have been the various accountancy professions represented in a so-called European Study Group it is suggested to check the results of their efforts against academic assessment. This seems to be even more necessary when one realizes that harmonization activities to date were without reliance on conceptual frameworks. Accordingly, it remains doubtful as to whether a sufficiently perceptive approach has been taken in the various attempts to reduce the differences between national financial reporting requirements (McComb 1979; Choi 1979).

The aim in the long range would be to develop a "decentralized" European accounting system with only limited harmonization modules. These should not only allow for alternative accounting measurements and methods. Rather decision models should be designed which would advise about the most efficient financial measurement and reporting practices in diverse accounting environments.

As a first step in this direction the present paper attempts to design a conceptual framework which allows for a more differentiated analysis of the respective environmental forces which influence national or regional accounting requirements. By use of such a model it should be possible to develop European standards in a more sensible way than only by aggregating what is considered to be good accounting practice in different countries or by designing standards based on the least common denominator of a political bargaining exercise. Obviously, the result of this type of approach would not be a system of uniform European standards but rather a set of regionally integrated standards where the criteria for boundaries need not necessarily be of a geographical nature. Rather similarities among accounting environments could lead to useful and meaningful "accounting clusters".

2. State of European Accounting Harmonization

The harmonization of accounting requirements was certainly not the primary objective of the European Communities (EC)*. This only forms part of the legal program included in the Rome Treaty of 1957 (Article 54/ (3) (g)) which represents the legal basis for the EC. Community law in the form of directives would specify certain minimum standards with which all national member states' laws would have to comply within a period of two years. The so-called Fourth Directive on the Annual Accounts of Certain Types of Companies (Commission of the European Communities 1978) requires minimum standards as to the form and contents of the annual accounts of private and public limited companies (about 1 500 000) covered. It includes the substance of the information to be published with particular reference to the balance sheet, valuation of related items, the income statement, and the notes. Specific disclosure requirements are contained in the First Directive of 1968, group accounts are dealt with in the Seventh Directive of 1983, organizational structure of companies and rights, duties, and liabilities of directors and auditors in the second draft of the proposed Fifth Directive of 1983, the qualification of auditors in the Eighth Directive of 1984, internal disclosure to employees in the proposed so-called "Vredeling"-Directive of 1983, and the Structure of Groups in the proposed Nineth Directive of 1985.

The implementation of the Fourth Directive will bring about major changes in the accounting laws and reporting practices of the member states of the EC. Some will be required to introduce for the first time a comprehensive set of legal rules with respect to the form and contents of annual accounts. Others will have to amend and complete their legislation, besides they will have to introduce the concept of the overriding obligation to provide a "true and fair view" of a company's situation. New requirements will cause considerable difficulties in terms of acceptance and operation by the preparers and users of financial information. On the other hand, there is much leeway as regards adoption of accounting and in particular measurement methods. There is extra disclosure of profit items required and reduced publication and audit requirements allowed for small companies. Banks and Insurance Companies are exempt from the provisions of the Directive. This again points at the central focus of the nature of harmonization of accounting standards.

The important requirements relate to the standardization of formats for the published balance sheet and profit and loss statement. There is a choice

* Twelve member states including Belgium, Denmark, the Federal Republic of Germany, France, Greece, Ireland, Italy, Luxembourg, the Netherlands and the United Kingdom, and another two, namely Portugal and Spain, as of 01-01-1986.

Assets

A Subscribed capital unpaid
B Formation expenses
C Fixed assets
- Intangible assets
- Tangible assets
- Participating interests and other financial assets
D Current assets
- Stocks
- Debtors
- Securities
- Cash
E Repayments and accrued income
F Loss for the financial year

Liabilities

A Capital and reserves
- Subscribed capital
- Share premium
- Revaluation reserve
- Reserves
- Profit/loss brought forward
- Profit/loss for the financial year
B Provisions for liabilities and charges
C Creditors
D Accruals and deferred income
E Profit for the financial year
(unless required to be shown as a reserve)

Details, as specified in the directive, would need to be shown in the notes

Figure 1a: Minimum format of the balance sheet

between the "statement" and "account" form and a choice of presentation for the trading account. (Fig. 1a and b)

Regrouping and summarization of items is possible. There are a number of calls for notes, particularly with respect to disclosure of the effect of taxation on the accounts which will be relevant for analyzing German and French financial statements. Apart from disclosure requirements on related companies in the notes there are no requirements for group accounts in the Fourth Directive. On the other hand does the Seventh Directive require such accounts including the case of foreign subsidiaries. Member states may permit or require a type of inflation accounting but there is no standardization on current cost or current purchasing power adjustments, and no regulation as to whether adjusted statements should be the main or supplementary ones or whether merely

A Charges

1. Cost of sales (including value adjustments)
2. Distribution costs (including value adjustments)
3. Administrative expenses (including value adjustments)
4. Value adjustments in respect of financial assets and of investments held as current assets
5. Interest payable and similar charges, with a separate indication of those concerning affiliated undertakings
6. Tax on profit or loss on ordinary activities
7. Profit or loss on ordinary activities after taxation
8. Extraordinary charges
9. Tax on extraordinary profit or loss
10. Other taxes not shown under the above items
11. Profit or loss for the financial year

B Income

1. Net turnover
2. Other operating income
3. Income from participating interests, with a separate indication of that derived from affiliated undertakings
4. Income from other investments and loans forming part of the fixed assets, with a separate indication of that derived from affiliated undertakings
5. Other interest receivable and similar income, with a separate indication of that derived from affiliated undertakings
6. Profit or loss on ordinary activities after taxation
7. Extraordinary income
8. Profit or loss for the financial year

Figure 1b: Minimum format of the profit and loss account

adjusting notes should be provided. Only the difference between adjusted and historic values must be shown.

Under rigorous criteria of corporate financial reporting one might be critical about the fact that the Directive is silent on the question of a "legal set-off" and the problem of "hidden reserves". The first is related to the prohibition of any set-off between assets and liabilities on the basis of which one might conclude that the practice of letters of set-off is rendered illegal. The possibility of building up hidden reserves is not completely eliminated by the Directive but limited by way of restrictions of under-valuation in the balance sheet and with respect to compensatory netting in the profit and loss statement.

Furthermore it is unsatisfactory that some eminent accounting problems are not sufficiently or not at all covered. These are the reporting of foreign currency translation, of leasing, and of the sources and application of funds. While there

	OECD	European Communities
Degree of codification	guidelines	compulsory legal requirements comprising national rights of options
coverage	multinational corporations	private and public companies with certain (national) exemptions
form and contents of balance sheet		required structure with a choice between statement and account form of presentation details of items of the balance sheet e. g. – disclosure of creditors becoming due and payable within one year – intangible assets
form and contents of profit and loss statement		required detailed structure with a choice between statement and accounts form of presentation
valuation		historical cost principle; national options of different types of inflation accounting; lower of cost or market rule for current assets, in exempt cases a still lower valuation; national options of revaluation for financial fixed assets;
	requirement to inform about the methods of drawing up the balance sheet	disclosure of valuation method
group accounting		consolidation required with certain national options (7th Directive) structure of group accounts under requirements of 4th Directive
	disclosure of information on the entire corporation and the important group companies	disclosure of information on holding company and group companies
		disclosure of the companies included in the group accounts
	disclosure of consolidation policy	disclosure of valuation methods used while drawing up group accounts
		disclosure of information on non-consolidated companies and related companies application of equity method subject to 20% ownership criterion

	OECD	European Communities
publicity	publication of financial statements of the entire corporation, recommendation to include funds statement and R & D statement;	publication of balance sheet, profit and loss account, notes directors report and audit report (4th Directive)
	publication of accounting, consolidation and transfer pricing policy	publication of valuation and revaluation methods
		publication of group accounts, directors group report and audit report for the group (7th Directive)
	publication of segment reports, breakdown of turnover for regions and divisions	publication of segment reports, breakdown of activities and geopraphical market segments
	disclosure of new capital investments and of the number of employees in the various regions	disclosure in the notes, e. g. – basis of foreign currency translation methods – equity investments – pension agreements and agreements with related companies – average number of employees – salaries of the directors and the supervisory board – amount of creditors due and payable within more than 5 years.

Figure 2: Comparative Description of some Important Contents of OECD Guidelines and EC Accounting Directives

is some guidance included in the Fourth Directive with respect to the first problem area there is no mention of the two latter problems in the Directive (Petite 1984).

The OECD, a 24 nation organization has issued a Code (cf. OECD 1976, amended 1979) with respect to the behavior of multinational corporations. Among the Code's many provisions there are specific financial disclosure guidelines relating to such items as operating results and turnover by geographical area and lines of business, as well as research and development expenditures for the business as a whole. Although considerable political and moral suasion supports the OECD the guidelines may not be too effective because of its voluntary nature. Fig. 2 contains a comparative description of the major requirements both of OECD guidelines and the European accounting directive.

The European example provides evidence for reluctance of national member states of the EC to accept the harmonized provisions of the Fourth Directive.

This was shown by the tedious and troublesome process of passing this directive. Besides, some of the member states hastily passed own national accounting legislation before the Directive was enacted as a European Law in 1978. The compulsory transformation of this law into national legislation has been dealt with reluctantly by most of the member states that have failed to meet the official deadline considerably.

Until now only Denmark, the U.K., France and Luxembourg have implemented the Directive in full and Belgium in parts. Moreover, there are clear indications that wherever there is leeway in form of options these will be used as far as possible. For instance, the proposed German transformation law (Bilanzrichtlinie-Gesetz i.d.F. von 1985) does not require inflation accounting despite a counter proposal of the German Institute of Public Accountants. At the extreme other end will price variation accounting form one of the most important requirements in the Dutch transformation law. How then is it possible to develop European standards in a more meaningful way when one accepts that the EC's Common Industrial Policy of 1970 has failed to establish a unified European economic and business environment. The establishment of a 'Contact Committee' of the EC and national civil servants is certainly a sign of the perceived obstacles of harmonization but no proper means to cure the problems. This committee is to look at practical problems arising from the implementation of the directives and to make suggestions for amendments. On an overall scale it is intended to advise where national laws are inflexible to changing circumstances and attitudes.

3. Conceptual Model

In order to take into account the existing environmental diversities in the various nations within which the accounting requirements are to operate a conceptual approach is suggested. This framework contains a system of variables related with the goals, the means, the context, and the efficiency of financial measurement and reporting. Goal variables include financial reporting objectives; means variables represent the variety of accounting methods and instruments of reporting; contextual variables relate to the accounting environment including the rule-making bodies; finally, efficiency variables measure the quality of accounting information in terms of the objectives.

As a first step this model can be used for descriptive purposes in order to improve the understanding of different accounting environments in the harmonization process. It may on the other hand serve predictive purposes as well so that the four sets of variables can be mutually related in order to form a complex system of hypotheses. The latter step is, however, not the intention of the present paper.

3.1 Objectives of Financial Reporting

Although, the discussion about objectives of financial reporting has had a long tradition it cannot claim to have provided a satisfactory solution yet. Maybe the reason for this negative outcome is that there is not much sense in attempting to solve this question in a *generally* acceptable way. Rather it may be more useful to analyze and test various national definitions of objectives of financial reporting against the historical context in which they were developed. In this way, the underlying reason for particular definitions and thereby the necessity for changes of the latter may become more explicit. Comparing for instance the German and the British opinions on objectives of financial reporting will result in disagreement. While these objectives are nowhere explicitly defined in Germany there is a rather flexible requirement contained in company law which could be interpreted as the informational purpose of annual accounts. Under § 119 (1) AktG* such accounts should disclose a company's results and net assets as fairly as possible within the framework of the valuation requirements. A secondary purpose refers to the determination of a company's annual income. This is a conflict-regulating mechanism which limits on the one hand the distribution of the annual profit by allowing the management board to retain up to 50 percent of it (§§ 58, 150 AktG) and, on the other hand, guarantees a minimum distribution to minority shareholders (§§ 58, 254 AktG). Apart from this there is a built-in conflict between these two basic purposes which the law-maker does not resolve. Moreover, they represent a rather conservative standpoint in terms of the societal function of financial reporting – very similar to the U.S. attitude.

Under FASB Statement of Financial Accounting Concept No. 1 the objective of financial reporting is to provide "information to help investors and creditors and other users assessing the amounts, timing, and uncertainty of prospective cash receipts from dividends or interest and the proceeds from the sale, redemption, or maturity of securities or loans". The opinion which directs financial reporting specifically to information needs of shareholders and potential investors is based upon the classical economic model of the firm rather than upon the way of business operations in developed industries (McComb 1979). This theory can be considered as a naive model of the motivational forces operating in large business organizations. The British attitude towards objectives of financial reporting is also concernd with communication of economic measurements of and information about the resources and performance of the reporting entity but does explicitly deny that distributable profit be the primary

* Aktiengesetz 1965 (Company Law)

performance indicator in corporate reports. It accepts multiple responsibilities of a business which are to be reported to those having reasonable rights to the information (Accounting Standards Steering Committee 1975). Clearly, catering for such disparate objectives accounting standards will be doomed to ineffectiveness from the very start. Accordingly objectives would have to be harmonized. This on the other hand does not seem to be feasible because of the diversity among and incompatibility of existing accounting objectives. This means that the question of objectives of the businesses themselves in the various countries will have to be raised if it holds true that it is the compatibility between corporate objectives in each country which limits the scope of harmonization. As a consequence national variations in the perception of the objectives, and national differences in ranking of the objectives of financial measurement and reporting of the business should be analyzed (McComb 1979).

3.2 Financial Reporting Environment

Analysis of disparate objectives in turn requires careful study of the underlying accounting environments because public perception of corporate objectives and the related interests in information about the corporation are largely influenced by the societal, i.e. social, political, economic etc. environment. Moreover, environmental analysis may provide useful information about the forces at work influencing financial measurement and reporting either directly or indirectly. Variables such as the level of industrialization, the degree of international integration of the economy, the quality of the capital market may be taken to exert a general influence on national accounting systems. Another class of variables which have a direct influence on national systems are normally referred to as financial reporting authorities. These may be the law, accounting practice, the accountancy profession, the stock exchange, governmental agencies, the bureaucracy, trade unions, boards of industries, and even accounting academics. These in turn reflect the national societal structure at large.

Some examples of different national accounting environments which are discussed below may provide a rough understanding about the accounting objectives followed, the accounting methods used, and the resulting accounting efficiency.

3.3 Methods of Financial Reporting

In the balance sheet, formats are diverse and definitions as to what does and does not constitute an asset varies from country to country. As regards the format the German and French examples of the prescribed structure of financial

Germany

Balance Sheet

Assets		
I. Capital subscriptions outstanding: showing the amount for payment		xxx
II. Fixed assets:		
A Fixed assets and intangibles	xxx	
B Investments	xxx	xxx
III. Revolving assets		
A Inventories	xxx	
B Other revolving assets	xxx	xxx
IV. Prepaid expenses and deferred charges		xxx
V. Deficit		xxx
		xxx
Liabilities		
I. Share capital		xxx
II. Reserves		xxx
III. Valuation reserves		xxx
IV. Estimated expense reserves and accrued liabilities		xxx
V. Liabilities with terms of at least four years		xxx
VI. Other liabilities		xxx
VII. Deferred income	xxx	
VIII. Profit		xxx
		xxx

Profit and Loss Statement of the Year	
Gross sales	xxx
Total	xxx
Net	xxx
Net income or loss for the year	xxx
Profit/loss carried forward	xxx

France

Balance Sheet

Assets		
I. Organisational expenses		xxx
II. Fixed assets		
A Property, plant and equipment	xxx	
B Other fixed assets	xxx	xxx
III. Current assets		
A Inventories	xxx	
B Other current assets	xxx	xxx
IV. Results		xxx
V. Amount of guarantees received		xxx
		xxx

Liabilities		
I. Capital and reserves		
A Capital	xxx	
B Reserves	xxx	
C Earned surplus/(deficit) brought forward	xxx	
D Equipment subsidies received	xxx	
E Reserves for losses and charges	xxx	xxx
II. Long and medium-term debts		xxx
III. Current liabilities		xxx
IV. Results	xxx	
V. Amount of guarantees given		xxx
		xxx

Profit and Loss Account for the Year	
Expenditure	
I. General trading account	xxx
II. Profit and loss account	xxx
Income	
I. General trading account	xxx
II. Profit and loss account	xxx

Figure 3: Required structure of German and French Financial Statements under AktG 1965 and Plan Comptable Général 1947, amended 1957 (the French requirements were adjusted to EC standards in 1982)

statements before the enactment of the Fourth Directive may illustrate some striking differences.

For private limited companies in France any change in the form of or principles of valuation in financial statements must be approved by the shareholders on the basis of reports of management and auditors, and on the basis of financial statements for the year being submitted in both the old and new forms. Depreciation reserves and necessary provisions must be set up, irrespective of whether there are profits or losses. Organization expenses must be fully written off before any dividends may be distributed. Goodwill is rarely depreciated. Expenses for increase of capital must be fully written off not more than five years after they have been incurred.

An appropriation of 5% of net profit of the year less prior losses brought forward if any is required to be made each year until a legal reserve equal to 10% of the capital is built up. This legal reserve cannot be distributed as a cash dividend and may only be used to absorbe losses. Cash dividends for any year must be paid not later than nine months after the closing date of the period.

On the contrary German private limited companies under Publicity Law of 1969 are not required to set aside an annual legal reserve as public companies have to do in Germany. A special feature in Germany is that the provision for liabilities of future pension payments are only optional. With few specific exceptions charges relating to the future cannot be deferred; rather they have to be fully written off against the income of the period in which they are incurred. Goodwill, only if purchased on acquisition of a business may be (not obligatory) recorded as an asset item, and in this case must be written off by annual charges to income of at least 20%. All liabilities must be fully provided for, receivable balances on deferred tax accounts which for instance arise through timing differences may not be carried in the books.

In conclusion it should be stressed that in both countries tax laws contain numerous requirements to the extent that they refer to general accounting matters and are usually considered as a part of good accounting principles.

The event that tax auditors (which often turn up rather infrequently and on very short notice in order to check the books and accounts of a company) would find deficiencies as regards these requirements could result in serious consequences. One of these could be expected to be the disallowance of tax concessions, a second the estimation in whole or in part of the taxable profits of the respective company by the tax authorities to the best of their ability. An even more serious consequence would be that where the accounting records have been rejected for a period in which the company has incurred a loss, it could forfeit the right to carry forward the loss against taxable profits of a later period.

German and French valuation provisions insofar as they relate to the prevention of an overstatement of net assets and net income apply to all business enterprises. Fixed assets in both countries are to be stated at cost less appropriate depreciation. There are detailed rules of the computation of depreciation charges in both countries. Earned assets are to be stated at the lowest of cost, net realizable value, or replacement, or lower if taxpurposes or a reasonable business judgement allow for this in Germany, whereas in France current assets must be simply valued at the lower of cost or market. Cost is usually to be determined by using the moving average method. LIFO is not permitted in France, and only permitted for tax purposes in Germany providing that the physical movement corresponds to the method used. Tangibles in Germany may only be carried if they were required from third parties; in France the may only be recorded if they were required for valuable consideration. The application of German and French tax law leads to an understatement of assets, especially where special depreciation rates for tax purposes for some types of fixed assets and inventory reserves up to 20 or 30% on certain imported products are allowed.

Comparing European accounting methods by including the other countries one finds that assets may include various types of leases, tax loss carry-forwards, and losses associated with foreign currency borrowings. Valuations of assets may be at historic cost or various types current values. Provisions for known liabilities such as pension agreements, or estimated losses, e.g. on long-term purchase commitments are not always taken up. On the other hand are liability definitions frequently used in order to understate reported earnings and to "hidden reserves". There is also great diversity with respect to the treatment of shareholders' equity. In some countries all transactions, except those relating to shareholder contributions, are required to flow directly to the income statement, while in others non-recurring gains or losses are permitted to be treated as adjustments to shareholders' equity.

European companies frequently use balance sheet reserves as a means of managing the trend in reported earnings. The practice that purchased goodwill is recorded as an asset and periodically charged to expense is seldom followed in Europe. Also due to a principle that financial and tax reporting should agree in some countries there is no deferred tax accounting.

3.4 Efficiency of Financial Reporting

The above discussion has shown that internationally harmonized standards simply may not apply in specific national contexts. When requiring international standards in those cases then not only the quality of information would be distorted; rather there is a danger of misallocation of resources.

Looking at the European standards on disclosure policy there is some doubt as to whether these are appropriate to regions in which debt financing via credit institutions is paramount compared to public equity financing as is the case in nearly all European countries apart from Britain and may be The Netherlands. It is true that France took a stand by suggesting that disclosure is necessary to develop capital markets because it would attract investors. Yet, inspite of making disclosure requirements much more restrictive the French have failed to increase the efficiency of their capital market. The reason for this may be that the mere fact that information about companies and their performance is improved will never attract investors to the stock exchange unless there is also a fundamental change in their attitudes towards equity investment. At the same time a basic structural change of financial institutions and intermediaries would be necessary in order to create the appropriate infrastructure which is geared to equity investment. Both such preconditions are for instance not available in some European countries. Also the consolidation requirements of the Seventh Directive (Commission of the European Communities 1983) may only be useful in cases where ownership of shares is widely spread. Another controversial issue with respect to efficiency is the European Fourth and Seventh Directives' 20% ownership criterion as a condition for use of the equity method of accounting for non-consolidated subsidiaries. This does not make such sense in cases where the shares of related companies are in the hands of say few medium or small businesses, or even family-type related owners. The latter often have stronger links than those based on formal parent-subsidiary relationships. As both cases are typical of certain European countries the Directives' requirements may be inefficient when applied in those countries.

To raise a "reverse" issue, i.e. one which was not taken up yet by the European standard setters, probably because of their tendency to mainly rely on professional impetus rather than societal interests, the problem of corporate social reporting (CSR) shall be mentioned briefly. Although this kind of disclosure certainly meets a large group of public interests it is not in the forefront of European programmes. Cognizant of this lack we are inextricably led back to the problem of accounting goals. Had the European standard setters thought about goals in the first place, they might have ranked the topic of CSR higher in their priority scale. Finally, defining objectives would make the problem of putting European standards to test in terms of their efficiency much easier, because it would be possible to measure the informational value against standards. As we are left with speculative assumptions about the underlying norms of proposed and required European standards their efficiency is difficult to assess; also the range for criticism is wide open. At the moment the extent of disclosure seems to be the primary efficiency criterion. We have already argued that even this is debatable from the standpoint of particular user interests.

4. Quest for Decentralized Solutions

It is obvious that in the context of our present societal development accounting does not only serve economic purposes but a complex set of interests. This has not yet been recognized by the European standard setting organizations. So far they have failed to appreciate multiple interests in accounting information. In order to make European standards more useful so that they might satisfy multiple interests it is imperative to analyze these interests and subsequent information requirements first, and only then develop standards.

Accordingly, empirical research based on and controlled by a conceptual model will be necessary in order to obtain valid knowledge about these interests. In order to understand and make them operable in accounting terms they will have to be interpreted with respect to their historical development and actual context (Nobes and Parker 1985; Macharzina and Scholl 1984). Because of the diversity of environmental forces and interests a system of harmonized standards seems to be necessary which would comprise decentralized solutions on a regional basis. This can certainly be effected by a central coordinating international body, representation of which should be designed towards respective interest groups.

We are on the brink of a new understanding of international harmonization of financial reporting: harmonization by sound conceptual reasoning rather than by false political compromise.

Bibliography

Accounting Standards Steering Committee, *The Corporate Report.* London 1975.

Choi, F. D. S.: Asia-Pacific Dimensions of Accounting Harmonization. In: Proceedings of the Academy of International Business. *Asia-Pacific Dimensions of International Business.* Honolulu 1979, pp. 199–206.

Commission of the European Communities, *Official Journal of the European Communities.* Vol. 21, No. L 222, 1978 pp. 11–31.

Commission of the European Communities, *Official Journal of the European Communities.* Vol. 26, No. L 193, 1983, pp.1–17.

Macharzina, K./Scholl, R. F.: Internationale Vereinheitlichung der Rechnungslegung. *Die Betriebswirtschaft,* Vol. 44, 1984, pp. 229–252.

McComb, D.: The International Harmonization of Accounting: A Cultural Dimension. *The International Journal of Accounting,* Vol. 14, No. 2, 1979, pp. 1–16.

Nobes, C. W./Parker, R. H.: *Comparative International Accounting 2nd ed.,* Oxford 1985.

OECD, *Code of Conduct for Multinational Enterprises.* Geneva 1976.

OECD, *International Investment and Multinational Enterprises,* revised ed., Paris 1979.

Perridon, L.: Internationales Kolloquium über die Harmonisierung der Abschlußprüfung von Gesellschaften in der Europäischen Wirtschaftsgemeinschaft. *Journal UEC,* Vol. 10, 1975, pp. 178–180.

Petite, M.: Future Developments in EEC Accounting Harmonisation. In: Gray, S. J./Coenenberg, A. G. eds.: *EEC Accounting Harmonisation: Implementation and Impact of the Fourth Directive.* Amsterdam 1984, pp. 131–139.

Personnel Management in Western Europe – Development, Situation and Concepts –

Andreas Remer

Summary

Nowadays it is generally acknowledged that it is wrong even start looking for the "right" approach to personnel management in a company. There is now widespread acceptance of the fact that managing a business necessarily involves both a generalized understanding of, and a specialized skill in fields like organization, leadership and personnel management, depending on the situation obtaining at any one point in time. This poses the question as to which concepts might be suitable for the particular situation. The example of the "situational theory of organization" shows that there is a need for some order in view of the actual multiplicity of characteristics relating to these situations and concepts. For those engaged in the academic study of personnel management this gives rise to a challenge to describe conceivable or probable situations in a simplified and comprehensive manner, to discover their causes and thereby to make it possible to forecast them, as well as to examine their effects on personnel management and to develop appropriate concepts within this field.

This paper concentrates on providing a broad outline of this task, above all by trying to present typical situations and their historical development in the context of personnel management. The situation in the Federal Republic of Germany is accorded a place of central importance. For the management of a company, the value of a presentation of this kind can be seen in the fact that it is thereby able to recognize the present state of developments, to draw logical conclusions regarding developments with conditions in the future and to draft appropriate concepts for personnel management. The analysis and classification of situations in personnel management can also serve as a reference point and guide to circumstances in Europe which still reveal a great variety of regional differences.

1. Basic Concepts

1.1 Personnel Administration as an Element of General Management

In this context, human resource management is understood to be a process which aims at the planned organisation of the structure of personnel (Wunderer/Mittmann 1983, p. 630). "Personnel" is deemed to be those persons bound to a company by contractual or other means (March/Simon 1976, p. 86 ff.).

If one looks at the company or economy (Luhmann 1970, p. 204 ff.; Grochla 1978, p. 8 ff.) as an *event* delimited by certain points of view, then business management encompasses everything which serves the organisation of this occurrence (Ulrich/Fluri 1978, p. 37). In the context under discussion, it is interpersonal events as opposed to purely mechanical and technical ones which are deemed of importance. Seen from this point of view, business management can also be defined as the organisation of social systems (Kolbinger 1972, p. 7 ff., 14 ff.). In this context, a difference can be established between two major elements of business management: on the one hand we have programmatic organisation in the form of policy-making and scheduling, and on the other instrumental organisation in the form of administration, personnel management and leadership (Ulrich/Fluri 1978, p. 39 f.).

The *instrumental* nature of personnel administration lies in the fact that it is a means to certain managerial ends. As an element of business management it is connected in many different ways to all other elements of the system of management, and for this reason it cannot be implemented or changed without taking account of the whole system of management. Its *function* in business management generally consists of mediating between the organisation and individuals; in the first instance the question as to which point of reference is accorded the greater priority must be left open. As an *institutionalised form* of business management, personnel administration is made up of organisational arrangements, individuals and codified procedures (Remer/Wunderer 1979, p. 10 ff.).

1.2 Situation and Adaptation of Personnel Management

The *situation* of personnel management is characterized by the organisational conditions obtaining at any one point in time. By this we mean by and large those factors which have a decisive effect upon personnel management e.g. the economy, technology, society, employers, politics, law as well as science and culture (Eckardstein/Schnellinger 1973, p. 35 ff., Bisani 1976, p. 29 ff.). On the one hand these factors influence the organisational and human demands made on personnel management, or the way these demands are fulfilled, and on the other hand they are linked to certain ideas as to what a firm is and what its management problem consists of (Fig. 1) (re consequences for personnel administration see Remer 1978b, p. 524 ff.).

The process of *adaptation* in personnel management can be viewed from an instrumental, institutional and functional point of view (Fig. 2).

Adaptation to the system of personnel management becomes necessary when there are normative, logical or factual discrepancies between personnel management and the situation in question. The personnel manager is faced with the

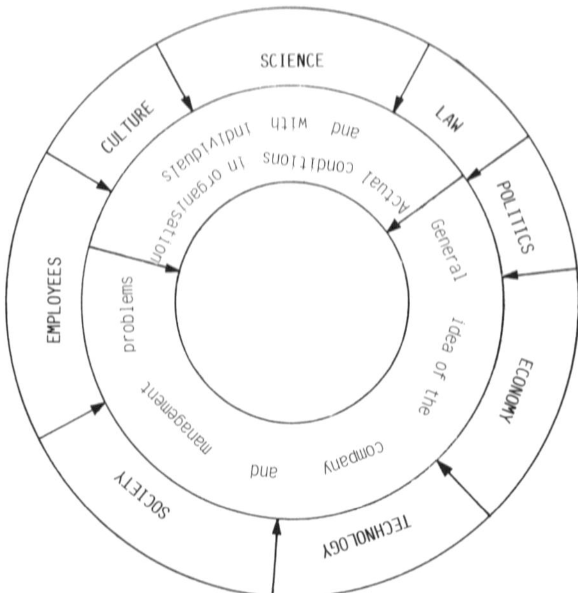

Figure 1: Situational characteristics of personnel management

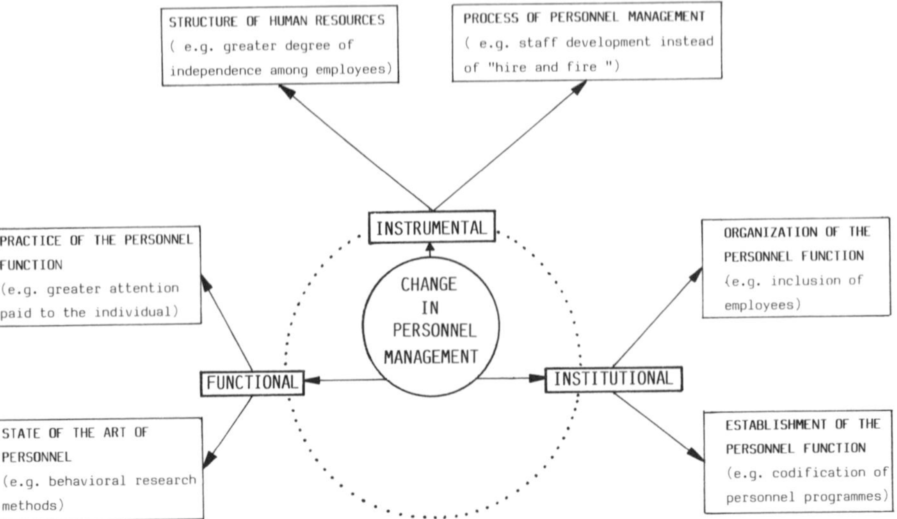

Figure 2: Change in personnel management

particular problem of being able to recognize or indeed forecast the need to adapt the system. This would not only presuppose a deep theoretical understanding of personnel management but also the ability to discover and interpret critical symptoms in situations. Of course, this process is made very much easier if reference can be made to ideas about *typical* situations and developmental tendencies.

What follows is a sub-division of personnel management into classical, neoclassical and modern forms, in which a situational model is expounded which is well known in literature (Massie 1965; Scott 1961; Mayntz 1964, Hoffmann 1973; Staehle 1980), and which unites situational aspects with those derived from logic. The basic idea behind this scheme is that it is possible in personnel management – just as in other fields like organisation and planning or in science, art and culture etc. – to observe the course of its development from "birth" and full development through modifications to degeneration or mutation. Each of these "phases" is based upon changes in external conditions and calls for different concepts, as is the case with personnel management.

In this connection it is essential that the development can be refined and promoted with regional variations and differences relating to the specific needs of companies. For this reason, any comparisons between USA and Europe or comparisons made within Europe (e.g. Bisani/Friedrichs 1979, p. 157 ff.) and even within the Federal Republic of Germany reveal very different situations in personnel management terms, and these differences call for different concepts, at least in broad terms.

2. Development and Concepts of Personnel Management in Western Europe

2.1 Classical Personnel Management

2.1.1 Classical Situation

From a historical point of view, the main focus of classical human resource management lies in the period from 1850 until the Second World War (Eckardstein/Schnellinger 1973, p. 35 ff.). However, in regional terms, classical personnel management can still be found wherever the situational characteristics depicted in Fig. (3) are a dominant feature of the scene.

In a situation like this the dominant company model is that of the "machine". According to this view of things, a firm "consists" of human and material factors which are installed in their entirety and as fixed items just as one might locate a piece of machinery with a specific job to do (e.g. Luhmann 1971,

Economy	Geared to production, problem-free labour markets, reliable mechanisms & rules, low volume, expansionist and positive without any shadow of doubt
Technology	Machine-based, beginnings of modern transport and communications systems, first large machines
Society	Differences in education, standards & opportunities still great, new freedom through professional work in sight, excess labour, few highly qualified workers
Employers	Owners or sole proprietors, mainly engineers or financiers. Sole-control and one-man planning still possible, main interest – profit and thinking in terms of costs
Politics	Nationalistic, economic and materialistic, use and promotion of nation's economic and military potential, new ideas on hierarchy
Law	Freely negotiated wages and contracts, property system and employers' rights, at best physical protection for employees
Science	Increased tendency to application for material purposes, rise of engineering sciences, Darwinism
Culture	Sense of duty, economic sense, materialism, pioneering spirit, utilitarianism as central values

Figure 3: Important characteristics of the classical management situation

p. 27 f.; March/Simon 1976, p. 18 ff.; Leibenstein 1960, p. 138 ff.). Management's control problem consists of creating an effective factor system which, at the press of a button, produces work and controll processes according to plan (e.g. Taylor 1947, Fayol 1916).

It is characteristic of the situation of classical personnel management that:

- people in the labour market can be incorporated into every area of the company relatively easily and show a very limited aptitude for more complex tasks, and
- organisational structures embody the entrepreneurial process in a clear, unambiguous and lasting manner and allow individual freedom of movement in very few positions.

In this example, the function of personnel management, i.e. mediation between organisation and personnel, can only take on the following form; the translation of organisational demands into corresponding staffing characteristics and the provision of a "corps of personnel" whose constituents are matched to each other and employed like the parts of a machine. When reduced to common terms, this form of "mediation" means fitting people into jobs.

2.1.2 Classical Concept

Classical concepts of personnel management are based upon a simple corps of personnel with whom very precise demands regarding output can, and indeed have to be laid down. Less attention is paid to planning the staffing structure than to the cheapest possible means of securing planned output. The organisation and implementation of personnel management is not considered a problem, since it is an integral component of a leader's role (Dahrendorf 1957; Büschges 1974, p. 141). The firm has at its disposal output potential in the form of simple, cheap employees lacking all power. This finds expression in the abrupt hiring and firing of staff. The programme is supplemented by technical supervision of the work and by simple administration of staff. During the era of industrialization, this classical set of instruments was, of course, extended and refined by systematizing the appointment of staff, disciplinary procedures, training programmes, arrangements for health and safety at work, wages structure and costly administration. Nowadays this classical form of personnel management is to be seen in a form more in keeping with the times as the doctrine of the provision of the "production factor: labour" (Gutenberg 1966, p. 11 ff.). In both practical and theoretical terms, adaptation to the new situation remains defensive when viewed from a purely external position.

2.2 Neo-classical Personnel Management

2.2.1 Neo-classical Situation

The situation has changed on many fronts since this classical beginning. Symptoms of this change could be detected e.g. in certain mistakes and failings by classical management or e.g. in insatisfactory production and output figures and resistance among staff. Since the Second World War, industrialized nations in Western Europe have had to cope with a series of phenomena which represent a stage of development in the history of their own civilisation, in which contact with other economic and social systems has played an important role. Compared with the classical structure, the neo-classical management situation reveals a series of distinctly different characteristics (Fig. 4).

The dominant company model under these new conditions is that of the "sociotechnical system". As far as personnel management is concerned it is particularly worth noting that the company is now conceived as a social operation and is not therefore made up of factors but of actions. The individual thereby becomes an extremely problematic element and not one which can be planned and installed in engineering terms. Management's central problem is to achieve conformity and to effect action with plans and programmes of an ever more diffuse nature e.g. under the slogan "Performance and Satisfaction".

Economy	Emergence of large firms, buyers' markets, international economic integration, shift to growth, ambitious programms
Technology	Capital-intensive mass technology, completion of modern systems of communication and transport, partial automation of production
Society	Society as a faceless mass, with an increase in horizontal and a decrease in vertical distinctions, growth of social needs
Employers	Excessive demands on individuals. Sales revenue takes the place of thoughts on costs, more and more managers without any personal investment in the firm, greater pressure on their role in society, higher professional standards, more diffuse distribution of interests and power
Politics	Pluralism, ironing out of inequalities in society, move towards competition, foreign policy strongly geared to economic interests, growth in democracy
Law	Support for market mechanisms, marked extension of legislation governing employment and co-determination, amendment and adaptation of many laws to the changes brought about by economic and technological developments
Science	Full development of technological research in the social science field, increase in scientific positivism, growth of international and pluralistic trends in research
Culture	Principle of efficiency, scientific approach, security, liberalism, progress as key values

Figure 4: Important characteristics of the neo-classical management situation

Managing by pressing a button is no longer sufficient to meet the needs of the situation; much more emphasis needs to be placed upon the staff's own initiative and willingness to shoulder responsibility.

This situation occurred somewhat later in Western Europe than in the USA (Barnard 1938; Roethlisberger 1941; Mayer 1951). But from the very start, this change has had the hall-mark and importance of a development in society and it reaches far beyond the problems purely associated with management. This is to be seen, inter alia, in the fact that this theme is treated in Western Europe not from a mainly psychological but much more from a sociological angle. The situation of neo-classical personnel management is characterized by:

- individuals in the labour market who, on the one hand, can carry out highly complex tasks in an independent, professional manner and who, on the other hand, feel themselves less tied to the company and who have to be motivated to participate in its activities, and
- organisational structures which are neither highly standardized nor completely explicit but which, in part, allow considerable scope for individual

responsibility, initiative and even obstruction, in order to allow a company the chance of operating on a relatively effective footing.

Under these circumstances, the mediation function of personnel management can no longer be interpreted from just one perspective; what is required is for the differences existing between the organisation and the individual to be ironed out. Of course, different courses of action are taken in the USA and in Western Europe. In the USA, mediation between the organisation and the individual is carried out in a purposive manner from an economic point of view and this is the reason why it has no consequences for the company's social structure, by and large. In contrast to this situation, intellectual and cultural traditions in Western Europe – and since the 1950's in terms of social policy and co-determination laws – have led to a split in considering the problem from a purely economic point of view and have introduced the alternative perspective of social values to the function of personell management (Kolbinger 1972, p. 14 ff.).

2.2.2 Neo-classical Concept

The change to the neo-classical conept of personnel management is first to be seen in the fact that detailed statements can now be made not only about the process but also about the structure of staffing. In the matter of the composition of the staff in particular, much more weight is now placed on a high level of aptitude in different subject areas and on personal qualities, and arguments concerning profits are pushed into the foreground alongside those concerned with expenditure in any assessment of the structure (also the use of investment theories in human resource management, Ackermann 1969, p. 161 ff.). As far as the process of organising staff is concerned, one finds numerous changes in methods, new activities and a re-evaluation of the importance of individual measures. One striking feature is the ever-growing importance of measures for personnel development, the selection of staff and the attention devoted to human relations in the company. A survey carried out in 1978 among West German personnel directors, department heads and works councils cited e.g. developments in patterns of behaviour as the most problematic area (Remer/Wunderer 1979, p. 202), whereas French personnel directors found the development of relations between people to be the most important question (Funke 1965, p. 74), and three subsequent investigations revealed that measures concerned with personnel development in the widest sense nowadays call for priority of attention (Büschges 1974, p. 143; Bisani 1979 p. 24, Deutsche Gesellschaft für Personalführung 1974, p. 52).

Essential neo-classical demands on personnel management do not seem to be attainable by staffing measures of a structural nature, especially since these demands are in part contradictions in themselves or because they presuppose far too great a sense of harmony between company and employees. To this end the concept of leadership style has been developed in the USA and this was successful in introducing the first element of mediation between the contradictions existing between work and work-force. However, in the Federal Republic of Germany and in other industrialized countries in Europe (Bisani/Friedrichs 1979, p. 157 ff.), mediation problems of this kind can hardly be solved on the basis of leadership styles, since the economy in these countries is increasingly seen as a social institution (and not the reverse!). To a certain extent this also applies to Japan which differs from Europe in so far as Japanese society has traditional values and structures which are extremely useful to the economy (e.g. Tominaga 1977, p. 21 ff.). This is the reason why the question of leadership style has never acquired the dominant role in Europe that it enjoys in the USA and why labour law, social legislation and social policy have been the subject of much more development in Europe.

The institutional side of personnel management has also undergone a neo-classical change. One example of this lies in the demands made on the personnel director in terms of subject specialism and character; these demands have changed in a manner which reveals a greater need for social aptitude for this kind of work (Brutzer/Schittek 1970, p. 120 f.; Remer/Wunderer 1979, p. 178). In addition, throughout the whole of Western Europe, there is a clear enhancement of the status of the personnel director and a growth in personnel departments in a manner comparable to trends in the USA (Remer/Wunderer 1979, p. 33 ff.; Bisani/Friedrichs 1979, p. 125 ff.). Over and above this trend, co-determination laws in West Germany have led to the creation of additional institutions in personnel management (e.g. the worker-director on the managing board and the works council) and these laws have laid down certain procedures (e.g. dismissal). In contrast to the USA, most West European countries reveal neo-classical relations in company constitutions, which at least suggest a trend towards socialisation among managers. Even in the United Kingdom, where co-determination seems on the face of it to have reached a similar stage to that obtaining in the USA, it is apparent as elsewhere in Europe that co-determination is by and large more a social question than an economic one (Schmidt-Dorrenbach 1981, p. 114, 118 ff.), to such an extent that many an American manager is often amazed at how little store is set by European employees on the purely financial improvement of their standard of living.

For personnel management as an element of general management, the consequences of the neo-classical concept are primarily to be seen in the fact that there is now an organisation at senior management level which provides for the representation of employers' problems. This process means that certain considerations are demanded of the organisation, and, in the final resort, of the whole management, without there being any need to pose fundamental questions about its basic role of aiming to hit targets.

2.3 Modern Personnel Management

The above account may be felt to be a description of a modern system, so that the idea of an even more modern set-up calls for much more imagination. Because of the danger that this may seem to be nothing but speculation, there is a need to attempt to give a brief outline of the beginnings of this modern trend.

2.3.1 Modern Situation

Neo-classical developments basically contain the seed of modern personnel management. All that is needed is to extend one's gaze along a path which has already been identified. As is becoming more and more apparent with each passing day, the economy in all industrialized countries is criss-crossed with many demands from the environments like politics, pressure groups, technology, law and science. Apart from in the scientific and technical fields, this process seems to be generally more advanced in Western Europe than in the USA, where it is occurring in a manner which is more natural material and direct than, e.g. in the Federal Republic of Germany with its host of social institutions and intellectual traditions which act as a brake. Of course it must be pointed out that the "economic" system in the USA was never at any time in its history as fundamentally separated off from other areas of society as in the Federal Republic of Germany, and Europe has had its period of existential disputes, even in the form of class struggles.

The modern situation of the company, at least in the fully industrialized countries of Western Europe, is characterized by the fact that operations have to be geared more and more to the total environment. Under certain circumstances this can even mean that the specific and 'original' reason for a company existing diminishes in importance (Schelsky 1979, Remer 1973, p. 77 ff.). For modern personnel management this development means:

- people who either cannot or will not make a clear distinction between their work and their social situation and, seeing this in reverse, who are able to see their participation in this society as work and to put this idea into practice, and
- organisational structures which do not incorporate a specific programme but rather highly complex, multi-faceted and changing problem-solving processes, which make demands on staff and which enable them to take part in these processes without degenerating into production factors.

The modern West European company consequently presents the image of a problemsolving system which is at once open to environmental forces and is a socio-economic complex. The participants in this system i.e. employers and staff as well as customers and the general public, become members in the sense of the company's constitution. Of course, this principle has been realized most of all in an East European country (Wolfstetter 1969, p. 743 ff.). The openness of this company system commences as soon as it seeks to fix its identity, which can change with environmental conditions.

Large European companies, which reveal considerable potential for causing friction in society, are already beginning to take on these characteristics. Their problem of management consists of hitting targets at the same time as adapting to changing environmental conditions; in the final resort their problem is to survive intact in an extremely problematic environment. As can be seen, this is not to be equated with any technical or rational pursuit of goals. On the contrary, more and more examples reveal that classically-structured and effective companies can land in difficulties and that ineffective companies survive (Luhmann 1971, p. 40 ff.) or that systems change their raison d'être without having to be built up again from scratch (Rice 1963, p. 188 ff.).

Personnel management has the job of defusing clashes between the organisation and the individual, not only on account of their consequences, as characterized by neo-classicism, but also of effecting "integration" between the organisation and the individual by acting as a mediator between the two parties. The motto for a modern approach to the function of personnel management could be: individuals mature enough to organize themselves, organisational structures which enable the individual to realize his self-potential.

2.3.2 Modern Concept

It is clear even with large European concerns that management's problems regularly do not fit into the pattern described above. But as long as there are indications of this trend then a modern concept of human resource management must amount to something more than a mere development of neo-classical methods. What is the point of personnel planning, which is becoming more and more comprehensive in scope, personnel selection, which is an ever more carefully considered process, and more intensive staff development etc. in companies whose programmes and organisational structures are seen to becoming more and more diffuse and variable? At the very least, modern personnel management has to come to a new arrangement with the function of the organisation (Müller-Nobiling 1969, p. 321 ff.; Schären 1976, p. 146 f.). This could perhaps mean that staff participation in the organisational process and an orientation of the staff to organisational structures whose dynamism owed much to their receptivity to external environmental factors might be more feasible now than was the case in the past. The latest concepts of organisational theory have paved the way along this road by making self-organisation and orientation to the environment easier. Personnel management is currently following this development, as became clear in a workshop of European academics in this field held in Brussels in 1983, and it is taking, much more notice of the problems and solutions provided by organisational theory than was the case in the past. A report from Sweden, for example, indicated that "organisation of work, the working environment, co-determination, administration and management" are the principal duties of the *personnel director* (Sigge 1979, p. 200), while "job-design and job-organisation" are deemed to be the essential task facing the *personnel* department (Isachsen 1979, p. 163) in Norway in the future, and in the Federal Republic of Germany, personnel directors already believe in part that organisational problems are more explosive than personnel ones (Remer/Wunderer 1979, p. 203). But even personnel problems are accorded more significance in modern personnel management. One of management's central problems is how to build up a work-force of the right quality and quantity which is flexible in both time and space dimensions but which is also stable. This means that procedures for personnel development and selection have to be geared much more to essentially more abstract and less specifically defined demands than was the case in the past. This leads to personnel work seeming to the majority of the staff to be a process of organising membership, perhaps similar to comparable processes in societies, cooperatives or clubs.

Institutional consequences of this modern concept of personnel management can be expected in the form of the widespread general enhancement of the status of administrative- and personnel departments. The classical division into line-management and managerial consultancy could be resolved in future with the result that administration and personnel management need no longer be looked upon instruments independent of each other in the management programme (Remer 1978, p. 16 ff.). Much to the contrary, these two areas will reveal their claim to playing a more fundamental and leading role in the management process – indeed, this is a development which has already occurred in a good many countries (Bisani/Friedrichs 1979, p. 124 ff.). In addition, personnel management will be expected to identify with a much broader front, going far beyond the principle of ownership. In the Federal Republic, for example, the personnel management process is already spread over several areas e.g. personnel director, works-director, personnel specialists, other staff departments like organization, as well as department heads, works council, individual employees, unions and consultants. Legislation governing co-determination provides for this in many European countries e.g. Sweden, Holland, France or Germany (Remer/Wunderer 1979, p. 12 f., 48; Deutsche Gesellschaft für Personalführung 1972; Wächter 1979, p. 86 ff.). In the final resort, the modern personnel manager has to see his job more and more as representing a certain sector of the environment, the staff, and in this sense he needs to direct events in the company from outside in a spirit which combines both competition and cooperation with other managers like, for example, the marketing manager (Luhmann 1964, p. 88, 220 ff.; Remer 1978a, p. 18 ff., 35 ff.).

3. Consequences for a Form of Personnel Management Suited to the Situation

By way of conclusion it is appropriate to pose the question as to what demands will be made on personnel management by the situation now obtaining in Western Europe and that of the immediate future. As should have become clear from the above, this question cannot be answered in a general manner. The conditions and circumstances within Western Europe are too different, even though, when taken as a whole, they stand out as being distinct from other economic areas like the USA, USSR or Japan. For this reason it seems appropriate to look at personnel management from the point of view of what is actually happening in this field (e.g. Candau 1980).

In Western Europe there is general acceptance of the rule that the shift from the classical to the modern is occurring on a scale which depends on the growth of a country's civilisation and the stage of industrialization it has reached. This rule could however also be applied to the USA so that – given certain qualifications, one could profit there from an analysis of developments in Europe. In this process, legal codification e.g. in the form of complicated acts of legislation (e.g. co-determination) probably plays a less significant role than is frequently thought (Wächter 1979, p. 105). There are more fundamental and more meaningful indicators for the management situation or for changes in the offing. These are, for example, various acts of legislation and legal judgements, changes in the economic system (e.g. structure of demand), changes in society (e.g. education) and political tendencies (e.g. social democracy).

Measured in these terms, it is possible to localize differences in trends and situations in Western Europe (Bisani/Friedrichs 1979). In a number of countries it is still possible to find a relatively high proportion of companies whose general situation swings like a pendulum between classicism and neo-classicism. This is seen in their simple, hierarchical, clear and invariable organisational structures and in the structure of the labour market. In this connection it is possible to talk of a North-South divide in Europe, which even occurs within individual companies, as for example in the Federal Republic, where the regions in the south tend to reveal classical characteristics. On the other hand, countries with a long cultural tradition like Italy or Greece, have in part extremely complex social relationships in the field of the labour market and in personnel work, which in many ways call for modern personnel management. But because the organisational structures in these countries (e.g. greater need for independent decisions) more often than not do not lend themselves to suggesting the need for changes in personnel policy to the employer, there are considerable differences of opinion and conflicts between classical and modern claims in these countries.

A different situation obtains in those countries in which companies have devised organisational models which allow staff more scope for action. In so far as this applies mainly for reasons of expediency, as, for example, is frequently the case in the Federal Republic, then an extreme neo-classical concept of personnel management is probably right for the situation. In Scandinavian countries (Bisani/Friedrichs 1979, p. 157 ff., 193 ff.), as well as in many large concerns in Central Europe, there are already clear indications to be seen of a modern situation which demands that personnel management should be much more involved in thinking through the relationship between the system and the environment.

It is, of course, necessary to attach certain reservations to this outline. In Germany, for example, there is a tendency for differences in situations to be seen not only on a regional basis but mainly with regard to the size of the company. This becomes all too clear in situations, for example, where dismissals in large companies exceed a certain percentage of the workforce; this has tended to turn into a socio-political issue which can no longer be resolved by the company acting on its own.

The development of personnel management in Western Europe, and in countries like the Federal Republic in particular, does not, however, stop at certain differences in detail. A fundamental change in companies seems to be occurring in a manner which seems to be independent of factors like location, size, branch or operational level. Based upon the events of the past 100 years then it is becoming clear that a modern era is dawning on personnel management in Western Europe.

In part this finds expression in the recommendations for the training of West German personnel managers (Remer/Wunderer 1979, p. 150 ff.) Nowadays both academics and practitioners involved in training place considerable priority on those topics which affect the social system (personality, human relations, labour laws, rules of management etc.). In addition, personnel managers, line-managers and works councils demand that specialists in the personnel field should have qualities like social awareness, a sense of social responsibility and social sensitivity. On top of this, questions of staffing structure (e.g. personnel planning) and increasingly organisational structure are seen to be important constituents of training programmes for personnel managers. In contrast, classical topics like remuneration procedures and personnel administration are clearly declining in importance in personnel work. Taken as a whole, the modern demands on Western European personnel managers can be characterized by a high level of socialization and social awareness among management in general and by the personnel function in particular. This calls for aptitudes – namely an understanding of and commitment to society – which go far beyond any personnel manager training programmes which have a purely technical orientation.

Bibliography

Ackermann, K. F.: Betriebliche Ausbildung von Arbeitskräften – Sozialleistung oder Investition. In: Marx, A. (Ed.): *Personalführung,* Bd. I, Wiesbaden 1969.

Barnard, C.: *The Functions of the Executive.* Cambridge/Mass. 1938.

Bisani, F.: *Personalwesen. Grundlagen, Organisation, Planung.* Opladen 1976.

Bisani, F./Friedrichs, H. (Eds.): *Das Personalwesen in Europa.* Königsstein/Ts. 1979.

Brutzer, S./Schittek, D.: Die Anforderungen an den Personalleiter in Stellenanzeigen. *Personal,* 4, 1970, pp. 102 ff.

Büschges, G.: Berufsbild und Berufspraxis der Personalleiter in erwerbswirtschaftlichen Großunternehmen. *Arbeit und Leistung,* 6, 1974, pp. 141 ff.

Candau, P.: *Pour une Analyse Radicalement Contingente de la Fonction Personnel.* Beitrag zum Kongreß der Association des Sciences Administrative du Canada, Montréal, Mai 1980.

Dahrendorf, R.: *Soziale Klassen und Klassenkonflikt.* Stuttgart 1957.

Deutsche Gesellschaft für Personalführung (Ed.): *Die personalpolitischen Konsequenzen des neuen Betriebsverfassungsgesetzes.* Neuwied – Berlin 1972.

Deutsche Gesellschaft für Personalführung (Ed.): *Das Funktions- und Berufsbild des Leiters des Personalwesens.* Schrift Nr. 34, Neuwied – Berlin 1974.

Eckardstein, D. v./Schnellinger, F.: *Betriebliche Personalpolitik.* München 1973.

Fayol, H.: *Administration Industrielle et Générale.* Bulletin de la Société de L'Industrie minérale, Paris 1916.

Funke, P.: Zur Funktionsanalyse des Personalleiters im internationalen Vergleich, Teil II: Zukünftige Schwerpunkte. *Arbeitswissenschaft,* 3, 1965, pp. 74 ff.

Grochla, E.: *Einführung in die Organisationstheorie.* Stuttgart 1978.

Gutenberg, E.: Grundlagen der Betriebswirtschaftslehre, Bd. I. *Die Produktion.* Berlin 1966.

Hoffmann, F.: *Entwicklung der Organisationsforschung.* Wiesbaden 1973.

Isachsen, K.: Der gegenwärtige Stand der Entwicklung des betrieblichen Personalwesens in Norwegen. In: Bisani, F./Friedrichs, H. (Eds.): *Das Personalwesen in Europa.* Königstein/Ts. 1979, pp. 157 ff.

Kolbinger, J.: *Das betriebliche Personalwesen,* Bd. I, 2. ed., Stuttgart 1972.

Leibenstein, H.: *Economic Theory and Organizational Analysis.* New York 1960.

Luhmann, N.: *Funktionen und Folgen formaler Organisation.* Berlin 1964.
Luhmann, N.: Wirtschaft als soziales System. In: N. Luhmann (Ed.): *Soziologische Aufklärung.* Opladen 1970, pp. 204 ff.
Luhmann, N.: Zweck – Herrschaft – System. Grundbegriffe und Prämissen Max Webers. In: Mayntz, R. (Ed.): *Bürokratische Organisation.* Köln/Berlin 1971, pp. 36 ff.
March, J. G./Simon, H.: *Organisation und Individuum.* Wiesbaden 1976.
Marx, A. (Ed.): *Personalführung,* Bd. I. Wiesbaden 1969.
Massie, J. L.: Management Theory. In: March, J. G. (Ed.): *Handbook of Organization.* Chicago 1965, pp. 387 ff.
Mayer, A.: *Die soziale Rationalisierung des Industriebetriebs.* München/Düsseldorf 1951.
Mayntz, R.: The Study of Organizations. *Current Sociology,* 13, 1964, pp. 94 ff.
Mayntz, R. (Ed.): *Bürokratische Organisation.* Köln, Berlin 1971.
Müller-Nobiling, H. M.: Zur Interdependenz von Organisation und Personalwirtschaft. *Zeitschrift for Organisation,* 8, 1969, pp. 321 ff.
Remer, A.: *Ansätze zu einer Theorie des Personalmanagement.* Diss., Augsburg 1973.
Remer, A.: *Personalmanagement.* Berlin/New York 1978(a).
Remer, A.: Organisationstheoretische Entwicklungen und ihre Bedeutung für das Personalwesen. *Zeitschrift für betriebswirtschaftliche Forschung,* 1978(b), pp. 513 ff.
Remer, A.: *Instrumente unternehmenspolitischer Steuerung.* Unternehmensverfassung, formale Organisation und personale Gestaltung. Berlin/New York 1982.
Remer, A./Wunderer, R.: *Personalarbeit und Personalleiter im Großunternehmen.* Berlin 1979.
Rice, A. K.: *The Enterprise and its Environment.* A System Theory of Management Organization. London 1963.
Roethlisberger, F. J.: *Management and Morale.* Cambridge/Mass. 1941.
Schären, F.: Management heute – Seine Führungsmittel im Bereich von Personal und Organisation. *Management-Zeitschrift/Industrielle Organisation,* 1976, pp. 145 ff.
Schelsky, H. (Ed.): *Zur Theorie der Institution.* Düsseldorf 1970.
Schmidt-Dorrenbach, H.: Die Beeinflussung der Unternehmenseffizienz durch Mitbestimmungsregeln aus ausländischer Sicht. In: Säcker, F. J./Zander, E. (Eds.): *Mitbestimmung und Effizienz.* Stuttgart 1981, pp. 85 ff.
Scott, W. G.: Organization Theory. An Overview and an Appraisel. *Academy of Management Journal,* 4, 1961, pp. 7 ff.
Sigge, E.: Der gegenwärtige Stand der Entwicklung des betrieblichen Personalwesens in Schweden. In: Bisani, F./Friedrichs. H. (Eds.): *Das Personalwesen in Europa.* Königstein/Ts. 1979, pp. 193 ff.
Staehle, W. H.: *Management.* München 1980.
Taylor, F. W.: *Scientific Management.* New York 1947.
Tominaga, K.: Rolle des Wertsystems für die Industrialisierung Japans. In: Ichihara, K./Takamiya, S. (Eds.): *Die japanische Unternehmung.* Opladen 1977.
Ulrich, P./Fluri, E.: *Management.* Stuttgart 1978.

Wächter, H.: Das Personalwesen in der Bundesrepublik Deutschland unter dem Einfluß von Betriebsverfassung und Mitbestimmung. In: Bisani, F./Friedrichs, H. (Eds.): *Das Personalwesen in Europa.* Königstein/Ts. 1979, pp. 75 ff.

Wolfstetter, E.: Die betriebliche Arbeiterselbstverwaltung in Jugoslawien. Ein Beitrag zum Problem der betrieblichen Mitbestimmung. *Zeitschrift für Betriebswirtschaft,* 1969, pp. 743 ff.

Wunderer, R./Mittmann, J.: 10 Jahre Personalwirtschaftslehren – Von Ökonomie nur Spurenelemente. In: *Die Betriebswirtschaft,* 1983, pp. 623 ff.

Public Administration and Civil Service in Europe – Approaches to Reform –

Walter A. Oechsler

Summary

Public administration in Europe is marked by a long bureaucratic tradition. A consequence of this historical perspective has been a massive resistance to change. Neither in the Federal Republic of Germany nor in such other major European countries as the United Kingdom and France has any systematic reform taken place. Reform strategy has given way to piecemeal engineering which has negatively influenced the effectiveness and efficiency of public administration and management. Reform deficiencies are clearly illustrated in a comparison with the U.S. Civil Service Reform.

1. The State of Public Administration and Civil Service and the Need for Reform

Public Administration and management in Europe as a whole cannot be described here in detail, as they vary too greatly from one country to another, nor can they be systematically examined in all European countries. The aim of this paper is to outline approaches to civil reform in three European countries. The Federal Republic of Germany, the United Kingdom and France have been chosen as large European countries and are examined here with regard to their approaches to civil service reform and their efforts towards more successful public management.

As stated above, European public administration has a long bureaucratic tradition. This is especially true for *Germany*, where first Prussian administrators put bureaucracy into practice and later the theoretical foundations of bureaucracy were laid by Max Weber (Weber 1956). Civil Service in Germany is still remarkably dominated by the institution of permanent civil servants (Beamte), who serve their country loyally and who have the advantage of such benefits as medical care. It is regulated by federal law and is based on traditional principles of professional civil service that are constitutionally guaranteed. State and local governments also employ non-permanent blue and white collar workers. Their compensation and working conditions are regulated by bargaining processes between government and unions (Perridon 1976).

The focus here is on civil servants, whose educational background, compensation and career development are determined by federal law. German civil service consists of four career groups established according to specified academic standards. Each of these career groups comprises a certain sequence of positions with corresponding increases in salary.

The major determining factors for career decisions in these groups are seniority and performance evaluation, which is conducted at maximal intervals of five years. This rigid bureaucratic career pattern makes possible the promotion of civil servants without prescribing more highly qualified functions and is an underlying motive for the decision to initiate civil service reform in Germany. Included in the reform discussion here are not only civil service, but also functional, procedural, budgetary and territorial reforms. The necessity for this discussion lies in the fact that public activities in Germany encompass a wide range of executive responsibility and operations in addition to service functions. The major objective of reform here is to introduce more economic thought to public activities (Oechsler 1984).

While public and civil law in Germany are very clearly distinguished, such a differentiation in the *United Kingdom* is relatively unknown. Federal law covers only non-industrial civil servants with regard to retirement questions and the obligatory observance of secrecy. Most regulations are passed by the Cabinet and the Civil Service Department and are based on agreement between state authorities and civil service organizations outside of or within the Whitley Council. The most important regulations are included in the "Establishment Code". Whereas it is possible in England to remove civil servants from their posts, they can on the other hand, actually attain establishment positions which might be compared with the permanency of German civil servants.

In addition to establishment positions, there are also "temporaries", who receive no retirement benefits. Then there are industrial civil servants, who are comparable with managers in private industry. They run state enterprise and are selected and compensated according to agreements between local governments and civil service organizations.

France represents the classic type of a centrally administrated country. The majority of its civil servants (fonctionnaires) is ruled by public law (Ordinnance). Their rights and obligations are similar to those of German civil servants. On the one hand they are subject to disciplinary rules, on the other they receive social benefits such as social security, leave and pension. Comparable to this group are the titled local civil servants, who fall under the jurisdiction of the "Code de l'administration communale".

As well as civil servants, state and local governments also employ auxiliaries, temporaries and employees (agents contractuels), who are subject to both public and civil law (Laubinger 1976).

This short summary describes the different ways in which civil service is administered in this one part of Europe. Whereas the legal structures ruling public personnel management in each of these countries are quite different, all three have experienced similar problems eventually leading to civil service reform. Increased public activities and a lack of financial resources combined with the inflexibility of bureaucratic public personnel management have given rise to a public demand for reform activities producing more effective public administration.

This tendency can be observed in all other European countries, as well – even such small countries as Switzerland have developed approaches to civil service reform.

2. Approaches to Reform

2.1 Federal Republic of Germany

In Germany the only partially successful civil service reform up to now has been a regional reform at the communal level where the number of local authorities was drastically reduced in order to establish larger administrative units. Other attempts, such as a reform of federal government and administration which would have included functional, procedural and personnel aspects have been unable to reach any stage beyond that of literary discussion. This is especially true with regard to civil service reform. A "Study Group for the Reform of Civil Service" was established in 1969. Its results were published in 1973 and consisted of approximately a dozen volumes, in which for the most part members of the academic profession reported on methods and instruments for use in public personnel management. These methods and instruments were those used in private industry and were recommended by the study group without their having considered the unique conditions inherent to civil service and how these might influence the application of such methods (Studienkommission 1973). Rating scales for performance appraisals and personnel selection tests consisting of performance and personality tests were among those recommendations made by the commission. The adequacy or inadequacy of such methods had not even been discussed yet, as the civil service reform discussion up to then had concentrated on the question of which legal procedure was to be applied and had come to a halt at that stage. This question was whether public personnel should fall under the jurisdiction of federal law or only that of bargaining processes between government and unions, or whether the present state, a mixture between both systems, should be retained. It was here that the discussion ended with the conclusion that there was no reason to alter the present system, and that as a consequence civil service reform was unnecessary.

The civil servants' lobby was successful enough to prevent the realization of these reform proposals. Needless to say, there was no objection to this outcome, for the reform proposals were poorly thought out and would hardly have been suitable for meeting the requirements of public personnel management (Oechsler 1982).

By the end of the 1960's it had already become clear that the efficiency of public administration was suffering from the weight and complexity of its functions and from a steadily increasing number of government operations. The federal government set up an "Interministerial Project Group on the Reform of Government and Administration" which worked from 1969 to 1975 in co-operation with the Federal Minister of the Interior. The project group analyzed organizational and procedural aspects of the cabinet, the ministries and subordinate authorities. A reduction in the number of ministers and a new distribution of functions were the results of this analysis. A proposal for the installation of a governmental policy planning system led at least to a better information system at the federal level. Further suggestions concerning, among other things, the more flexible assignment of personnel were made to promote an increase in the efficiency of ministerial departments (v. Oertzen 1983).

Consequently, civil service reform in Germany seems to be a slow and constantly necessary process of altering bureaucratic positions. As long as bureaucracy is able to dominate governmental and administrative policy, efficient reforms cannot take place.

2.2 United Kingdom

Public sector management reform in the United Kingdom was also started in the 1960's. In contrast to most continental states, Britain's central and local governments operate as distinct services with different constitutional and managerial traditions. Central government reform has expanded control over local government by meeting the aims of modernization and economy, i.e. by finding new institutional ways for handling crises in investment, in unemployment and the regional distribution of growth and by striving to economize on the consumption of national resources by the public sector in an age of recession.

In *central government* the agencies responsible have in most cases been brought in from outside of public administration and outside of political institutions. In one case the chancellor of a university (Fulton) was chosen. In a later case a commercial director of a retail firm (Sir Derek Raynar) was appointed to examine specific parts of government operations. A topdown notion in operation here was that the public sector management would not be trusted to carry out reform from within without the assistance and prestige of a top persons' panel and the reputation of other agencies outside government to stimulate them (Ledgerwood 1982).

The approaches have varied from the global and radical to the detailed and incrementalist of recent years. Permanent civil service was at the center of this discussion. The Fulton inquiry into the structure, recruitment and management of the civil service was an attack on the cult of the "generalist" civil servant and supposed that by innovating new segments, new agencies, within the system the system itself could be gradually reformed. The central organizational recommendation of the Fulton report was the removal from the Treasury of the responsibility for managing civil service and the creation of a new Civil Service Department (CSD). This was to symbolize the new importance attached both to the new style of management and to changing the skills and style of the service as a consequence. As part of the latter a new self-contained Civil Service College was established. Besides this, a new "Programme Analysis and Review" (PAR) process was introduced, which was a modified British version of the American Planning-Programming-Budgeting System (PPBS). Another new structure was the "Central Policy Review Staff" (CPRS), a small, multidisciplinary unit located in the Cabinet Office and intending to offset the fragmented, centrifugal quality of government, in which the proposals and actions of individual departments and agencies tend to relate more closely to their own sectional objectives than to those of the government as a whole. While the PAR programme in 1979, by the time the Conservative Government came to power, was practically defunct and ended shortly afterwards, the CPRS programme survived two changes of government and seems to have become a permanent institution and represents one of the most important administrative reforms in British government (Plowden 1983).

Furthermore, by the Conservatives' reform in the 1980's civil service was to be reduced to some 14 per cent over five years, and waste and inefficiency were to be eliminated throughout the public sector. As means for the latter served audit and accountability programmes. Among these was the requirement, embodied in legislation, that local authorities shall publish certain information concerning the costs and nature of the services they provide for the benefit of local voters and taxpayers. The same philosophy underlies the creation of the so-called "Audit Commission", an independent institution which emerged from the insight that it was not good for local authorities to be able to appoint their own auditors. The result of this was the tendency to make public sector managers more accountable and, as a consequence, the slow erosion of the independence of local authorities in the face of continuing intervention by central government in their management. Control was accompanied by co-ordinative corporate planning and the performance review of specific expenditure areas. The efforts towards eliminating inefficiency in local governments were accompanied by the

"Rayner" reviews, which were a form of consultancy in order to find out scopes of potential savings within the federal government system.

The last major development marks the abolition of the "Civil Service Department", which was created as part of the process of modernizing the civil service in the wake of the Fulton report. It was abolished largely because it was seen as having succeeded all too well in this task and because this task meanwhile was seen as secondary to the reduction of size and costs of the civil service. CSD mainly helped to win pay increases for civil servants. For this reason its responsibilities for civil service members, pay, superannuation and conditions of service have been returned to the Treasury. Its responsibilities for personnel management, recruitment, training, management systems and performance review have been given to a new "Management and Personnel Office", grouped with the Cabinet Office (Plowden 1983).

In conclusion it can be said that the senior civil service, with its close connections to the "establishment", has never viewed reform as a major threat to its power and privileges. The general climate of turbulence has produced an introverted, poorly motivated public service at the national level, which, even while it sheds manpower, also departs from an older atmosphere of dedication and of collegial and ethical trust (Ledgerwood 1982).

2.3 France

Whereas the tendency in the United Kingdom has been towards centralization, administrative reform in France aims to increase decentralization. This is because centralization has long been considered one of the defining characteristics of the French state, part of a tradition reaching back to monarchy and reinforced by the Napoleonic Empire and 'jacobin' republicanism (Keating 1983). In fact, the legal system supports this notion. At its base are the 'communes', governed by elected mayors together with communal councils (conseils municipales). Above these are councils (conseils généraux) for the 95 'départements', also directly elected, but until the recent reforms, without any executive of their own. Then there are the regional councils, which were founded in 1972 and also had no executive of their own prior to 1982. While 'communes' and 'départements' had universal jurisdiction, regions, with the more limited status of 'etablissements publics', were restricted in their functions. In each département there was traditionally a prefect, a central government official who was able to exercize control over communal activities. The prefect of the main département in each region was the executive for the regional council, as well (Keating 1983). This prefect system gave the federal government in Paris a great amount of influence and prevented real local democracy.

Beginning in 1946 government and legislation continuously worked towards adapting the described system to the needs of modern government and administration. Aside from slight shift of power from the central government to the prefects and limited communal participation in central economic planning, reforms mainly intended to achieve a more efficient local implementation of federal government policies. For this purpose the communes were enlarged and the départements were joined together in regions, each region consisting of two to seven départements. These changes led to a decrease in the autonomy of local governments due to their having become financially bankrupt and thus more dependent upon federal government (Fromont 1983).

After the election of Francois Mitterand in 1981 a number of acts were passed to attain more local democracy, and the Ministry of the Interior was changed to "Ministre de l'Intérieur et de la Décentralisation". The most important acts in this area were "loi relative aux droits et libertés des communes, des départements et des regions" (2. 3. 1982) and "loi relative à la réparation des compétence entre les communes, les départements, les régions et l'État" (7. 1. 1983). A new Ministry of Civil Service and Administrative Reform is carrying out programmes that emphasize decentralization, planning and improvements in the relations between public officials and citizens. The act of 1982 introduced new structures to the regions in order to attain more democratic processes in local government. At the same time, central federal control was weakened to gain more autonomy for local governments so that they could fulfill their new functions. Local governments also attained more authority for pursuing their own local economic policies. The act of 1983 introduced new rules for the distribution of authority in local and federal government and consists of a list of the responsibilities to be transferred from federal to local governments which is to be confirmed by another act presently in preparation (Fromont 1983).

These efforts aim towards producing a more decentralized political and administrative system which is able to meet the needs of a democratic society, which strengthens the position of citizens in the face of state authorities and which develops new modes of participation of citizens in administrative decision making processes (Bellon 1983).

Although it is too early to evaluate the effects of French reform acts for decentralization, decentralization, it is already evident that the favored vertical decentralization, e.g. a shift of activities and of authority from the top level of hierarchy to the bottom, has not been realized. Instead, a horizontal redistribution of competence at the commissaire (former préfect) and local government levels has taken place. This tendency is confirmed by the redistribution of public personnel at a rate of between 20 and 40% from the commissaire to local governments. Another negative effects is that democratically elected members of parliament interpret the process of decentralization as one of diminishing public activities and federal jurisdiction. Consequently, they no longer consider themselves responsible for such problems as social security and increasing unemployment (Dupuy/Thoenig 1983).

3. Comparison with U.S. Civil Service Reform

A comparison of the three European approaches to civil service reform discussed here with that applied in the United States in nearly impossible. The above analysis showed that even among European countries legal and historical backgrounds differ so widely that their approaches to reform obviously must vary accordingly.

As explained above, attempts at federal civil service reform in Germany stagnated in the 1970's, whereas in the U.K. and especially in France they are still going on. In view of the difficulty of comparing different reform proposals in different cultural contexts, an analysis of the formal reform process in each of these countries, the course of its institutionalization and the support it could or could not gain might give some insight into the effectiveness of such reforms.

The literary discussion on reform in Germany, conducted by study and project groups lacking in political competence, exemplifies an approach to reform that was predestined to fail – aside from its comparatively minute success at the local territorial level. In the United Kingdom external authorities were mobilized to initiate the reform process which was then institutionalized in public administration by means of creating the Civil Service Department or the Central Policy Review Staff. In France the socialist party programme for decentralization was effected in two major acts. The examples of the above three countries show that the degree of institutionalization and implementation of reform corresponds to the actual willingness to carry out change.

U.S. civil service reform demonstrates a way of both institutionalizing and implementing reform processes. In nearly all approaches to civil service reform illustrated here, the reform process was planned by some type of commission. In the USA it was the "Civil Service Reform Commission" whose work resulted in the Civil Service Reform Act of 1978 (Steinberg 1979). In Germany the discussion whether the civil service should fall under the jurisdiction of public law, of bargaining processes or of a mixture of both exhausted all potential for reform. In the USA and France this problem was solved by simply passing public laws.

The Civil Service Reform Act defines merit principles and prohibited personnel practices. *Merit system principles* symbolize a personnel policy which must be put into practice. This can only be effective if institutions responsible for the transfer of a policy and programs which convert policy statements into workable courses of action are established. Such institutions, which now replace the former Civil Service Commission, are the "Office of Personnel Management" (OPM), "Merit Systems Protection Board" (MSPB), and "Federal Labor Relations Authority" (FLRA) (Campbell 1978).

The *Office of Personnel Management* is responsible for most parts of the reform project. It administers a number of programs, such as affirmative employment programs executive personnel and management development, intergovernmental personnel programs, staffing services, agency compliance and evaluation and work force effectiveness and development.

These programs and activities show the main objectives of civil service reform, that is, increasing the efficiency of civil service. Another reform objective is the balance of interest between agency employees and management officials. Here, the *Merit Systems Protection Board* is responsible for adequately protecting the public interest in a civil service free of prohibited personnel practices.

Finally, the *Federal Labor Relations Authority,* amon other things, prosecutes those guilty of prohibited personnel practices and resolves issues relating to the regulation of bargaining in good faith (Oechsler 1982).

These institutions were established in order to ensure the realization of the cicil service reform concept. In addition to this institutional background the Civil Service Reform regulates staffing procedures, merit pay and the Senior Executive Service (SES). The Senior Executive Service is a separate personnel system for the men and women who establish policy and administer programs at the top levels of government. It is designed to hold executives accountable for their performance so that good performers can be rewarded and continually poor performers can be removed. Career executives who receive a rating of fully successful or better may receive a lump sum bonus of up to 20% of their basic salary and may even presented with honorary ranks and stipends (meritorious executive: $ 10,000; distinguished executive: $ 20,000) (OPM 1979).

In order to make such a system work, valid and reliable performance appraisal systems are necessary. In contrast to civil service reform in Germany, where one kind of performance appraisal system was suggested for the entire civil service, performance appraisal systems in the USA are developed at agency level on the basis of the critical incident technique. An agency can even introduce two or more performance appraisal systems, if necessary, and OPM assists in developing these systems. Thus, performance appraisals tend to concentrate on critical work factors which can be observed and discussed. The German approach led to abstract criteria which would have resulted in performance appraisals with poor validity and reliability (Oechsler 1982 a).

Recent studies on the implementation of performance appraisal, however, show that with a change in Office of Personnel Management policy, problems in the form of supervisory resistance to the significantly increased workload and potential for conflict associated with the new procedures have arisen (Demarco/Nigro 1983). There are many reasons for critical statements on US civil service reform (Stanley 1982). First of all, the short time frame in the Civil Service Reform Act for putting appraisal systems and merit pay into effect was clearly a mistake, and secondly, it was not foreseen that agency budgets would be cut so deeply (Nigro 1982).

In summary, the US approach to civil service reform, from a formal point of view at least, seems to be a logical process consisting of the formulation of personnel policies (merit system principles), the establishment of institutions which are responsible for programs meeting the policy (OPM, MSPB, FLRA), and, finally the evaluation of the effects of reform. A five-year evaluation program is planned to show whether reform objectives have been met in the course of the reform process.

Another significant aspect of successful approaches to civil service reform seems to be decentralization, a concept which not only means the shift of competence to subordinate authorities, but also a decentralized development of instruments and methods (e.g. performance appraisal systems). Finally, it must be added that historically founded bureaucratic systems, such as civil service in Germany, the United Kingdom and France, produce considerably more resistance to reform and change than such systems as the U.S. civil service, which has been much better assimilated into business administration and management.

Bibliography

Bellon, M.: New Directions in Administrative Reform. *Revue Internationale des Sciences Administrative* 1, 1983, pp. 105–108.

Campbell, J. A.: *Civil Service Reform.* Office of Personnel Management, Washington D.C. 1980.

Demarco, J. J./Nigro, L. G.: Implementing Performance Appraisal Reform in the United States Civil Service. *Public Administration,* 61, 1983, pp. 45–57.

Dupuy, F./Thoenig, J.-C.: La Loi Du 2 mars 1982 sur la décentralisation. *Revue Française de Science Politique,* 33, 1983, pp. 962–986.

Fromont, M.: Die französischen Dezentralisierungsgesetze. *Die öffentliche Verwaltung,* 10, 1983, pp. 397–402.

Keating, M.: Decentralization in Mitterand's France, *Public Administration,* 3, 1983, pp. 237–251.

Laubinger, H. W.: Öffentlicher Dienst. In: Bierfelder, W. (Ed.): *Handwörterbuch des öffentlichen Dienstes,* Stuttgart 1976, pp. 1069–1088.

Ledgerwood, G.: *Public-Sector Management Reform in the United Kingdom 1962–82*. Working Paper, Graz 1982.

Nigro, L. G.: Civil Service Reform in the United States. *Public Administration,* 60, 1982, pp. 225–233.

Oechsler, W. A.: Personalentwicklung im öffentlichen Dienst. In: Kossbiel, H. (Ed.): *Personalentwicklung,* ZfbF Sonderheft 14, 1982, pp. 94–106.

Oechsler, W. A.: Vergleichende Analyse der Dienstrechtsreform in der Bundesrepublik Deutschland und der Civil Service Reform in den USA. *Verwaltungsarchiv 2,* 1982 a, pp. 196–215.

Oechsler, W. A.: Betriebswirtschaftslehre der öffentlichen Verwaltung. In: v. Mutius, A./Friauf, K. H./Westermann, H. P. (Ed.): *Handbuch f. d. öffentliche Verwaltung,* Vol. 1, Neuwied 8.

Oertzen v.: New Direction in Administrative Reform. *Revue Internationale des Sciences Administrative,* 1, 1983, pp. 108–109.

Office of Personnel Management: *Senior Executive Service.* Washington D.C. 1979.

Perridon, L.: Öffentliche Wirtschaftseinheiten, Sonderheiten des öffentlichen Personalwesens. In: Bierfelder, W. (Ed.): *Handwörterbuch des öffentlichen Dienstes.* Stuttgart 1976, pp. 1088–1103.

Plowden, W.: New Directions of Administrative Reform. *Revue Internationale des Sciences Administrative,* 1, 1983, pp. 96–101.

Stanley, D.: Civil Service Reform in the United States Government (1). *Revue Internationale des Sciences Administrative,* 3–4, 1982, pp. 305–322.

Steinberg, R.: *Politik und Verwaltungsorganisation,* Baden-Baden 1979.

Studienkommission für die Reform des öffentlichen Dienstrechts, Baden-Baden 1973.

Weber, M.: *Wirtschaft und Gesellschaft.* 4th Edition, Tübingen 1956.

The Authors

Adelberger, Otto L.

Dr. oec. publ., Dipl.-Kfm. Munich University, Professor of Business Administration at the University of Essen. 1979 Visiting Professor, Finance Department, University of Michigan, Ann Arbor. Major publications, e. g. "Simulfin. Die Finanzwirtschaft der Unternehmung als Simulationsexperiment", 2 Vols. (1976).

Albrecht, Hellmut K.

Chairman of the board of management, Schmalbach-Lubeca AG, largest packaging company of the European continent; formerly Vice President Finance & Administration, The Continental Group of Europe, Brussels; Three years in the U.S.A. as senior staff manager and management consultant; Chairman, Association of Metal Packaging Manufacturers, Germany. – Ph. D. in business administration; thesis: "The organization structure of international companies"; published numerous articles in journals and collective works.

Boisot, Max

Associate Professor at the Ecole Supérieure de Commerce de Paris; currently involved in an EC sponsored management training project in the People's Republic of China. – Doctorate from Imperial College, London University.

Published several articles, e.g. to technological strategies also as the genesis and diffusion of knowledge in organizations in Management International Review and Journal of Management Studies.

Borrmann, Werner A.

Member of the Management Board of A. T. Kearney GmbH, Management Consultants, Düsseldorf (Germany). Coordinating Vice President of Kearney's Corporate Strategy Practice in Europe. Vice President and Partner of the US parent company A. T. Kearney Inc., Chicago; Joined A. T. Kearney in Germany 1973. Consulting work mainly in the areas of strategy and organization development, capital goods marketing, and corporate turnaround projects in Germany, Austria, Netherlands, Great Britain and USA. Numerous publications concentrate on these areas of professional experience; Prior to Kearney: Internal Management Organization Consultant with Chrysler International S. A. in London (Great Britain). – Doctoral and Masters's degrees of Business Administration from the University of Munich (Germany).

Brauchlin, Emil A.

Full Professor for Business Administration and Vice Dean of the Department of Business Administration at the University of St. Gallen, Switzerland. – Published several books and articles especially about decision-making, management in the national and international context, e.g. "Problemlösungs- und Entscheidungsmethodik" (1978, 2nd ed. 1984); "Transnationale Unternehmungen und nationale Interessen als unternehmenspolitisches Problem." In: Lück/Trommsdorf, Internationalisierung der Unternehmung (1982).

Gaitanides, Michael

Professor at Hochschule der Bundeswehr Hamburg. – Graduated from the Munich University and doctorates at the universities of Augsburg and Darmstadt. – Major publications are: "Industrielle Arbeitsorganisation und technische Entwicklung" (1975); "Planungsmethodologie: Vorentscheidungen bei Formulierung integrierter Investitionsplanungsmodelle" (1979), "Prozeßorganisation" (1983).

Ghertman, Michel

Professor of Strategic Management and International Business at CESA (HECISA), Jouy-en-Josas, France; also consultant to the top management of multinational corporations and to international organizations. – Published numerous books and articles in English and French, e.g. "An Introduction to the Multinationals" (1984); "Decision-making in Multinational Enterprises. Concepts and Research Approaches" (1984); "Les Multinationales en Mutation" (1983).

Hochmuth, Milton S.

Professor of International Business at the Ecole Supérieure de Commerce de Paris. – Before 1982: Visiting Professor of Business Administration at Amos Tuck School of Business, Dartmouth College; Professor of Management and International Business and Director of the Institute of International Business at Georgia State University and Professor of Business Policy at the Centre d'Enseignement Superieur des Affairs (C.E.S.A.). – Published several books and articles about the management of transnational enterprises, e.g. "Organizing the Transnational: The Management of Transnational Enterprise in Advanced Technology" (1974); "Revitalizing American Industry: Lessons from Our Competitors" (1985).

Hörnell, Erik

Secretary of the Swedish Government's Committee for Direct Investments. – Doctorate at the Department of Business Administration, Uppsala University. – Written several articles and books in international marketing and industrial policy.

Hood, Neil

MA, MLitt, Professor of Business Policy at the University of Strathclyde, co-Director of the Strathclyde International Business Unit and Associate Dean of Strathclyde Business School. – Academic positons in the UK. U.S. and Europe; worked in both the private and public sectors in the UK; consulting appointments with a variety of business and UK government departments and agencies, and a range of international bodies including the World Bank and the UN. – Published (together with Stephen Young) a large number of articles and six books on multinationals and related topics including "Economics of Multinational Enterprise" (1979) and "Multinational in Retreat: the Scottish Experience" (1982).

Kogut, Bruce

Assistant Professor at the Wharton School, Department of Management. – Visiting Assistant Professor at the Stockholm School of Economics in 1983; worked for the Rand Corporation, UNESCO, and, as an intern, at the Council of Foreign Relations. – AB University of California at Berkeley, MIA Columbia University, Ph. D. Sloan School of Management, Massachusetts Institute of Technology. – From his various articles there are to be mentioned, e.g. "Foreign Direct Investment as a Sequential Process". In: Kindleberger/Audretsch: The Multinational Corporation in the 1980s (1983); "Normative Observations on the International Value-added Chain and Strategic Groups". In: Journal of International Business Studies (1984).

Macharzina, Klaus

Dr. oec. publ., Dipl.-Kfm. Munich University, Professor and Director, Institute of Business Administration at the University of Hohenheim, Stuttgart, Germany. – Editor of "Management International Review"; among his many publications in the areas of corporate management, organization, accounting, and international management are "Personnel Management", 2 Vols. (1977, with W. A. Oechsler); "Management of Discontinuities in International Business" (1984); "Financial Management in International Business" (1985).

Negandhi, Anant R.

Professor of International Business at University of Illinois, Champaign. – Ph. D. Michigan State University. – Published more than 60 scholary articles in various journals and is the author, co-author, or editor of 30 books, including "Quest for Survival and Growth: A Comparative Study of American, European, and Japanese Multinationals" (1979) and "The Functioning of Complex Organizations" (1981) and "Tables are Turning: German and Japanese Subsidiaries in the United States" (1981).

Oechsler, Walter A.

Prof., Dr. rer. pol., Dipl.-Kfm., Chair of Personnel Management, University of Bamberg/Germany. – Publications: "Personalmanagement", 2. Vol. (1977, with K. Macharzina); "Konfliktmanagement, Theorie und Praxis industrieller Arbeitskonflikte" (1979); "Zweckbestimmung und Ressourceneinsatz öffentlicher Betriebe" (1982); "Führungsgrundsätze und Führungsmodelle" (1982); "Erfolgreiche Führung in Wirtschaft und Verwaltung" (co-editor); "Personal und Arbeit" (1985).

Remer, Andreas

Dr. rer. pol., University of Augsburg, Professor of Business Administration at the University of Bayreuth. Major publications include "Personalmanagement" (1978), "Strukturelle Instrumente unternehmenspolitischer Steuerung" (1982).

Rugman, Alan M.

Director of the Centre for International Business Studies at Dalhousie University, Halifax, Nova Scotia, Canada; Professor of Business Administration. – 1982 Visiting Professor at the Graduate School of Business, Columbia University, New York. – Recent major publications include e.g. "Multinationals in Canada" (1980); "Inside the Multinationals" (1981); "New Theories of the Multinational Enterprise" (1982) and "Multinationals and Technology Transfer" (1983).

Staehle, Wolfgang H.

Director of the Institute of Management at the Free University, Berlin; Dr. oec. publ., Dipl-Kfm. University of Munich; Professor of Business Administration. Vice-Chairman, German Industrial Relations Association. Editor of 'Mensch und Organisation'. Recent major publications include e.g. "Management" 2nd ed. 1985, "Management-Functions" 1983, "Analysis of Work Situations" 1982 (with P. Karg).

Steiner, Manfred

Dr. rer. pol., University of Augsburg, Professor of Business Administration at the University of Bremen. Major publications include "Ertragskraftorientierter Unternehmenskredit und Insolvenzrisiko" (1980), "Finanzwirtschaft der Unternehmung" 3rd ed. 1984 (with L. Perridon).

Stopford, John M.

BA Oxon, SM MIT, DBA Harvard University, Professor of International Business and Director of the Centre for Business Strategy at the London Business School; Director of the InterMatrix Group and several small companies. – Non-executive Director of Shell (UK) Ltd until 1977. An engineer by initial training, worked with Baker Perkins and Shell Chemicals (UK) before managing a Booker McConnell subsidiary in Guyana; he has been with the United Nations and on the faculty of the Harvard and Manchester Business Schools. – The most recent of his many publications in the fields of corporate strategy and international business is (with John H. Dunning) "Multinationals: Company Performance and Gobal Trends" (1983).

De la Torre, José

D.B.A. Harvard University, M.B.A. Pennsylvania State University, Professor of International Business at INSEAD, Fontainebleau. – Up to 1975: Associate Professor of Management at the Georgia State University, Atlanta and Visiting Professor at Universidad de Valle, Cali, Colombia. – Among his books, monographs and articles there are especially to be mentioned the recently published "Clothing Industry Adjustments in the Industrialized Countries" (1984); "A la recherche d'une politique: Intervention des Pouvoirs Publics dans les secteurs industrielles en declin" (1984); "Adjusting to Import Competition: Private and Public Responses in the Industrialized Countries" (1984).

Tsurumi, Yashihiro

MBA and D.B.A. Harvard University, Professor of International Business at Baruch College, the City University of New York; leading consultant to many governments, the International Monetary Fund, and various multinational firms and President of the Pacific Basin Center Foundation, New York, which is a research and educational institute devoted to the improved relationships of the U.S. with other Pacific Basin nations. – Author of eight books including "The Japanese are Coming" (1976) and "Multinational Management" (1977, 2nd Edition in 1983).

Young, Stephen

B Com, MSc, Senior Lecturer in the Department of Marketing, University of Strathclyde and co-Director of Strathclyde International Business Unit. – Worked as an international economist with the Government of Tanzania and with the British food organization; Consultant to the IFC on the automobile industry and consulting work fot the UNCTC and a variety of UK government departments. – Published together with Neil Hood six books and numerous articles on the topics of multinationals and industrial policy, the most recent of the former being: "Multinational Investment Strategies in the British Isles" (1983).

Van den Bulcke, Daniel

Professor at the Economische Hogeschool Limburg and the State University of Antwerp; teaches also special courses about multinational enterprises at ICHEC and EHSA (Brussels) and the College of Europe (Bruges); past-chairman of the International Trade Invest Institute (1981–1984). – Ph. D. University of Ghent, Belgium and M/A University of Toronto, Canada. – Published extensively about the activities of multinational enterprises in Belgium and Western Europe and conducted studies for several national and international organizations, e.g. "European Headquarters of American Multinational Enterprises in Brussels and Belgium" (1984); "Employment Decision-making in Multinational Enterprises: Survey Results from Belgium" (1984); "Employment Effects of Multinational Enterprises: A Belgian Case Study" (1979); "Investment and Divestment Policies of Multinational Corporations in Europe" (1979).

ORGANIZATION STUDIES

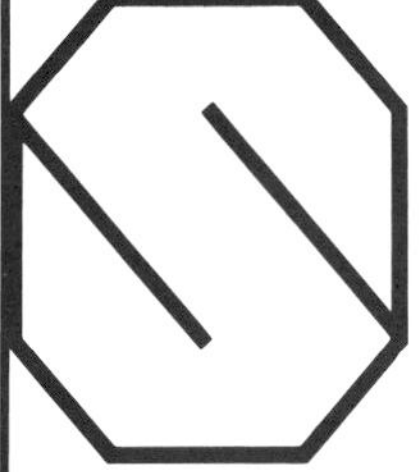

An international multidisciplinary journal devoted to the study of organizations, organizing and the organized in, and between societies.

Organization Studies is a supranational journal, based neither on any one nation nor on collaboration between any particular nations. Its aim is to present diverse theoretical and empirical research from all nations, spanning a broad view of organizations and organizing. Its current Editorial Board is drawn from thirteen nations, and its contributors are worldwide.

O. S. is published in English because that language is the most widely read in this field of research. But manuscripts in other languages can be reviewed in those languages prior to translation. O. S. reviews books published in languages other than English to bring them before its international readership, and News and Notes cover conferences and research in many countries.

O. S. has published papers by authors from sociology, political science, management and public administration, psychology and economics. Some among the range of titles are listed overleaf. O. S. is not only about the study of "the organization", though that is central. It is also about the processes of organizing people, whether in business, public services, or public administration and government; and it is about the response of "the organized". It is not only about the contemporary scene, especially differences around the world, but also about the historical developments which have led to that scene.

Subscription rates 1986

Per volume of four issues. Libraries and institutions **DM 118,– /** approx. US $43.70. Individuals (except FRG and Switzerland) **DM 59,–** / approx. US $21.85 (DM-prices are definitive, $-prices are approximate and subject to fluctuations in the exchange rate).

Published in collaboration with the European Group for Organizational Studies (EGOS) and the Maison des Sciences de l'Homme, Paris by

WALTER DE GRUYTER · BERLIN · NEW YORK

Verlag Walter de Gruyter & Co., Genthiner Straße 13, D-1000 Berlin 30, Tel.: (0 30) 2 60 05-0
Walter de Gruyter, Inc., 200 Saw Mill River Road, Hawthorne, N. Y. 10532, Tel.: (914) 747-0110